D1646382

An Introduction to
Personality, Individual Differences and Intelligence

LIVERPOOL JMU LIBRARY

3 1111 01502 0108

SAGE Foundations of Psychology

Series editors:
Craig McGarty, Murdoch University
Alex Haslam, University of Queensland

Sage *Foundations of Psychology* is a series of texts intended to provide an introduction to key areas of psychology. Books in the series are scholarly but written in a lively and readable style, assuming little or no background knowledge. They are suitable for all university students beginning psychology courses, for those studying psychology as a supplement to other courses, and for readers who require a general and up-to-date overview of the major concerns and issues in contemporary psychology.

Published titles:

Research Methods and Statistics in Psychology (2nd edition)
S. Alexander Haslam & Craig McGarty

An Introduction to Child Development (3rd edition)
Thomas Keenan and Subhadra Evans

Statistics with Confidence
Michael J. Smithson

Health Psychology
Hymie Anisman

Second Edition

An Introduction to Personality, Individual Differences and Intelligence

Nick Haslam, Luke Smillie and **John Song**

Los Angeles | London | New Delhi
Singapore | Washington DC | Melbourne

Los Angeles | London | New Delhi
Singapore | Washington DC | Melbourne

SAGE Publications Ltd
1 Oliver's Yard
55 City Road
London EC1Y 1SP

SAGE Publications Inc.
2455 Teller Road
Thousand Oaks, California 91320

SAGE Publications India Pvt Ltd
B 1/I 1 Mohan Cooperative Industrial Area
Mathura Road
New Delhi 110 044

SAGE Publications Asia-Pacific Pte Ltd
3 Church Street
#10-04 Samsung Hub
Singapore 049483

© Nick Haslam, Luke Smillie and John Song 2017

First edition published 2007

Reprinted 2008, 2010, 2011 (twice), 2012 (twice), 2013, 2015 (thrice)

This second edition published 2017

Apart from any fair dealing for the purposes of research or private study, or criticism or review, as permitted under the Copyright, Designs and Patents Act, 1988, this publication may be reproduced, stored or transmitted in any form, or by any means, only with the prior permission in writing of the publishers, or in the case of reprographic reproduction, in accordance with the terms of licences issued by the Copyright Licensing Agency. Enquiries concerning reproduction outside those terms should be sent to the publishers.

All material on the accompanying website can be printed off and photocopied by the purchaser/user of the book. The web material itself may not be reproduced in its entirety for use by others without prior written permission from SAGE. The web material may not be distributed or sold separately from the book without the prior written permission of SAGE. Should anyone wish to use the materials from the website for conference purposes, they would require separate permission from us. All material is © Nick Haslam, Luke Smillie and John Song 2017

Editor: Luke Block
Editorial assistant: Lucy Dang
Production editor: Imogen Roome
Proofreader: Jill Birch
Marketing manager: Lucia Sweet
Cover design: Wendy Scott
Typeset by: C&M Digitals (P) Ltd, Chennai, India
Printed by CPI Group (UK) Ltd, Croydon, CR0 4YY

Library of Congress Control Number: 2016944598

British Library Cataloguing in Publication data

A catalogue record for this book is available from the British Library

ISBN 978-1-4462-4962-8
ISBN 978-1-4462-4963-5 (pbk)

At SAGE we take sustainability seriously. Most of our products are printed in the UK using FSC papers and boards. When we print overseas we ensure sustainable papers are used as measured by the PREPS grading system. We undertake an annual audit to monitor our sustainability.

Contents

Contents

Contents

Author biographies

Nick Haslam is Professor and Head of the School of Psychological Sciences at the University of Melbourne, Australia. He received his PhD in clinical and social psychology from the University of Pennsylvania, and taught at the New School for Social Research in New York City for several years before returning to Australia in 2002. Nick's academic interests span personality, social and clinical psychology. His research has explored the classification of mental disorders, the basic forms of social relationships, stigma, and the nature of dehumanization and other forms of prejudice. He is also interested in the psychology of morality and in refugee mental health. Nick has published over 200 scholarly articles and book chapters, and he also writes regularly for a general audience in outlets including *The Conversation*, *The Guardian* and *The Washington Post*. In addition to this volume he has published several other books, including *Introduction to the Taxometric Method*, *Values and Vulnerabilities: The Ethics of Research with Refugees and Asylum Seekers* and, most recently, *Psychology in the Bathroom*, an only partly tongue-in-cheek study of the psychology of excretion. Nick is a Fellow of the Academy of the Social Sciences in Australia and is currently President of the Society of Australasian Social Psychologists.

Luke Smillie is a Senior Lecturer in Psychology at the University of Melbourne and director of the Personality Processes Lab. He received his PhD from the University of Queensland and completed postdoctoral research fellowships at the University of London. He has published over 50 articles on a range of topics in personality, including neurobiological and motivational accounts of individual differences, and the impact of personality on social behaviour. He is a consulting editor for the *Journal of Research in Personality*, and a member of the International Society for the Study of Individual Differences.

John Song received his PhD from Swinburne University, Australia, in 2003. He worked as a lecturer in Australia before moving to the UK where he is currently a senior lecturer in psychology at De Montfort University. He teaches intelligence, personality, and research methods, and in 2016 he co-led a successful study and cultural-exposure trip for a group of psychology students to Taiwan to explore cross-cultural concepts around intelligence. He is also the programme leader of four undergraduate psychology programmes at De Montfort University. His research interests are in the field of individual differences. His PhD research focused on brain electrical activity during completion of an intelligence test. Current interests include intelligence-related cognitive processes and also individual differences variables such as morningness and creativity. He has published book chapters on topics such as intelligence, personality, and assessment, and in 2015 received the Vice-Chancellor's Distinguished Teaching Award at De Montfort University.

Acknowledgements

Several people deserve special credit for making the second edition of this book a reality. Luke Block, Lucy Dang and the team at SAGE showed consistent support and encouragement for the project through its long gestation. Series editors Craig McGarty and Alex Haslam reinforced the project's value and clarified its goals.

In addition to these fine individuals, Nick Haslam would like to thank Vikki, his colleagues at the University of Melbourne, and the many students who gave feedback on the strengths and weaknesses of the first edition.

Luke Smillie is grateful to Kristelle for her support, and to the various colleagues and students with whom he has explored the field of personality and individual differences.

John Song thanks his colleagues at De Montfort University for their encouragement and useful informal discussions during the process of writing.

SAGE companion website

Visit the SAGE companion website at **https://study.sagepub.com/haslam2e** to find a range of free tools and resources that will enhance your learning experience.

For students:

- **PowerPoint slides** featuring figures and tables from the book, which can be downloaded and customised for use in your own presentations.
- **Test your knowledge!** Take an interactive quiz and get the feedback you need to help you succeed in your assignments and exams.
- **Chapter summaries** to help you understand key points from each chapter.

Introductory remarks: The psychology of individual differences

This book is not like other books. It differs from them in its subject matter, its length, its shape, its price, its publisher, and in many other ways as well. At the same time, this book is just like other books. It is something that is meant to be read, that aims to inform, that is published and that might be found in libraries. It is a unique individual, but it is also an example of a general kind of thing.

The same goes for people, of course. Each of us is a unique individual, different from everyone else. But each of us is also a member of humankind who has the shared characteristics of our species; what might be called our human nature. This book is all about that duality, exploring how humans differ psychologically from one another and what these differences tell us about our shared human nature. It examines what psychologists call 'individual differences' – the ways in which people vary in personality and mental abilities – and how psychologists have developed scientific generalizations about this kind of human diversity.

The psychology of individual differences is fascinating and fundamental. Capturing the richness of human psychological variation and individuality is very challenging, and psychologists have developed many ways of describing these differences. They have also developed numerous theories to explain these differences, invoking factors as diverse as genes, brain systems, cultural factors and early childhood experiences. They have applied an enormous variety of research methods to develop and test these theories, ranging from brain imaging studies to psychological biographies. And in the process they have come to very dissimilar visions of what it is to be human: what we have in common in the midst of all our differences.

In the pages that follow we will introduce you to the fundamental issues, concepts and theories of the psychology of individual differences, and present research findings that illuminate them. The book doesn't aim to cover the field exhaustively, hoping instead to give you a first taste of individual differences – focusing on the psychology of personality and abilities – that will stimulate your appetite and make you want to come back for more. We will be more than satisfied if this book makes you a little more inquisitive, more introspective, more reflective, or more critical in your everyday thinking about people.

We will even be happy if you emerge at the other end of the book more confused about the psychology of persons than when you started. After all, confusion is a sign of a mind in ferment, actively thinking through ambiguities and puzzles in search of some sort of truth or clarity. Out of confusion often comes curiosity, insight and the will to learn, things that every teacher prizes. But it is also true that confusion sometimes breeds frustration and a disappointed turning of one's back on whatever it is that produced the confusion. We will be sorry if that is how you feel at the end of this book. Either we will have failed in our goals, or perhaps the psychology of individual differences is just not for you.

The book is organized into four sections, the first three of which explore the psychology of personality. The first section has to do with the basic questions of how personalities should be described. For example, what do we mean by 'personality'? How should we characterize people's individuality? Is there a universal vocabulary or framework for capturing differences between them? All of these questions are fundamental. However, working out how to describe something is only a first step towards really understanding it. To do that, we need explanations and theories that account for *why* things are as they are. So the second section of the book focuses on theoretical approaches to the study of personality, approaches that tell quite different stories about the roots, causes and underpinnings of individual differences in personality.

Personality psychology is not simply an abstract, academic enterprise of describing and explaining differences between people, however. It is intimately connected to a variety of practical activities in contemporary society, such as the treatment of mental disorders, the selection of job candidates, and the making sense of lives in biographical writing. These applied and practical aspects of personality psychology are discussed in the book's third section.

The book's fourth and final section shifts focus from personality to intelligence and cognitive ability, including emotional intelligence, a domain of abilities that has attracted increasing attention in recent years. This section of the book examines many of the same topics discussed in the three preceding sections, but in relation to intelligence: how differences in cognitive ability should be described, how they should be explained, how they should be assessed in practice and how they have a variety of important real-world implications.

Each chapter contains several features that can help you direct and consolidate your learning and exploration. Each one starts with a set of learning objectives to guide your reading, and a brief chapter summary that captures the main topics to be covered. Every chapter ends with a summary of the main points, and an annotated list of suggested further readings, most of which are very recent works accessible to the beginning student of personality. Each chapter (except Chapter 1) also presents a recent piece of research that illustrates the chapter's themes, using studies conducted in many diverse countries. Key concepts are defined and explicated in a Glossary at the end of the book.

So without further ado, let's begin our journey by trying to understand what personality is.

Section 1

Describing Personality

What is Personality?

Learning objectives

- To develop an understanding of how the concept of 'personality' has developed over the course of history.
- To understand how personality is conceptualized within psychology and how personality differs from other forms of psychological variation.
- To distinguish between personality and related concepts, such as character and temperament.
- To recognize how personality psychology fits within psychology as a whole and how it differs from related subdisciplines.
- To develop an overview of the book's organization.

This chapter introduces and clarifies the concept of 'personality', which defines the subject matter of personality psychology. The historical background and alternative meanings of the concept are discussed, followed by an analysis of how personality relates to and is distinct from other kinds of differences between people, such as those that are physical rather than psychological, or transient rather than lasting. Personality is distinguished from the related concepts of character and temperament, and the place that the study of personality occupies in psychology as a whole is examined. Personality psychology is argued to be distinguished by its emphasis on individual differences, and by its focus on whole persons as behaving, thinking, and feeling beings. Finally, an overview of the book's organization is presented.

A friend of one of the authors once told him a sad story about a boy he knew as a child. Apparently, this boy's mother took him aside at an early age, looked him in the eye, and addressed to him the following words: 'Son, you're not very good-looking, you're not very smart, you have no personality, and you'll probably never have many friends, and I thought I should tell you this while you are young so you don't develop any unrealistic hopes for the future.'

This rather harsh assessment immediately raises a few questions. What kind of harm did the boy suffer from this statement? Did he grow up to be an alcoholic, an axe murderer, a dentist? What kind of mother would say this to her child? Is this story made up? However, one question that may not have struck you is this: What would it mean to have no personality? Or, turning the question around, what does it mean to have a personality?

The concept of personality

To answer this question we have to explore the meanings of the word 'personality', because it turns out that there are several. One particularly instructive way to sort out these meanings and to think through their implications is to examine the word's history. People have always had personalities and all ancient thought traditions made judgements about human personality (Mayer, Lin, & Korogodsky, 2011), but the concept of personality itself is relatively recent and has undergone some significant changes. Once upon a time, personality was something everyone had. When the word first appeared in English in the 14th century, it meant the quality of being a person, as distinct from an inanimate thing. 'Personality' referred to the capacities – such as consciousness and rational thought – that were believed to give humans a special place in creation (Williams, 1976). In this theological sense, then, personality refers to our shared humanity.

In time, however, this sense of personality as personhood gave way to one that has a more modern feel to it. Over a period of centuries, personality came to refer less to the human capacities that we share and that distinguish us from animals, and more to the characteristics that give each one of us our individuality. In this sense, personality implies a focus on the individual human being: the 'person'. Interestingly, however, the word 'person' did not originally refer to the individual in the way we tend to use it today. Instead, 'person' came, via French, from the Latin word '*persona*', which referred to the mask worn by an actor to portray a particular character. In this theatrical sense, personality has to do with the role or character that the person plays in life's drama. The person's individuality, in this sense, is a matter of the roles or characters that he or she assumes.

While 'personality' gradually acquired the sense of individuality, it sometimes took on a more specific connotation. Rather than referring equally to all kinds of individuality, it increasingly referred to vivacity or charisma. As a popular song of the 1960s by Lloyd Price put it: 'I'll be a fool for you, 'Cause you've got – [ecstatic chorus] Personality! – Walk – Personality! – Talk – Personality! – Smile – Personality! – Charm – Personality!', and so on. People who had these qualities in abundance were said to have more personality, and self-improvement books gave directions for acquiring this precious quantity. Presumably it is in this sense that our unfortunate boy was said to have 'no personality', and why celebrities are commonly referred to as 'personalities'.

Clearly 'personality' has had several distinct meanings: personhood, individuality, and personal charm. These are all meanings that laypeople understand and use in their everyday speech. But what does personality mean in the specialized language of psychology, the science that should, presumably, have something to say about human individuality, and what it is to be a person? What is it, precisely, that personality psychologists study?

'Personality' in psychology

If you ask an ornithologist or an architect what their fields are basically all about they will probably give you a simple, unhesitating answer: birds and buildings. Ask a personality psychologist and you are likely to hear a pause, an embarrassed clearing of the throat, and then a rather lengthy and abstract formulation. Ask ten personality psychologists, and you may well hear ten different formulations. Personality is a slippery concept, which is difficult to capture within a simple definition. In spite of this, a common thread runs through all psychologists' definitions. Psychologists agree that personality is fundamentally a matter of human individuality, or 'individual differences', to use the phrase that most prefer.

However, this definition of personality as human individuality immediately runs into problems unless we flesh it out a little. For a start, it is obvious that not all differences between people are differences of personality. We differ in our physical attributes, our ages, our nationalities, and our genders, and none of these differences really seems to be about personality. Of course, it is possible that these differences are in some way *related* to personality, but they are not themselves differences of personality. We are sometimes told that men are from Mars and women from Venus – the former aggressive and dominating, the latter loving and nurturing – but even if these crude stereotypes were true, biological sex would not be a personality characteristic. So we must immediately qualify our definition so that personality refers only to *psychological* differences between people, differences having to do with thought, emotion, motivation, and behaviour.

Even here our definition is not quite sufficient as far as most psychologists are concerned. Traditionally, psychologists have considered certain psychological differences between people to be outside the realm of personality, specifically those involving *intelligence* and *cognitive abilities*. For many years psychological researchers and theorists have tried to understand and measure people's intellectual capabilities, individual differences that predict successful performance on a variety of tasks, and particularly those that involve formal schooling. Individual differences of this sort will be examined in a later section of this book (Chapters 12–14), and are certainly of interest to many personality psychologists, but they are generally treated separately from individual differences in personality. Excluding these ability-related differences, then, we are left with a definition of personality as non-intellectual psychological differences between people.

If this distinction between intellectual and non-intellectual differences makes you uneasy, you are not alone. Many psychologists consider it to be somewhat arbitrary. Which side of the conceptual divide does creativity fall on, for example? It seems to be partly a matter of mental abilities, and partly a matter of non-intellectual qualities such as openness to new experiences, mental flexibility, and drive. In addition, some psychologists argue that certain personality differences – differences that do not involve competencies in particular cognitive tasks – can be fruitfully understood as abilities or intelligences. For instance, some psychologists have recently proposed interpersonal and emotional intelligences. Nevertheless, although the boundary between the intellectual and non-intellectual domains is a vague and permeable one, it is a boundary that most psychologists continue to take seriously.

Have we finished our conceptual labour now that we have a working definition of personality as non-intellectual psychological differences between people? Sadly, not quite. Consider the case of emotions and moods. Emotions and moods are non-intellectual states of mind, and at any particular time individuals differ on them (you may be angry, another person anxious, yet another person content). Shouldn't emotions and moods therefore be aspects of personality? Psychologists argue that they are not, precisely because they refer to fleeting *states* rather than to enduring characteristics of the person. Only characteristics that have some degree of stability and consistency – characteristics that can be thought of as lasting *dispositions* of the person – are considered to be aspects of personality. Once again, people's emotional states may *reflect* enduring emotional dispositions (e.g., you might be an anger-prone person) or they may be *related* to their personalities in a specific way (e.g., you might be angry now because you are the sort of person who is quick to take offence). However, emotional states are too short-lived to be considered as aspects of personality themselves.

A related issue arises with psychological characteristics such as attitudes (e.g., being for or against immigration restrictions), beliefs (e.g., whether or not God exists), tastes (e.g., preferring hip hop or Haydn), and habits (e.g., going to bed early or late). All of these characteristics, unlike emotions and moods, are at least somewhat stable over time, and they clearly reflect non-intel-lectual differences between people. However, psychologists still do not usually consider them true components of personality. The reason this time is that attitudes, beliefs, tastes, and habits are normally quite narrow and restricted in their psychological relevance. Attitudes and beliefs concern specific propositions, tastes concern specific experiences, and habits concern specific actions. Personality characteristics, in contrast, have relatively broad relevance; they refer to *generalized patterns* of psychological functioning. For instance, people might be said to have 'authoritarian' personalities if, in addition to their specifically anti-immigration sentiments, they hold a variety of prejudiced, repressive, and highly conventional attitudes. Similarly, people who go to bed late might be said to be ambitious if this habit is part of a larger pattern of hard work and competitive striving, or extraverted and sensation-seeking if it is part of a pattern of relentless partying.

As you can see, the understanding of personality that psychologists employ is quite complex. The appealing simplicity that 'individual differences' implies is a little deceptive. From the perspective of personality psychology, that is, personality refers to those individ-ual differences that (1) are psychological in nature, (2) fall outside the intellectual domain, (3) are enduring dispositions rather than transient states, and (4) form relatively broad or generalized patterns. This set of distinctions is presented schematically in Figure 1.1.

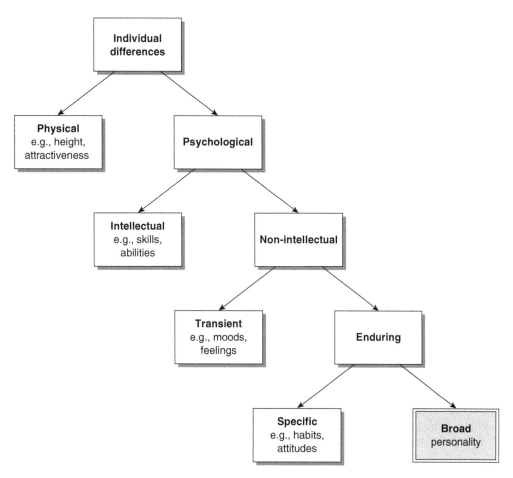

Figure 1.1 A classification of individual differences

Does this complex set of distinctions add up to a satisfactory definition of personality? It certainly comes close. However, we need to make one more important addition to it. Some psychologists argue that the definition of personality should not only refer to individual differences in dispositions, but should also refer to the underlying psychological mechanisms and processes that give rise to them. That is, someone's personality is not simply a set of *characteristics* that they possess, but also a set of *dynamics* that account for these characteristics. If we allow for this sensible addition, then it is hard to do much better than Funder (1997), who defines personality as 'an individual's characteristic pattern of thought, emotion, and behavior, together with the psychological mechanisms – hidden or not – behind those patterns' (pp. 1–2).

After reading all of the conceptual distinctions we have made so far while defining personality, the definition that we have come up with may seem to narrow personality down to a small and insignificant subset of the differences between people. However, if you think about it for a minute, you might change your mind. In fact, those aspects of your psychological individuality that are enduring, broad, and non-intellectual are particularly important ones.

If you were asked to describe yourself, you would probably mention many attributes that are not aspects of your personality – such as groups you belong to (e.g., national, ethnic, gender, age) and physical descriptions – but you would almost certainly mention quite a few personality characteristics. Indeed, psychologist Deborah Prentice (1990) asked a sample of university students to describe themselves and found that personality characteristics such as **traits** and **values** were among the most common attributes that the students mentioned. It is unlikely, on the other hand, that you would mention many of the psychological characteristics that we excluded from our definition of personality, such as current mood states, specific attitudes, or particular habits. Imagine how you would feel if someone responded to a request to describe who she is by stating that she feels worried, thinks that Justin Bieber is a fine singer, and brushes her teeth five times a day. You would probably think that this person wasn't really answering the question appropriately: she isn't really giving you a good sense of who she is as a person and seems to be referring to incidental details of her life.

This is an important point. The reason why personality characteristics as we have defined them are particularly significant is that they seem to be central to who we are as persons, rather than merely being minor or incidental details. Why this is so is no great mystery. Characteristics that are not enduring dispositions are, almost by definition, not very informative about who we are as persons: our transient psychological states may well not reflect how we normally are. Characteristics that are highly specific are usually not central to our sense of ourselves because they also tend to reflect isolated features of our make-up rather than ways in which our behaviour and our identity are coherent. Even if we did think of ourselves in terms of a list of specific attitudes, tastes, beliefs, and the like, it would be such a long and formless list that it would not amount to any good sense of who we are as individuals. This is why we tend to define ourselves in terms of broader patterns of thinking, feeling, and behaving: in short, personality characteristics. Even the distinction between intellectual and non-intellectual differences is relevant to our sense of self. People tend to define themselves much more in terms of a vast range of (non-intellectual) personality characteristics than the relatively narrow domain of cognitive abilities (although almost all of us, of course, think of ourselves as 'intelligent').

Personality characteristics are important not only for how we define ourselves, but also for how we perceive other people. Social psychologists have shown that when we form impressions of others we try to extract information about their personality attributes from how they look and act: whether they are friendly, trustworthy, emotional, dominant, and so on. Impression formation is all about making what are known as 'dispositional inferences' about other people's personalities. Similarly, the stereotypes that we hold about particular social groups are saturated with personality characteristics. Whether accurate or inaccurate, these stereotypes represent personality portraits of group members, such as whether they are happy-go-lucky, aggressive, socially awkward, greedy, and so on. Once again, personality characteristics matter to us as social perceivers because they are such centrally important aspects of people.

To summarize, personality is a particularly important domain of individual differences, even if on the surface it seems to be rather narrow according to our definition. It is important because it encompasses the sorts of psychological characteristics that are most informative about who we and others are as individuals, individuals whose behaviour is coherent, patterned, and governed by a stable sense of self or personal identity.

Related concepts

Having closed in on a sense of what personality is, it may be helpful to compare the concept to others with related meanings. Two concepts that quickly come to mind are '**temperament**' and '**character**'. In everyday language these terms are sometimes used more or less interchangeably with 'personality', and historically they have often been used in contexts where, in more recent times, 'personality' would be employed. Within psychology, however, they have somewhat distinct meanings. Temperament usually refers to those aspects of psychological individuality that are present at birth or at least early in child development, are related to emotional expression, and are presumed to have a biological basis. In short, temperamental characteristics are thought to be grounded in bodily processes.

Character, on the other hand, usually refers to those personal attributes that are relevant to moral conduct, self-mastery, will-power, and integrity. Someone of 'poor character', that is, might be deceitful, impulsive, and shiftless. Whereas temperamental characteristics are commonly assumed to have a biological basis, character is often assumed to be the result of socialization experiences, aspects of the person's psychological make-up that depend on learning socially appropriate forms of self-control and 'prosocial' conduct. Both assumptions are only partially true.

How do temperament and character relate to personality as we have defined it, and as it is understood by psychologists? Although the two concepts have rather distinct connotations, psychologists now tend to think of them as referring to different sorts of personality characteristics. In short, psychology's concept of personality contains temperament and character within it, and recognizes that personality characteristics can spring from biological and social influences, from genes and experiences, and, most often, both. We will have a lot more to say about this in later chapters.

Putting it together

Figure 1.2 tries to lay out the basics of our emerging sense of personality, as it is understood by personality psychologists. To the left is a set of psychological mechanisms and processes that produce enduring psychological differences between people. These differences can be roughly divided into those that are intellectual (i.e., involving cognitive abilities) and those that are not, with a grey area of ambiguous characteristics in the middle. Some personality differences can be considered aspects of character or temperament. Enduring psychological differences are, in addition, related to more transient and specific behaviours, cognitions, and emotions.

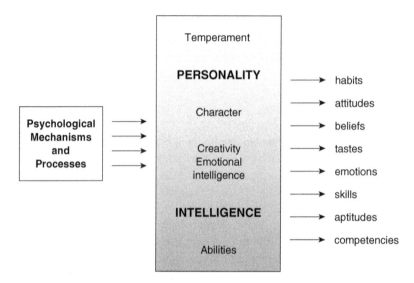

Figure 1.2 Psychology's model of individual differences

Personality psychology's place in psychology

The definition of personality that we have been mulling over is psychology's. It may not correspond exactly to yours or anyone else's. However, it does define the subject matter of one of psychology's basic subdisciplines or areas of study, alongside cognitive, developmental, social, and physiological psychology, among others. So how is the psychology of personality, defined in this way, distinct from these other subdisciplines? Three distinctions are most important.

First, personality psychology is all about differences between people, as we have seen, whereas the other subdisciplines generally are not. Most psychological areas of study investigate what people have in common: the mechanisms, processes, and structures that we all share by virtue of being human. Cognitive psychologists may study how we perceive objects, social psychologists how we form stereotypes, and physiological psychologists how our brain chemicals are associated with our moods, where 'we' and 'our' are understood to refer to people in general. The focus of the studies that these psychologists conduct is usually on the average pattern of response that a group of study participants manifests. Variations among participants around that average are usually ignored and treated as a nuisance ('random error'). To personality psychologists, in contrast, such variations between people are precisely what is most interesting. Of course, understanding how we are all the same is at least as important as understanding how we differ, but personality psychology is virtually alone within psychology in focusing on questions of the second kind.

A second distinctive feature of personality psychology is that its focus is on the whole person as an integrated individual. This probably sounds rather vague and fluffy, but it is in clear contrast to some other areas of study in psychology. Most subdisciplines address a specific psychological function or domain, one piece of what makes up the functioning individual. These functions and domains include perception, thinking, emotion, and language. These are all important aspects of human psychology, of course, but they are also in some sense 'sub-personal', referring to components that are integrated into a coherent system that we call a person. Personality psychology, which takes individuals rather than their components as its subject matter, aspires to be broader and more encompassing. Arguably, social and developmental psychology, by studying people in their social interactions and contexts and investigating their changes over time, share this focus on the whole person, although they do not usually emphasize individual differences. This is one reason why personality, social, and developmental psychology are all sometimes disparaged as 'soft' psychology, their methods seen as less rigorous and their findings less objective and reliable than those of the 'harder' subdisciplines. Because personality psychology and its allied subdisciplines deal with people in all their complexity – as creatures with social, cultural, and biological dimensions – they face greater scientific challenges than those subdisciplines that can isolate and study one part of the psyche.

A third distinctive feature of personality psychology contrasts it with social psychology. Personality and social psychology are close neighbours in some ways: many psychologists identify themselves with both, many professional journals are devoted to both, and both tend to share a focus on the whole person. However, as we have seen, personality psychology focuses on enduring characteristics of the person that are consistent across different situations. In contrast, social psychology tends to pay attention to those aspects of the person's thinking, feeling, and behaving that change over time and under different circumstances. Social psychologists are interested in how our mind and behaviour are shaped by the social contexts in which we are embedded and the social interactions in which we participate. Consequently, social psychologists emphasize the extent to which our attitudes, beliefs, emotions, and behaviours are malleable products of our social environment, and personality psychologists emphasize the extent to which they are stable attributes of the person. One way to think about this is that personality psychologists have a tendency or bias to see psychological phenomena as being due to *internal* factors – influences intrinsic to the person – whereas social psychologists have a corresponding tendency to see them as due to *external* factors located in the social environment.

In summary, then, the psychology of personality is an important and distinctive area of study within the broader field of psychology. It is distinctive in its focus on psychological variation, on the whole person or individual as the unit of analysis, and on the determinants of thinking, feeling, and behaving that are intrinsic to the person.

Overview of the book

In the remaining chapters of the book we will explore the psychology of personality, keeping in mind the issues that have arisen in this introduction. In the remainder of this first section of the book ('Describing personality'), we discuss the efforts that psychologists have made to *describe* personality, that is, to define what it is and determine how its variations should be mapped out. Once we have decided that personality is essentially about certain kinds of differences between people – human individuality – we have to decide how these differences are most usefully characterized and classified. What units should we use to describe personalities, and can they be organized into an encompassing framework of personality description? Chapter 2 presents the tradition of psychological research that has attempted to characterize personality in terms of units called 'traits'. Psychologists who work in this tradition argue that traits provide the best language for describing personality variations, and that a few fundamental traits underlie these superficially limitless variations. The chapter reviews this psychology of traits as well as some of the challenges that have been posed to it. Chapter 3 then examines the psychological processes that give rise to personality; the mechanisms behind the patterns that we call traits.

Having reviewed attempts to *describe* personality, we turn in the book's second section to attempts to *explain* it. It is one thing to establish *how* something should be characterized, quite another thing to account for *why* it is as it is. For instance, to describe a landscape we might draw a map of its physical features (e.g., peaks, valleys, rivers, lakes), its vegetation (e.g., forests, woods, grasslands), and the incursions that people have made on it (e.g., settlements, roads, power-lines, district boundaries). However, to explain why the landscape is as it is, we need to go beyond and beneath its visible topography. Our explanation might refer to any number of influences, such as the geological forces that buckled and carved the surface of the land, the climate that surrounds it, and the historical, economic, and political realities that affected how humans modified it. In short, there may be many ways to account for why a phenomenon – a landscape or a personality – is the way it is.

The second section of the book ('Explaining personality') therefore reviews a variety of personality theories and kinds of explanation, which offer quite different answers to this 'why' question. Chapter 4 discusses psychoanalytic theories, which account for personality in terms of child development, unconscious **motives**, and psychological defences and conflicts. Although linked in the popular mind with one man, Sigmund Freud, we discuss the many ways psychoanalytic theory has developed since he originated it and the many ways in which it accounts for personality processes and characteristics.

We then examine biological theories of personality, which maintain that personality variation is underpinned by individual differences in genetic inheritance and brain functioning. In Chapter 5 we review evolutionary approaches to personality and what 'behavioural genetics' can tell us about the sources of personality. In Chapter 6 we also consider the degree to which fundamental traits are rooted in brain structure and function, such as the extent to which fundamental traits have a neurochemical basis.

Chapter 7 introduces cognitive theories of personality, which explain personality variation as the result of differing patterns of thinking, perceiving, and believing. These patterns range from beliefs that guide our individual ways of understanding the world, to the strategies we employ in trying to accomplish our goals and plans, to the ways we think about that special somebody, the self.

The first two sections of the book focus on the fundamental concepts, theories, and findings of personality psychology. However, personality psychology is not simply an abstract science of how and why people differ psychologically. It also has important practical applications, which we will discuss in the book's third section ('Applying personality'). The book's first two sections therefore provide a conceptual foundation for exploring these applications. Chapter 8 discusses the ways in which personality psychology can illuminate psychological development, and help us to understand personality stability and change. Does personality change in adulthood, or is it set in plaster during childhood? Can you predict adult personality from child temperament? What stages do people go through in personality development, and what are the characteristic themes and preoccupations of each stage?

Chapter 9 reviews the ways in which personality can be measured, and the contexts in which personality assessment has a very real impact on people's lives. Increasingly, personality tests are finding their ways into the selection of employees, as a supplement to interviews and other criteria. Personality testing is also commonly performed by clinical psychologists who need to evaluate the progress of clients in therapy, to diagnose their problems, or to assess their suitability for treatment. Many different forms of personality assessment have been developed, and their strengths, weaknesses, and goals are discussed at length in the chapter.

Chapter 10 discusses the various roles that personality plays in mental disorders, such as creating vulnerabilities for particular psychiatric conditions. The chapter also examines the destructive ways in which personality disturbances can manifest themselves, with a focus on the so-called 'personality disorders'. Chapter 11 critically reviews attempts to apply personality theory to the study of individual lives, a controversial practice known as 'psychobiography'. In discussing the difficulties, risks, and limitations of psychobiography – how hard it is to 'put it all together' and formulate persons in their entirety – we will come to an appreciation of the complexity of human lives and personalities.

The book's fourth and final section ('Intelligence') contains three chapters on the psychology of ability. Chapter 12 discusses intelligence and cognitive abilities, reviewing evidence on how individual differences in abilities should be described (i.e., the structure of ability) and how they should be explained (i.e., the role of environmental and genetic factors).

Chapter 13 focuses attention on practical issues surrounding the study of abilities, such as the nature of intelligence testing, as well as demonstrating the many ways in which the study of intelligence can be applied in the real world of schools and workplaces.

Finally, Chapter 14 broadens out the study of abilities to include emotional intelligence, a proposed set of abilities that relate to competent perception, understanding, and reasoning about emotional states rather than narrowly cognitive ability. Emotional intelligence is shown to have wide-ranging implications for many domains of life.

Chapter summary

- 'Personality' is a complicated concept that has had several distinct meanings over the course of history. Within psychology, however, it refers to individual differences in psychological dispositions: that is, enduring ways in which people differ from one another in their typical ways of behaving, thinking, and feeling. These differences often reflect core features of who we are as persons, and are central to our self-concepts.
- This understanding of personality often excludes individual differences in intelligence and cognitive ability, although these are also of interest to many personality psychologists.
- In addition, personality psychologists are interested not only in individual differences, but also in the underlying causes or dynamics that explain these differences between people.
- Personality can be loosely distinguished from character (morally-relevant dispositions having to do with self-control, will, and integrity) and temperament (biologically-based dispositions that often involve emotional expression and are present early in life).
- Within psychology, the study of personality is distinctive for its focus on human individuality and its concern for the person as a functioning whole. It differs from social psychology, a neighbouring subdiscipline, by emphasizing the contribution that the person's internal dispositions make to behaviour, rather than the contribution of the person's external situation or context.

Further reading

Major reference works

For students wishing to obtain a more thorough and advanced review of personality psychology, the following major handbooks may be of interest:

Corr, P. J., & Matthews, G. (2009). *The Cambridge handbook of personality psychology*. Cambridge, UK: Cambridge University Press.

John, O. P., Robins, R. W., & Pervin, L.A. (Eds.) (2010). *Handbook of personality: Theory and research* (3rd ed.). New York: Guilford Press.

Journals

To get a sense of current research in personality psychology, and the sorts of research methods that it uses, you should take a look at recent issues of prominent scientific journals such as the following:

- *European Journal of Personality*
- *Journal of Personality*
- *Journal of Personality and Social Psychology*
- *Journal of Research in Personality*
- *Personality and Individual Differences*
- *Personality and Social Psychology Bulletin*
- *Personality and Social Psychology Review*

Trait Psychology

Learning objectives

- To develop a working understanding of the concept of 'personality trait' and the hierarchical structure of traits.
- To understand how psychologists have developed models of the dimensional structure of personality traits, including the statistical methods employed.
- To comprehend the 'Big Five' personality dimensions and their differences from existing three-factor models.
- To recognize the importance of trait taxonomies for advancing psychological understanding and prediction.
- To develop a balanced understanding of the merits and limitations of personality traits as units of personality description.
- To recognize some of the controversies and criticisms surrounding personality traits and trait models of personality.

This chapter turns to the fundamental question of how individual differences in personality should be described. The concept of personality 'trait' – the primary unit of personality description – is introduced and defined, and the hierarchical nature of traits is explained. The long-standing efforts to uncover the structure or organization of personality traits, by reducing the bewildering variety of possible traits into a few basic personality dimensions, are then explored. Along the way, the statistical methods used to conduct this reduction are presented. One prominent outcome of this work, the Big Five model of personality, is presented, and contrasted with a rival model that proposes three rather than five basic dimensions along which people vary. We discuss the value of dimensional systems such as these, and demonstrate the many phenomena that one illustrative dimension helps to illuminate. Finally, we see that, in addition to such broad personality dimensions, a variety of more specific traits also offer valuable ways of capturing meaningful differences between people.

The previous chapter left us with an abstract understanding of what personality psychologists study. Our rather unwieldy definition tells us what personality is, according to the psychologists who study it. However, it does not even begin to tell us how to characterize a personality. How are we to describe the individual differences that make up people's personalities?

Description is a fundamental problem for any science, and personality psychology aspires to be scientific. Chemistry has its periodic table of elements, zoology its taxonomy of biological species, physics its classification of elementary particles. These systems of description systematically lay out the sorts of things that scientists encounter and work with when explaining phenomena. They describe the *structure* or *organization* of the world from the perspective of the respective sciences, and provide the units of analysis for theoretical and empirical work. So how are we to describe the structure of personality, and what are the proper units of description?

What is a trait?

Many psychologists think that the best unit for describing personalities is the **trait**, and that the structure of personality is the organization of traits. At one level, the concept of trait is a simple one: a trait is a characteristic form of behaving, thinking, or feeling, such as 'friendliness', 'rigidity', or 'anxiousness'. At another level the situation is more complicated, and several important aspects of the concept need to be spelled out. Some of these should remind you of our discussion of the concept of personality in Chapter 1:

- A trait must be a relatively enduring characteristic of the person, as distinct from a transient state. Although vague, the 'relatively' is an important qualification here. Traits may change over time, but they shouldn't change rapidly or chaotically; they should tend to be stable attributes of the person.
- A trait represents a pattern of behaviour, thinking, or feeling that is relatively consistent over a variety of different situations. If a person behaves in a very different manner when in similar situations – being very outgoing in some and very reserved and shy in others, for example – we should not attribute a trait to him or her. Once again, the 'relatively' is important because traits do not entail total situational consistency in a person's behaviour. People need not be shy in *all* social situations for it to be appropriate to call them shy.
- A trait is a way in which people differ from one another – it is, as scientists would say, a 'variable' – so that different individuals will manifest different levels of the trait. To simplify communication, we may say that someone either has or doesn't have a particular trait, but psychologists typically assume that people differ by degrees on

traits. People may have greater or lesser degrees of shyness, and in principle these degrees can be quantified.

- Traits are dispositions. That is, a trait is best thought of as a probabilistic *tendency* that a person has to act in a certain way when placed in a certain kind of situation. Cats, for instance, have dispositions to hiss and scratch, but will only express these dispositions in particular circumstances, and even in these circumstances they may not always do so. Consequently, a trait may remain unexpressed and unobserved if a person encounters few situations in which it might be expressed.

- Traits vary in their generality. Some traits only bear on narrow domains of life, and others are relevant to a very large proportion of the person's everyday activities. We can talk about a hierarchy of traits, with relatively specific traits that relate to a small number of behaviours falling under broader traits. For instance, shame-proneness could be considered one component of a more general trait of 'negative emotionality', the disposition to experience unpleasant emotional states. Such a hierarchy could have several levels, with particular behaviours or habits representing the bottom level: placing a raunchy personals advertisement is a behaviour that may reflect a narrow trait of sexual sensation-seeking, which is one component of a medium-level trait of sensation-seeking, which is itself a component of a high-level trait of extraversion. This hierarchical arrangement is illustrated in Figure 2.1.

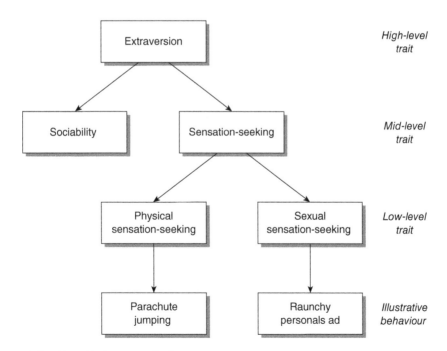

Figure 2.1 The hierarchical structure of traits

Defining the trait universe: Part 1

Our discussion so far should make it clearer how personality psychologists conceptualize traits. Defining what a trait is and choosing the trait as the unit of personality description is only the beginning, of course. To go further towards a system of personality description, we need a way to map the trait universe. In other words, we need to find a way to characterize the range of personality variation that traits cover. Does this universe of traits have any fundamental dimensions, groupings, coordinates, or axes, and what might they be?

A first step towards answering this question by English-speaking psychologists was taken in 1936 by Allport and Odbert, who followed research in German by Baumgarten. Allport and Odbert sought to define the boundaries of the trait universe by collecting an exhaustive list of personality descriptors (see John, 1990, for more details). They did this by patiently combing through a large dictionary, containing about 550,000 entries, for terms that referred to ways in which one person's behaviour could be distinguished from another's. By this means they obtained almost 18,000 terms, an astonishing number if you think of it. As you might imagine, after reading Chapter 1, not all of these terms were personality characteristics. In fact, about three-quarters of them were not, according to the authors' understanding of personality. Some referred to physical characteristics, cognitive abilities or talents, transient states such as moods, specific behaviours, social roles, or highly evaluative terms used to describe people's effects on others rather than consistencies in their own behaviour (e.g., 'irritating'). Nevertheless, after all of these non-personality terms were removed from the list, roughly 4,500 trait terms remained.

Allport and Odbert's work creates a dilemma. If there really are 4,500 different trait terms circulating in English, and similar numbers in other languages, does this mean personality psychologists have to pay attention to all of them? That would seem to be a daunting task, and any descriptive system that needs 4,500 different terms would seem to fail an important scientific criterion: to be an economical and practical way to describe the phenomena of interest, in this case, human personalities. Surely, also, many trait terms are redundant with others and refer to the same sorts of people. It is possible to draw subtle conceptual distinctions between 'hostile', 'aggressive', 'fierce', and 'belligerent', for example, but their meanings clearly overlap and it would be more than a little odd to hear someone described as 'hostile and aggressive but not at all fierce or belligerent'. If this is the case, it makes sense to imagine that hidden within the vast expanse of the trait term universe there might be a smaller number of fundamental personality characteristics, like constellations in the night sky. But how many such basic traits are there, what might they be, and how on earth might we be able to discover them?

A statistical digression

Before we answer the first two of these questions we need to address the third, the 'methodological' question of how basic traits are to be determined. And to answer this question, we need to embark on a short digression into statistics. If the mere sight of this word makes your stomach turn, be reassured that this little excursion will not be technical. However, like all sciences, personality psychology has a significant quantitative component, and psychologists interested in determining the fundamental traits of personality have relied very heavily on two statistical procedures in particular. Statistical methods are indispensable to personality psychology as it has developed, because as it is impossible to grasp efforts to examine personality structure without them.

The first procedure is called the *correlation coefficient* or **correlation** for short. A correlation represents the degree of association between two variables (i.e., things that vary) and is measured on a scale from –1 to +1. 'Association' refers to the degree to which one variable is *related to* or *predictable on the basis of* another. If I know that you are of above average height, for example, I can predict that you will be of above average weight too, because height and weight are associated in this sense. My predictions may be wrong in particular cases – there are plenty of heavy shorter people and skinny tall ones – but on average they should be better than chance (i.e., predicting randomly). This association of height and weight is a positive one, because the higher the quantity of one variable, the higher the quantity of the other is likely to be. A negative association – such as between a place's latitude and its average temperature – means that the higher the quantity of one variable, the lower the quantity of the other tends to be. When there is no association between two variables – such as shoe size and intelligence – they have a correlation of 0 and do not enable any prediction of one another at all. A very large proportion of research in personality psychology involves looking for associations among variables, using the humble correlation coefficient.

The magnitude of a correlation coefficient matters a great deal. A positive association may exist between two variables, so the correlation is somewhere between 0 and +1, but the implications of it being .1 or .9 are very different. If it is .9, then each variable allows confident prediction of the other: the correlation is almost perfect. If it is .1, on the other hand, the two variables will yield prediction of one another that is barely above chance. By convention in psychology, correlations of .1, .3, and .5 are considered small, moderate, and large, respectively (Cohen, 1992). Correlations much higher than about .6 are quite rare, except between alternative measures of the same variable (e.g., two tests of depression). Because the size of correlations will be referred to on a few occasions throughout this book, it is worth getting some sense of what these values mean. Consider the three hypothetical situations presented in Table 2.1, each of which represents 200 people measured on two variables, A and B. Each person's level on each variable is represented as being either 'above average' or 'below average', in the sense of falling in the top or bottom half of the 200 people. (Strictly speaking, this average is called the 'median'.) Note that this is a simplification: usually measures of personality variables take a continuous range of numerical values rather than crudely dichotomizing people.

Table 2.1 illustrates small, medium, and large correlations. Look at data set 1 first, which represents a small correlation of .1. If I know that someone is above average on Variable A, I can predict that he or she will also be above average on Variable B, because this is somewhat more likely (55%) than the reverse. However, this prediction is obviously not one that I can be very confident about, as it will be wrong 45% of the time. Still, it is better than nothing, because if I predicted at random I would be wrong 50% of the time.

Table 2.1 Hypothetical data sets illustrating correlations of different sizes

Data set 1: small correlation (.1)

		Variable B		
		Above average	Below average	Total
Variable A	Above average	55	45	100
	Below average	45	55	100
	Total	100	100	200

Data set 2: moderate correlation (.3)

		Variable B		
		Above average	Below average	Total
Variable A	Above average	65	35	100
	Below average	35	65	100
	Total	100	100	200

Data set 3: large correlation (.5)

		Variable B		
		Above average	Below average	Total
Variable A	Above average	75	25	100
	Below average	25	75	100
	Total	100	100	200

Data set 2, which illustrates a .3 correlation, is quite a bit better than nothing. Knowing that someone is above average on A allows us to predict that he or she will be above average on B with more assurance. We will be correct 65% of the time, almost twice as often as we are incorrect (i.e., 65 ÷ 35 = 1.86). Data set 3, showing a strong .5 correlation, allows us to be correct 75% of the time: the odds of our prediction being correct are now 3:1. As you can see, the magnitude of a correlation has clear implications.

The little tables we've used to illustrate the meaning of correlation are called binomial effect size displays (BESDs; Rosenthal & Rubin, 1982). If you want to get a sense of what a correlation means in practical terms, a simple calculation lets you convert it into this way of thinking. All you need to do is divide the correlation by two and then add 0.5. This number estimates the proportion of cases who are above average on one variable who will be above average on the other, for example:

Table 2A

Correlation	Divide by 2	Add .5
.4	→ .2	→.7
−.2	→ −.1	→.4
.7	→ .35	→.85
0	→ 0	→.5

In these four examples, then, about 70%, 40%, 85%, and 50% of people, respectively, who score above the average on one variable will be above average on the other.

So much for the correlation coefficient, a simple measure of association that is the first statistical procedure that we need to review before returning to our exploration of personality structure. The second procedure that has been central to the study of personality structure is called **factor analysis**. In essence, factor analysis is a method for finding patterns within a group of correlations. It is perhaps best illustrated by a hypothetical example. Table 2.2 presents what is called a 'correlation matrix', which lays out correlation coefficients for all pairs of variables in a set. One half of the matrix is empty because the correlation between B and C, for example, is the same as the correlation between C and B, so there is no need to present both. Correlations falling on the diagonal are all +1 because a variable always correlates perfectly with itself.

Looking at Table 2.2 what you probably see is a big mess. Some variables correlate quite strongly, some not much at all, some negatively, and some positively. This is where factor analysis enters the scene. What it attempts to do is find patterns of correlations within the matrix that may not be readily obvious to the observer (i.e., what psychologists sometimes facetiously call 'eyeball analysis'). The technical and computational details of factor analysis need not concern us here, but in this particular correlation matrix the procedure would find clear evidence of two distinct groups of variables. Variables A, C, and F form one group, and variables B, D, and E the other. Table 2.3 simply rearranges Table 2.2 to demonstrate the patterns that factor analysis would uncover.

Table 2.2 Hypothetical correlation matrix for variables A to F

	A	B	C	D	E	F
A	1.0					
B	.1	1.0				
C	.5	−.2	1.0			
D	.2	.5	.1	1.0		
E	−.1	.4	−.1	.6	1.0	
F	.4	.1	.6	.2	−.2	1.0

Table 2.3 Rearranged correlation matrix

	A	C	F	B	D	E
A	1.0					
C	.5	1.0				
F	.4	.6	1.0			
B	.1	−.2	.1	1.0		
D	.2	.1	.2	.5	1.0	
E	−.1	−.1	−.2	.4	.6	1.0

As you can see, all of the correlations among variables A, C, and F are relatively strong and positive, averaging .5, as are the correlations among variables B, D, and E. However, the correlations of variables from one group with variables from the other, shown in the square at the lower left of the table, are all relatively weak, some positive and some negative, and they average close to 0. This indicates that there is no systematic pattern of association between the two variable groups: they are distinct and unrelated. In the language of factor analysis, these groups define separate factors.

Factor analysis searches through correlation matrices in an effort to locate variable groupings such as these. When it does so, it allows us to make certain inferences. First, we can guess that concealed within – or perhaps 'beneath' – the large set of variables, there is a smaller set of more basic 'latent' variables. Second, we can guess what these latent variables might be by paying attention to what the variables within each group seem to have in common. If variables X, Y, and Z belong to one factor, that factor's identity or meaning can be guessed at by thinking about how the three variables are conceptually similar or about what they might jointly reflect.

As you may have guessed by now, factor analysis seems like a perfect way to begin the task, interrupted by this statistical digression, of uncovering and characterizing the fundamental traits that may underlie the wild profusion of trait terms.

Defining the trait universe: Part 2

Sure enough, the first attempts to simplify the trait universe and discover the latent structure of personality relied heavily on factor analysis, and thus on correlation coefficients. The trail-blazer in this effort was Raymond Cattell, who tried to distil a smaller number of basic personality factors from Allport and Odbert's lengthy list of trait terms. Such a reduction could not easily be done by statistical means alone, so Cattell (1943) began by sorting the terms into semantically similar clusters of synonyms or near-synonyms, according to his personal judgement. He then sorted these clusters into pairs that appeared to be semantic opposites, or antonyms. In this fashion he derived 160 clusters, to which he added a few more from the psychological literature, and selected a representative term from each cluster.

At this point, the trait list drastically reduced from 4,500 to 171, statistical methods played their first, minor role. Cattell had 100 people rate one or two people they knew on the 171 trait terms, and then examined the correlations among the terms to identify a smaller set of 60 clusters. These were further reduced to 35, according to Cattell's judgement of which clusters were supported by the psychological literature. Only now did he employ factor analysis, again using a group of people's ratings of others' personalities. Through a complicated procedure, Cattell derived 12 factors from this analysis, to which he later added four more factors based on additional studies. At the end of this long and complicated process, then, we are left with 16 personality factors on which Cattell built a theory of personality.

Cattell's efforts to uncover the fundamental dimensions were Herculean, especially given the computational limitations of his time. Contemporary researchers can perform large factor analyses with a few pecks of a keyboard or clicks of a mouse, but in the mid-20th century analyses of moderately large data sets might take weeks of pencil-and-paper calculation. Cattell's work lives on in the tradition of factor-analytic research he pioneered, and in a still-popular personality test, the 16PF. Nevertheless, it has been eclipsed in recent personality psychology for three main reasons. First, many researchers have found Cattell's procedure for distilling his 16 factors to be somewhat arbitrary, relying on several steps that seem to involve too much subjective judgement. They have also had trouble replicating his factors in their own studies. Second, although 16 factors allow a much more economical description of personality than 4,500 trait terms, that number still seems too large for most theorists to juggle. It is certainly hard to keep so many dimensions in mind at once, leading many theorists to hope that a simpler system of description might emerge. Finally, many of Cattell's factors seemed to correlate, just as the trait terms within each factor correlate with one another. This fact raises the possibility that even more basic dimensions, or 'superfactors', might underpin Cattell's 16 factors. Ideally, perhaps, trait terms could be boiled down to truly independent, uncorrelated factors that are irreducible to any others.

The search for this bedrock of fundamental trait dimensions began with Fiske (1949) and was continued by many psychologists in the ensuing decades. Over time, researchers began to notice that factor analyses of personality ratings frequently converged on just five broad factors. Recognizing this regularity took some time, in part because different investigators chose different labels for their factors. Although factor analysis can tell researchers how many factors seem to be present in a correlation matrix, it is sadly incapable of telling precisely what they mean. Researchers must bestow a name, which they do based on some mixture of intelligent guesswork and theoretical predilections. Nevertheless, the recurrence of similar factors in many studies, using different methodologies and large and diverse samples of personality raters, eventually led some psychologists to dub them the '**Big Five**'. These five factors, it is claimed, represent the five fundamental ways along which people's personalities vary: the core of your personality can be represented by your position on these five dimensions. The primary label for each factor, alternative factor labels, and some trait terms that

Table 2.4 Summary of the Big Five personality factors (after John, 1990)

Standard name	Alternative names	Illustrative trait terms
I. Extraversion	Surgency	sociable, assertive, enthusiastic, energetic, forceful, talkative
		quiet, reserved, shy, retiring
II. Agreeableness	Social adaptability	warm, modest, kind, appreciative, trusting, affectionate, helpful
		cold, quarrelsome, unfriendly
III. Conscientiousness	Dependability, Prudence, Will to achieve	efficient, organized, thorough, planful, reliable
		careless, irresponsible, frivolous
IV. Neuroticism	Emotional instability	tense, irritable, shy, moody, nervous, high-strung
		stable, calm, contented, unemotional
V. Openness to Experience	Culture, Intellect	imaginative, intelligent, original, insightful, curious, sophisticated
		narrow interests, simple, shallow

illustrate each factor, are presented in Table 2.4. Terms in italics represent the opposing pole of each factor.

Extraversion is a term that originated in the personality theory of Carl Jung, who meant by it an orientation to the outside world rather than to private experience, which he dubbed introversion. In the Big Five its connotations are somewhat different. As the table indicates, Extraversion is best exemplified by traits involving sociability, in particular a preference for large groups. However, it is much broader in scope than sociability, encompassing traits that involve energy and activity levels (hence the alternative title 'surgency'), sensation-seeking, interpersonal dominance, and a tendency to experience positive emotional states. Introverts tend to have low levels of these same traits.

Agreeableness, like Extraversion, primarily has to do with interpersonal qualities. Unlike Extraversion, it involves cooperativeness, altruism, and a generally warm, compliant, and trusting stance towards others. Disagreeable individuals are characterized as cold, callous, selfish, calculating, hostile, and competitive in their motivations.

Conscientiousness is a factor whose name has been the focus of some disagreement. However, there is little disagreement about the traits that characterize it, which generally reflect self-control, planfulness, and being organized, efficient, and deliberate in one's approach to tasks. Unconscientious people tend to be impulsive, disorganized, oriented to the present rather than the future, and careless towards their responsibilities. Conscientiousness is therefore a matter of caring about one's long-term goals and **interests**, resisting impulses that threaten to sabotage them, and harnessing one's efforts to accomplish these goals and interests competently. Different names for the factor draw attention to one or other of these aspects:

'dependability' emphasizes self-control and predictability, 'prudence' emphasizes planning and foresight, 'will to achieve' emphasizes the driven pursuit of goals.

Neuroticism has to do with people's emotional instability. Although 'neurosis' is an almost obsolete psychiatric term referring to pathological manifestations of anxiety, Neuroticism refers to a considerably wider range of negative emotions, including anger, sadness, shame, and embarrassment. It also does not imply the presence of any mental disorder. In this expanded sense, neurotic people are more prone to experience negative emotions, to be psychologically maladjusted and vulnerable, and to have low self-esteem. In contrast, people who are low in Neuroticism are emotionally stable, calm, and able to cope well with stress.

Openness to Experience is a somewhat vague term for a factor that has proven to be controversial and difficult to name. Metaphorically, 'openness' implies a willingness to adopt novel and unconventional ways of thinking and behaving, manifest in such traits as creativity, imaginativeness, curiosity, and aesthetic appreciation. Open people are heavily invested in cultivating new experiences, and have a mild tendency to score relatively high on measures of intelligence. People who fall at the other end of this factor are conventional and narrow in their interests, and conservative and sometimes rigid in their approach to life's challenges and opportunities.

This set of 'Big Five' personality factors, which is sometimes referred to as the **'five-factor model'**, is probably the dominant model of personality structure in contemporary personality psychology. It is pleasingly economical, but also seems to leave few regions of the trait universe uncovered. Most of the trait terms we use in everyday speech can be related to the high or low end of these five factors, and most of the personality scales or tests that psychologists have developed seem to be measuring one or more of them to varying degrees. Research indicates that the factors can be derived from trait terms from several languages besides English, that they emerge reliably in studies of self-ratings as well as ratings of other people, that they are stable over time, and that they can predict many forms of behaviour. Several questionnaire measures of the factors, the NEO PI-R, NEO-PI-3, and the NEO-FFI (e.g., Costa & McCrae, 1992), are among the most widely used personality measures. All told, the discovery of the five factors has been hailed as a major integrating achievement of personality psychology, a structure as objectively real as the seven continents.

Alternatives to the Big Five

Although it has been widely adopted as a descriptive framework, the Big Five is not universally celebrated by psychologists working in the trait psychology tradition. Several alternative models have been propounded, the most well-supported of which propose that there are only three fundamental dimensions of personality. However, before we get to the details of these alternatives, we need to turn a critical eye on the origins of the Big Five. You will recall that the five factors emerged from statistical reductions of Allport and Odbert's list of trait terms. At the time you may not have questioned the merits of this list as a starting point for the exploration of personality structure. However, the idea that a language's repertoire of trait terms is the best place to search for basic personality dimensions can be challenged.

This idea is a key assumption of what has been called the *lexical* approach to personality description, from the Latin for 'word'. The lexical approach assumes that personality can be adequately encompassed by single words in natural language, and that languages encode in trait terms the personality distinctions that matter for their speakers. Every important personality characteristic should therefore be represented in the trait vocabulary, or 'lexicalized'. Is this so obvious? Might it not be the case that some important personality characteristics have evolved no corresponding term? Perhaps some characteristics, or traits, are not recognized or talked about by members of a language community, or maybe some are communicated about only by phrases or sentences. If this were true, and the trait term repertoire does not comprehensively reflect the trait universe, then factor analyses of trait terms might fail to capture some basic domains of personality, or might misrepresent others.

If the lexical approach is potentially flawed in this way, how else might the basic dimensions of personality be discovered? One approach is to examine people's responses to personality questionnaires rather than to trait lists. For at least a century psychologists have been developing scales or 'tests' to assess personality characteristics, which commonly contain a number of questionnaire items. These items usually take the form of statements to which people respond by endorsing one of a set of alternatives (e.g., yes/no, true/false, 1 = *strongly disagree* to 5 = *strongly agree*). Items might refer to a person's behaviours, feelings, attitudes, or beliefs. People's ratings of themselves or others on such items, or on the scales that are composed by combining multiple items, can be factor analyzed, just like trait terms.

Advocates of this questionnaire approach to the study of personality structure argue that questionnaire items have one main advantage over trait terms. Simply put, they propose that items should be able to assess a greater range of personality characteristics. The greater semantic complexity of whole sentences should allow items to assess characteristics that have no corresponding single trait term, if such characteristics exist. This complexity also allows items to assess traits in particular contexts, whereas trait terms are context-free. Compare the task of rating how 'sociable' you are, which requires you to make a judgement that is abstracted from particular circumstances, with responding to 'I like to meet new people when I know I probably won't see them again'. Arguably statements such as these come closer to our ways of thinking about ourselves and others than lists of traits. It is therefore possible that people might respond in importantly different ways to questionnaire items and trait terms, and that using items might uncover traits to which the lexical approach is blind.

The most famous proponent of this questionnaire-based approach to personality description is Hans Eysenck. Eysenck was a colourful and very influential German-born English psychologist noted for his prolific, wide-ranging, and often controversial writings on such topics as the genetics of intelligence, psychoanalysis, crime, psychotherapy, and astrology. He is best known among psychologists for developing a two-factor model of personality. These factors, Extraversion–Introversion and Neuroticism, are now familiar to you, but they were first recognized and rigorously investigated by Eysenck (1947). On the strength of extensive factor-analytic research, he proposed that Cattell's 16 trait dimensions, many of which were moderately correlated, could be reduced to these two uncorrelated factors. In addition, he theorized that these factors were rooted in variations in the functioning of the nervous system, as we shall see in Chapter 6.

In subsequent work, Eysenck found a need for a third factor, which he labelled '**Psychoticism**'. By his account, the traits that composed this factor included aggressiveness, coldness, egocentricity, antisocial tendencies, creativity, lack of empathy, and tough-mindedness. These traits, according to Eysenck, reflect an underlying dimension stretching from psychological normality to psychotic disorders such as schizophrenia, which are marked by disabling symptoms such as hallucinations and bizarre delusions. Other theorists have disputed this understanding of the factor, proposing that it is more closely linked to 'psychopathic' tendencies – such as callousness, violence, and ruthlessness towards others – than to psychosis. Although some evidence supports Eysenck's proposed link between Psychoticism and schizophrenia, the factor's nature remains rather obscure. Its status is made more controversial by the factor's somewhat unreliable emergence in factor-analytic studies.

Despite the questions that surround Psychoticism, other psychologists have developed three-factor models of personality that closely resemble Eysenck's triad. Tellegen (1985), for example, found evidence for factors that he dubbed Positive Emotionality, Negative Emotionality, and Constraint. The first two are closely associated with Extraversion and Neuroticism, respectively, and emphasize the emotional susceptibilities associated with each. Constraint has a strong negative association with Psychoticism, representing a tendency to inhibit and control the expression of impulses and antisocial behaviour. Traits that illustrate Constraint include carefulness, cautiousness, reflectiveness, and lack of spontaneity. Watson and Clark (1993) developed a very similar model – cheekily dubbed the 'Big Three' – labelling their three factors Positive Temperament, Negative Temperament, and Disinhibition. Disinhibition's opposing pole, in this model, is Constraint. Although this profusion of factor names may seem confusing at first, they clearly converge on three distinct conceptual domains, and questionnaire measures of the corresponding factors all correlate strongly.

Three factors or five?

There is considerable empirical support for three-factor as well as five-factor models of personality, and proponents of each often find themselves in opposition. You might well ask, though, whether the differences between these models are really so deep. After all, three-factor and five-factor models both recognize that Extraversion and Neuroticism are fundamental dimensions of personality. Their real disagreement is therefore confined to a choice between a single Psychoticism, Disinhibition, or Constraint factor on the one hand, and distinct Agreeableness, Conscientiousness, and Openness to Experience factors, on the other. It turns out that Constraint or Psychoticism, from the three-factor models, seem to correspond to a combination of the Big Five model's Agreeableness and Conscientiousness factors. People who score high on Constraint, for example, are typically agreeable and conscientious, and those who score high on Psychoticism are disagreeable and unconscientious. In short, Constraint or Psychoticism can be seen as a broad trait dimension that encompasses two Big Five model factors. Indeed, measures of Agreeableness and Conscientiousness tend to correlate positively with one another. This suggests that the two Big Five dimensions have the sort of affinity that makes it not entirely unreasonable to combine them into a superordinate dimension, although it is also true that they usually emerge as distinct factors in factor-analytic research.

The three-factor and five-factor models of personality are therefore not as different as they might first appear. They share two factors, and the three-factor model's third factor can be interpreted as a combination of two Big Five model factors. (Alternatively, these two factors can be seen as aspects, facets or components of this third factor.) Three-factor model advocates prefer the combined factor, which yields a more economical system of personality description and reduces the correlations among the system's factors. Big Five model advocates, in contrast, prefer to keep Agreeableness and Conscientiousness conceptually distinct, even if they are empirically related. This distinction between 'lumpers' and 'splitters' – theorists who prefer fewer or more categories, respectively, when making classifications – appears frequently in personality and abnormal psychology. Here, as elsewhere, neither lumpers nor splitters have a monopoly on the truth, and judging who is right cannot be based exclusively on timeless 'facts'.

Only Openness to Experience is left out of the integration that we have laid out. It has no obvious home in the three-factor model, although its creativity component falls within Eysenck's understanding of Psychoticism. If you consider Openness to be an indispensable component of any system for describing personality, you will tend to favour the Big Five model. If, on the other hand, you find it to be of relatively minor importance to personality description, you will consider its exclusion from three-factor models to be a reasonable omission. Whichever stance you take, however, what is not in doubt is that Openness to Experience is a meaningful broad personality factor. Only its importance is in question.

At this point you might be tempted to think that all of this quibbling about how many personality dimensions there are and how they should be characterized demonstrates either the irresolvable nature of the problem or the arbitrariness of psychologists' answers. Before you give in to this temptation, consider a couple of things. First, the five- or three-factor solutions have been obtained again and again by many independent researchers, with many different research populations, and using diverse sets of trait adjectives and questionnaires. Researchers don't tend to find two, four or six dimensions, and when they find three or five their composition almost always resembles those presented in this chapter. This is an impressive record of replication, a vital component of good science and a sign – although not a perfect one – that the solutions that have been reached are not arbitrary.

Further evidence against arbitrariness comes from studies that show quite consistently that factors akin to most of the Big Five can be detected in a variety of non-human animals (Gosling & John, 1999). These studies, which attempt to describe individual differences evident in ratings of animals' behaviour, find that factors closely resembling Extraversion, Neuroticism, and Agreeableness are detectable in most of the species studied. For example, Agreeableness-related factors have been obtained in chimpanzees, hyenas, dogs, pigs, rats, and five other species, but not in guppies and octopuses. Openness-related factors have emerged in seven of the 12 species studied, but Conscientiousness has only appeared in chimpanzees, our closest evolutionary relatives. Might these findings be due to the 'anthropomorphic' projection of human traits onto other animals? This possibility seems remote because studies have employed careful and objective ratings of specific behaviours – such as frequency of vocalization and number of nose contacts as indicators of piglets' 'extraversion' – rather than loose, subjective impressions. On balance, these findings provide remarkable support for the cross-species generality, and hence non-arbitrariness in humans, of most Big Five trait dimensions.

Whether there are three or five fundamental dimensions of personality, or some other number, is not a trivial issue, and it is possible that it will be conclusively resolved in the years to come. Hopefully you will now recognize that some of the differences between the rival models of personality structure are not so unbridgeable as they might seem, and that they are differences of theoretical predilection as much as fact. This should only increase our appreciation of just how far trait psychologists have moved towards their goal of understanding personality organization.

How do models of basic traits advance the field?

As we have seen, there is as yet no consensus among psychologists about the fundamental structure of personality, but there is substantial agreement and most of the disagreements that remain are not radical. At this point we need to ask what is gained by determining the structure of the trait universe. Is a model of personality structure just a descriptive classification – a factual statement about personality, equivalent to saying that there are two broad types of dinosaur or 94 chemical elements – or does it also promote our understanding of personality in other ways?

Before we explore this question we should remember that an empirically sound model of personality structure is a substantial intellectual achievement, and would remain substantial even if it did little more than enumerate and describe the fundamental ways in which personalities differ. Descriptive models and classifications are indispensable for science, and are interesting in and of themselves. Nevertheless, models of the basic trait dimensions go beyond simple classification in a number of valuable ways.

The first way in which models of personality structure advance the study of personality is by providing a conceptual net for capturing specific personality characteristics. If this sounds loose and metaphorical, imagine that you are beginning a study of a little-researched trait such as cynicism or envy-proneness. If you want to understand how your trait relates to other better-known traits, you would be well advised to find out whether a measure of it correlates with fundamental personality dimensions. Because these dimensions are broad and cover the personality domain comprehensively, they provide a framework for locating your trait. Perhaps it correlates with only one factor, as cynicism might correlate negatively with Agreeableness, for instance. In this case you could infer that your trait is similar to others that are associated with that factor, and that theory and research that apply to the factor – for example, ideas about its causes and correlates – may also apply to your trait. Or perhaps your trait correlates with two or more factors, suggesting that it represents a mixture of distinct characteristics. Shyness, for example, correlates negatively with Extraversion and positively with Neuroticism. This suggests that shyness represents a blend of lack of social interest (Introversion) and social anxiety (Neuroticism). Alternatively, shy people may come in two varieties: those who prefer being alone but tend not to be uncomfortable when in company, and those who are the reverse. Either way, locating the shyness trait's relationship to basic personality dimensions helps to clarify it. In principle then, models of personality structure can provide coordinates for any particular personality characteristic on a multidimensional map, and these coordinates can enlighten us about the nature of that characteristic.

A second way in which models of personality structure promote psychological under-standing is closely related to the first. Just as the Big Five model or Eysenck's three factors provide frameworks for locating specific personality traits, they can help to understand psy-chological phenomena other than traits. Let's say there is a phenomenon that we want to be able to understand better, such as illegal drug use, or psychological well-being, or proneness to depression. The number of personality characteristics that might predict (i.e., correlate with) these phenomena is vast and unwieldy, but the basic personality dimensions offer an economi-cal way to cover the personality domain. A researcher can therefore investigate whether any of these dimensions correlate with the phenomenon of interest, and possibly draw some helpful inferences about it.

Imagine, for example, that we want to understand vulnerability to depression. We could assess a group of people on a measure of the Big Five and on their history of depressive epi-sodes. Let's say we find that people with more depression in their histories have relatively high levels of Neuroticism and low levels of Extraversion and Openness. These findings would not allow us to say that these broad trait dimensions cause people to become depressed: maybe they are just associated with vulnerability. Nor could we confidently claim that these dimensions are the best way to conceptualize vulnerability: depression-proneness might be better understood in terms of more specific personality characteristics rather than broad fac-tors. However, the findings would strongly suggest that personality characteristics linked to neuroticism, introversion, and lack of openness are associated with depression-proneness, and support more focused investigations of these characteristics. The findings would also count against any theory proposing that depression-proneness is a matter of having poor self-control or being overly competitive, because the factors associated with these characteristics (i.e., low Conscientiousness and Agreeableness) are not correlated with it. The broad trait dimensions can therefore help to clarify phenomena that could not be so easily clarified without them.

A third benefit that models of personality structure bring is that they point to the under-lying *causes* of personality variation. If differences in people's observable behaviour reliably reveal a set of basic dimensions, it is reasonable to infer that there are distinct underlying processes or structures that give rise to these dimensions. The basic personality dimensions are clearly not arbitrary – they must have some objective basis – and just like any other psychological phenomena it should be possible to locate their underpinnings. Models of personality structure therefore guide the search for explanations of personality. If there is a trait dimension of Extraversion, for example, there ought to be some psychological or biological structures and processes whose variations underlie variations in extraversion-related behaviour. Conversely, a satisfactory explanation of Extraversion must be capable of accounting for all of the forms of psychological variation that it encompasses (e.g., sociability, interpersonal dominance, high activity levels, sensation-seeking, positive emotionality, etc.). In short, models of personality description advance our knowledge of personality explanation.

Specific traits

From reading this chapter so far you may think that trait psychology consists entirely of efforts to determine the broad fundamental dimensions of personality structure. This has indeed been a major focus for researchers and theorists, but a great deal of trait psychology focuses on more specific traits. Many psychologists working within the tradition of trait psychology aim to clarify, explain, and determine the correlates of personality characteristics that refer to more delimited patterns of behaviour, feeling, and thinking. All it takes to work within this tradition is a belief that traits are useful units of personality description and a commitment to assess and study them, whether or not one clings to a particular model of basic personality dimensions.

There are two main reasons why psychologists are often inclined to focus on specific traits rather than broad personality factors. The first has to do with the *descriptive inadequacy* of broad factors, and the second with their *predictive inadequacy*. You have probably already had some doubts about the descriptive adequacy of models such as the Big Five. Are five dimensions really enough to characterize a personality in all its richness? The answer is obviously a resounding 'No'. As Allport and Odbert showed, human languages often supply vast numbers of trait terms to capture the subtle shades of meaning that people have found helpful in capturing one another's individuality. To believe that the Big Five is sufficient to describe individual personalities is to imagine falsely that the 4,500 trait terms are essentially synonyms of ten basic personality characteristics (i.e., high and low on each factor). We usually aren't satisfied to know that a person is relatively high in Neuroticism, but want to know in what forms and under what circumstances this emotionality is expressed (e.g., is the person typically shy, angry, jumpy, moody, sad, tense, guilty, high-strung, under-confident …?).

The predictive adequacy of broad personality factors may not have struck you as being as questionable as their descriptive adequacy. However, it is often true that broad personality factors correlate less strongly with psychological phenomena than the more specific traits that define them. For example, Paunonen and Ashton (2001) found that Conscientiousness and Openness to Experience predicted performance in an undergraduate psychology course modestly or not at all (correlations were .21 and –.04, respectively). However, narrower traits that were related to these factors – 'achievement' and 'need for understanding' – correlated somewhat more strongly (.26 and .23). Similarly, DeNeve and Cooper (1998) investigated personality predictors of subjective well-being, and found that Neuroticism and Extraversion correlated –.27 and .20, respectively. However, several specific traits demonstrated stronger correlations, including desire for control, hardiness, trust, repressive-defensiveness, and a tendency to think that events are primarily due to chance (the last two traits correlated negatively with well-being). In short, broad personality factors are often outperformed as predictors by the traits that are supposedly less basic.

These descriptive and predictive limitations of broad models of personality are unquestionably real. However, they are not really failures of the models, although personality psychologists who are opposed to them sometimes make this claim. The Big Five model and others make no claims to provide a sufficient set of dimensions for characterizing individuals or predicting particular psychological phenomena. They are organizing frameworks only, ways of classifying personality characteristics in an economical and encompassing fashion that aspires to reveal some deeper truth about the underlying structure (and maybe also the causes) of individual differences. Advocates of broad factors are not claiming that specific traits are *nothing but* the factors that they are associated with, just as no one claims that parrots and penguins are nothing but birds. Instead, they argue that each specific trait has its own specific content as well as some degree of overlap with broad factors, and that these factors reflect ways in which specific traits tend to go together. By analogy, parrots and penguins each have their own distinctive features, but they also share certain underlying similarities which make them both examples of the broad grouping of birds.

Similarly, advocates of broad personality factors make no claims about the predictive superiority of these factors. In fact, it would be surprising if more specific traits were *not* frequently better predictors of behaviour than broad factors. First, such factors comprise many specific traits, and unless every trait is equally predictive of the behaviour in question, some traits must be more predictive than the factor of which they are a part. Second, specific traits refer to narrower patterns of behaviour than traits, so they should be able to predict relatively narrow or context-specific kinds of behaviour in a more focused and hence stronger manner. Consider the case of sensation-seeking, presented in Figure 2.1 near the beginning of this chapter. If the behaviour to be predicted were taking out a raunchy personal ad in a magazine, then the specific trait that is narrowly focused on the sexual domain (i.e., sexual sensation-seeking) should predict better than the broader, less domain-focused trait (i.e., sensation-seeking). By incorporating non-sexual domains of sensation-seeking, whose relevance to sexuality is weaker than sexual sensation-seeking, the broader trait's capacity to predict sexual behaviour will be diluted. Extraversion, whose coverage of behavioural domains and contexts is even broader than sensation-seeking, should have an even more diluted capacity to predict sexual adventurism. By this reasoning, broader traits tend to predict specific behaviours more weakly than certain narrow traits. But by the same reasoning, as you may have noticed, broader traits will tend to predict a greater range of behaviour: more behaviours fall within their field of relevance. Thus, although broad personality factors often predict behaviour less strongly than specific traits, this is neither an embarrassment to proponents of these factors nor a sign of their overall predictive inferiority.

In any event, given that broad personality factors like the Big Five have some limitations, both in allowing fine-grained personality description and in predicting specific behaviours, psychologists have energetically pursued the study of specific traits. Often they have done so in the hope of illuminating a particular set of psychological phenomena. The number of traits that have been investigated is huge, but a small selection of some of the most interesting examples offers a flavour of the enterprise.

Authoritarianism

Authoritarianism is a specific trait that has been investigated by psychologists who want to understand the roots of prejudice. This programme of work was begun by Adorno, Frenkel-Brunswik, Levinson, and Sanford (1950), who sought to explain the extreme and genocidal hatred of the Nazi regime towards Jews, Gypsies, homosexuals, and others. By their working understanding, embodied in a popular questionnaire (the California F-scale), the trait had several distinct components. These include an uncritical and submissive acceptance of societal authorities, deeply conventional values, thinking that is based on superstition and rigid categories, a tendency to project one's own impulses onto others and be punitive towards them, cynicism and misanthropy, and a reluctance to introspect. Although this formulation and the F-scale are controversial, recent work has shown right-wing authoritarianism to be a strong and reliable predictor of individual differences in prejudiced attitudes (Sibley, Robertson, & Wilson, 2006). In Big Five terms, authoritarianism appears to be characterized primarily by low Openness and high Conscientiousness (Heaven & Bucci, 2001).

Attachment styles

Attachment style refers to a set of personality characteristics that are particularly relevant to close relationships. Inspired by developmental psychology research on the different ways in which infants and toddlers react to separation from their caregivers, studies of attachment styles in adults present them as basic orientations to intimate relationships. Three styles are often recognized, each marked by distinctive approaches to forming and conducting emotional bonds, and responding to challenges to them (Hazan & Shaver, 1987). People with a 'secure' attachment style are comfortable with closeness and mutual dependency and are not preoccupied with the possibility of abandonment. The 'avoidant' style is associated with a lack of trust in others, and a reluctance to become close to or dependent on another. 'Anxious/ambivalent' people, finally, tend to desire more intimacy than their partner and want it more quickly, and are concerned about being abandoned or not loved enough.

These three traits are associated with a host of intriguing differences in psychological phenomena within close relationships. Not surprisingly, secure individuals experience the most trust, satisfaction, and commitment in their romantic relationships. Anxious/ambivalent people have the lowest self-esteem and satisfaction with their romantic relationships, are most prone to jealousy, obsessive preoccupation with and sexual attraction to others, and belief in love at first sight, and report having had fathers who were unfair. Avoidant people have the strongest fear of closeness, fail to seek support from a partner when under stress, and report having cold and rejecting mothers. When brought into a lab to discuss a relationship problem with their romantic partners (Simpson, Rholes, & Phillips, 1996), they show little negative emotion, remain distant and unsupportive (especially men), and report no change in feelings of love and commitment after the discussion. Anxious/ambivalent people, in contrast, show anger and upset during the discussion and reduced love and commitment after it, and securely attached people showed little distress and then more positive evaluations of the relationship.

In one fascinating study, Fraley and Shaver (1998) examined a setting where romantic couples frequently separate, and where attachment behaviour might therefore be particularly notable. They had a research assistant approach couples at an airport and ask them to complete a short questionnaire, which included a measure of attachment styles. Unknown to the couples, another research assistant then observed them until one or both of them departed, coding specific kinds of attachment-related behaviour. Fraley and Shaver found a number of correlations between participants' attachment styles and these behaviours for separating couples. More avoidantly attached women, for example, engaged in less 'contact seeking' behaviour (e.g., kissing, embracing, turning back after leaving), less 'caregiving' (e.g., stroking, whispering 'I love you'), and more 'avoidance' behaviours (e.g., looking away from the partner, breaking off contact, hurrying the separation). In short, attachment styles reveal themselves in naturalistic settings, and are clearly important specific traits for making sense of close relationships.

Type A

Type A personality is a characteristic that has been most intensively studied by psychologists interested in predicting risk for coronary heart disease, a major cause of death in most industrialized societies. Cardiologists had long suspected that people who suffered from heart disease tended to have a distinctive personality style, and Type A was an attempt to capture it (Friedman & Rosenman, 1974). Type A personalities are described as competitive, given to excessive achievement striving, vigorous in their activity and speech patterns, hostile, and impatient and pressured in their attitude towards time. Research has repeatedly linked Type A to a moderately increased risk for the development of heart disease, and suggests that hostility is the most toxic of its components, the one most strongly associated with coronary risk. This association may be partly due to an increased engagement in health-damaging behaviours and partly due to more direct physiological effects of chronic hostility on the body. Whereas Type A may put people at risk of heart disease, another supposed type, Type D personality, has been shown to predict poor outcome in people who have heart disease (Denollet, Sys, Stroobant, Rombouts, Gillebert, & Brutsaert, 1996).

The specific traits sketched here illustrate a tiny fraction of the personality characteristics that have been studied by trait psychologists. Note how they illuminate psychological phenomena in specific domains – attitudes towards outgroups, close relationships, physical health – by focusing on specific kinds of thinking, feeling, and behaving. Note also how none of these specific traits corresponds precisely to any trait term in English. Instead, they are theoretical entities or 'constructs' that have been proposed, assessed, and studied by researchers. Specific traits need not be drawn from the everyday lexicon, which clearly does not exhaust the trait universe.

Challenges to trait psychology

Trait psychologists have made great progress in developing ways of describing personality with a few basic trait dimensions. To have reached a virtual consensus on the fundamental dimensions of personality is no small accomplishment. Every field of study needs to develop ways of describing and classifying the phenomena of interest to it. Some of the most important achievements of the sciences have been systematic ways of describing nature: the periodic table of elements in chemistry, the enumeration of elementary particles in physics, and the classification of species in biology. Just as these systematic descriptions provide foundations for their sciences, trait psychology aspires to be a foundation for the study of personality. However, the strength of this foundation has not gone unchallenged. Indeed, psychologists have raised many criticisms of trait psychology, and questioned whether it offers a firm ground on which to build a science of personality. In the remainder of this chapter we will review some of these challenges.

Do traits exist and do they matter?

It seems intuitively obvious that people differ from one another in their typical ways of behaving, and that these differences matter. Most of us are implicit trait psychologists, thinking about one another in terms of general dispositions and using trait terms extensively in our daily lives. However, the most fundamental challenge to trait psychology argued that we are all quite mistaken: traits are much less solid and powerful than we, and academic trait psychologists, imagine.

This challenge, which came to be known as '**situationism**', was launched by Walter Mischel in a controversial book published in 1968. In his book, Mischel reviewed a large number of studies of behavioural consistency, the extent to which a person's behaviour is consistent in different situations or according to different measures. Although trait psychology assumes a high level of consistency, Mischel repeatedly found that behaviours expressing a single trait in different settings often correlated quite weakly (i.e., rarely more than .30). Another way of saying this is that there is a great deal of 'within-person variability' of behaviour across different situations. For instance, a well-known study of children's moral behaviour found that their likelihoods of cheating, lying, and stealing were only marginally correlated when assessed in diverse classroom, home, and social settings. Different children behaved immorally in different situations, and most individual children were not consistently moral or immoral. Similarly, Mischel found that alternative measures of particular traits rarely reached high levels of consistency, and usually correlated quite modestly. He concluded that behaviour is influenced only weakly by traits, and that situational determinants are usually more powerful. Behaviour is, in short, highly specific to situations, rather than springing from general dispositions as people tend to imagine. Consequently, even if such dispositions exist – a claim he never denied – they are of little practical value in predicting behaviour.

Needless to say, Mischel's conclusions were met with a chorus of disagreement from personality psychologists. (In contrast, social psychologists, who focus on situational determinants of behaviour, tended to applaud.) Mischel had, after all, cast doubt on the large and apparently successful research enterprise of trait psychology, as well as on the livelihood of psychologists who practised personality assessment in clinical, educational, and industrial settings. As a result, his findings were subjected to numerous criticisms over many years. Some psychologists argued that his review of the literature was selective, others that it focused too much on studies performed in artificial laboratory situations which might not generalize to everyday life. However, two criticisms are particularly telling.

First, is it true, as Mischel maintained, that the levels of behavioural consistency revealed in his review are too low to be practically useful? Some psychologists have argued that .30 correlations of the sort he dismissed may actually have considerable practical value. Remember that such a correlation allows a 30% reduction in prediction errors and raises the odds of correct prediction from 1:1 to almost 2:1. In many practical settings these figures are very respectable. An extreme example comes from the study that first showed the role of aspirin in preventing heart attacks. In this case, a correlation of .034 between aspirin consumption and heart attack was enough to lead researchers to call off the study and announce their findings to the world (Rosenthal, 1990). Modest correlations can clearly be of great importance.

Second, it may well be that Mischel significantly under-estimated the degree to which behaviour can be predicted by traits. The studies that he reviewed correlated specific behaviours measured on a single occasion with one another, or with psychological tests. However, psychologists are often interested not in predicting single instances of particular behaviours, but in predicting *tendencies* to behave in a certain general manner over a period of time (i.e., 'aggregated' behaviour). A personnel psychologist assessing the conscientiousness of potential employees is usually not aiming to predict a specific occasion of dishonesty, for instance, but hopes instead to predict *patterns* of unconscientious behaviour (e.g., lying, lateness, absenteeism, theft, drinking on the job). Now, aggregated behaviour is more predictable than specific instances, because the many unpredictable factors that influence each instance tend to even out in the long run. Think about how much less accurately you would probably predict the maximum temperature on this day next year than the average maximum temperature for this month next year. For this reason, aggregated behaviour is more consistent, and more strongly correlated with trait measures, than Mischel claimed.

It is now generally accepted that traits survived the 'person–situation debate' with few lasting injuries. Evidence for the consistency of behaviour has accumulated, and growing evidence for the stability of personality traits over time has strengthened the position that traits are influential and predictively valuable sources of behaviour. At the same time, trait psychologists have developed a healthy recognition of the level of inconsistency or within-in-person variability (Fleeson, 2001) in behaviour and the vital importance of the context in which behaviour occurs. Some have acknowledged the role of the situation and reconciled it with the trait approach in a variety of ways. For instance, some note that traits will tend to predict behaviour best in situations that are not governed by constraining rules and expectations (e.g., extraversion levels are unlikely to predict the behaviour of students in lecture theatres, where outgoing behaviour is generally frowned upon). Others propose what has been called '**interactionism**', according to which people's traits express themselves in ways that are situation-specific, so that behavioural consistency is to be found in particular *combinations* of traits and situations. For instance, some people are consistently anxious in social settings, others in settings involving physical danger. All in all, then, trait psychologists have learned from the situationist critique, and its challenge has been successfully rebutted.

Are trait dimensions culturally universal?

Trait psychology aspires to give us a universal language for describing differences between people. Trait theories such as the Big Five model aim to provide a map of *human* personality, rather than one that is only appropriate to members of a particular cultural, national, or linguistic group. Some psychologists have challenged this claim of universality, arguing either that Western trait dimensions are not appropriate to particular non-Western cultures, or, more radically, that the trait concept itself is not applicable in these cultures. Such challenges – which represent what can be called the *relativist critique* – are important ones. If they are valid, they imply that trait theories apply only within rather narrow cultural and geographical boundaries, and have more to do with culturally-specific beliefs and ways of life than with the fundamentals of human nature.

There are certainly reasons to suspect that there might be significant cultural variations in the ways in which personality is conceptualized. Anthropologists and cultural psychologists have pointed out many differences between Western and non-Western people's typical ways of understanding themselves, their minds, and their behaviour, ways that may collectively be called their 'folk psychologies'. Compared to Westerners, non-Western people tend (1) to explain their behaviour in terms of 'external' factors such as the situation in which it occurred, and the social constraints and relationships that influenced it; (2) to talk about concrete behaviour without referring to underlying psychological causes such as intentions, desires, and traits; and (3) to possess relatively restricted trait vocabularies (see Lillard, 1998, and Fiske, Kitayama, Markus, & Nisbett, 1998, for reviews). In contrast, Westerners tend to interpret behaviour in terms of an elaborate folk psychology of dispositions and mental

39

processes. That is, they tend to see people as autonomous agents whose actions spring from abstract internal attributes that distinguish them from one another. On the surface, then, trait psychology would seem to be less appropriate to non-Western cultures, with their preference for contextual and situational explanations and their less individualistic values.

All of this evidence suggests that Western trait psychologies could in some respects be specific to their cultural origins. But is it true, for instance, that trait theories such as the Big Five model only hold up in Western contexts? This turns out to be quite a difficult question to answer. On the one hand, when standard personality tests are translated into non-Western languages, they usually yield more or less identical underlying factors, suggesting that Western trait dimensions are indeed universal and can be exported with confidence. For example, questionnaire measures of the Big Five have yielded factors closely resembling these dimensions when translated from English into Chinese, Croatian, Dutch, Filipino, French, German, Hebrew, Japanese, Korean, and Spanish. Translated versions of Eysenck's measure of Extraversion, Neuroticism, and Psychoticism have yielded quite consistent factors in an even wider variety of languages. Although this evidence for universal factors is generally strong, however, it is also worth noting that it is somewhat less strong for non-European samples. For instance, there is some indication that the Big Five Extraversion and Agreeableness factors do not appear in Filipino, Japanese, and Korean samples, but seem to be replaced by factors that might be better labelled Love (a blend of Extraversion and high Agreeableness) and Dominance (a blend of Extraversion and low Agreeableness).

Translated versions of Western personality measures provide evidence that trait dimensions proposed by Western psychologists are reasonably general, and also reveal some subtle cultural variations. However, it can be argued that such translations are not the best places to look for cultural differences in personality structure. After all, these measures contain items that have been selected by Western psychologists to reflect the characteristics that they consider to be most relevant for describing individual differences within their own cultures. For this reason, some psychologists have claimed that translations of Western measures essentially impose a restricted and potentially quite alien set of descriptions on the non-Western people who respond to them. Consequently, translation of imported Western measures may exaggerate the consistency of personality structure across cultures. More importantly, it may fail to detect trait dimensions that are specific to a culture because items relevant to these dimensions are not included in the original Western measure. In response to these problems, some cross-cultural psychologists have proposed investigating personality from an *indigenous* perspective, studying personality characteristics and trait terms that are recognized *within* the culture of interest.

Studies of indigenous personality characteristics typically begin with the collection of trait terms that occur naturally in the language of interest, often following a detailed 'ethnographic' analysis of the characteristics that are most culturally salient. Participants then rate themselves or others on the resulting terms, and correlations among these are examined for evidence of broader dimensions, whose resemblance to those obtained in other cultures can be assessed. Several such 'lexical' studies have now been performed and the findings are very interesting. On the one hand, they show a fairly high level of consistency with the Big Five dimensions in many cases, especially in European languages. On the other hand, they are often inconsistent, failing to yield equivalents of specific Big Five dimensions or yielding indigenous dimensions that resemble Big Five dimensions in some respects but differ in others. For instance, the Big Five dimension of Openness to Experience is not consistently represented in an assortment of European languages, and a study of Chinese trait terms yielded dimensions such as 'optimism' and 'self-control' that clearly overlap with the Big Five but do not obviously correspond to them in a one-to-one fashion. Most strikingly, some indigenous research has yielded entirely unique dimensions, such as a dimension of 'Chinese Tradition' (incorporating 'harmony', 'relationship orientation', and 'thrift') among Chinese people, and a dimension of 'Filipino Cultural Norms' (incorporating 'respectfulness', 'restraint', 'perseverance', 'responsibility', and 'humility') among Filipinos. Studies of indigenous personality dimensions therefore pose a challenge to the universality of Western trait theories. Although the dimensions that they produce are often similar to those developed by Western psychologists in broad outline, they differ significantly in the finer detail.

In sum, all cultures use trait terms to describe differences between people, and do so in ways that reveal a moderate to strong level of consistency. This consistency indicates an encouraging but by no means overwhelming cross-cultural generality for the broad trait dimensions advocated by Western trait psychologists. However, the inconsistencies that remain are significant, especially when traits are investigated from an indigenous perspective, and they show that trait psychology cannot at this stage claim to have conclusively demonstrated universal personality dimensions. This conclusion neither invalidates trait theories such as the Big Five model nor does it imply that measures of these traits should only be used in Western cultures. It simply means that trait psychology may not have identified the fundamental dimensions of human nature, possibly because such universal dimensions do not exist.

Traits or types?

In essence, traits are ways in which people differ from one another. When psychologists talk about a trait, they are thinking of a dimension on which people differ: some people are very high on the dimension, some are very low, and most vary by degrees in the intermediate range. A trait is therefore understood to be a continuum, so that scores on a personality test correspond to approximate positions on the underlying trait that it measures. In short, traits are differences that are *differences of degree*, differences that can be thought of as *continuous*, *dimensional* or *quantitative*, like the weight of an object, the brightness of a light, or the volume of a noise.

Although this view of traits often goes unchallenged, some psychologists have pointed out that not all differences between people are differences of degree. Some differences – like biological sex and blood type – are not continuous variations on a dimension, but involve a small number of discrete alternatives (e.g., blood types A, B, AB, and O). In differences of this sort, people either belong to one kind or to another. Differences such as these are therefore called *differences of kind*, and may also be described as *discontinuous*, *categorical*, *typological*, or *qualitative* (Meehl, 1992).

Several psychologists consider that some personality characteristics are better thought of as **types** rather than dimensions. The concept of Type A personality described a few pages ago is one example: its proponents argue that people either belong to this type or they do not, categorically. Similarly, the psychologist Carl Jung wrote a book titled *Psychological Types* (1921/ 1971) and proposed that introverts and extraverts were discrete types: any person must be either one or the other. His ideas live on in the popular Myers-Briggs Type Inventory, a personality test that is very widely used in the consulting industry and that sorts people into personality types based on four Jung-inspired dichotomies. Depending on their responses to a series of questions, people are categorized as Introverts or Extraverts, INtuiters or Sensers, Thinkers or Feelers, and Judges or Perceivers. Combine these four dichotomies and you get 16 possible types, usually identified by a four-letter code (e.g., INTJ or ESTP, etc.).

If personality types or categories such as these exist, but traits are usually understood as differences of degree, then the trait concept does not adequately characterize some personality differences. The possibility that some differences between people are better understood as types rather than traits has been examined in many studies using a statistical method called 'taxometric analysis'. This analysis rigorously tests between categorical and dimensional models of personality characteristics. A recent review of several hundred scientific studies using it (Haslam, Holland, & Kuppens, 2012) suggests that personality types are very rare, if they exist at all. Although personality psychologists have proposed a number of personality types, most of them, including Type A personality, seem to be better understood as continuous trait dimensions (e.g., people vary along a continuum of Type A tendencies, rather than either belonging or not belonging to the type). There is no evidence that Jungian 'types' are, in fact, types. The one possible exception to the conclusion that personality tends to be a matter of degree is a personality characteristic called 'schizotypy'. This characteristic, which puts people at risk of developing the mental disorder schizophrenia and involves social awkwardness and having odd experiences, will be examined further in Chapter 10.

In conclusion, the idea of personality types does not seem to pose a significant challenge to trait psychology. Types are vanishingly rare and most personality variation can be captured better by trait dimensions. The fact that we differ from one another by degrees rather than belonging to different categories – shades of grey and more or less, not black or white and either/or – is a valuable lesson of personality psychology.

Do traits explain behaviour?

Some trait psychologists take it as a given that traits explain behaviour. After all, psychological tests that measure traits generally predict behaviour to some extent, and you might think being able to predict something implies being able to explain it. In addition, traits are conceptualized as general dispositions that underlie specific behaviours, and it seems reasonable to explain the specific events, such as behaviours, by the more general tendencies. Gravity, for example, involves a general disposition for things to move towards the ground: knowing about gravity allows us to predict with high confidence that a spilled drink will fall to the floor rather than float around the room or splash upon the ceiling, and allows us to explain why. Is the explanation of behaviour by traits any different?

Some psychologists have argued that it is quite different, in several respects. First, trait explanation can often seem rather circular. Does it really explain a person's agreeable behaviour to say that he or she has a high level of trait agreeableness? This sounds a little bit like the medieval thinkers who argued that fire heated things up because it had 'calorific power', where this power was defined as the tendency to heat things up. Similarly, agreeableness just *is* the tendency to act agreeably; it is not a cause or explanation of the agreeable behaviour. In short, to refer to the trait may not really offer an explanation of the agreeable behaviour, but be just an observation that the behaviour is consistent with a pattern that the person has displayed in the past.

A second objection to the explanatory power of traits involves a fundamental question about what a trait is. Two main alternative views can be distinguished (Wiggins, 1997). On one view, traits are hypothetical 'latent variables': we cannot observe them but on the basis of regularities in someone's observable behaviour we hypothesize that they exist as explanatory entities within the person. To attribute a trait to someone involves inferring something that underlies and accounts for their behaviour. This is somewhat like how we explain the dropped drink: we infer the existence of an unobserved force (gravity) that causes the drink to fall. On the other view (Hampshire, 1953), however, traits are not inferred hypothetical entities. They do not cause behaviour, but simply provide a summary description of it. To attribute agreeableness to a person is not to infer something unobservable that resides within them, but just to state that in the past the person has tended to behave in an agreeable manner. Such a summary of past behaviour cannot explain present or future behaviour, but only point to its consistency or inconsistency with that behaviour.

A third criticism of the capacity for traits to explain behaviour argues that traits are static (i.e., fixed) attributes or entities that tell us very little about the *processes* that underlie behaviour. Even if we accept that traits are underlying variables and not mere behavioural summaries, there is often still something unsatisfying about explanations of behaviour that refer to traits: they don't tell us about the multiple steps and mechanisms that gave rise to that behaviour. You can explain why a car moves fast by referring to its horsepower or number of cylinders – both fixed attributes – but this explanation does not help to understand the many processes and mechanisms that combine to enable the car to move quickly. Similarly, if a researcher found that people high in neuroticism were less likely to get tested for a disease than those lower in neuroticism, this would not enlighten us about the processes that might underpin that difference in behaviour. Perhaps more neurotic people worry more about receiving an undesirable test result and therefore avoid testing, or perhaps they estimate defensively that they have a lower risk of having the disease (i.e., denial) and so don't bother getting tested. As a static attribute of the person, neuroticism is certainly relevant to the explanation of this behaviour, but a fuller explanation requires some added detail about psychological processes. These issues will be examined in Chapter 3.

All of these criticisms of the explanatory power of traits have some merit, but it is important to put them in perspective. Trait explanations are certainly not always circular, for example. If we refer to a trait to explain a behaviour that is not merely an example of that trait – using Conscientiousness to explain longer life, for instance (Friedman, Tucker, Tomlinson-Keasey, Schwartz, Wingard, & Criqui, 1993) – then there is no circularity. Living longer is not an example of Conscientious behaviour; it appears to be an outcome or consequence of it. Similarly, most personality psychologists would argue that traits are not just summaries of past behaviour, that they allow the prediction of future behaviour, and that there is nothing unusual about inferring unobservable entities and giving them explanatory power, as we do with gravity. Finally, most psychologists would accept that traits can play an important role in the explanation of behaviour, even if it is only a partial explanation that needs to be supplemented by other psychological processes.

These issues surrounding the explanatory adequacy of trait psychology are also relevant to all of us in our daily lives. There is plenty of evidence from social psychology that laypeople – particularly in Western countries – make sense of one another's behaviour in much the same way as trait psychology, and with some of the same limitations and biases. We often under-estimate the extent to which other people's behaviour is due to situational factors, over-estimate the extent to which it is due to their traits, and act as if describing people in terms of their traits is a sufficient explanation for their behaviour. When a shop assistant responds to a question with an unhelpful comment or an annoyed expression, we are often quick to explain that behaviour in trait terms – they acted in this way *because* they are 'arrogant' or 'stuck-up' – without considering that they might be tired, caffeine-deprived, or responding to our own unpleasant tone of voice. This tendency has been referred to as 'lay dispositionism': people tend to see behaviour (especially other people's behaviour) as caused by static, unchanging dispositions. Just as it is important for us to recognize the limitations of the trait approach to personality – to remember that situational factors are important, that people's behaviour is quite variable, that traits cannot always explain behaviour satisfactorily – it is important to be wary of our own tendencies to jump to conclusions about other people's traits.

Conclusions

The psychology of traits starts from some intuitively sensible premises. It assumes that personality characteristics encoded in ordinary language are useful units of personality description, and that their structure can be determined by studying empirical consistencies in thinking, feeling, and behaving. On these pillars – the trait lexicon and the humble correlation coefficient (and its factor-analytic descendant) – elaborate and robust accounts of personality structure have been built. In addition, a great assortment of specific traits has been investigated. The language of personality description that has emerged from this enterprise seems to be both systematic and comprehensive. Its practical utility is shown by an enormous research literature that demonstrates the capacity of traits to predict a wide range of psychological phenomena. Trait psychology would appear to give us a solid foundation for personality description.

Nevertheless, that solid foundation has received several challenges. Some of these have been successfully addressed, but others must be taken seriously. In particular, it is important to recognize that behaviour has a great deal of within-person and cross-situational variability, that there are important cross-cultural variations in trait dimensions, and that traits have limitations as explanations of behaviour. Another potential challenge that is discussed in the following chapter is that there may be more to personality than traits. Despite all of these challenges, trait psychology offers an unquestionably important perspective for describing and understanding personality.

Chapter summary

- A major task of personality psychology is to develop systematic ways of describing and classifying individual differences, or determining the 'structure' of personality.
- A major unit for the description of personality is the 'personality trait', an enduring disposition (or tendency) to think, feel, or behave in a particular, patterned way. Traits vary in breadth, some relating to very specific or narrow types of behaviour and others to wide ranges of behaviour, and broader traits may incorporate more specific traits.
- Personality psychologists have made efforts to classify the structure of traits for more than 70 years, starting from the thousands of trait words available in everyday language and distilling these, using correlations and factor analysis, into a smaller number of broad trait dimensions.
- Factor-analytic research first distilled traits into 16 factors or dimensions, and then further reduced them to five. The five factors have increasingly come to represent the scientific consensus on personality structure and are referred to as the 'Big Five' or the 'five-factor model'.
- The five factors are Extraversion, Agreeableness, Conscientiousness, Neuroticism, and Openness to Experience. They serve as a useful framework for personality description and explanation, and they are associated with a wide variety of psychological phenomena.
- Although broad factors play an important role in personality description, many more specific traits have also been the focus of personality research and theory. These specific traits may be more effective in predicting behaviour than broader traits.
- Although the psychology of traits has made major contributions to the study of personality, it has also come under criticism on a variety of fronts. For example, some psychologists have argued that behaviour is not very consistent across different contexts, and that it is therefore determined primarily by the situation in which it occurs rather than by enduring traits. However, traits can predict behaviour well when the behaviour is assessed as aggregate patterns rather than single actions.

(Continued)

(Continued)

- Other psychologists have argued that trait dimensions are not culturally universal, and that explaining behaviour with reference to personality is characteristically Western. Research tends to support the view that broad factors are reasonably universal, with a few exceptions. However, there is also evidence of cross-cultural variation in the structure of traits.
- Trait psychologists usually assume that individual differences in personality fall along continuous dimensions: they are matters of degree, like height. Although some psychologists have proposed categorical personality 'types', most personality variation is dimensional.
- It has been controversial whether traits explain behaviour rather than merely describing or summarizing behaviour patterns. However, personality traits can play a role in explaining behaviour in the same, non-circular way that other inferred variables do.

Further reading

Heine, S. J., & Buchtel, E. E. (2009). Personality: The universal and the culturally specific. *Annual Review of Psychology, 60*, 369–94.
This is an excellent review of the role of culture in personality and of how basic personality characteristics, such as motives and traits – and even the relevance of personality for understanding self and others – may vary across cultures.

John, O. P., Naumann, L. P., & Soto, C. J. (2010). Paradigm shift to the integrative Big Five trait taxonomy: History, measurement, and concepotual issues. In O. P. John, R. W. Robins, & L. A. Pervin (Eds.), *Handbook of personality: Theory and research* (3rd ed.) (pp. 114–58). New York: Guilford Press.
This chapter lays out the historical development of the five-factor model of personality and reviews relevant research and theory on the nature of the factors and their optimal measurement.

Matthews, G., Deary, I. J., & Whiteman, M. C. (2009). *Personality traits* (3rd ed.). New York: Cambridge University Press.
This is a thorough, up-to-date and readable presentation of contemporary personality psychology from the trait perspective.

McCrae, R. R., & Costa, P. T. (2005). *Personality in adulthood: A five-factor theory perspective* (2nd ed.). New York: Guilford Press.
For those who want a more comprehensive discussion of the five-factor model of personality, this book offers a useful review of an enormous body of research.

Meehl, P. E. (1992). Factors and taxa, traits and types, differences of degree and differences in kind. *Journal of Personality*, *60*, 117–74.
This is a conceptually difficult but nevertheless valuable discussion of the distinction between dimensional and categorical (i.e., type) views of personality, and of why that distinction matters.

Wiggins, J. S. (1997). In defence of traits. In R. Hogan, J. Johnson, & S. Briggs (Eds.), *Handbook of personality psychology* (pp. 95–115). New York: Academic Press.
Wiggins vigorously defends the concept of personality traits against some of the criticisms discussed late in this chapter, arguing that most of these criticisms are weaker than some had supposed.

Personality Processes

Learning objectives

- To understand the Big Five as the major dimensions of covariation among most personality *traits*, and therefore as a useful organizing framework for the many trait constructs in personality psychology.
- To describe personality traits in terms of a hierarchically organized system of *meta-traits*, *domains*, *aspects*, and *facets*.
- To understand traits as coherent patterns of basic psychological processes (chiefly, *affect*, *behaviour*, and *cognition*).
- To understand how a variety of methods can be used for illuminating the affective, behavioural, and cognitive components of traits, including content analysis and models of personality judgements.
- To appreciate the limited resolution of traits for describing personality and to understand two higher-resolution levels of personality description – notably, *characteristic adaptations* and *integrative life narratives*.

The last chapter introduced the notion that personality can be usefully described in terms of traits, and that a broad consensus has been reached regarding the usefulness of one trait taxonomy in particular, the Big Five. This chapter explores the trait approach in greater detail, with the aim of providing a deeper understanding of what it is that trait taxonomies such as the Big Five describe, and what aspects of our personality lie beyond the scope of such taxonomies. After reading this chapter, you will hopefully share our view that the personality descriptions provided by the Big Five are more complex than first impressions might suggest.

The simplistic view that we wish to dissuade you of is that the Big Five are analogous to basic physical dimensions such as height and weight, or length, breadth, and depth. It is sometimes said that the Big Five provide the 'latitude and longitude' of personality structure. To some extent, geographical coordinate systems do provide a useful metaphor for the personality trait systems: just as you would be able to comprehensively describe the location of a person in space using geographical coordinates, you can describe someone's location in 'trait space' in a reasonably comprehensive manner using the Big Five. Nevertheless, the analogy is a rough one and breaks down upon closer examination, for at least three reasons. First, while characteristics such as height are one-dimensional and irreducible, the same cannot be said for any of the Big Five. As we will see, the Big Five are *complex composites* of individual differences in **affect** (how we feel), behaviour (what we do), and cognition (what/how we think) – what are sometimes called the ABCs of personality. Second, while height is a rigid and unchangeable – we do not get taller or shorter throughout the day – a personality factor is a *summary* of a dynamic psychological system. That is, describing someone as 'extraverted' says something about how they *typically* behave, feel, and so on, but not how they are 100% of the time. Finally, while geographical coordinates are completely sufficient for specifying the locations of objects in physical space, trait systems are insufficient for describing personality in all its richness of detail. This means we need additional ways of describing people, beyond traits, to provide a complete picture of anyone's personality.

Looking inside the Big Five

What exactly are we describing when we say that someone is highly extraverted? Or agreeable? Or low on Openness to Experience? One of the first things we learned about the Big Five in the previous chapter is that traits can be organized in terms of a hierarchy, in which illustrative behaviours are nested within lower-level (or *narrow*) traits, which are in turn nested within higher-level (or *broad*) traits (see Figure 2.1). Therefore, when we describe someone as 'extraverted', it is quite different from describing someone as 'tall'. Height is an irreducible physical dimension; there is no way to elaborate on or 'unpack' the statement that a person is 198 cm in height, or that such an individual would be considered tall considering the average height of a human being. Extraversion, in contrast, is a way to describe someone who is sociable, or talkative, or adventurous – or all of the above. We can elaborate on what we mean by describing someone as 'an extravert', and there is more than one way to be extraverted, because extraversion is a broad trait construct under which other narrower traits can be grouped. Recognizing the hierarchical structuring of traits also helps us avoid a common misconception about the Big Five, which is to view them as a definitive list of *THE* five traits that are more 'legitimate' than other trait descriptors. There are tens if, not *hundreds* of, traits that can be legitimately studied in personality psychology, most of which are not named among the famous five (e.g., impulsiveness, authoritarianism, narcissism, shyness, optimism, etc). The Big Five serves as an *organizing framework* for these countless traits, rather than a finite 'set of' traits *per se*. More precisely, the Big Five represent the major patterns of *covariation* among all kinds of different personality traits. For instance, 'Conscientiousness' is a broad term that captures a cluster of characteristics that tend to covary – or 'go together' – in the population overall. People who tend to be orderly tend also to be hard-working, and hard-working people are typically not impulsive. Conscientiousness is a useful umbrella term for organizing this cluster of interrelated characteristics.

Research suggests that there are probably four major levels of the trait hierarchy, known as *meta-traits*, *domains*, *aspects*, and *facets* (Figure 3.1). The Big Five are located at the *domain* level. Trait domains represent the major dimensions of personality uncovered via factor analyses of trait terms and personality questionnaire items. Most major trait constructs can be located somewhere within the multidimensional space provided by these Big Five domains. For instance, trait anxiety – the tendency to experience nervousness, tension, and worry – can be clearly located within the Neuroticism domain. Positive emotionality – the tendency to experience higher levels of positive affect – can be located within the Extraversion domain. Some traits will overlap with multiple domains, such as shyness, which may be described in terms of low Extraversion as well as high Neuroticism. For some time, the Big Five were thought to lie at the highest level of the personality hierarchy, meaning that they provided the broadest desciptive dimensions of personality. From the late 1990s, however, evidence began to accumulate for two even broader *meta-traits* at a level above the Big Five. These have been suggested to reflect broad processes that are common to Agreeableness, Conscientiousness and (low) Neuroticism on the one hand, and Extraversion and Openness on the other. DeYoung (2006) labelled these two meta-traits *stability* and *plasticity*, for reasons that will be discussed later in this chapter. Moving down in the trait hierarchy, each trait domain can be divided into exactly two correlated *aspects* (DeYoung, Quilty, & Peterson, 2007). Figure 3.1 presents all ten aspects of the Big Five domains. Among other arguments for the usefulness of the aspect level of the hierarchy is the fact that it helps resolve some long-standing debates among prominent Big Five researchers regarding the conceptualization of each of the trait domains. For example, while Costa and McCrae preferred the label 'Openness to Experience' (capturing various traits concerning imaginativeness and creativity), Goldberg preferred the label 'Intellect' (capturing various traits concerning curiosity and intellectual engagement). It actually appears that these labels are *both* valid, corresponding to the two separate aspects of the broader 'Openness/Intellect' domain. Finally, each aspect of the Big Five domains can be broken down into a number of *facets*. Some taxonomies suggest that there are around six facets per Big Five domain, but the precise number and nature of personality traits is indeterminate and most lists of facets are at least partly arbitrary. In summary, the Big Five domains provide a set of organizing constructs for traits, located near to the top of a hierarchical system of trait descriptors.

The hierarchical nature of traits helps us to appreciate the fact that each Big Five domain is a complex composite that can be unpacked in terms of increasingly more finely grained constructs. We can say in broad terms that someone is highly agreeable, or more specifically that they are compassionate, or even more precisely that they are charitable. We can also meaningfully interpret research on almost any trait in terms of which trait domain(s) it might belong to, and where in the trait hierarchy it might be located. Of course, understanding trait constructs in terms of narrower and narrower component traits constructs – like a set of nested Russian Dolls – does not ultimately illuminate the contents of any of these trait descriptions. At some

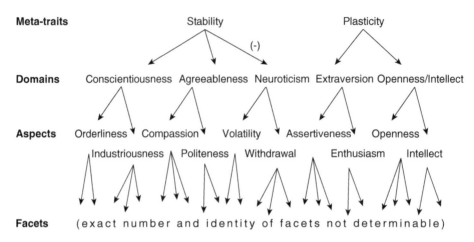

Figure 3.1 The hierarchical structuring of meta-traits, domains, aspects, and facets (from DeYoung, 2015)

point, a trait must be understood in terms of components other than further, narrower traits. In Chapter 2, we saw that narrow traits might be understood in terms of specific behaviours, such as talkativeness in the case of Extraversion. In fact, we can expand on this to suggest that all trait constructs describe coherent patterns of *basic psychological processes*. As originally discussed by Hampshire (1953), these processes can be grouped in terms of affect (valenced feelings), behaviour (all kinds of actions and activities), and cognition (patterns of thought) – the 'ABCs' of personality. (Some researchers prefer to add a 'D', which stands for desire or motivation. However, these processes could alternatively be considered part of affect and behaviour.) While psychology as a whole can be defined as the study of affect, behaviour, and cognition, personality psychology can be defined as the study of *regularities in*, or *stable differential patterns of* these processes, usefully organized in terms of the Big Five.

A systematic effort to articulate the basic psychological processes captured by each of the Big Five trait domains was undertaken some years ago by Pytlik Zillig and colleagues (2002). The authors brought together three teams of 'judges' (30 undergraduate students, 10 graduate students specializing in personality psychology, and three professors in personality psychology) who each read over nearly 500 questionnaire items from four popular questionnaires used to assess the Big Five. For each item, the experts had to indicate in percentage terms the extent to which that item referred to an affective, behavioural, or cognitive process. This kind of study is called a 'content analysis', because it involves systematically describing the item content of the scales being analyzed. The authors gave the example of an Extraversion item '*I see myself as someone who generates a lot of enthusiasm*', which was judged to reflect an even 50/50 balance of affect and behaviour, and to be unrelated to cognition (Pytlik Zillig, Hemenover, & Dienstbier, 2002, p. 851). This enabled the authors to calculate to what extent measures of each Big Five domain provide self-reported samples of affect, behaviour, and cognition. The full results from this study are summarized in Table 3.1, and offer a number of insights about what basic psychological processes are reflected in the major domains of personality. For instance,

Table 3.1 Results from a content analysis of Big Five personality questionnaires (Pytlik Zillig et al., 2002) showing how each trait domain describes differing patterns of affect, behaviour, and cognition

	Affect	Behaviour	Cognition
Extraversion	38%	**52%**	10%
Neuroticism	**70%**	18%	12%
Agreeableness	27%	**43%**	30%
Conscientiousness	6%	**68%**	26%
Openness/Intellect	22%	17%	**61%**

it is clear that most personality-related differences in affect are captured by Neuroticism and Extraversion; that regularities in behaviour are largely subsumed by Extraversion and Conscientiousness; and that differential patterns of cognition fall mainly within the Openness/ Intellect domain. We can see that the large majority of the content of Neuroticism scales concerns affective processes, while Agreeableness, in contrast, captures a fairly balanced mixture of affective, behavioural, and cognitive processes. So, when we describe someone as highly open, we are largely describing what kind of person they are in cognitive terms – what and how they think, the way in which they understand and interpret the world around them. On the other hand, to describe someone as an 'introvert' is to say something primarily about their behavioural tendencies – specifically, that they are less active, bold, talkative, and dominant than the average person. In the next three sections we will explore the ABCs of personality in greater detail.

Personality and affect

In examining the relation between personality and affect, one should first be aware of how 'affect' is typically defined in the literature, and distinguished from other feeling-constructs, such as *emotions* and *moods*. Emotions are said to be relatively short-lived feeling states that involve the evaluation – positive or negative – of events or stimuli (e.g., good or bad news, praise or criticism, reassurances or threats). Moods are often distinguished from emotions for being longer-lasting, generally less intense, and less connected to particular events. A person can experience a state of mild happiness or anxiety that lasts much of the day and arises for no easily apparent reason. With these definitions in mind, we can then conceptualize affects as the building blocks of both emotions and moods. Specifically, affects can be defined as our most basic, consciously-accessible feeling-states. At any point in time, we can describe our affective state, even if we are not experiencing an emotional episode or 'in a mood'. On the other hand, an emotional episode will be accompanied by particular affects, but also by cognitions and possibly behaviours. A person who is feeling tense or irritable at a particular moment is experiencing an affective state. If this state was relatively prolonged, and perhaps accompanied by cognitive activity (e.g., rumination) and behaviour (e.g., pacing, sighing), we would say they were experiencing a mood. If this feeling state was elicited by a specific event (e.g., an argument), and the feelings and cognitions were directed towards that triggering event (e.g., irritation at the person involved, rumination about what they had said), then this person would be experiencing an emotional episode. These distinctions may sound somewhat arbitrary, and they are not always adhered to in the literature, but many researchers have found them useful for distinguishing between different forms of affective experience.

In much the same way that the structure of personality traits can be organized in terms of the Big Five, researchers have attempted to determine the basic dimensions of affective states. Although there has been some controversy over how these dimensions should be conceptualized (Barrett & Russell, 1999; Tellegen, Watson, & Clark, 1999), factor-analytic evidence indicates that a two-factor model provides a parsimonious and relatively comprehensive system for describing affects. The most popular and consistently supported model labels these 'Big Two' dimensions Positive and Negative Affect (Watson & Tellegen, 1985). Like traits, both of these broad dimensions incorporate more specific affective states in a hierarchical fashion. Positive Affect involves feeling states such as enthusiastic, alert, and interested, whereas Negative Affect includes states such as nervous, afraid, and irritable. These two dimensions reliably appear across cultures and in analyses of how people report feeling at a single moment, over a short period (e.g., 'today'), or over an extended time (e.g., 'for the past few weeks'). Interestingly, and perhaps contrary to your intuitions, the two dimensions of affect are generally uncorrelated: the extent to which people currently or generally experience positive affective states is unrelated to the extent to which they experience negative states. Moreover, people can experience *mixed* affective states, which shows that positive and negative affects are not polar opposites or mutually exclusive states. For example, on graduation day, many university students experience mixtures of positive and negative affect, an experience often referred to as 'bittersweet' (Larsen, McGray, & Cacioppo, 2001).

Researchers have examined whether the broad dimensions that capture individual differences in personality traits might be associated with these two affect dimensions. One consistent finding in this area is that two of the Big Five traits converge closely with the two dimensions of affect (Larsen & Ketelaar, 1991; Meyer & Shack, 1989). Neuroticism is associated with the tendency to experience negative affects, and Extraversion with the tendency to experience positive affects. This is consistent with the results of the content analysis by Pytlik Zillig and colleagues, summarized in Table 3.1. Contrary to what is implied by the term 'emotional stability', which is often used to describe low levels of Neuroticism, people scoring high on traits within this domain are not more 'emotional' in general terms but more specifically are prone to the experience of *negative* emotions. Of course, emotional stability is still a reasonable description of low levels of Neuroticism, given that the frequent experience of stress, worry, and anxiety will have a destabilizing effect on psychosocial functioning. Affective processes are also relevant to the other major domains of personality, albeit to a lesser extent than Extraversion and Neuroticism. For example, one study found that negative affective states involving hostility are associated with low Agreeableness as well as high Neuroticism, and that positive affective states are associated with some traits within the

Conscientiousness domain (achievement-striving) as well as with Extraversion (Watson & Clark, 1992a). Also, major measures of Openness often include a trait facet concerning the extent to which one engages with their feelings and emotions. Nevertheless, it is quite clear that Extraversion and Neuroticism have particularly intimate associations with the two major dimensions of affect.

If measures of Extraversion and Neuroticism include items related to positive and negative affect, then isn't it inevitable that these two domains of personality will be associated with the two major dimensions of affect? That is, is it a circular and meaningless exercise to correlate personality measures with affect measures? There are good reasons why we should not arrive at this conclusion. First, in the early research that helped establish the Big Five as a robust taxonomy of traits, emotion words were explicitly excluded from all analyses (Waller, 1999). Later work then showed that emotion terms could also be accommodated within this same structure (Markon, Krueger, & Watson, 2005). This means that the Big Five subsume affect-related constructs, but can nevertheless be identified independently of such constructs. Second, many researchers have show that the associations between trait domains and affect dimensions are similar in strength when affect-related items are removed from the personality scales (e.g., Lucas & Fujita, 2000). This shows, for example, that the correlation between Extraversion and positive affect is not the simple result of similar items appearing on both questionnaires. All in all, the literature suggests that the major dimensions of affect can be integrated with the major trait domains of personality. Some writers have gone so far as to propose that the convergence of these separate descriptive systems is so close as to indicate an affective 'core' to Extraversion and Neuroticism, and that they might instead be named 'positive affectivity' and 'negative affectivity' (Watson & Tellegen, 1985). Of course, this terminology might place too much emphasis on the affective components of personality, while neglecting behaviour (which is particularly relevant to Extraversion, see Table 3.1) and cognition.

ILLUSTRATIVE STUDY

Personality traits and emotion regulation across cultures

'Emotion regulation' is the ability to manage emotional reactions in order to achieve one's goals. People are often faced with situations when it is desirable to modify or suppress the expression of an emotion: failing to do so may lead us to give up on an important task, say something offensive, escalate an argument, or do something socially inappropriate. Emotion regulation is also something on which cultures may differ. It has been argued, for example, that some cultures discourage emotional expression more than others, or require that individual emotion be subordinated to collective demands.

(Continued)

(Continued)

The American cross-cultural psychologist David Matsumoto (2006) examined differences in emotion regulation between Americans and Japanese. Previous research had suggested that Japanese participants score lower on emotion regulation than Americans, and Matsumoto aimed to explain why this might be. There is reliable evidence of mean differences in Big Five traits between cultures, and Americans have been found to score higher on average than Japanese on Extraversion and Conscientiousness, and lower on Neuroticism. Given the role of Extraversion and Neuroticism in emotionality, these cultural differences in mean levels of personality traits might account for cultural differences in emotion regulation.

Matsumoto assessed large samples of Japanese (6,409) and American (1,013) adults on a questionnaire measure of the Big Five and two questionnaires measuring emotion regulation. As in previous research, he found that Americans scored higher on emotion regulation – although the Japanese scored higher on a scale assessing emotion suppression – and he replicated the cross-cultural differences on the three personality factors. More significantly, analyses showed that the cross-cultural differences in emotion regulation were explained by the cross-cultural differences in personality traits.

One interesting implication of Matsumoto's study is that some psychological differences between cultures may not be due to culture *per se*. Rather than explaining differences in emotion regulation between Japan and the USA in terms of culture – shared beliefs, values, and social norms – perhaps we should refer to different average levels of traits. Such trait differences might themselves be partly grounded in culture, as our personality is in part shaped by our environment and experiences (see Chapter 5). Even so, this study shows how personality trait dimensions may illuminate the sources of some cross-cultural phenomena.

Personality and behaviour

Unlike personality traits and major dimensions of affect, there appears to be no widely accepted system describing the structure of behaviour. Researchers are typically interested in how personality relates to specific behavioural outcomes, ranging from job performance to the use of contraceptives. If one's research is concerned with predictors of volunteering, for example, then it is understandable that one's focus tends to be narrowly constrained to that class of behaviour. As a result, relatively little attention is given to the development of overarching taxonomies for organizing all kinds of different behaviours. Nevertheless, many personality researchers have attempted to understand, in broad terms, how behaviour is reflected in major personality traits.

One notable effort to illuminate the behavioural processes underlying personality was the Act Frequency model proposed by Buss and Craik (1983). The basic premise of this model is that personality traits are, in large part, summaries of frequencies of behaviours or 'acts'.

A person who we describe as 'bold' is a person who engages in particular acts (e.g., approaching a stranger to ask for a date) more often than a person who we describe as 'shy'. Because these acts are the building blocks of traits, the structure of personality itself may provide an organizing framework for behavioural acts. In one illustrative study, Grucza and Goldberg (2007) administered an extensive list of 400 behavioural acts (e.g., read a book; drank in a bar; hugged someone) grouped in terms of 60 clusters of related acts. Participants rated how frequently they had performed each act on a scale from 1 (never in my life) to 5 (more than 15 times in the past year). The researchers selected six of these behavioural clusters in order to examine associations between personality traits and two sets of socially undesirable activities (e.g., drug use), two sets of socially desirable activities (e.g., friendliness) and two neutral sets of behaviours (e.g., communication). This study was perhaps most remarkable for its inclusion of 11 multi-scale personality inventories. However, for brevity, we will focus specifically on findings for measures of the Big Five. On average, measures of personality correlated in the region of .45 with the various behavioural acts. This level of association seems reasonably high, given that traits are not exclusively comprised of behavioural processes (contrary to what is implied by the Act Frequency model). Some notable associations include that between Extraversion and more frequent instances of drug use (e.g., took a hard drug), Conscientiousness and fewer instances of 'undependability' (e.g., arrived at an event more than an hour late), and Openness in relation to more frequent creative acts (e.g., played a piano or other instrument).

Efforts to 'unpack' the affective, behavioural, and cognitive components of major personality traits can facilitate the construction of theories regarding the underlying causes of personality, and also help to conduct tests of those theories. This process is nicely illustrated in a study by Hirsh and colleagues (2009), who used the behavioural acts protocol employed by Grucza and Goldberg (2007). These authors set out to test a theory regarding the behavioural processes that characterize the two meta-traits residing at the highest level in the personality trait hierarchy – stability and plasticity. Stability comprises Agreeableness, Conscientiousness and (low) Neuroticism, all of which appear to be characterized by stabilizing influences on psychosocial functioning. For instance, low levels of Neuroticism are associated with more calm affective states, as opposed to the *psychologically destabilizing* feelings of tension, anxiety, and worry. High Conscientiousness can be characterized in terms of *motivational stability* (DeYoung, 2015), to the extent that conscientious individuals tend to stay more focused on their goals and resist distraction. The polite and compassionate components of Agreeableness, in turn, appear to facilitate interpersonal harmony, thereby maintaining *stability of social relationships*. One could characterize stability with the injunction to 'keep calm (low Neuroticism), stay on track (high Conscientiousness) and be nice (high Agreeableness)'. Based on this conceptualization of stability, Hirsh and colleagues predicted that this meta-trait would show a disproportionately high number of negative associations with a wide range of behavioural acts, this being indicative of processes that constrain or regulate behaviour. Indeed, of the 91 behavioural acts associated with stability, 90% of these correlations were negative. For instance, individuals high in stability reported less frequent instances of staying up all night, losing their temper, or becoming intoxicated.

The other personality meta-trait, plasticity, is so named because it is thought to comprise processes that allow for behavioural exploration, flexibility, and growth. This is because the two trait domains nested within this meta-trait are associated with the tendency to be outgoing and adventurous (Extraversion), and curious and creative (Openness/Intellect). This should allow for greater *plasticity of psychosocial functioning* through tendencies to try new things, meet new people, and explore more of what life has to offer. Based on this reasoning, Hirsh and colleagues (2009) predicted that plasticity would show a disproportionately high number of positive associations with various behavioural acts, this being indicative of behavioural exploration and engagement. Again, their prediction was supported. Of the 126 behavioural acts associated with stability, 98% of these correlations were positive. Individuals high in plasticity reported more frequent instances of planning a party, decorating a room, and – our personal favourite – lounging around the house without any clothes on.

Another way we can think about the organization of behaviour is through the lens of basic motivational dimensions. Motivation can be defined in terms of the effortful direction of behaviour, and can be organized in terms of two major dimensions – *approach* and *avoidance* (Elliot, 2008). These dimensions describe behavioural responses to the two major classes of motivational stimuli – *rewards* and *punishments*. We can define a reward as any stimulus for which an individual will expend effort to move towards, or approach, while a punishment is any stimulus for which an individual will expend effort to move away from, or avoid. Motivation is often also termed 'motivated action', which makes the relevance of behaviour to motivation more explicit. In fact, there can arguably be no motivation in the absence of some kind of behaviour. Imagine two students who both claim that they really want a good mark on their final exam – that they are both *really motivated* to do well. However, one spends the week before the exam lounging idly on the couch, while the other spends time reviewing lecture notes, printing out articles, and completing practice exams. In a very important sense, only one of these students is 'motivated' to obtain a good mark on their exam. The fact that both students feel a certain longing to do well might be described in terms of affect rather than motivation. Similarly, we might mope about the fact that our degree or our career was not all we had hoped for, but unless we actually *did* something to change this state of affairs (e.g., switch majors, change jobs), our experience would best be described in terms of affect, not motivation. Motivation, in short, is the process that drives behaviour.

One important paper examining the relation between personality and motivation was published by Elliot and Thrash (2002), whose findings indicated a strong overlap among the two major dimensions of motivation (approach and avoidance), the two major dimensions of affect (positive and negative) and two of the major dimensions of personality (Extraversion and Neuroticism). This research extends the work on personality and affect structure that we have already discussed, and illuminates the relevance of personality to motivated action. Specifically, Extraversion may consist in large part of the tendency to experience positive affect and approach desired goals, while Neuroticism may comprise the tendency to experience negative affect and avoid undesirable goals. In Chapter 6 we will encounter a theory of personality, called *reinforcement sensitivity theory*, which attempts to explain these motivational aspects of personality.

In broad terms, this picture of the affective and motivational/behavioural components of personality has largely stood the test of time, and is particularly relevant to a number of major biological theories of personality that we will encounter in Chapter 6. However, the picture is also incomplete, due to the fact that behaviour and motivation is also linked to each of the other Big Five domains (Corr, DeYoung, & McNaughton, 2013). Conscientiousness is patently concerned with motivation and is measured using questionnaires that are comprised largely of behavioural content (Table 3.1). Conscientiousness seems to be concerned primarily with the *regulation* of motivated action – recall that earlier we described Conscientiousness in terms of motivational *stability*. In other words, your level of Conscientiousness may help explain why you persist in your efforts to reach a goal, but it may be less involved in the kind of goal that you select in the first place. Openness/Intellect also appears to reflect specifically approach motivation, to the extent that individuals high on this domain are strongly characterized by curiosity and engagement with intellectual and aesthetic experiences. Finally, Agreeableness appears to reflect a complex mix of approach and avoidance motivation in relation to interpersonal stimuli. Specifically, agreeable people are motivated to help others, to prevent harm being done to others, and to maintain interpersonal bonds. Unfortunately, most research concerning the motivational bases of personality has focused on Extraversion and Neuroticism, and as a result our understanding of how motivation is linked with the other domains of personality is more limited.

Personality and cognition

Cognition is a broad term that refers to various mental processes such as perception, thinking, knowing, reasoning, learning, and memory. As an aspect of our experience, cognition is perhaps most usefully contrasted with affect. Affective states are *valenced*, which means they involve *feelings* of various intensities. In contrast, cognitions are largely non-valenced mental events. They include performing arithmetic, identifying as a member of a particular group in society, or perceiving a map of Italy as boot-shaped. Cognition is often described in terms of 'cold' information processing, in contrast to 'hot' affective processes. Of course, cognition and affect will often interact, such as when we find ourselves thinking over and over about a difficult problem and feel increasingly stressed (i.e., when we ruminate). Our understanding of how personality relates to cognition has been somewhat obscured by a long tradition that has drawn a sharp distinction between personality and cognition. More specifically, it has been suggested that individual differences in cognition are described by constructs such as intelligence (the focus of Chapters 12 and 13 of this book), and that these are separate from personality. Indeed, personality is sometimes described explicitly in terms of 'non-cognitive traits'. Another relevant distinction suggests that intelligence and other cognitive abilities relate to *maximal performance* (i.e., what you *can* do), whereas personality traits concern *typical performance* (i.e., what you *usually* do). This is reflected in the way we assess intelligence and personality; the former with challenging items that have only one right answer, and the latter with self-descriptions that we are free to endorse or oppose. The fact that the book you are reading is called 'Introduction to Personality, Individual Differences *and* Intelligence' is a clear reflection of this tradition. Nevertheless, a number of theorists argue that the personality–intelligence/cognition dichotomy is a false one, and that intelligence satisfies the definition of a personality trait because it describes a regular aspect of (cognitive) experience. Moreover, there is now plenty of evidence that personality traits capture individual differences in cognition.

As we saw earlier, Pytlik Zillig and colleagues (2002) found that one of the Big Five domains, Openness/Intellect, is conspicuously related to cognitive phenomena (see Table 3.1). Typical terms that appear on scales measuring Openness/Intellect include, *intellectual*, *perceptive*, and *innovative*. Perhaps the most compelling evidence linking Openness/Intellect with cognition is a fairly consistently observed correlation of .30 with measures of intelligence and other cognitive capacities, such as working memory capacity (Ackerman & Heggestad, 1997). This has given rise to the theory that this domain – in particular, the *intellect* aspect – reflects the extent to which one engages with ideas, information, and intellectual matters, and that intelligence can even be thought of as facet of intellect, residing at the lowest known level of personality structure (DeYoung, 2014). Openness/Intellect has also been associated with a particular kind of learning known as *latent inhibition*. Latent inhibition is often referred to as a sensory-gating mechanism, which means that it is a process that prevents sensory information from entering our conscious perception. We need such mechanisms because the world is extremely complex, and we need a means to 'tune out' the innumerable stimuli clamouring for our attention. To ensure that we are overwhelmed by all of these sights, sounds and smells, we screen-out or 'gate' any information that is not important. It turns out, however, that individuals high in Openness/Intellect seem to do this to a reduced extent. Experiments show that such individuals are more likely to notice, or incorporate into their thinking, stimuli and information that the average individual has learned to ignore or treat as irrelevant (Carson, Peterson, & Higgins, 2003; Peterson & Carson, 2000). This suggests that, in cognitive terms, 'open' people really are more *open-minded* – they are characterized by greater 'breadth, depth, and permeability of consciousness' (McCrae & Costa, 1997, p. 826).

Another broad cognitive process to which Openness/Intellect has been robustly linked is creativity. Creativity can be defined as the generation of products or works that are valuable (i.e., either useful in a practical sense or held in some esteem by others) but also novel and original. Openness/Intellect is the Big Five domain that has been most robustly associated with various measures of creativity and creative achievement. A simple laboratory test of creativity is the alternate uses task, which is a test of *divergent thinking*. In the alternate uses task, participants are asked to list as many uses they can think of for seemingly mundane objects (e.g., a brick or a pencil). Several studies have shown that high scorers on Openness/Intellect can think of a larger number of uses for such items, and also that these uses are often highly novel and original (e.g., using a brick as a coffin for a Barbie doll funeral diorama) (Silvia et al., 2008, 2009). Openness/Intellect has also been associated with actual creative achievement in real life. In one recent study, Kaufman and colleagues (2015) surveyed over 1,000 participants regarding their creative achievements in the arts (e.g., music, dance, creative writing) and sciences (e.g., inventions and scientific discoveries). These achievements were scored in terms of seven levels of achievement based on, for example, awards won for one's creative outputs. Consistent with laboratory studies of creativity, Openness/Intellect was the strongest predictor of creative achievement out of all Big Five domains. Perhaps most interesting was the finding that Openness was a unique predictor of creative achievement in the arts while Intellect was a unique predictor of creative achievement in the sciences. Kaufman and colleagues suggest that this may indicate that Openness reflects cognitive processes that are more experiential and intuitive, while Intellect reflects cognitive processes that are more rational – again linking Intellect with intelligence.

Although it is clear from Table 3.1 that Openness/Intellect is the trait domain most closely connected with cognition, the other Big Five domains have also been associated with cognitive processes. For example, Agreeableness has been associated with tests of 'theory of mind' that involve understanding the mental states of others (Nettle & Liddle, 2008). This suggests that highly agreeable people are better able to take the perspective of others and appreciate their point of view. Another example is trait anxiety, which is closely related to the withdrawal aspect of Neuroticism and has been robustly associated with biases in visual attention. Specifically, anxious individuals seem to have a sensitive 'radar' for threatening stimuli, which will more easily capture and hold their attention (Mathews & MacLeod, 2002). Conscientiousness, as we have seen, is strongly related to the regulation of motivated action, a process that is sometimes referred to as *cognitive control*. Conscientious people appear better able to resist distractions, focus their thoughts on a task at hand, and are less susceptible to mind-wandering or 'zoning out' (e.g., Jackson & Balota, 2012). Only Extraversion appears largely unrelated to cognitive processes, although some links have occasionally been drawn here (see Lieberman & Rosenthal, 2001). All in all, the common claim that personality traits are 'non-cognitive' is patently unsustainable.

Perceiving personality processes

The previous sections provide a glimpse of the various affective, behavioural, and cognitive processes that are reflected in personality traits, as shown by studies in which personality scales are correlated with measures of these basic psychological processes. Another way we can gain a sense of how these processes are manifest in personality is through research into personality judgements. This field explores how people make judgements about the personalities of others, as well as how accurately they do so. In such studies, participants (or 'judges') provide personality ratings of other individuals (or 'targets') using exactly the same items that appear on measures of regular, self-assessed personality. Research generally shows that how you describe your own personality on such questionnaires is at least moderately related to how other people who know you well describe your personality (Funder, 1995). This is a testament to the *inter-rater reliability* of major personality questionnaires, which simply means that multiple raters (e.g., self and other) achieve reasonable levels of consensus when describing an individual's personality traits.

Intriguingly, levels of consensus remain well above chance even when the other-rater is a complete stranger – at least for some traits. In a typical study of this kind (Borkenau & Liebler, 1992), 100 individuals were videotaped for approximately two minutes while reading a short script (a weather report). Twenty-four participants viewed the clips and completed personality ratings for the persons who had been filmed. Despite the fact that the judges and the targets had never even met one another, levels of consensus were quite respectable, and for some traits even reached the levels attained by close acquaintances. How do people make such accurate judgements of a stranger's personality? They do so by correctly detecting the affective, behavioural, and cognitive 'cues' that are relevant to personality, and can be perceived even within a relatively short video clip. In the study by Borkenau and Liebler, extraverted targets tended to read the script in a louder and more powerful voice, they tended to have a more friendly and self-assured expression, they looked directly into the camera, and – when walking to the chair on which they would sit to read their script – they walked in a more relaxed way and were more likely to swing their arms. All of these behavioural cues were detected by the judges, whose ratings of Extraversion were higher if the targets being recorded spoke in a louder voice, appeared more self-assured, and so on. So, just as we know that traits in the Extraversion domain describe individuals primarily in terms of their behaviour, people also form judgements about an individual's extraversion by attending to the behaviours exhibited by that individual.

Knowledge of the basic psychological processes captured by major domains of personality traits leads to an interesting inference concerning personality judgements. Specifically, it helps us understand why some traits are more easily judged than others. Typical studies in personality judgements show that extraversion is the most easily judged personality trait. If you think for a moment about someone you have met recently and still don't know very well, you'll probably find it reasonably straightforward to describe them in terms of their level of Extraversion. In contrast, it is probably trickier to describe them in terms of their levels of Neuroticism or Openness/Intellect. This is because the tendencies described by Extraversion are largely behavioural in nature, and behaviour is highly visible to others. In contrast, other aspects of our personality are less visible to the outsider – how we are feeling (e.g., Neuroticism), or what we are thinking (e.g., Openness/Intellect). These processes are not always easy to see when observing others. For instance, in the study by Borkenau and Liebler (1992), accuracy for judgements of Neuroticism were close to chance levels. This makes good sense when you think about the likely appearance of more neurotic individuals in the video clips. Even if they felt a little bit nervous, it seems unlikely that this would have created visible signs of worry, such as stammering or shaking. After all, the task of reading a simple prepared script is not the most anxiety-provoking situation in which to find oneself. Many of the cues to the tendencies of a highly neurotic individual, which primarily consist of negative emotions, would probably have been minimal, if not completely absent, in this context. Of course, as we really get to know someone, and observe him or her in a wider range of situations, we may gradually get a better sense of their emotional stability.

This brings us to a further important insight about what exactly we are describing when we describe somebody as high or low on a particular trait. Specifically, it is not the case that people who score relatively high on Neuroticism *constantly* shake like a leaf and sob in despair. Agreeable people do not wear a perpetual benevolent smile, showering kindness and rainbows on everyone around them, and extraverts can regularly spend their evenings quietly reading a book without sending ripples of confusion throughout personality science. Many years ago, some psychologists did wonder if the tendency for people to behave and feel differently in different situations might undermine the existence of stable personality characteristics (e.g., Mischel, 1968). In more recent years, a broad consensus has emerged around the idea that the processes described by traits are at least somewhat situationally specific. That is, the affects, behaviours, and cognitions described by any trait domain are more likely to occur in some situations than in others. Extraverts tend to be bold, talkative, and assertive in *social* situations. Indeed, it is hard to imagine anyone reading in an assertive manner, or boldly sleeping. Similarly, more neurotic individuals tend to feel more anxious, worried, and tense in situations that provoke such emotions. Again, this explains why it is easier for us to judge another person's level of Extraversion (i.e., we typically observe other people in social situations) than their Neuroticism (i.e., we might need to know someone for a long time before we ever see them in a stressful or emotion-provoking context). In short, personality traits describe *regularities* in behaviour and experience, not *absolute*, *constant levels* of behaviour and experience. That is, our behaviour and experience varies considerably over time and space, and in accordance with the kinds of situations in which we find ourselves, but these patterns of variation are different for different people.

A recent study on personality judgements by Hirschmüller and colleagues (2015) demonstrates the situational specificity of personality processes related to Neuroticism. The authors reasoned that judgements of Neuroticism between non-acquainted individuals would be more accurate when made in a *trait-relevant situation* – one that was more likely to provoke the kinds of emotional affects and behaviour that are described by Neuroticism. Fifty individuals were videotaped giving a brief introduction about themselves to a group of peers, who they had been told would be subsequently rating them in terms of likability. This evaluative situation was intended to be at least mildly anxiety-provoking, and thereby elicit visible individual differences relating to Neuroticism. Indeed, accuracy of Neuroticism judgements in this situation was well above chance, and appeared to be based on visual and vocal signs of nervousness displayed by the judged individuals. In contrast, ratings made for videotaped individuals serving in a control condition (involving some small talk between the judged individual and the experimenter) were about half as accurate. This appeared to be because the videotaped individuals displayed less trait-relevant signs of nervousness in this fairly benign situation. The two conditions in this experiment may provide a snapshot of daily life for the archetypal person scoring high on Neuroticism. Specifically, in many situations, neurotic individuals are *not* more tense, worried or anxious than their emotionally-stable counterparts – at least not to the point where this is visible to other people. However, in situations involving stressors and other emotion-provoking stimuli, neurotic tendencies bubble up to the surface, both in terms of the individual's experience and in terms of what is visible to others around them.

A final point to note about research in personality judgements concerns how we might interpret discrepancies between self-ratings and the other-ratings provided by judges. Self- and other-ratings are never perfectly correlated, so clearly they are never perfectly accurate. But where two ratings differ, how do we know which is the more accurate? Imagine that a friend, who has known you very well for many years, rates you as lower on Agreeableness than you rate yourself. You might argue that their ratings are inaccurate because, although they know you well, they surely do not know you as well as you know yourself. Or do they? Researchers in personality judgements argue that the discrepancy between self-ratings and other-ratings may not necessarily be due to the inaccuracy of the judge, because self-ratings are also prone to error and distortion. For example, people differ in terms of their awareness of their own emotionality, as described by the trait *alexithymia* (Vorst & Bermond, 2001). Highly alexithymic individuals find it difficult to identify, describe, and distinguish their emotions. People also differ in their tendency to self-deceive, such that they may maintain particular beliefs despite being exposed to contradicting evidence (Mele, 1997). There are also situations in which we may be motivated to present an overly positive image of ourselves, such as when undergoing psychometric testing as part of an employment procedure. These factors can introduce bias and inaccuracy into self-descriptions of our personality. There is also evidence that other-reports can *add information* to personality descriptions based on self-reports, and that the predictive validity of traits increases when personality is assessed using multiple raters. For example, estimates of the impact of genetic factors on personality – which we will discuss in more detail in Chapter 5 – increase substantially when multiple raters are used to assess personality (Riemann & Kandler, 2010). Such studies show that our personalities can be validly, though imperfectly, viewed from multiple vantage points – from the inside and from the outside. These different sides of the personality 'coin' are sometimes referred to as our *identity* (how we see ourselves) and our *reputation* (how others see us).

Regularities in behaviour and experience

Throughout this chapter we have asked, what exactly are we describing when we describe someone in terms of a personality trait? We have conceptualized personality in terms of regularities in behaviour and experience – stable patterns of affect, behaviour, and cognition. As we have seen, there is a wealth of data demonstrating how personality traits reflect different, coherent patterns of affect, behaviour, and cognition. We have also seen that these patterns vary over different situations, and in response to different stimuli: people scoring high in Neuroticism don't constantly behave in a 'neurotic' way, but they are relatively more likely to be visibly anxious and emotional when they are in a stressful situation. A person who scores highly on Neuroticism will often have very calm, unemotional experiences – just as relatively hot cities will often have several cool spells each year. Just as climate is a summary of regularities in weather, personality traits summarize regularities in behaviour and experience.

The notion that personality traits capture regularities in dynamic states is formalized more rigorously in William Fleeson's (2001) 'distribution density hypothesis'. According to this model – which has some similarity to the Act Frequency model discussed earlier – we can think of an individual's affects, behaviours, and cognitions as forming a frequency distribution throughout a given time period. For example, in a given week, almost everyone will spend some time being very talkative and some time being completely silent, whether or not they are highly extraverted. The interesting question, from a personality perspective, is to ask how the properties of this distribution of states vary from one individual to the next. For many people, their distribution of states over time might form a classic 'bell curve' (see Figure 3.2b), suggesting that they are sometimes very talkative, sometimes very quiet, but that mostly they are at least somewhat talkative. Other individuals may have a negatively skewed distribution with a very high mean – they spend most of their time up the more talkative end of the scale (see Figure 3.2c). This captures one of the key characteristics referred to when we describe someone as an 'extravert'; they *tend* to be more talkative than the average person. Similarly, if you spent most of your time during an average week up the less talkative end of the scale, you would be less talkative than the average person, and might be described as relatively less extraverted (see Figure 3.2a). The distribution density hypothesis states that personality traits reflect these properties of distributions of affect, behaviour, and cognition. Specifically, the place where a given individual's distribution is at its most dense – its *central tendency* – corresponds to their standing on the relevant trait.

The distribution density hypothesis may make sense in principle, but in practice is it an accurate portrayal of the dynamic processes captured by major personality traits? In fact, good support for Fleeson's model has been gathered using Experience Sampling Methods (ESMs). In such studies, individuals report on their behaviour and experience multiple times per day via a mobile device, typically for around two weeks. This enables researchers to empirically construct the state distributions depicted in Figure 3.2. Fleeson and Gallagher (2009) conducted a meta-analysis of 15 such studies in which participants provided these momentary reports for various personality states (e.g., behaviours relating to Extraversion, affects relating to Neuroticism, etc.), several times a day for up to three weeks. In line with the distribution

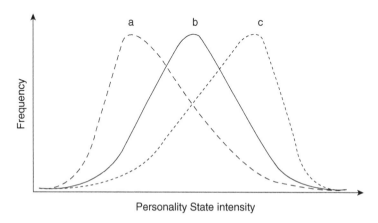

Figure 3.2 Distributions of personality states for three individuals. According to the distribution density hypothesis (Fleeson, 2001), personality *traits* correspond to the long-term averages of corresponding personality *states* (lowest for person a, middling for person b, highest for person c)

density hypothesis, the data showed that participants did indeed vary widely over time in terms of their personality states. However, measures of the central tendency of the distributions of these states (i.e., the *mean*, *median*, and *mode*) were strongly related to measures of the Big Five personality traits. For example, across the 15 studies in the meta-analysis, the correlation between scores on trait Agreeableness and mean levels of agreeable behaviour and experience was .55. Therefore, individuals who describe themselves as highly agreeable on a personality questionnaire are more likely, on average, to find themselves behaving in an agreeable way or experiencing emotions and cognitions relating to Agreeableness throughout their daily life. Furthermore, a person's average levels of personality states are extremely stable from one week to the next, even though they vary from moment to moment throughout each week (Fleeson, Malanos, & Achille, 2002). In other words, while all individuals will be talkative in some situations and quieter at other times, some individuals tend more often to be talkative, while others are typically less talkative – and these regularities are a key part of what is captured by measures of trait Extraversion. Overall, research in this area has shown that the clusters of behaviour and experience captured by each of the Big Five are highly flexible and changeable. At the same time, however, each individual's particular *pattern* of behaviours and experiences is highly stable and consistent over time.

We can briefly summarize the ideas we have explored in this chapter so far as follows: First, the Big Five provide a useful system for organizing most trait constructs. These trait domains can be thought of as broad umbrella terms that capture clusters of narrower, inter-related personality trait descriptors (i.e., aspects and facets of personality). Second, these traits describe patterns of basic psychological processes comprising affect, behaviour, and/or cognition – the ABCs of personality. To describe someone in terms of their dispositional traits is to describe them in terms of how they typically feel, behave, and/or think. Third, the different patterns of affect, behaviour, and cognition captured by each of the Big Five are illuminated by studies concerning how people make personality judgements. We can more accurately judge an individual's standing on certain traits (i.e., those that concern highly visible, behavioural tendencies) and when observing that individual in certain situations (i.e., in contexts that are likely to evoke visible, trait-relevant tendencies). Finally, while the processes captured by personality traits are dynamic and changeable, an individual's standing on any trait measure captures certain *regularities* in the patterning of behaviour and experience. Specifically, traits appear to reflect the long-term averages – or distribution densities – of fluctuating patterns of affect, behaviour, and cognition.

Are traits sufficient for describing personality?

Considering that traits reflect complex blends of multiple, dynamic psychological processes, an individual's trait profile can be surprisingly uninformative. Imagine a person who scores above average on Agreeableness and Extraversion and average on Neuroticism, Conscientiousness and Openness/Intellect. What do we really know about this person based on these five numbers? As they have elevated scores on the two major interpersonal domains within the Big Five, we might expect them to be relatively sociable and good-natured. But otherwise we don't have much distinctive information to go on. Ironically, this is partly because the processes underlying these five numbers are so complex – a high score on Agreeableness could indicate higher levels of compassion and empathy, or a tendency to be polite, or a modest and humble disposition (or all of the above). Now imagine two males who score very low on Extraversion but are more or less average on the remainder of the Big Five. The first person, a young, mild-mannered automotive mechanic, happily interacts with customers and colleagues, but is fairly quietly spoken and short on conversation. He has some good friends and socializes often, even though he tends to keep in the periphery. In contrast to this, the second person – a middle-aged schoolteacher – often appears surprisingly extraverted. Specifically, he seems to have the knack for controlling classrooms of rowdy students, capturing their attention, and communicating with firm authority and eloquence. It is only once he has returned home for the day that his other side is revealed – his quieter, more retiring side. Outside work he doesn't socialize so much at all, spending most weekends gardening and listening to public radio. The mechanic and the teacher are two individuals with very similar trait profiles who, nevertheless, have very different kinds of personalities. The clear implication of this example is that traits may not be sufficient for fully describing personality.

Traits have clear limitations. Although few psychologists deny that traits provide an important, even essential vocabulary for describing individual differences, even fewer would argue that traits encompass all that we need to consider when describing human individuality. In other words, traits are necessary but they are not sufficient. Many theorists have identified a wide variety of descriptive units, concepts, and structures that purportedly lie beyond the realm of traits. Collectively, these are often referred to as *characteristic adaptations*; aspects of your personality that reflect how you have adapted to your particular life circumstances. Unfortunately, the definition, scope, and boundaries of characteristic adaptations have been neither clear nor consistent in the personality literature. In reading this literature, one often gets the sense that any construct that does not seem to clearly fit the definition of a trait is labelled as a characteristic adaptation by default. As a result, the universe of characteristic adaptations tends to resemble a 'lost property' box. Dan McAdams (1995) notes that constructs as varied (and seemingly unrelated) as *values*, *talents*, and *attachment styles* can be lumped together under the umbrella term of characteristic adaptations. Similar, seemingly arbitrary collections of constructs have been described elsewhere, encompassing *interests*, *roles*, *attitudes*, and *habits*, and many others. In short, and in contrast to trait psychology, there is currently no robustly established system for describing and organizing characteristic adaptations.

According to McAdams (1995), the key difference between traits and characteristic adaptations is that the latter are highly contextualized with respect to *time* (i.e., developmental period in life), *place* (i.e., the specific situation or environment), and or *role* (i.e., a particular function or duty we may perform). In the case of our two introverts described above (the mechanic and the school teacher), the differences in their personalities seem more easily articulated if we think about matters of time, place, and role. The mechanic's professional role is to maintain and repair vehicles, and he does this in an environment that allows for a reasonable degree of solitude. The patterns of behaviour and experience that are likely to suit this state of affairs are reasonably consistent with his relatively introverted disposition. We might say that the mechanic has adapted to his life circumstances by identifying a career that fits comfortably with his basic traits. Contrastingly, the schoolteacher's primary role is to *teach*, which requires a lot of talking, as well as leading and motivating a large group of individuals. The teaching environment demands interaction, and highly introverted behaviour is not going to be very useful to the teacher or to his class. To perform effectively as a teacher, an introverted person would probably need to adapt in various ways, and cultivate characteristic ways of behaving that are appropriate to this place and role – even if this is not consistent with their dispositional tendencies. Finally, with respect to time, recall that in our example the mechanic is at an earlier stage of his life, which may explain why he is more sociable when not at work (e.g., he may be single or dating). In contrast, the teacher is much older and may have 'settled down' a long time ago.

Many of the constructs that have found their way onto various lists of characteristic adaptations seem to fit McAdams' notions of time, place, and/or role. For example, one aspect of personality that seems to complement trait psychology concerns individual differences in *vocational interests.* These **interests** represent the preferences people have for particular lines of work – the function they wish to serve in society (i.e., role) and the environment in which they would like to be employed (i.e., place). One popular model of vocational interests was developed by Holland (1997), who proposed that there are six main interest types. The typical characteristics and most suitable occupations for these interests are laid out in Table 3.2. Holland's model underlies a popular assessment tool for career counsellors to assess people's profiles of interests – people rarely have interests that are specific to one interest type – and can help to illuminate the reasons why people may fail to adapt successfully to their work environments. If their interests are a poor fit to their work role or environment – for instance, someone with artistic interests working in a position more suited to someone with conventional interests, or in an organization that adopts an inflexibly conventional workplace culture – then they may grow dissatisfied and perform poorly at their job. In the specific context of jobs and careers, therefore, an individual's patterns of interests are an important aspect of their personality in addition to their basic traits.

Vocational interests appear different from traits in terms of being concerned narrowly with one particular aspect of human life, but it is not hard to spot the similarities between the characteristics listed in Table 3.2 and the traits depicted in Figure 3.1 (and described in detail in Chapter 2). For example, the characteristics of the enterprising individual seem remarkably similar to those of the extravert. Consistent with this observation is the fact that Extraversion predicts performance in sales and management – the occupations to which enterprising individuals are thought to be suited. Similarly, the characteristics of investigative and artistic individuals seem to chime closely with the two complementary aspects of Openness and Intellect (see Figure 3.1). As we saw earlier, Intellect predicts creative achievement in the sciences while Openness predicts creative achievement in the arts – the exact careers linked with investigative and artistic interests. This clear overlap demonstrates the fact that the distinction between traits and characteristic adaptations is

Table 3.2   Summary of Holland's model of vocational interests

Interest type	Typical attributes	Occupations
Realistic	Hard-headed, conforming, practical, materialistic; prefers work with physical objects	Mechanic, electrician, farmer
Investigative	Analytical, rational, curious, cautious, critical; prefers work involving systematic observation and problem-solving that is not too social or repetitive	Scientist, lab assistant, anthropologist
Artistic	Intuitive, independent, open, imaginative, idealistic, impractical; prefers work that is creative and varied	Artist, musician, writer
Social	Friendly, kind, empathic, responsible; prefers work that involves helping or teaching others	Teacher, clinical psychologist, nurse
Enterprising	Outgoing, energetic, optimistic, ambitious, confident; prefers work involving leadership and power	Executive, manager, salesperson
Conventional	Orderly, efficient, pragmatic, careful; prefers work that is systematic and unambiguous	Financial analyst, book-keeper, accountant

still fuzzy and imperfect. A construct that appears to add information to a trait profile might do so simply because it is a narrower, more specific trait within the trait hierarchy – in other words, it might be a facet of personality masquerading as a characteristic adaptation. Even when a construct is highly contextualized, such as Holland's vocational interests, this may not disqualify it from being a trait. As we have discussed earlier in this chapter, traits are not completely decontextualized (e.g., neurotic people are more tense and anxious in emotion-provoking situations). While McAdams (1995) and others identify context-dependence as the distinguishing feature of characteristic adaptations, an alternative view is that characteristic adaptations are only *relatively* more context-dependeent than personality traits. That is, the issue of context-dependence may be a matter of degree, not 'all or none'.

An attempt to provide a sharper demarcation between traits and characteristic adaptations has recently been made by DeYoung (2015). First, DeYoung defines traits as regular patterns of behaviour and experience 'in response to classes of stimuli that have been present in human cultures over evolutionary time' (p. 35). This definition makes explicit the view that traits are at least partly context-dependent. He also suggests that the reason traits *appear* to be decontextualized is that trait-relevant stimuli form extremely broad classes. For example, relevant eliciting stimuli for extraverted behaviour and experience might include 'social' stimuli – a vast stimulus category and highly regular feature of daily life for most people. The same might be said for anxiety-provoking stimuli (relevant to Neuroticism). Second, DeYoung defines characteristic adaptations as 'relatively stable *goals*, *interpretations* and *strategies*, specified in relation to an individual's particular life circumstances' (2015, p. 38). Goals refer to any representation of a desired future state (e.g., to be a parent), interpretations are representations of any current state (e.g., 'my career is going well'), and strategies are plans and actions that allow one to move from one state to another (e.g., learning to play the guitar). So, for example, while being adventurous and venturesome is a trait, a lifelong dream to scale Mount Everest (a goal) is a characteristic adaptation. Having low self-esteem is a trait, while fretting throughout high school that one is a bad kisser (an interpretation) is a characteristic adaptation. Being conscientious in general is a trait, while always clearing one's email inbox at the end of the working day (a strategy) is a characteristic adaptation.

DeYoung's (2015) distinction between traits and characteristic adaptations may provide a clearer means for determining whether a given personality construct is a trait or a characteristic adaptation. For example, one set of constructs that historically have been distinguished from traits are **values**. Values are abstract principles or beliefs that motivate or guide people to behave in a way that pursues or expresses it. The most popular psychological model of values was developed by Schwartz and colleagues (e.g., Schwartz et al., 2012), which includes 10 distinct values including Hedonism, Achievement, Tradition, and Security. If you value Achievement, for example, you believe it is important to strive for success in all that you do, and you will be more ambitious and hard-working than someone who does not hold this value. Conversely, if you value Security, you will identify the safety and stability of your self, your family, or even your nation, as being of utmost importance, and this value will guide your behaviour in such a way that maintains states of harmony and order. Values are often described as characteristic adaptations, but, once again, we can see some clear similarities with traits (e.g., valuing achievement seems highly conceptually related to Conscientiousness). According to DeYoung's definitions, the values in Schwartz's model clearly *are* traits: they describe stable patterns of behaviour and experience that relate to very broad classes of stimuli (e.g., pleasure, safety). Schwartz's model has also been shown to generalize across different cultures, suggesting that the relevant stimulus classes may indeed have been universally present throughout human ancestry. Despite this, DeYoung's framework would allow for other kinds of values to be characteristic adaptations. On the one hand, placing a relatively high value on Benevolence (honesty, tolerance, concern for others) would be a trait – most likely falling under the Big Five domain of Agreeableness. But, on the other hand, explicitly identifying these values as central to one's self concept (an interpretation), or seeking counselling and self-help resources (a strategy) in order to become a kinder and more tolerant spouse (a goal) would satisfy DeYoung's definition of a characteristic adaptation. Similarly, valuing tradition in general would be a trait, while being a staunch defender of the second amendment of the constitution of the United States of America would be a characteristic adaptation (a goal). As these examples show, DeYoung's framework has the potential to greatly clarify the identification and description of aspects of personality beyond traits.

It is important to briefly mention one further level of personality description beyond characteristic adaptations: *life narratives*. The importance of the life narrative to personality comes from the insight that persons are more than just lists of human attributes. Rather, it is argued that the construction of the self ultimately takes the form of a story or 'personal myth' (McAdams, 1995). When we think deeply about who we are, we don't simply think about being shy, disliking horror films, or whatever the case may be. We think about *why* we are this way. We think about our history, our memories, the people and events that shaped us, how we got to this point in our lives and where things will go from here. Like any story, we understand ourselves in terms of plots, themes, settings, and other characters. Importantly, the life narrative is at least partly a work of fiction: rather than a factual, verbatim record of our experiences, it is a constructive process that we engage in to derive a sense of meaning and coherence in our lives. The study of life narratives, as you might imagine, is an intensive and highly individualized process – not unlike the task of writing a biography. The value of studying personality at this highest, most detailed level of resolution, and also the challenges one faces in doing so, will be discussed in more detail in Chapter 11.

To conclude: there is more to personality than traits. People are intuitively aware of this, which is perhaps why so many of us regard personality testing with scepticism. If you have ever taken a personality test, you have probably quibbled with your scores, or felt that it provided little more than a rough sketch of who you are. Indeed, it would be absurd to suggest that a person can be reduced to a set of scores on the Big Five, even though those scores will capture some general dispositional tendencies. Although psychologists sometimes write as if traits are all there is to personality – or that personality *is* traits – this is simply because the trait approach is one of the largest and most successful strands of personality research. Because they are the best-understood aspects of our personality, this book does have a tendency to focus strongly on traits. However, later chapters will also consider constructs that may lie beyond traits, including defence mechanisms (Chapter 4), personal constructs, explanatory styles, and the self (Chapter 7). We will also consider in greater depth the study of life narratives – the broadest and most individualized way of describing our personalities (Chapter 11).

Chapter summary

- While the Big Five are currently the most widely used taxonomy of personality traits, this is not at the exclusion of other personality traits. Rather, the Big Five represent the major dimensions of covariation among all personality traits, and therefore serve as an organizing framework for a diverse range of trait constructs.
- Personality traits can be arranged in a hierarchy, ranging from very broad 'meta-traits' (stability and plasticity), through the 'domains' and 'aspects' of the Big Five, to much narrower 'facets'. In principle, it should be possible to locate all personality traits somewhere within this hierarchy.
- Personality traits are complex composites of basic psychological processes consisting of affect, behaviour, and cognition. Content analyses show that measures of each Big Five domain are made up of items concerning different kinds of behaviour, and different kinds of cognitive and affective experience.
- Models of the structure of affect have been closely integrated with the structure of personality traits. Specifically, the Extraversion domain largely subsumes positive affect while the Neuroticism domain largely subsumes negative affect.

(Continued)

(Continued)

- The structure of personality traits provides a system for organizing individual differences in behaviour. Traits within the meta-trait of plasticity (Extraversion and Openness) are generally related to instances of behavioural exploration, while traits within the meta-trait of stability (Conscientiousness, Agreeableness and low Neuroticism) are generally related to instances of behavioural constraint and regulation.
- Motivation, which can be understood in terms of the confluence of affect and behaviour, is structured in terms of approach (action directed towards rewards) and avoidance (action directed away from punishment). Individual differences in approach and avoidance motivation are largely captured by Extraversion and Neuroticism, respectively.
- The claim that personality is separate from cognition is incorrect. Cognition is most clearly represented within the Openness/Intellect domain, which appears to reflect processes concerning cognitive exploration. This is illustrated by the relation this domain has with creativity and creative achievement.
- Knowledge of the affective, behavioural, and cognitive components of major personality traits enables us to understand why some traits are more readily perceived than others, and the kinds of situations in which certain traits will become more visible.
- The processes described by personality traits are not static; they vary widely across time and space. What is much more stable is the average tendencies of these processes. Tests of the distribution density hypothesis of personality confirm that one's score on a personality trait corresponds to one's average levels of particular affects, behaviours, and cognitions sampled over a period of time.
- Traits are not the only units that can be used to describe personality, and psychologists have developed useful models of several alternative units that have collectively been termed characteristic adaptations. At an even higher level of resolution are life narratives – the evolving *story* that individuals construct about who they are, and the broadest and most individualized way of describing personality. These higher level ways of describing personality complement the psychology of traits.

Further reading

Fleeson, W., & Gallagher, P. (2009). The implications of Big Five standing for the distribution of trait manifestation in behavior: Fifteen experience-sampling studies and a meta-analysis. *Journal of Personality and Social Psychology*, 97, 1097–14.
This meta-analysis shows that personality traits reflect average levels of behaviour and experience. This not only formalizes the way in which we conceptualize personality traits, but also demonstrates that personality questionnaires validly reflect what we suppose them to.

Gosling, S. D. (2007). *Snoop: What your stuff says about you*. New York: Basic Books.
An entertaining, popular book on personality showing how personality processes spill over into our everyday environments. Your bedroom, your desk, your bookshelf, and your music collection – all of these environments are shaped by the behaviours that make up your personality, and therefore can reveal what you are like.

Little, B. R. (2008). Personal projects and free traits: Personality and motivation reconsidered. *Social and Personality Psychology Compass*, *2/3*, 1235–54.
'Free traits' is an alternative conceptualization of characteristic adaptations, focusing specifically on how we can cultivate ways of behaving that are contrary to our dispositional traits (e.g., when we 'act out of character').

McAdams, D. P. (1995). What do we know when we know a person? *Journal of Personality*, *63*, 365–96.
A highly readable paper providing one of the first, broad conceptualizations of personality at the level of traits, characteristic adaptations (referred to here as 'personal concerns'), and integrative life narratives.

Pytlik Zillig, L. M., Hemenover, S. H., & Dienstbier, R. A. (2002). What do we assess when we assess a Big 5 trait? A content analysis of the affective, behavioral, and cognitive processes represented in Big 5 personality inventories. *Personality and Social Psychology Bulletin*, *28*, 847–58.
This paper illuminates the contents of the major trait domains of the Big Five in terms of the affective, behavioural and cognitive processes that are summarized by these measures.

Section 2
Explaining Personality

Psychoanalytic Approaches to Personality

Learning objectives

- To understand the historical development of psychoanalytic theory.
- To understand the multiple 'models' that make up the psychoanalytic account of the mind and the Freudian account of personality development.
- To develop a basic understanding of the directions that psychoanalytic theory has taken in different schools of post-Freudian psychoanalysis.
- To recognize the theoretical limitations of psychoanalytic theory and the problematic nature of its evidence base from the point of view of scientific method.
- To come to a balanced understanding of the weaknesses of psychoanalytic theory as well as its unique vantage point on human personality.

This chapter presents psychoanalytic theory, an influential but controversial account of the structure, functioning, and development of personality. After describing the origins of psychoanalysis in Sigmund Freud's clinical work with hysterics, we review three distinct 'models' of the mind that he developed: the topographic model, which presents the different levels of mental life; the structural model, which proposes three different and often conflicting mental agencies; and the genetic model, which lays out the stages of childhood development that form the adult personality. Along the way, the nature of psychological conflict and the ways in which people protect themselves against undesirable thoughts and desires ('defence mechanisms') are explained. Psychoanalysis does not end with Freud, however, so several post-Freudian schools are presented. We then turn to criticisms of psychoanalytic theory, focusing on its account of motivation, on the problematic nature of the evidence on which the theory is based, and the deficiencies of the theory from a scientific viewpoint (e.g., whether it can be tested or falsified).

In the first section of this book we discussed how individual differences in personality should be described and represented. Now we move on to consider the ways in which these differences can be explained. To explain a phenomenon is to give an account of how and why it arises. However, explanation is not a simple concept and explanations may take a variety of forms. To explain phenomena such as flight in birds and mechanical alarm clocks, for instance, it may be appropriate to refer to *structures* (e.g., feathers, hollow bones, and wing muscles; cogs, wind-up motors, and clock-hands), underlying *processes* or *mechanisms* (e.g., coordinated patterns of muscle contraction and relaxation; the interconnections of the rotating components), and *functions* (e.g., to allow swift escape from predators and access to distant or inaccessible food; to tell time and wake people up). All of these elements of explanations – structures, processes, and functions – contribute to a full account of why a phenomenon is as it is, and how it is produced. To explain personality differences, then, we must account for the structures, processes, and functions that underlie them. In the four chapters that make up the second section of this book we will explore a wide variety of explanatory approaches, beginning with psychoanalysis.

In 1896, Sigmund Freud was a Viennese neurologist specializing in the treatment of hysteria. The cause of this condition, which was most often diagnosed in women, was something of a mystery. The ancient Greeks believed it to result from the uterus becoming dislodged and roaming malevolently through the body, and the doctors of Freud's day debated several alternative theories. The manifestations of the condition were also puzzling and often bizarre. Freud wrote about one patient, Anna O., whose symptoms included loss of feeling in her limbs; inability to drink water; medically unexplained pains, paralyses, and muscular twitches; hallucinations of slithering black snakes; failure to see or hear nearby things; loss of the capacity to speak her native German while retaining facility with English; and 'absences' in which she lapsed into a trance-like state.

Freud treated his hysterics using hypnosis and noticed that in the hypnotic state many patients recalled childhood memories of a sexual nature. He found that when his patients were led to recount these memories, a flood of emotion was often released and their hysterical symptoms often vanished. Intrigued about what these apparent therapeutic successes might imply about the nature and origins of hysteria, Freud set about developing a theory of the condition. His first attempt, usually referred to euphemistically as the 'seduction' theory, proposed that hysterics suffered from traumatic memories of childhood sexual abuse, typically perpetrated by fathers. Soon after, however, Freud abandoned this theory for a number of reasons, including his doubts that childhood 'seductions' could be as common as the theory implied. Instead, he argued that the origins of hysteria were to be found not in memories of actual events but in childhood fantasies. These fantasies, in turn, expressed and satisfied the child's perverse sexual wishes and impulses. Hysterics suffered not from memories, as Freud had first thought, but from the disowned products of their childhood desires.

This episode, which took place when Freud was just embarking on the work that would make him a household name, captures in a nutshell many of the distinctive properties of the psychoanalytic theory of personality. First, both of Freud's accounts of the origins of hysteria propose that the sources of the condition are to be found in phenomena that are outside the person's consciousness. The hysteric is a mystery to herself, her disturbed experience and behaviour produced by causes of which she is unaware, and which are accessible only by special procedures such as hypnosis. Second, these underlying causes are proposed to be meaningful psychological phenomena. Rather than being explained by neurochemistry – or a wandering uterus – Freud argued that the source of hysteria could be traced back, often circuitously, to interpretable experiences, whether real or imagined. Third, Freud's second theory of hysteria implies that the mind is a place of conflict: the hysteric has wishes that are forbidden and perverse, and that she cannot consciously acknowledge. The price of this conflict between the wish and the social prohibition that forbids it is suffering and symptoms. Fourth, childhood experience is given a privileged place in the explanation of adult behaviour. Fifth, the sexual dimensions of experience are also given a large role in psychoanalytic explanation, with Freud maintaining that children are not innocent of sexual desires and experiences. These basic elements of psychoanalytic theory – the unconscious, the meaningfulness of behaviour, and the importance of psychological conflict, childhood experience, and sexuality – give it its distinctive flavour. A sixth property of psychoanalytic theory that the seduction theory episode demonstrates might also be mentioned at this point: it is unfailingly controversial.

Biographical details

Psychoanalysis was, from the beginning, the brainchild of Sigmund Freud. Freud was born to a middle-class Jewish family in Freiburg, Moravia (then Austria-Hungary), in 1856, moving in early childhood to Vienna, where he lived for most of his life. A good and intensely curious student, he entered university for medical training and soon became fascinated with biological research. His first research was on the sexual organs of the eel, but he subsequently became interested in the nervous system and spent several years doing laboratory science on its anatomy. Following graduation Freud did several years of clinical work with patients suffering from neurological disorders and continued to conduct research on questions including the possible medical uses of cocaine. After a period of study with the famous neurologist Jean-Martin Charcot in Paris, he commenced a private practice in which he primarily treated hysteria and other neuroses, using hypnotic methods that were controversial at the time.

Following the abandonment of the seduction theory of hysteria, Freud began to develop psychoanalytic ideas in numerous books and papers. After publishing an early volume on hysteria, his next three books, the first to be truly psychoanalytic, were on topics that appeared to be incidental to personality and mental disorder. Nevertheless, these studies of dream interpretation, slips of the tongue and related errors, and jokes, laid out a systematic psychology and showed how even apparently trivial phenomena such as these seemed at the time could be richly revealing about mental life. His later writings continued to develop and popularize his ideas, including his clinical writings on the psychoanalytic treatment of mental disorders. Meanwhile, Freud cultivated a group of thinkers and clinicians interested in his work and aggressively strove to develop a world-wide psychoanalytic movement with their help. Although some of his early supporters, most famously Carl Jung and Alfred Adler, had bitter breaks with this movement, within a couple of decades institutes for the training of Freudian psychoanalysts were widespread in Europe and the USA. When the Nazis invaded Austria in 1938 Freud escaped to London, where his daughter Anna went on to a distinguished career in the psychoanalysis of children. In 1939 he died of throat cancer, probably due to smoking the cigars about which, in reference to his theories of symbolism, he famously said, 'Sometimes a cigar is just a cigar'.

Elements of psychoanalytic theory

Before we begin our examination of psychoanalytic theory, it is important to recognize that the theory has an unusually broad focus. Psychoanalysis certainly contains a theory of personality, but it also offers theoretical tools for understanding culture, society, art, and literature. It is also a clinical theory that aspires to explain the nature and origins of mental disorders, and that is associated with an approach to their treatment. To give a sense of Freud's breadth, consider that he wrote extensively on topics as diverse as the meaning of dreams and jokes, the origins of religion, Shakespeare's plays, the psychology of groups, homosexuality, the causes of phobias and obsessions, and much more besides. Even as a theory of personality, psychoanalysis is primarily an account of the processes and mechanisms of the mind, rather than an account of individual differences.

In addition to its breadth of focus, Freud's psychoanalytic theory has many distinct components, making it difficult to integrate into a unitary model of the mind. Although they are all interconnected in complex ways, these theoretical components – often referred to as 'models' – are best introduced individually. To do justice to the richness and complexity of psychoanalytic theory, we will discuss three of these models.

The topographic model

The first model of the mind that we will consider is called the 'topographic' model because it refers to levels or layers of mental life. Freud proposed that mental content – ideas, wishes, emotions, impulses, memories, and so on – can be located at one of three levels: Conscious, Preconscious, and Unconscious. Before we examine each of these levels, it is important to understand that Freud used these terms to describe degrees of awareness or unawareness, but also to refer to distinct mental systems with their own distinct laws of operation. Unconscious cognition is categorically different from Conscious cognition, in addition to operating on mental content that exists beneath awareness. To convey this point, Freud often referred to the three levels of his topographic model as the 'systems' Cs., Pcs., and Ucs.

The Conscious

According to Freud, consciousness was merely the proverbial 'tip of the iceberg' of mental activity. The contents of the Conscious are simply the small fraction of things that the person is currently paying attention to: objects perceived, events recalled, the stream of thought that we engage in as a running commentary on everyday life.

The Preconscious

Not all of our mental life occurs under the spotlight of attention and awareness, of course. There are many things to which we could readily pay attention but do not, such as ideas or plans we have set aside or memories of what we were doing yesterday. Without any great effort these things, which in the present are out of consciousness, can be made conscious. They form the domain of the **Preconscious**.

The boundary between the Conscious and the Preconscious is a permeable one. Thoughts, memories, and perceptions can cross it without great difficulty, according to the momentary needs and intentions of the individual. They also share a common mode of cognition, which Freud called the 'secondary process'. Secondary process cognition is the sort of everyday, more-or-less rational thinking that generally obeys the laws of logic.

The Unconscious

The **Unconscious** is perhaps Freud's most celebrated theoretical concept. He did not invent or 'discover' the unconscious as is sometimes claimed – versions of the concept had been floating around intellectual circles for some time – but he gave it a much deeper theoretical analysis than anyone before him. Freud distinguished between mental contents and processes that are *descriptively* unconscious and those that are *dynamically* unconscious. The former simply exist outside consciousness as a matter of fact, and therefore include Preconscious material that can become conscious if it is attended to. Freud's crucial contribution was to argue that some thoughts, memories, wishes, and mental processes are not only descriptively unconscious, but also *cannot* be made conscious because a countervailing force keeps them out of awareness. In short, mental life that is dynamically unconscious is a subset of what is descriptively unconscious, one whose entry to consciousness is actively thwarted. The Freudian Unconscious corresponds to the dynamic unconscious in this sense.

Freud held that the Unconscious contains a large but unacknowledged proportion of mental life that operates according to its own psychological laws. The barrier between it and the Preconscious is much more fortified and difficult to penetrate than the border between the Preconscious and Conscious. In addition, it is policed by a mental function that Freud likened to a 'censor'. The censor's role is to determine whether contents of the Unconscious would be threatening or objectionable to the person if they became conscious. If the censor judges them to be dangerous in this way, the person will experience anxiety without knowing what caused it. In this case, these thoughts, wishes, and so on, will normally be repelled back into the Unconscious, a process referred to as 'repression'. Unconscious material, by Freud's account, has an intrinsic force propelling it to become conscious. Consequently, repression required an active opposing force to resist it, just as effort is required to prevent a hollow ball from rising to the surface when it is submerged in water.

Under the unremitting pressure of Unconscious material bubbling up towards the Preconscious, the censor cannot simply bar entry to everything. Instead, it allows some Unconscious material to cross the barrier after it has been transformed or disguised in some way so as to be less objectionable. This crossing might take the form of a relatively harmless impulsive behaviour, or in the form of private fantasy, the telling of a joke, or in a slip of the tongue, where the person says something 'unintentionally' that reveals to the trained eye their repressed concerns and wishes. Psychoanalytic training teaches how phenomena such as these can be interpreted, a process that involves uncovering the unconscious material that is concealed within their disguises.

To Freud, dreams represent a particularly good example of the disguised expression of Unconscious wishes. They offered, he wrote, 'a royal road to the Unconscious'. One reason for this is that during sleep the censor relaxes and allows more repressed Unconscious material to cross the barrier. This material, given a less threatening form by a process referred to as the 'dream-work', then appears as a train of images in the peculiar form of consciousness that we call dreaming. By Freud's account, each dream has a 'latent content' of Unconscious wishes that is transformed into the 'manifest content' of the experienced dream. This transformation must allow the Unconscious wishes to be fulfilled while concealing their threateningness. If it fails to conceal the latent content sufficiently, the sleeper will register the threat and be awoken. To avoid this, the dream-work may change the identities of the people represented in a wish. For example, if a person has an Unconscious wish to harm a loved one, the dream-work might produce a dream in which the person harms someone else or in which the loved one is harmed by another person. Neutralized in this way, the Unconscious wish finds conscious expression.

Dreams also showcase the distinct form of thinking that operates in the Unconscious. 'Primary process' thinking, unlike the secondary process that governs the Conscious and Preconscious, shows no respect for the laws of logic and rationality. In primary process thinking, something can stand for something else, including its opposite, and can even represent two distinct things at once. Contradictory thoughts can co-exist and there is no orderly sense of the passage of time or of causation. Described in this way, primary process thinking captures the magical, chaotic quality of many dreams, the mysterious images that seem somehow significant, the fractured story lines, the impossible and disconnected events. To Freud, dreams are not simply night-time curiosities, but reveal how the greater part of our mental life proceeds beneath the shallows of consciousness.

The structural model

The topographic model of the mind was part of Freud's psychoanalytic theory almost from the beginning, the Unconscious being one of the fundamental concepts of the theory. Several decades later, in 1923, Freud proposed another three-way dissection of the mind, this time defined in terms of distinct mental functions instead of levels of awareness and their associated processes. In English, these three mental structures were translated as the Id, Ego, and Super-Ego, forbidding terms that encourage a mistaken view of the structures as mental organs or entities. In Freud's original German, the terms – das Es, Ich, and Über-Ich; literally the It, I, and Over-I – come across as less alien and thing-like. As we examine each of these structures, it is important to remember that they were not proposed as real underlying entities, but rather as a sort of conceptual shorthand for talking about different kinds of mental processes. Although it is convenient to talk of the Ego, Id, or Super-Ego 'doing' such-and-such or being 'in charge of' so-and-so, remember that they were not intended to refer to distinct sub-personalities within the individual.

The Id

The **Id** represents the part of the personality that is closely linked to the instinctual drives that are the fundamental sources of motivation in Freudian theory. According to Freud, these drives were chiefly sexual and aggressive in nature. On the one hand, he proposed a set of 'life instincts' concerned with preserving life and with binding together new 'vital unities', the foremost expression of this concern being sexual union. Opposed to these life instincts are a set of 'death instincts', whose corresponding concern is with breaking down life and destroying connections, its goal a state of entropy or nirvana, the complete absence of tension. The clearest expressions of these instincts were aggressiveness expressed inward towards the self or outward towards others. Freud proposed that the instinctual drives were powered by a reservoir of instinctual 'psychic energy' grounded in basic biological processes. The sexual form of this energy was referred to as the libido.

Although Freud proposed that the Id has a biological underpinning, its contents are psychological phenomena such as wishes, ideas, intentions, and impulses. These phenomena are therefore sometimes described as 'instinct-derivatives'. Some of these phenomena are innate, whereas others have been consigned to the Id by the process of repression. All of the Id's contents, however, are unconscious.

Freud proposed that the Id operated according to what he called the 'pleasure principle'. Simply stated, this principle states that the Id's urges strive to obtain pleasure and avoid 'unpleasure' without delay. Pleasure, in Freud's understanding, represented a discharge of instinctual energy which is accompanied by a release of tension. In short, the Id strives to satisfy its drives by enabling the immediate, pleasurable release of their instinctual energy. Its essence is nicely captured by a quote from a friend of one of the authors' charming young son: 'I want my ****ing sweets, and I want them now!'

The Ego

The **Ego** complicates this cheerful picture of immediate gratification. According to Freud, this 'psychic agency' arises over the course of development as the child learns that it is often necessary and desirable to delay gratifications. The bottle or breast does not always appear the instant that hunger is first experienced, and sometimes it is better to resist the urge to urinate at the bladder's first bidding if one is to avoid the unpleasure of wet pants, embarrassment, and a parent's howls of dismay. The Ego crystallizes out of this emerging capacity for delay, and in time becomes a restraint on the Id's impatient striving for discharge. It cannot be an inflexible restraint, however. Its task is not to delay the fulfilment of wishes and impulses endlessly, but to determine when and how it would be most sensible or prudent to do so, given the demands of the external environment. It operates, that is, on the 'reality principle', which simply requires that the Ego regulate the person's behaviour in accordance with external conditions.

Freud emphasized that the Ego is not the dominant force in the personality, although he believed it should strive to be. (His famous statement of the goal of psychoanalytic treatment is 'Where Id was, there Ego shall be'.) By his account, the Ego not only emerges out of the Id in the course of development – beforehand, the infant is pure Id – but it also derives all of its energy from the Id. Freud had a gift for metaphor, and he likened the Ego's relation to the Id as a rider's relation to a wilful horse. The horse supplies all of the pair's force, but the rider may be able to channel it in a particular direction.

Fortunately, this rider has a repertoire of skills at its disposal. Freud proposed that the Ego could employ a variety of '**defence mechanisms**' in the service of the reality principle. A few of these mechanisms are presented in Table 4.1. Despite their diversity, they all represent operations that the Ego performs to deal with threats to the rational expression of the person's desires, whether from the Id or the external environment. Although the table presents situations in which Freud believed the mechanisms to be especially prominent, he proposed that they were common processes in everyday mental life.

Table 4.1   Selected Ego defence mechanisms

Denial	Refusing to acknowledge that some unpleasant or threatening event has occurred; common in grief reactions.
Isolation of affect	Mentally severing an idea from its threatening emotional associations so that it can be held without experiencing its unpleasantness; common in obsessional people.
Projection	Disavowing one's impulses or thoughts and attributing them to another person; common in paranoia.
Reaction formation	Unconsciously developing wishes or thoughts that are opposite to those that one finds undesirable in oneself; common in people with rigid moral codes.
Repression	Repelling threatening thoughts from consciousness, motivated forgetting; common in post-traumatic reactions.
Sublimation	Unconsciously deflecting sexual or aggressive impulses towards different, socially acceptable expressions; central to artistic creation and sports.

ILLUSTRATIVE STUDY

Defence mechanisms and social adjustment

American psychologists Marlene Sandstrom and Phebe Cramer (2003) sought to investigate the defence mechanisms people employ in response to experiences of rejection, and whether socially maladjusted people respond differently from others. Their chosen study sample contained 50 grade-four girls, who first completed a 'sociometric' interview in which they reported who among their classmates they liked or disliked. The data from this interview enabled the researchers to classify the girls according to their levels of popularity or social rejection. Each girl was then run through a procedure in which she was told that she would later have a chance to communicate over 'closed circuit TV' with another girl who was doing the study at the same time in another location. In fact this girl was a child actor who had been videotaped making a standard presentation. The actual participant was instructed to describe herself to this bogus participant over the TV, and then watched that participant 'respond' with her own, pre-recorded presentation. The actual participant was then instructed to ask the bogus one to join her for a play session, to which the bogus participant 'responded' as follows: 'No, I don't think so … I don't want to play'.

Both prior to and following this harrowing rejection experience, the girls told stories about what was going on in a series of ambiguous images. (These images were chosen from the TAT, a well-known 'projective' personality test that aims to assess hidden psychological dynamics; see Chapter 9.) These stories were scored for the presence of two defence mechanisms using an established and validated coding manual. Denial was coded when, for instance, a story omitted major characters in the images or overly minimized negative aspects of the image, and projection was coded when, for instance, hostile feelings were attributed to characters in the image.

Sandstrom and Cramer's findings indicated that more socially maladjusted girls used more defences after the rejection experience than the more popular girls, but did not use more defences prior to that experience. By implication, the maladjusted girls were more disturbed by the rejection and therefore responded in a more defensive manner. Doing so might have negative implications, furthering these girls' rejection by their peers.

You will be relieved to hear that no little girls were harmed (at least in any lasting way) by this research. Before the study was over, each girl was told that the bogus participant actually thought she was 'a really neat kid', and wasn't able to play with her because she 'wasn't allowed to', not because she didn't want to.

The Super-Ego

As we have seen, the Ego's task is to regulate the expression of the Id's impulses in response to the demands and opportunities of the external environment. However, this task is complicated by the emergence of a third psychic agency during childhood. This agency, the **Super-Ego**, represents an early form of conscience, an internalized set of moral values, standards, and ideals. These moral precepts are not the sort of flexible, reasoned, and discussable rules of conduct that we tend to imagine when we think of adult morality, however. Internalized as they are in childhood – under developmental conditions that will become clearer when we discuss the next of Freud's models of the mind – they tend to be relatively harsh, absolute, and punishing; adult morality as refracted through the immature and fearful mind of a child. The Super-Ego therefore represents the shrill voice of societal rules and restrictions, a voice that condemns and forbids many of the sexual and destructive wishes, impulses, and thoughts that emerge from the Id.

The Ego now becomes the servant of three masters: the Id, the Super-Ego, and the external environment. It is not enough now to reconcile what is desired with what is possible under the circumstances. The Ego now also needs to take into consideration what is socially prohibited and impermissible. Instinctual drives must still be satisfied; that is a constant. However, the Ego now attempts to satisfy them in a manner that is flexibly 'realistic' – that is, in the person's best interests under existing conditions – but also socially permitted. These prohibitions are often quite unreasonable and inflexible, rejecting any expression of the drive with an unconditional 'No', either because the moral strictures of a culture are intrinsically rigid or because the child's internalization of these strictures is starkly black-and-white.

Given the multiple demands it faces, the Ego can either find a way to express the Id's desires successfully, or its attempts to arbitrate can fail. In this case, psychological trouble is likely to follow. If the Id wins the struggle, and the desire is expressed in a more-or-less unaltered form, the person may experience guilt or shame, the Super-Ego's sign that it has been violated, and may also have to pay the price of a short-sighted, impulsive action. If the Super-Ego dominates, the person's conduct may become overly rigid, rule-bound, anxious, and joyless. The forbidden desires may well go 'underground' and manifest themselves in symptoms such as anxieties and compulsions, or in occasional 'out-of-character' impulsive behaviour or emotion.

Freud's account of the Id, Ego, and Super-Ego implies that conflict within the mind is inevitable, a view that has led some to describe his theoretical vision as 'tragic'. The demands of society – or 'civilization' as he preferred to say – are inevitably opposed to our natural drives. Indeed, intrapsychic conflict is one of the fundamental and defining concepts of psychoanalysis. For Freud, conflict is at the root of personality structure, mental disorder, and most psychological phenomena.

Before we proceed to the next model, the relationship between the first two should be clarified. Although the structural model is conceptually distinct from the topographic model, they do map onto one another to some degree. The content of the Id, of course, lies firmly within the Unconscious, forbidden entry to consciousness unless disguised in the form of dreams, slips of the tongue, symptoms, and so on. However, the Ego also has an Unconscious component, given that a great deal of psychological defence is conducted out of awareness and is inaccessible to introspection. The Super-Ego also has an Unconscious fraction, reflecting as it does an often 'primitive' and irrationally punishing morality at least as much as it reflects our reasoned beliefs and principles.

The genetic model

The third model that we will explore is usually called the 'genetic' model, a term that in this context means 'developmental' rather than having anything to do with DNA. Freud proposed that the developing child proceeded through a series of distinct stages on its way to adulthood, each with its own themes and preoccupations. What is truly novel about Freud's stage theory is that the stages are understood to be organized around the child's emerging sexuality. As we have seen in our discussions of the structural model, 'sexuality' meant more than adult genital sexuality to Freud, referring broadly to pleasure in the body and to sensuality. He believed that adult sexuality merely represented the culmination of an orderly set of steps in which the child's 'psychosexual' focus shifted from one part of the body to another. These body parts or 'erotogenic zones' all have orifices lined with sensitive mucous membranes. (The nose alone lacks its own stage, although Freud did briefly speculate on nasal erotism.) Initially the infant's sensuality is centred on the mouth, followed by the anus and then the genitals in early childhood. After some interesting dramas at about age 5, the child's sexuality goes under-ground for a few years, reappearing with a vengeance when puberty hits. We will examine each stage in turn.

The oral stage

According to Freud, the infant's voracious sucking is not purely nutritional. Although the infant clearly has a basic need to feed, it also takes a pleasure in the act of feeding that Freud did not hesitate to call sexual. Babies appear to enjoy the stimulation of the lips and oral cav-ity, and will often happily engage in 'non-nutritive sucking' when they are no longer hungry and the milk supply is withdrawn. Beyond being an intense source of bodily pleasure – an expression of sexuality in Freud's enlarged sense – sucking also represents the infant's way of expressing love for and dependency on its feeder, normally its mother. It also signifies a general stance that the infant takes towards the world, one of 'incorporation' or the taking in of new experience.

In addition to this lovingly incorporative mode, the **oral stage** also has an aggres-sive component. This 'oral-sadistic' component involves the infant's pleasure in biting and devouring. Both of these themes – incorporation and sadism – are important elements of the oral stage.

The anal stage

With the **anal stage**, we move to the other end of the digestive tract. At around the age of 2, the child is developing an increasing degree of autonomous control over its muscles, including the sphincters that control excretion. After the incorporative passivity and dependency of the oral stage, the child begins to take a more active approach to life. According to Freud, these themes of activity, autonomy, and control play out most crucially around the anus. The child learns to control defecation, and finds that it can control its environment, in particular its parents, by expelling or withholding faeces. Moreover, it takes pleasure in this control, pleasure that Freud recognized as 'anal erotism'. An important conflict during this stage involves toilet-training, with struggles taking place over the parents' demand that the child control its defecation according to particular rules. However, the anal stage represents a set of themes, struggles, pleasures, and preoccupations that cannot be reduced in any simple way to toilet-training, as they sometimes are in caricatures of Freudian theory.

The phallic stage

Eventually, but still in the early childhood years, the primary location of sexual pleasure and interest shifts from the anus to the genitals. The little boy becomes fascinated with his penis and the little girl with her clitoris. However, Freud referred to this stage as 'phallic' rather than 'genital' because he maintained that both sexes were focused on the male organ; 'phallus' referring not to the actual anatomical penis but to its symbolic value. Briefly stated, the little boy has it but, knowing that girls lack it, believes he could possibly lose it. The little girl, in contrast, knows that she lacks it, and wishes she had it. This is the first time that the difference between the sexes, and the contrast between masculinity and femininity, really becomes an issue for the child, according to psychoanalytic theory. It is also the first stage at which Freud's psychosexual theory recognizes sexual differences, and marks the crucial point at which, according to the theory, children become gendered beings.

The little boy's and girl's differing relation to the phallus plays a vital role in an unfolding drama that takes place within the family during this stage, somewhere around the age of 3 to 5. It is dubbed the 'Oedipus complex', after the Greek legend in which Oedipus unwittingly kills his father and marries his mother. The little boy is proposed to direct his phallic desires towards his mother, his original love-object after all, and is consequently jealous of his father, who seems to have his mother to himself. The boy's fearful recognition that he could lose his prized penis – 'castration anxiety' – becomes focused on the idea that his father could inflict this punishment if he recognizes the boy's desire for his mother. Faced with this fear, the boy renounces and represses this desire and instead identifies with his father, becoming his imitator rather than his rival. In this way the little boy learns masculinity and internalizes the societal rules and norms that the father represents (i.e., the Super-Ego).

The little girl's case is a little different. According to Freud, she feels her lack of a penis keenly ('penis envy') and blames her mother for leaving her so grievously unequipped. The father now becomes her primary love-object and the mother her rival. A similar process to the little boy's now takes place, resulting in the repression of the little girl's love for her father and an identification with her mother and hence with femininity. However, given that the girl is under no castration threat, this process occurs under less emotional pressure. Consequently, Freud proposed that the Oedipus complex was resolved less conclusively and with less complete repression in girls than in boys, and that girls internalized a Super-Ego that was in some ways weaker or less punishing. Needless to say, this last claim was highly controversial, and is one reason why Freud's account of the Oedipal conflict in women has been the subject of much criticism and revision.

Latency

After the upheavals of the Oedipus complex, the sexual drives go into a prolonged semi-hibernation. During the pre-pubertal school years, children engage in less sexual activity and their relationships with others are also desexualized. Instead of desiring their parents, children now identify with them. This interruption of childhood sexuality is largely a result of the massive repression of sexual feelings that concluded the phallic stage. One consequence of this repression is that children come to forget about their earlier sexual feelings, a major source, Freud claimed, of our general amnesia for our early childhoods. Social arrangements such as formal schooling reinforce the repression of sexuality during **latency**, leading children to focus their energies on mastering culturally valued knowledge and skills. Freud observed that the desexualization of latency-age children was less complete among so-called 'primitive' peoples.

The genital stage

The latency period ends with the biologically-driven surge of sexual energy that accompanies puberty. This issues in the final stage of psychosexual development which, if all has gone well, leaves the person with a capacity for mature, sexual love. The focus of sexual pleasure is once more the genitals, as it was before latency, but now it is fused with a capacity for true affection for the object of desire. In addition, both sexes are now invested in their own genitals rather than sharing a focus on the penis, as occurred in the phallic stage. The genital stage therefore sees the end of the 'polymorphous perversity' of childhood sexuality. These earlier erotic elements are not abandoned entirely but are instead subordinated to genital sexuality, often finding expression, for example, in sexual foreplay.

According to the genetic model, people pass through each of the psychosexual stages on the way to maturity. However, we do not pass through them unscathed. There are many ways in which people have difficulties in particular stages, and when this occurs a 'fixation' develops. A fixation is simply an unresolved difficulty involving the characteristic issues of the stage, and represents a fault-line in the personality. If the person did not receive reliable nurturance and gratification during the oral stage – or alternatively if they were over-indulged – a fixation on that stage may develop. When a person is confronted with stresses, they may revert to the typical immature ways of dealing with the world of that period, a process that Freud referred to as 'regression'. In some cases, fixations might also lead to fully-fledged mental disorders. Oral fixations are linked to depression and addictions, anal fixations to obsessive-compulsive disorder, and phallic fixations to hysteria.

Fixations do not only represent forms of behaviour and thinking that people regress to when faced with life's difficulties. The whole personality or 'character' – the term Freud preferred – may be organized around the themes of the stage at which people are most strongly fixated. As a result, Freud proposed a set of distinct stage-based character types. Oral characters tend to be marked by passivity and dependency, and are liable to use relatively immature ego defences such as denial. Anal characters tend to be inflexible, stingy, stubborn and neat, with a defensive style favouring isolation of affect and reaction formation. Phallic characters, finally, tend to be impulsive, vain and headstrong, with a preference for defence mechanisms such as repression. This three-part typology is the closest that the psychoanalytic theory of personality comes to being a psychology of individual differences.

Exploring a concept: The anal character

Freud first identified the anal character type in 1908, writing that its main features – the so-called 'anal triad' – are orderliness, obstinacy, and parsimony. People of this type therefore show traits such as conscientiousness, a preoccupation with cleanliness, stubbornness, perfectionism, rigidity, and miserliness with money. Freud believed that these traits tended to be found among people who recalled, as children, having an unusual concern with defecation. Indeed, he saw the traits as defences against these 'anal-erotic' wishes: anal characters sublimated their childhood interest in retaining faeces into an adult interest in holding onto money, and they became concerned with cleanliness and order as adults as a reaction-formation against their childhood fondness for filth.

Later psychoanalytic writers developed Freud's ideas about the anal character further. They proposed that these characters are often pedantic, have strong disgust reactions, cannot delegate work, are unable to relax, and are prone to collect or hoard things. They even proposed that the character style is associated with liking statistics, having good handwriting, being fascinated with tunnels, and not changing underclothes 'more than is absolutely necessary'.

The anal character has not attracted a great deal of attention from researchers, but what it has attracted is often memorable. One study by Rosenwald, Mendelson, Fontana, and Portz (1966) hypothesized that people with anal characters would have difficulty coping with situations that evoke supposedly anal anxieties. Study participants had to look at a picture of several objects, submerge their arm up the elbow in a liquid and identify by touch which of the objects was submerged in it. In one study condition the liquid was water, and in the other it was a revolting, faecal-like mixture of used motor oil and flour. Participants with anal personality traits performed especially badly on the faecal version of the task, supporting the researchers' claim anal characters cope poorly when faced with disgusting situations. Regrettably other studies found no link between childhood excretion patterns or toilet training and later anal character traits.

Although the anal character is not considered scientifically respectable in mainstream personality psychology, many psychologists study the traits that compose it. There are active research programmes on cognitive flexibility, perfectionism, hoarding, conscientiousness and disgust-proneness. There is also substantial research on obsessive-compulsive personality disorder (see Chapter 10), which shares many features with the anal character style. In sum, the anal character has not been consigned to psychology's scrap-heap of bad ideas: rather, it has been recycled into several smaller and better concepts (see Haslam, 2011).

Post-Freudian developments

Up to this point we have treated psychoanalytic theory as if it were the product of one remarkable and solitary mind. Although it is true that psychoanalysis owes more to its founder than any other major theory of personality, it would be a mistake to imagine that psychoanalysis ends with Freud. Indeed, the psychoanalytic movement has been very active since Freud's death in 1939, and has spun off many new theoretical developments rather than standing still. A complete review of these strands of thought is beyond the scope of this chapter, but brief reviews of some of the main historical trends and movements may give a sense of how varied Freud's legacy has been.

The first development to be considered is a loose group of so-called 'Neo-Freudian' theorists, most of them European immigrants to the USA following World War II, who took psychoanalytic thought in more accessible and socially-engaged directions. Erich Fromm, for example, wedded Freudian thinking about the formation of character with sociological and political ideas about human freedom and the good society. In his work, he proposed that people's needs extend beyond the Freudian drives to include loving relatedness to others and a sense of identity. He further argued that many social and political arrangements distort or fail to satisfy our basic needs, and that people often go along with their own oppression out of a fear of freedom and the insecurity it brings. In a similar fashion, Karen Horney wrote several popular books challenging Freud's views on female sexuality and development, including forceful critiques of the concept of penis envy. Rather than envying and feeling inferior to men on anatomical grounds, she argued, many women suffer more from an over-emphasis on love and a general lack of confidence. Like Fromm, Horney accepted that unconscious processes and conflict are central to personality, but they also argued that social conflict – conflict between people or between people and their wider social environments – was just as important for personality development and behaviour as the intrapsychic conflict that Freud emphasized. Similarly, she argued that human motivation goes beyond the instinctual drives to include needs for approval, achievement, and power.

A second, primarily American post-Freudian development was 'ego psychology'. Its main theoretical emphasis was on the functioning of the ego, a structure often described by Freud as at the mercy of the drives and responsible for the irrationality that repression and other defence mechanisms often generated. Ego psychologists such as Heinz Hartmann, Robert White, and George Klein gave a stronger role to the ego, presenting it as a source of psychological strength and potentially mature defence, and seeing in it a capacity to adapt to the demands of the outside world rather than merely resolving the mind's inner tensions. In addition to their emphasis on the adaptive capacities of the ego, these authors also argued that some of the ego's functions were relatively independent of psychic conflict, comprising the ego's 'conflict-free sphere'. The ego even had its own intrinsic drive towards competent mastery of tasks, rather than simply finding ways to channel sexual and aggressive impulses in socially acceptable and prudent ways, as Freud has proposed. Finally, the ego psychologists broke new ground by trying to subject psychoanalytic ideas to experimental tests and in studying psychoanalytically relevant traits (like 'cognitive style') empirically.

Ego psychology granted the ego a larger role in the theatre of mental life, but otherwise left much of classical Freudian psychoanalytic theory unchallenged. The person was still understood as a more-or-less solitary individual beset by forbidden wishes and impulses, punitive super-ego prohibitions, and the demands of the outside world. Although they remained faithful to many basic psychoanalytic doctrines, theorists of the **object relations** school that began to emerge in Britain in the 1950s challenged these aspects of classical psychoanalytic theory. These theorists, including Melanie Klein, Ronald Fairbairn, and Donald Winnicott, focused attention on the early, 'pre-oedipal' years of life when the infant and young child is experiencing intense relationships with its parents and developing an independent sense of self. Object relations theorists therefore place great emphasis on interpersonal relationships and on how our mental representations of other people ('object representations'), often forged in those early years of life, influence and distort these relationships. This emphasis on relationships extends to their theory of motivation. Unlike classical Freudians, object relations theorists propose that people have a basic drive to relate to others, not just aggressive and sexual instincts.

Our fourth and final post-Freudian development, especially popular in Europe and South America, was initiated by the colourful French psychoanalyst Jacques Lacan. Lacan developed psychoanalytic theory in radically new directions that relied heavily on linguistic theory and on other intellectual trends in late 20th-century France, such as the structuralist movement. He proposed that the Unconscious is structured like a language, so that its operations can be likened to linguistic phenomena (for example, he likened repression to metaphor). One consequence of this view is that to uncover unconscious material the psychoanalyst must decipher a chain of clues with a great deal of verbal cleverness. Half-flippantly, he once suggested that analysts could prepare for their profession by doing crossword puzzles. Lacan also held that the ego is not so much an organ of self-control and adaptation, as the ego psychologists maintained, but an unstable and ultimately illusory sense of personal unity. Our sense of self is, to Lacan, a tissue of identifications with people we have known, and the only wholeness we imagine ourselves to have is a fiction, a comforting and self-deceiving way of narrating our personal story. Our selves are profoundly 'de-centred'.

The four broad branches of psychoanalytic theory discussed here are only a sampling of the many schools of thought that have emerged since Freud. However, they should make it clear to you that there is a diversity of belief within psychoanalysis, and that contemporary psychoanalysis cannot be reduced to the worshipful preservation of Freud's legacy. Indeed, since Freud's death almost 80 years ago, psychoanalysis has not only diverged along several different lines, but has also shown a few broad trends. Generally speaking, contemporary psychoanalytic theory pays more attention to interpersonal relationships, gives less credence to Freud's account of drives, dispenses with outdated concepts such as psychic energy and instinct, and has made modest efforts to reconcile with empirical psychology.

Critiques of psychoanalysis

Psychoanalysis has been, without any doubt, the most criticized theory of personality, and perhaps the most criticized theory in psychology as a whole. The reasons for this are quite clear. Psychoanalysis has been around for a long time by the standards of most psychological theories, it makes many bold and challenging claims, and it was for a long time a dominant force in the study of personality and mental disorder. In short, it has been a large and juicy target. As a result, the list of critiques of psychoanalysis is a very long one, and impossible to review in a short space.

Thankfully, however, many of these criticisms are irrelevant for the purposes of evaluating the psychoanalytic theory of personality. For instance, criticisms of Freud as a person – for example, his shabby conduct towards some patients and stubborn and perhaps deceptive unwillingness to modify theories in light of new evidence – are not directly relevant to the adequacy of his theories, let alone those of other psychoanalysts. Similarly, criticisms of his clinical theory and practice – such as his dubious accounts of particular disorders and the limited evidence for the efficacy of psychoanalytic therapy – also have little bearing on the psychoanalytic theory of mental life as a whole. We shall focus instead on just a few major criticisms that have a more direct relevance to the psychoanalytic theory of personality. These include critiques of Freud's motivational theory, of psychoanalytic inference, and of the questionable scientific credentials of psychoanalytic theory.

The psychoanalytic account of motivation

Freud's account of human motivation, resting on his account of sexual and death instincts, has been a flashpoint for critics of psychoanalysis from the very beginning. Two of the earliest departures from the psychoanalytic movement were largely caused by disagreements over motivational concepts. Jung questioned the centrality of sexuality and argued the importance of spiritual motives, and Adler proposed a basic desire for social superiority and a 'will to power'. Later writers within the psychoanalytic tradition also sought to expand the theory of motivation to include drives for mastery and competence (i.e., ego psychologists) and for interpersonal relatedness (i.e., object relations theorists). Writers outside the psychoanalytic movement typically challenge the importance Freud ascribed to sexuality and the very existence of a death instinct.

These disputes can perhaps be broken down into two main issues. The first is whether the sexual and death instincts are plausible sources of human motivation. Second, we can ask whether they are sufficient explanations of motivation, or whether additional motives that are not reducible to these drives are needed.

With respect to the first issue, it is difficult to deny that sexual wishes and drives are powerful sources of motivation, especially if, following Freud, we include as 'sexual' desires for loving relationships and for bodily pleasure. From a biological or evolutionary standpoint, it could not be otherwise, as reproductive success is the basic currency of individual genetic fitness, not to mention species survival. From this perspective, the psychoanalytic emphasis on sexual drives, an emphasis shared by no other personality theory, is a strong point of the theory, even if we disagree about some of Freud's particular claims about sexual development or the antiquated idea of sexual 'energy'. From the same evolutionary standpoint, however, a death instinct makes no sense at all. It is entirely implausible that a creature would have a fundamental drive for its own destruction and decay. Note that this negative judgement on the death instinct, which is shared by many contemporary psychoanalysts, does not mean that we need to dispense with the idea of aggressive drives. Aggressiveness could be theorized not as a form of self-destructiveness, but as a way to strive for social dominance, to fend off attackers or intruders on one's territory, or to assert one's personal interests.

Our second issue is whether sexual and perhaps aggressive drives are broad enough to capture the full range of human motivations. At one level, the answer is clearly not. What about drives for achievement, social approval, non-sexual relatedness, creativity, self-esteem, and so on? More basically, are biologically-based motives that 'push' us towards certain kinds of behaviour sufficient? Do we not also need to include future-oriented motivational concepts, like goals and personal ideals, that 'pull' us towards desirable endpoints? When it is stated in this way, it becomes obvious that the Freudian account of human motivation is too limited in its scope, leaving out a range of motives that are socially shaped or personally determined, rather than being grounded in basic biological processes.

However, the issue is not quite so easy to resolve. Psychoanalysts might agree that motivations beyond the instinctual drives are needed to describe how our behaviour is guided, but argue that these motivations ultimately derive from the drives. For example, achievement striving could be understood psychoanalytically as a socially shaped motive that is underpinned and powered by aggressive urges. Similarly, creativity might be understood as a sublimated expression of the sexual drive, based on the sort of desire for unifying and making connections that Freud saw as the hallmark of the life instincts.

This issue is therefore complex. Most psychologists, and even many psychoanalysts, will tend to find any claim that human motivation is ultimately based on a few instinctual drives to be overly reductive. Even if this claim were true, it would probably still be more enlightening and accurate to describe a person's motivation in a more complex way. And the real problem is that there is really no way to establish that this claim *is*, in fact, true or false. The only reason to believe that motivations such as achievement striving or creativity are based on aggressive or sexual drives is a pre-existing commitment to psychoanalytic theory. Most psychologists therefore remain unconvinced that the Freudian account of motivation is adequate.

Psychoanalytic inference

Another focus of criticism of psychoanalysis reflects not so much the basic propositions of the theory, such as its claims about human motivation, but the way in which the theory is used to account for psychological phenomena. Critics often argue that inferences drawn from psychoanalytic theory – interpretations of dreams, symptoms, character traits, psychological test results, and other phenomena – are often not adequately supported by the available evidence. When psychoanalysts make judgements about what a phenomenon means, they argue, these judgements are not sufficiently constrained and objective, relying far too much on subjective interpretation. Consequently, judgements will often be wild, arbitrary, and over-confident, and different analysts will reach entirely different interpretations of the same phenomenon. Critics argue that if psychoanalytic inference is unreliable in this way, then there is little reason to place confidence in *any* psychoanalytic interpretation.

This criticism clearly has some merit. Psychoanalysts from different schools of thought often offer radically different interpretations of the same phenomena, and psychoanalytic clinicians frequently disagree strikingly about how to make sense of a patient's presenting difficulties. Similarly, examples of silly psychoanalytic inferences are not hard to find. For example, one of Freud's colleagues proposed that a patient developed a swelling on his knee to symbolize the swollen head of his father, who had died in a fall from a ladder. A psychoanalytic study of low productivity in the British coal-mining industry suggested that this was due to miners being hampered in their work by unconscious fantasies that they were tearing at their mothers' internal organs. If psychoanalytic inference can give rise to such flagrant absurdities, how can we have faith in others that seem superficially less ridiculous?

This critique of psychoanalytic inference is a serious one. Part of the reason for its problems is that psychoanalysis attempts to make sense of things that are intrinsically difficult to interpret. If the phenomena to be explained are in their very nature slippery – recollections of remote childhood events, dreams, baffling symptoms – attempts to grasp them will often lead to mistakes. However, the critique cannot be entirely brushed off by the intrinsic difficulty of psychoanalytic inference. The nature of psychoanalytic theory also makes wild and arbitrary inferences more likely. For a start, the concept of the Unconscious allows any phenomenon to be explained with reference to a cause that not only cannot be observed, but also cannot be verified in an independent, objective manner by someone other than the explainer. Explaining something in terms of unconscious processes therefore allows the explainer to make inferences that are not restrained by conventional standards of evidence. The concepts of primary process and of defence mechanisms also allow for a great deal of looseness in psychoanalytic inference in a similar fashion. If a phenomenon can mean something different from or even opposite to what it appears to mean, and if an idea or impulse can be distorted in myriad ways by reaction formation, projection, sublimation, and the like, it is inevitable that different interpreters will often come to different interpretations.

All of this places psychoanalysis in a dilemma. Some of its fundamental concepts, the ones that suggest that human psychology is more complex and mysterious than common sense would have it, are the very concepts that make inferences about human psychology unreliable and problematic. Psychoanalytic theory proposes that the Unconscious, defence mechanisms, and the like, are indispensable concepts for making sense of psychological phenomena, but as soon as we use them we seem to be vulnerable to real concerns about the adequacy of these explanations.

The scientific status of psychoanalysis

A final, and particularly crucial, set of criticisms of psychoanalytic theory concern its scientific status. These criticisms can be divided into two subsets. First, critics have questioned whether the kinds of evidence on which psychoanalytic theory was developed are sufficiently reliable to yield valid conclusions. Second, critics have argued that psychoanalytic claims either have not stood up well to scientific investigation or that they are not scientifically testable in the first place.

Psychoanalytic evidence

Freud ardently believed that psychoanalysis was a science, and he was an accomplished biological scientist before he developed his psychoanalytic theories. Biological ideas are woven throughout his work, as in his concepts of drive, instinct, and psychic energy. Nevertheless, the methods which he used to obtain evidence for his psychoanalytic proposals were very different from those he used as a laboratory scientist. As an anatomist and physiologist, he made systematic observations of living and dead organisms, and conducted controlled experiments. As a psychoanalyst, in contrast, he introspected and speculated about his own mental life, and listened closely to what his patients told him during sessions of psychoanalytic therapy. It goes without saying that dissecting an eel is importantly different from dissecting a personality, and that observing the stream of one's consciousness or another's speech is different from conducting a controlled experiment. Psychoanalytic evidence is clearly unlike the evidence on which most 'hard science' is based.

Many critics of psychoanalysis have pointed out the limitations of psychoanalytic evidence, and argued that much of it is too flimsy to serve as a foundation for developing or testing a scientifically adequate theory of personality. These limitations are several. First, whereas scientific evidence ought to be publicly available for checking by independent observers, most psychoanalytic sessions are intensely private and go unrecorded. Any reports on what happened in these sessions therefore cannot be independently re-examined and verified by people who might want to challenge how the analyst interpreted it. Second, scientific evidence ought to be objectively recorded, free from the possibility of distortion by the observer. Clearly this is not the case in the psychoanalytic session, where the analyst cannot help but interpret what is spoken according to subjective biases. Analysts, like everyone else, are prone to attend to and recall information selectively, to take heed of information that confirms their theoretical preconceptions, and to discount information that does not. Consequently, analysts' claims that their clinical experience repeatedly confirms a particular psychoanalytic hypothesis are scientifically tainted.

A third limitation of psychoanalytic evidence is more complicated. Even if the evidence of millions of psychoanalytic sessions were publicly accessible and objectively recorded, it would still be compromised by the nature of the psychoanalytic relationship between analyst and patient. What patients say in psychoanalytic sessions is influenced in often subtle ways by how the analyst responds to them and by their expectations for psychoanalytic treatment. This influence has been called 'suggestion', referring to the ways in which ideas can be insinuated into the mind. Suggestion can take a variety of forms. Most crudely, analysts might directly suggest to patients that they have a certain kind of wish, feeling, or recollection, and patients might oblige by reporting these things, perhaps even coming to believe in their reality. Less directly, the patient might infer from the thrust of the analyst's comments the sort of thing they ought to be saying, or learn to focus, even without being aware of it, on the sort of topic in which the analyst seems to take particular interest. In addition, it is a rare patient who comes to psychoanalytic therapy without being at least somewhat knowledgeable about psychoanalytic theory, and a large fraction of patients nowadays are training to be analysts. As a result, most patients enter psychoanalytic treatment with at least an implicit understanding of what is expected of them, with some familiarity with psychoanalytic ideas, and with a positive disposition towards psychoanalytic theory.

None of this implies that patients deliberately tailor their behaviour in psychoanalytic sessions to be consistent with psychoanalytic theory. However, under these circumstances it is clear that patients' reports of their experience in psychoanalytic sessions might conform to psychoanalytic hypotheses for reasons other than the truth of those hypotheses. It is no surprise, perhaps, that patients of Freudian analysts report Oedipal dreams, those of Jungian analysts report mythological and spiritual dreams, and those of Adlerian analysts report dreams about struggles for superiority.

Psychoanalysts are well aware of the problem of suggestion, and strive to assume a stance of 'neutrality' towards the patient, trying not to introduce any particular social demands or personal elements into the therapeutic relationship. Nevertheless, influential critics such as Adolf Grünbaum (1984) and Malcolm Macmillan (1997) have argued that analysts seriously under-estimate the problem. In their view, psychoanalytic evidence is deeply contaminated from a scientific standpoint, and claims by Freud and his followers that psychoanalytic hypotheses are confirmed by clinical experience are rather weak.

As we have seen, psychoanalytic evidence is problematic, and does not offer a very solid foundation on which to construct or test psychoanalytic theories. These criticisms aside, it is important to recognize that there is also something quite special about psychoanalytic evidence, for all its flaws. A completed psychoanalytic treatment may occupy four or five sessions each week over a period of several years, amounting to perhaps 1,000 hours in which the analyst listens closely to the patient's innermost thoughts. These thoughts, often too intimate and raw to be shared even with loved ones, range widely over the patient's personal history and lived experience. They are recounted in a wide variety of mood-states and frames of mind. These millions of spoken words and feelings may not represent the kind of systematically and objectively collected data on which a scientific theory of personality can easily be built. However, it is difficult to accept that the analyst does not understand the patient's personality better than someone who might interpret the patient's responses, dashed off in a few minutes, to a trait questionnaire. There *is* something valuable about psychoanalytic evidence, but it is devilishly difficult to build reliable theory out of it.

Scientific support and testability

The clinical evidence on which many psychoanalytic theories were developed is clearly problematic from the perspective of empirical science. Critics of psychoanalysis have also claimed that the theories themselves are often not scientifically testable. The influential philosopher Karl Popper argued that for a theory to be scientific its propositions had to be falsifiable – that is, capable of being refuted by evidence – and by this criterion, critics argued, psychoanalysis is not a science. We mentioned some of the reasons for this claim in the preceding section on psychoanalytic inference. The Unconscious and concepts such as defence mechanisms make it very difficult, if not impossible, to falsify any psychoanalytic claim, because the analyst can always explain away evidence that contradicts the theory. For instance, if a certain mental disorder is proposed to be caused by a certain kind of wish or childhood event and a patient with the disorder shows no evidence of the wish or event, it can always be claimed that these supposed causes have been repressed or disguised in some way.

Often accompanying this philosophical criticism regarding scientific testability is a factual criticism that psychoanalysts have seldom tried to test their theories scientifically. This criticism has some truth to it. Many psychoanalysts have responded to the call for more scientific research by asserting that it is unnecessary and that clinical evidence is quite sufficient. Other analysts have argued that scientific support for their theories is irrelevant. Psychoanalysis, they suggest, is not a science, so it is inappropriate to judge it by scientific standards. Some see psychoanalysis as a 'hermeneutic' discipline, an approach to interpretation rather like a school of literary criticism or biblical scholarship. To them, psychoanalytic theory is a way to decipher mental life, an interpretive technique for uncovering meaning. Its goal, they say, is to understand psychological phenomena in terms of their underlying reasons rather than explaining them scientifically in terms of causes. Some have gone so far as to suggest that the goal of psychoanalytic understanding is not to ascertain literal or scientific truth – for example, what 'really happened' in a person's past to make them the way they are today – but instead to formulate 'narrative truth', a story that gives coherent meaning to the person's experience (Spence, 1980).

Increasingly, however, some psychoanalytic thinkers and sympathizers are beginning to find ways to test psychoanalytic hypotheses in rigorously scientific ways, despite all the difficulties that this involves. This research is now very extensive, and is therefore difficult to summarize. However, two very broad conclusions can be drawn from it. First, specific Freudian claims typically fail to receive experimental support. For example, repression, castration anxiety, and penis envy cannot be experimentally demonstrated, dreaming does not seem to preserve sleep by disguising latent wishes, and there is very little evidence to back up the theory of psychosexual stages. However, more general Freudian concepts often receive a good deal of support.

For example, there is plentiful evidence for the existence of unconscious mental processes, for the existence of conflict between these processes and conscious cognition, and for the existence of processes resembling some of the defence mechanisms. Two illustrative studies can give a flavour of this work. First, Fazio, Jackson, Dunton, and Williams (1995) found that people who sincerely profess to having no racial prejudice can be shown to associate negative attributes with Black faces more than White faces in a laboratory task. This finding, which has been replicated countless times by social cognition researchers, shows that people's conscious attitudes may conflict with their 'implicit' attitudes. Second, Adams, Wright, and Lohr (1996) hooked male subjects up to a daunting instrument called a penis plethysmograph, which measures sexual arousal by gauging penile circumference. They found that men who reported strong anti-gay ('homophobic') attitudes demonstrated increased arousal when shown videos of homosexual acts, whereas non-homophobic men did not. This finding seems to reveal the defensive operations consistent with the psychoanalytic view that homophobia is a reaction formation against homoerotic desires.

None of these illustrative studies is conclusive, and all have been controversial and subject to different interpretations. For example, perhaps the increased penile blood flow of Adams et al.'s homophobic subjects was due to anxiety, shock, or anger rather than sexual arousal pure and simple. Nevertheless, they show that with enough ingenuity at least some psychoanalytic propositions can be scientifically tested. Doing so should contribute to the important task of sifting what is worth retaining in the psychoanalytic theory of personality from what isn't.

Conclusions

The psychoanalytic theory of personality is an enormously complicated and ambitious one. It aims to make sense of a much broader array of psychological and social phenomena than other theories, and does so with a large collection of explanatory concepts. If nothing else, the sheer scope of psychoanalytic theory – its aspiration to be a total account of mental life – needs to be recognized and applauded. By comparison, most other approaches to the study of personality look decidedly timid and limited in focus. Although other approaches generally have better scientific credentials, they tend to leave out much that we might want to include in a comprehensive theory of human behaviour. To many people, any account of personality that fails to acknowledge that we are something like how psychoanalytic theory sees us – driven by deeply rooted motives, inhabiting bodies that bring us pleasure and shame, shaped by our early development, troubled by personal conflicts, and often a mystery to ourselves – is fundamentally limited.

The price of all this depth and scope in psychoanalytic theory, of course, is some quite serious theoretical and empirical weaknesses, reviewed towards the end of this chapter. Many psychoanalytic claims are questionable, psychoanalytic evidence is often too contaminated to support the theories that have been developed from them, and these theories often permit the drawing of inferences that are unconstrained. Some of these problems are due in part to the intrinsic difficulty of what psychoanalytic theory tries to explain. Others could be at least partly overcome if researchers made a more concerted effort to determine which psychoanalytic ideas stand up to closer, scientific scrutiny. If we are to evaluate psychoanalytic theory only on the basis of its current scientific standing, most of it will be found wanting. However, it would be a mistake to abandon it impatiently, given how much a suitably revised and empirically updated theory of psychodynamics might deepen the future scientific study of personality.

Indeed, for all its failings, psychoanalysis is at least partly responsible for several important and scientifically respectable ideas. Although it may have originally presented these ideas in ways that have since been discredited, they had a kernel of truth that has been developed by other researchers. The psychoanalytic idea that childhood experiences determine adult personality has been abandoned by most psychologists, but increasingly the importance of those experiences is recognized. The genetic theory of psychosexual stages is no longer credible, but it gave rise to the very fruitful study of childhood attachment. Freud's dynamic Unconscious remains controversial, but the reality of unconscious cognition is now an uncontroversial idea in cognitive and social psychology, where huge volumes of research explore nonconscious or 'implicit' attitudes. Very few psychologists believe that human motivation can be reduced to sexual and aggressive instincts, but psychoanalysis reminds us that any adequate psychology of personality needs some kind of theory of what motivates people. Even if there is a great deal wrong with classic psychoanalysis, something worthwhile can be salvaged from it.

The last word goes to the psychodynamic psychologist Drew Westen (1998, p. 362):

> Grand theorists like Freud … are … the grandest purveyors of falsehood in the business. This reflects simple mathematics: The more propositions one advances (and the bolder these hypotheses are), the higher the probability that several will be wrong. But on some of the central postulates of psychodynamic theory, such as the view that much of mental life is unconscious, Freud has left an important … mark on human self-understanding. As psychology moves into its second century, we would do well to attend to and integrate some of these disavowed psycho-dynamic ideas.

Chapter summary

- Psychoanalysis is a theory of the underlying dynamics of personality that was originally developed by Sigmund Freud, whose theory consists of several distinct models of the mind and its functioning.
- The topographic model divides the mind's contents into levels of awareness, from conscious, potentially conscious ('preconscious') to unconscious. Unconscious content is not just out of awareness, but actively prevented from reaching awareness except in disguised form, as in dreams, jokes, slips of the tongue, and neurotic symptoms.
- The structural model describes three interacting mental 'agencies'. The Id is the repository of desires, wishes, and impulses that are connected with sexual and aggressive instinctual drives, and seeks expression of these desires and so on. The Super-Ego is a harsh and primitive form of conscience that opposes the expression of desire. The Ego mediates between Id, Super-Ego, and the constraints of reality.
- Among the Ego's tools for dealing with the conflicting demands of desire and prohibition is a repertoire of defence mechanisms.
- According to Freud's genetic model, children progress through a series of psychosexual stages that are referenced to different body parts: oral, anal, and phallic. Each stage has its distinctive themes, and failure to successfully negotiate each stage is associated with distinctive forms of disturbed personality.
- Psychoanalysis is often identified with Freud, but it has undergone numerous developments since his death, and is composed of several distinct theoretical schools.
- Psychoanalytic theory has drawn many criticisms. The sexual instinct-based account of motivation has been very controversial, and the reliability of psychoanalytic inference – the ability of interpretations to yield dependable knowledge about the mind – has been seriously challenged.
- Psychoanalytic theory is often difficult to test scientifically or to falsify, and much of its evidence base is problematic. Nevertheless, it is an ambitious theory that attempts to capture aspects of human motivation and cognition that have often been ignored by other theories.

Further reading

Freud, S. Just about anything.
Freud's work is more often criticized or adulated than read. It is an instructive exercise to read some of his work to get a flavour of the psychoanalytic approach, and an appreciation

(Continued)

(Continued)

of his stylistic brilliance. A good place to start is the 'Introductory lectures' or his case histories (e.g., the 'Rat-man', 'Anna O.', the 'Wolf-man').

Luborsky, L., & Barrett, M. (2006). The history and empirical status of key psychoanalytic concepts. *Annual Review of Clinical Psychology, 2,* 1–19.
Luborsky and Barrett defend the accessibility of some psychoanalytic concepts to scientific investigation, and review a (rather modest) body of evidence related to them. In general, they find a reasonable degree of support for at least some psychoanalytic propositions.

Macmillan, M. (1997). *Freud evaluated: The completed arc.* Cambridge, MA: MIT Press.
This book is pitched at a fairly advanced level, but presents a concerted critique of psychoanalytic theory and evidence that cannot be ignored.

Milton, J., Polmear, C., & Fabricius, J. (2011). *A short introduction to psychoanalysis* (2nd ed.). London: Sage.
An accessible and sympathetic introduction to psychoanalytic ideas, which also addresses psychoanalytic therapy.

Westen, D. (1998). The scientific legacy of Sigmund Freud: Toward a psychodynamically informed psychological science. *Psychological Bulletin, 124,* 333–71.
Westen is a clinical psychologist and personality theorist who is adamant that there is something worthwhile to be salvaged from psychoanalytic theory, despite is flaws and limitations. This article forcefully defends the possibility of a scientifically defensible form of 'psychodynamics'.

Biological Approaches Part 1: Evolution and Genetics

Learning objectives

- To distinguish proximal biological influences on personality (i.e., brain structure and function) from distal influences on personality (i.e., evolution and genetics).
- To understand and describe Darwin's theory of evolution by natural selection, along with key terms in evolutionary biology such as genotype and phenotype.
- To identify and understand major mechanisms through which pressures of natural selection may have shaped the genetic architecture of personality.
- To understand and describe the process of Mendelian inheritance.
- To identity the major methods used to estimate heritability in the field of behavioural genetics.
- To appreciate how behavioural genetics has illuminated not only the role of genes, but also the role of the environment, in shaping personality.
- To describe and understand major molecular genetic approaches to identifying the role that specific genes play in personality differences.

All affect, behaviour, and cognition is produced by living, embodied organisms – the objects of biological investigation. Psychologists do not view the mind as a separate entity to the brain – a perspective called 'mind-body dualism' – rather, psychological processes are produced and constrained by biological processes. Given this, it would be surprising if individual differences in personality did not have some relationship to biological differences. This notion is reflected in many common intuitions. For instance, it often seems that personality characteristics run in families – as when a grandparent remarks that a child is 'just like her mother was at that age!' It is also common to hear anecdotes of long-lost twin siblings who, upon being reunited, discover that they are similar in ways that go well beyond their physical appearance. It turns out that many of these anecdotes are borne out by the scientific evidence.

Biological approaches to personality have attracted a great deal of interest in recent years, both in academic circles and in the public sphere. It is relatively common to read newspaper articles reporting the discovery of a gene purportedly linked with some kind of human trait, whether it be sociability or religiosity. This reflects the growing influence and attraction of the field known as *Personality Neuroscience*. One reason for this trend is the recent surge in availability and affordability of methods for studying the brain. What was prohibitively expensive or simply impossible to do a few years ago is becoming increasingly easy to add to the personality researcher's tool-kit. Another reason is the view held by many people that biological approaches will help us answer questions that are difficult or impossible to answer through purely behavioural research methods. For those who hold this 'holy grail' view, the increasing visibility of biological approaches in the landscape of personality research methods is a cause for excitement and optimism.

However, not everyone is thrilled about the rise of biological psychology. Some psychologists object strongly to the implication that cultural, social, and other environmental influences on behaviour ('nurture') are over-shadowed by biological influences ('nature'). The nature–nurture debate has a complicated and heated history, and to approach the subject in an even-handed manner we should keep a few thoughts in mind. First, to say that biological differences influence personality is not to imply that environmental influences on personality are unimportant. Second, the division between biological and environmental influences and explanations is to some extent a false one. Unless we embrace mind-body dualism, we must accept that *both* nature and nurture influence behaviour via physical processes in the brain. Third, it is possible to investigate the biological bases of personality without claiming that they completely determine personality variation ('determinism'), or that personality can be entirely reduced to brain tissue and neurochemicals ('reductionism'). Biological accounts of personality simply represent one among several legitimate ways of understanding sources of human variation. These different levels of explanation are, in principle, mutually compatible. Most of the genuine debate concerns which level of explanation is most helpful or appropriate for understanding a particular phenomenon or issue.

We saw in Chapter 4 that explanations of personality may focus upon structures or functions, and this is also the case with explanations situated at the biological level. In the next chapter, we will see how studying the structures and functions of the brain can illuminate our understanding of personality at the biological level. Before this, however, we must consider the influences on those structures and functions. Like any other part of the body, the brain is produced by the combined influence of genes and the environment. Therefore, it is reasonable to ask to what extent personality traits are shaped by genetic influences. In turn, we know that our genetic make-up is the product of the evolution of our species. Our first question, therefore, concerns the extent to which individual differences in personality might have been shaped by evolution.

Evolution by Natural Selection

All life on earth can be traced back nearly four billion years to a single common ancestor. The diversity of life we see in the world today – from amoeba to zebras – is the result of evolution, a gradual process whereby the characteristics of species change over successive generations. When different groups of a single species become isolated, the gradual changes in characteristics experienced by both groups may proceed in different directions, eventually resulting in separate species (this process is called *speciation*). Evolution therefore explains the distinctive biological configuration of our species, and why life in general varies in a multitude of ways. The idea of evolution as an account for biological diversity became increasingly popular among scientists and naturalists during the 18th century, but it took some time for scientists to work out *how* life evolved. English naturalists Charles Darwin and Alfred Russel Wallace independently reached the solution in the mid-19th century. Both men presented their theories to the Linnean Society of London (concerned with taxonomy and natural history) in 1858. The following year, Darwin published, what he called, a 'hastily-written abstract' of the theory he had been meticulously developing for around 20 years, and only rushed to publicize when he discovered that Wallace had hit upon the same idea. The title of this book was *On the Origin of Species by Means of Natural Selection, or the Preservation of Favoured Races in the Struggle for Life* (later shortened to *The Origin of Species*), and is widely considered the founding work in modern biology.

Natural Selection is a process whereby characteristics that favour survival and reproduction are more likely to be passed down to offspring and future generations, therefore being retained or developed in the species as a whole. This is very similar to the process through which dog breeders have produced the diverse range of domestic breeds with which we are familiar today. In early times, humans recognized that dogs could be useful for different tasks (e.g., hunting or pulling loads). They selected and bred animals that best displayed particular characteristics while neglecting those that did not. This process continues in dog breeding today, although in many cases the key characteristics are desired for reasons of aesthetics rather than utility. A breeder may have the goal to preserve the defining characteristics of a purebred, such as the white tip on a Beagle's tail (initially favoured to help hunters locate their hounds in the field). A male pup that displayed this feature best of his litter might therefore be selected for mating with another, equally representative female. Breeders sometimes also want to develop new breeds that combine the desirable features of existing dogs. For instance, in 1988 Australian breeder Wally Conron sought to combine the placid nature and intelligence of the Labrador Retriever with the hypoallergenic coat of the Standard Poodle – as a result, we now have the remarkable Labradoodle. The domestication of animals illustrates the process of Evolution by Natural Selection so clearly that Darwin chose this topic for the first chapter of *The Origin of Species*. The crucial difference, however, is that there is no 'breeder' in Natural Selection, and the notion that characteristics are deliberately 'selected' is just a metaphor. What actually happens is that characteristics that increase the likelihood of reproduction and survival are maintained or promoted in the species, because those characteristics are most likely to be passed along to the next generation. Evolution works via blind and trial-and-error processes leading to gradual change within and divergence between species. This process is artfully captured in the title of Richard Dawkins' (1986) indispensable popular book on the subject, *The Blind Watchmaker*.

We have so far been talking as though Natural Selection acts directly upon observable characteristics such as strength or height – known as *phenotypes*. This is true to the extent that it is the phenotype that may or may not be adaptive. However, it is not this phenotype *per se* that is passed onto successive generations and so preserved in the species. The unit of selection is the genetic information that underlies this phenotype, while the sum of an individual's genes is their *genotype*. So when we use the phrase 'survival of the fittest' as a description of evolution by Natural Selection, we are talking about the fittest genes. To help illustrate this idea consider the following analogy. Suppose a group of friends – let's call them Harry, Sally, and Larry – decide to 'evolve' a new type of chocolate cake. Harry starts by trying to remember a chocolate cake recipe and comes up with three very similar approximations. He bakes all three cakes and then invites Sally to try a piece of each and select the tastiest of the three. After Sally has made her selection Harry reads her the winning recipe. Sally then goes home, tries to remember this recipe and, like Harry, writes out three approximations. She repeats the bake-and-taste test, and then asks Larry to identify the most delicious result, and passes the corresponding recipe along – verbally. As recipes are passed along, it is likely that the key elements of a delicious chocolate cake would be preserved or enhanced – cocoa and sugar for instance. It is also likely that, given enough time, the final cake in the sequence would be somewhat different from the first – it would have 'evolved'. The key point of this analogy is that the cakes are selected for their observable characteristics (taste) but the actual unit of selection is the information underlying these characteristics (the recipe). Genes are very similar to cake recipes in that they contain instructions that code for proteins and thus for building biological bodies. Although a phenotype such as running speed or binocular vision may confer *adaptive fitness*, it is the genes responsible for the phenotype that are passed down to the next generation.

A final but crucial piece of the evolutionary puzzle is *variation*. Dog breeders select a pup for mating from a litter that varies in certain attributes. There was also variation in the chocolate cake recipes that provided our analogy of *genetic transmission*. In this case, the reason for the variation in recipes is that imperfect copies were being made as a result of the recipes being passed on by word of mouth. This error-prone duplication of information is exactly what happens when genetic information is transmitted from parent to offspring. When there is an error in the duplication of a particular gene, this is called a *mutation*. When people first hear the word mutation, they often think of ghastly disfigurations such as *Proteus Syndrome* – the likely affliction of Joseph Merrick (the 'Elephant Man'), caused by a mutation in the gene responsible for cell growth regulation. Most mutations are not so extreme, and tend to have extremely small or null effects. Over millennia, however, very small genetic mutations are able to explain the gradual emergence of genetic variation, which is then subject to the discriminating hand of Natural Selection.

In summary, evolution by Natural Selection is the process whereby (1) genotypic variation is introduced into a species via mutations in inherited genes, (2) phenotypic variations that emerge from this genetic variation result in differences in adaptive fitness, and (3) greater adaptive fitness translates into greater likelihood of survival and reproduction, and thus greater likelihood of genetic transmission to the next generation. Because biological processes underlie all psychological processes, the evolution of mental adaptations (e.g., fear of snakes and spiders) is in many respects no different from the evolution of physical adaptations (e.g., fast-twitch muscle fibres). This is the central premise of the scientific field known as *Evolutionary Psychology*.

Evolutionary accounts of personality

Is personality shaped by Natural Selection? It is intuitively easy to see how a dog breeder, for example, could select for canine characteristics that are highly analogous to human personality. Placidness, loyalty, trainability, and fearlessness are all animal traits that can be selected for, and indeed were probably selected for in the domestication of the wolf (from which most domestic dogs are descended). Is it possible that a similar thing might have occurred during human evolutionary history? In other words, do personality traits contribute to adaptive fitness? Notice that this is not the same as suggesting that the behavioural systems on which personality differences are based are adaptive. For instance, in the next chapter we will see that Extraversion may partly reflect the functioning of a brain system that motivates us to pursue rewards, such as food and sex. It seems obvious that such a system would contribute enormously towards our adaptive fitness, but less obvious why *individual differences* in such systems might be favoured by Natural Selection.

In 1990, evolutionary psychologists Tooby and Cosmides published an influential paper that cast much doubt on the notion of adaptive personality traits. They argued that evolution has produced a universal 'human nature' that we all share. Just as all people – with a few pathological exceptions – are born with an identical configuration of bodily organs, our shared genetic constitution also endows us with an identical set of psychological mechanisms and capacities, or 'mental organs'. By analogy, when we say that a certain breed of dog has been 'bred for placidness', we recognize that the breeder's goal is to produce a group of relatively placid animals, rather than a group of animals which *vary* substantially on the trait dimension of placidness. Natural Selection has no 'goals', of course, but it similarly drives evolution towards optimal universals (albeit in a blind, error-prone fashion), such that most biological differences within a species reflect random variations, not adaptations. From this, Tooby and Cosmides argue that genetically-based personality traits are probably rather trivial differences of degree in the operation of universal psychological capacities – random 'noise' in an otherwise finely-tuned machine. As these trivial variations would not have any influence on adaptive fitness, they could escape selection pressures and progressively increase the variation in a characteristic. Penke, Denissen, and Miller (2007) refer to this process as *selective neutrality*, and give the example of the route taken by our tangled small intestine. Genetic mutations might give rise to any number of different 'gut-packing' designs that are all equally effective, and therefore are overlooked by the optimizing influence of Natural Selection.

In their highly influential paper, Penke and colleagues accept that selective neutrality is a viable explanation for *trivial* individual differences, but point out that personality traits do not have trivial consequences. While individual differences in gut-packing design seem unlikely to be associated with adaptive fitness, personality traits are associated with many fitness-relevant outcomes, including health, life expectancy and reproductive success (Ozer & Benet-Martínez, 2006). It therefore seems restrictive to assume that, throughout our evolutionary history, variations in personality have remained completely untouched by the discriminating hand of Natural Selection. So how might we otherwise account for the evolution of personality traits? The solution, according to Penke and colleagues, is *balancing selection*, which occurs when *both* extremes of a continuously distributed phenotype confer adaptive fitness in different ways or under different circumstances.

One way in which balancing selection might occur is via *antagonistic pleiotropy*, which is where a certain characteristic has a positive impact on one aspect of fitness and a negative impact on another. Daniel Nettle (2005) provides suggestive evidence for such a 'fitness trade-off' in the case of trait Extraversion. Consistent with earlier theory and research, he found that extraverted people tended to have had more sexual partners – an obvious boon for adaptive fitness. However, he also found that these extraverts were more likely to have been hospitalized for accidents and illness – presumably as a consequences of their more outgoing, 'no-holds-barred' behaviour. This may suggest that, in our evolutionary history, introverts were more likely to live long enough to reproduce, but extraverts who *did* survive to reproductive age had more offspring. Nettle (2006) builds further upon this idea with an evolutionary cost-benefit analysis of each of the Five Factors of personality. The idea of such fitness trade-offs is appealing, and fits nicely with the view that one set of personality characteristics is generally not 'better' than another. However, the difficulty with this theory is that it requires the pros and cons of fitness trade-offs to be exactly matched, and for this stalemate to generalize to all situations and environments. That is, the self-preserving characteristics of the introvert must perfectly, and consistently, cancel out the promiscuity of the extravert. According to Penke and colleagues (2007), this requirement might be too restrictive for antagonistic pleiotropy to offer a complete picture of the evolution of personality variation.

Another way in which balancing selection might occur is via *environmental heterogeneity*. This is a scenario in which genetically-based behavioural variations reflect different adaptive *strategies* that are specialized for different environmental niches. Niches may be spatially distributed – such as the availability of different kinds of food at any point in time – or temporally distributed – such as variations in the availability of food over time. As psychologist and popular science author Steven Pinker (2009) has put it: 'The early bird gets the worm, but the second mouse gets the cheese. An environment that has worms in some parts but mousetraps in others could select for a mixture of go-getters and nervous nellies.' Data that appear suggestive of personality adaptations to environmental niches has been described by Camperio Ciani, Capiluppi, Veronese, and Sartori (2007). They found that Italians whose families had resided on islands for at least 20 generations had lower Extraversion and Openness/Intellect scores than both coastal mainland Italians and those whose families had more recently settled on the islands. These findings could not be explained by cultural variables or personality-related lifestyle preferences, and numerous other potential confounding factors were carefully ruled out. Overall, it seems plausible that the two environments (islands versus the mainland coast) differentially favoured extraverted and open personalities.

Niches are also distributed throughout our highly heterogeneous *social* environments. In this case, balancing selection may explain the evolution of human personality in terms of specializations for different roles and activities within the social world. Penke and colleagues note that personality variations – including animal analogues of personality, such as boldness or skittishness – are especially pronounced in more social species. This may hint that adaptations to social structures are an especially fruitful means to understand personality evolution. For instance, more inhibited or introverted people may be specialized for acting in more structured social settings (e.g., large settled populations), whereas bolder, more extraverted people may be adapted to social settings in which greater spontaneity and tolerance of risk is required (e.g., nomadic groups) (see also Wilson, 1994).

A further example of balancing selection via social environmental heterogeneity is *frequency-dependent selection*. The idea here is that if all your neighbours are pursuing one strategy, it may pay off to pursue another. A world of laid-back Larries may favour the few nervous Nellies who respond more quickly to danger. On the other hand, if everyone around you is jumpy and hyper-vigilant, then you have the opportunity to take things easy and minimize your stress levels. Perhaps the best-known illustration of frequency-dependent selection is the classic 'Hawk-Dove game' (Maynard Smith, 1982). In this scenario, individuals compete for an environmental resource by adopting one of two strategies: 'Hawks' compete aggressively, not giving in until injured or until their opponent backs down, while 'Doves' give in as soon as their opponent initiates any aggressive behaviour. When Hawks and Doves compete, the Hawk always wins, suggesting that Hawks should slowly drive Doves out of the population. But this would result in a social landscape composed entirely of aggressive interactions, with each individual facing continually high odds of injury. When two Doves meet, the environmental resource is shared equally. A world composed entirely of Doves therefore seems ideal, but it would also be an ideal social landscape for a rogue Hawk to exploit. It turns out that neither the Hawk nor the Dove represents what is called an *Evolutionarily Stable Strategy (ESS)*, but a mixture of these strategies is stable.

Frequency-dependent selection has been suggested to explain the preservation in our species of apparently maladaptive personality characteristics such as psychopathy or antisocial personality disorder. Psychopaths are interpersonally callous, exploitative, remorseless, and deceitful. Such behaviour might serve as an effective adaptive strategy – especially, perhaps, as a way to acquire unearned resources and reproduce without commitment – provided not too many people adopt it (Mealey, 1995). Although psychopathy might be a profitable strategy when it is uncommon and most people are trusting and gullible, if it became common there would be fewer mugs left to cheat and deceive. As a result, the frequency of psychopathy should reach an equilibrium point at which the behavioural strategy that it represents is as adaptive as the alternative. This idea is an exact parallel to the Hawk-Dove game. Another possibility is that frequency-dependent selection accounts for the skewed distribution of Neuroticism in the normal population: low Neuroticism may be an adaptive trait, provided there are at least a couple of people around you who are vigilant for dangers and threats. It is important to keep in mind that these ideas are highly speculative and have proven difficult to substantiate with empirical data.

The different routes that balancing selection may have taken all involve optimization of some trade-off through inter-individual variation in a particular phenotype. A broader account of how different solutions to major trade-offs may produce individual differences in personality is provided by *Life History Theory* (Kaplan & Gangestad, 2005). According to this framework, the major challenge faced by all living things is how to 'capture' energy from the environment (e.g., via hunting or foraging) and 'allocate' it to activities that promote survival and reproduction (e.g., courtship or parenting). In other words, organisms must balance a limited energy budget. As in the case of a financial budget, this balancing act entails many trade-offs. For instance, a used car is cheap but a new car has a warranty; cheap products can be purchased today, but if you save up your money you can buy higher-quality products that last longer. Importantly, the way we resolve these trade-offs depends in part on our individual circumstances (e.g., the new car warranty might be less important to the expert mechanic). Life History Theory therefore suggests that the various strategic solutions to major trade-offs will vary as a function of the individual's unique situation, resulting in the clustering together of coherent strategies and dispositions that form distinctive life histories.

A fundamental trade-off discussed in Life History Theory is immediate versus future reproduction. One might delay reproduction due to inadequate safety or resources, but must then pay the 'opportunity cost' of not reproducing now, and gamble on the possibility of never reproducing. Wolf, van Doorn, Leimar, and Weissing (2007) use a computer simulation to demonstrate how different solutions to this problem might give rise to major personality variations. Their model begins with virtual organisms inhabiting a heterogeneous environment consisting of high- and low-quality food resources. Thorough foraging increases the likelihood of finding high-quality food resources but leaves less time for reproduction, while the reverse is the case for superficial foraging. The computer simulation confirms that this scenario results in the evolution of two stable foraging strategies: superficial foragers prosper through immediate reproductive success, while thorough foragers prosper through longer-term reproductive success. What we can see at this stage is an example of balancing selection via environmental heterogeneity, but Wolf and colleagues take things a step further. Specifically, they assume that individuals in this simulated environment face a number of risky encounters with conspecifics, modelled in terms of Hawk-Dove games. As described above, victorious Hawks receive a bigger piece of the pie than sharing Doves, but will often face heavy losses. Wolf and colleagues' simulation reveals that superficial foragers, who focus on immediate reproduction and therefore have invested less in their future, are far more likely to play the Hawk during risky encounters. Conversely, thorough foragers, who must live longer if they are to produce any offspring, are more likely to play the Dove. Over successive simulated generations, continuously distributed personality traits emerge (boldness and aggressiveness), arising from the intersection of an evolutionarily significant trade-off (immediate versus delayed reproduction) and adaptive strategies to environmental niches (superficial versus thorough foraging). This coherence of particular traits and characteristics forms the basis of distinct life histories.

Evolutionary approaches to personality explanation are intriguing and increasingly popular, and have wide-ranging implications for the study of individual differences. A central idea arising from the field is that we can think about personality differences in terms of 'strategies' for negotiating the gauntlet of Natural Selection. Of course, just as Natural Selection itself is a metaphor, so are the personality-related strategies that may confer adaptive fitness. What is meant is that certain personality characteristics may offer a *strategic advantage*, depending on when or where they are expressed, and may thus survive the test of evolutionary time.

Genetics

When Charles Darwin published *The Origin of Species* in 1859, he was well aware that he was missing a major piece of the evolutionary puzzle: his theory required that characteristics were inherited, but he did not know how inheritance worked. At the same time as Darwin's book was being published, Gregor Mendel, an Augustinian monk in the city of Brno (former Austro-Hungarian Empire, now Czech Republic), was conducting the experiments that would illustrate the process of inheritance. Mendel was using a common strain of pea plant to study the process of hybridization. He found that when purple-flowered peas were crossed with white-flowered peas the result was not a blend of the two colours – as when one mixes two different coloured paints – rather, the flowers of the offspring were all purple. Several such experiments targeting different phenotypes (e.g., seed shape, stem length) similarly argued against *Blending Inheritance*, which in Mendel's day was a widespread assumption. Mendel then self-pollinated his new generation of purple-flowered peas and made an even more interesting finding: while a majority of the resultant offspring had purple flowers, roughly one-quarter had white flowers. Again, he obtained the same results when he focused on other pea characteristics. It was clear from these experiments that the pea plants could somehow possess the potential for certain characteristics (and pass those down to their offspring), without expressing those characteristics themselves.

To explain the results of his experiments, Mendel derived a number of principles that formed the basis for the modern field of genetics. First, for a given characteristic there are two discrete units of inheritance, which we now know as *alleles* (different versions of a single gene), and offspring receive one allele from each parent. Second, one allele will be *dominant* over another with respect to expression of inherited characteristics, while a *recessive* allele will only be expressed if the dominant allele is not inherited. These principles formed Mendel's first law of genetics, the *Law of Segregation*, which states that alleles segregate

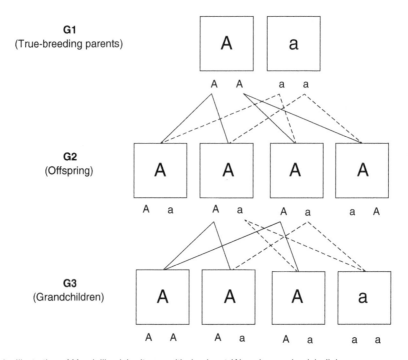

Figure 5.1 Illustration of Mendellian inheritance with dominant (A) and recessive (a) alleles

during the production of gametes (reproductive cells). Mendel's second law of genetics, the *Law of Independent Assortment*, stated that alleles of separate genes assort independently of one another. That is, the inheritance of a particular allele of one gene has no influence over the inheritance of an allele of another gene. It can be seen in Figure 5.1 that these principles were able to account for Mendel's observations of pea plant hybridization.

As impressed as you might be with Mendel's ability to explain the inheritance of pea characteristics, you might be sceptical that these principles apply to the inheritance of personality. The idea of two distinct alleles seems worryingly similar to the idea of personality 'types', which we roundly rejected in Chapter 2. When a highly-introverted person and a highly-extraverted person decide to have a family, is it really the case that all of their children are highly extraverted, as well as all but one quarter of their grandchildren (who are highly introverted)? Obviously not. In humans there are very few 'either-or' characteristics that are directly comparable to purple and white pea flowers.[1] What would Mendel have discovered if he studied pea characteristics that, like personality traits, are continuously distributed? About

---

[1]A frequently noted exception is Huntington's Disease (HD), a debilitating neurodegenerative disorder. HD is caused by a single genetic mutation, and the inheritance of HD is directly analogous to that of dichotomous pea characteristics.

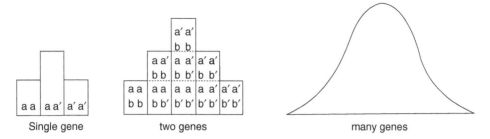

Figure 5.2 Continuously distributed phenotypes reflect multiple genetic influences. In the case of additive genetic influences, a single gene with two alleles (a and a') will produce three genotypes and phenotypes. Conversely, two genes that each have two alleles (a, a', b, b') will produce nine genotypes and five phenotypes. Phenotypes that are continuously and finely distributed – as are personality traits – are therefore likely to reflect the influence of many more genes.

ten years after Mendel's studies, Francis Galton – a cousin of Charles Darwin's – performed such studies, focusing on seed size. Galton showed that larger than average parent seeds have larger than average offspring seeds. He then went on to reproduce this same pattern of findings through studies of human height – on average, taller parents produce taller children. The apparent discord between Mendel's and Galton's data was for some time taken to indicate that Mendel's laws did not apply to continuously distributed traits. However, it was eventually realized that the crucial difference between a dichotomous characteristic like flower colour and a continuously distributed characteristic like seed size is the number of genes that are involved. As Figure 5.2 demonstrates, the greater the number of genes that influence a given characteristic, the more finely graded are variations in that characteristic. Moreover, while it is possible for a single gene to wholly *determine* an 'either-or' characteristic, it can only be *probabilistically* associated with more 'trait-like' characteristics. We should always be mindful of this fact when reading claims of a discovery of 'the gene' for aggression or altruism, shyness or boldness, that often appear in the popular press.

Behavioural genetics

The realization that multiple genes underlie continuously distributed traits is fundamental to the field known as behavioural genetics (also called *quantitative genetics*). Behavioural geneticists study the degree to which genes and environments influence phenotypes such as cognitive abilities, mental disorders, and personality traits. The **heritability** of a trait, h^2, refers to the proportion of variation in that trait which is accounted for by genetic influences. Methods for estimating heritability are all based on the knowledge that individuals who are more closely related share more genes. For instance, the 'first-degree' relatives of a particular family member – the person's siblings, parents, and children – share 50% of their genes. This is because offspring inherit half of their genes from each parent, and siblings therefore have

113

a 50% chance of inheriting the same allele from each parent. Conversely, 'second-degree' relatives – grandparents, uncles and aunts, nephews and nieces, and grandchildren – share 25% of their genes. As we move to more distant relatives we see further reduction in genetic similarity. Because of this, individuals who are more closely related will also be more similar to one another in terms of traits that are strongly influenced by genes. This is the guiding principle of the three main methods behavioural geneticists employ for estimating heritability: family studies, twin studies, and adoption studies.

Family studies assess the resemblance of family members on some trait – usually in terms of correlations between them on a personality questionnaire – as a function of their degree of genetic relatedness. If genes contribute to the trait of interest, then closer relatives should be more similar to one another on that trait, with unrelated people having no systematic resemblance at all. Although family studies can begin to establish genetic influences in this way, they have a significant deficiency in that they fail to disentangle these from environmental influences. Closer relatives – such as brothers, or parents and children – resemble one another more closely than distant relatives in their genes, but also in their family environment and social class. Consequently, their greater resemblance on the characteristic of interest may be due either to shared genetic influences, shared environmental influences, or both.

Twin studies offer an alternative means of estimating genetic contributions to a characteristic. They capitalize on the well-known distinction between identical twins (i.e., monozygotic; MZ) and fraternal twins (i.e., dizygotic; DZ) twins. Because MZ twins are derived from a single fertilized egg they are genetically identical – 'clones', if you like. Conversely, as DZ twins are derived from two separately fertilized eggs, they are no more genetically similar than non-twin siblings (50%). Therefore, genetic influence can be shown to the extent that MZ twins resemble one another more than DZ twins. Unlike family studies, twin studies are able to disentangle genetic influences from environmental influences; although MZ twins differ from DZ twins in terms of the proportion of shared genes, they are assumed not to differ in terms of shared environments (this is called the 'equal environments assumption'). Therefore, geneticists can be confident that differences in the resemblance of MZ and DZ twins are primarily genetic in origin.

A third form of behavioural genetic investigation is the *adoption study*, in which the resemblance of adopted children to their biological and adoptive parents is examined and compared. The extent to which children resemble the biological parents who gave them up at birth reveals the extent of genetic influence, because there should be little systematic environmental resemblance between them. Similarly, children's resemblance to their adoptive parents, with whom they have no systematic genetic similarity, reveals the extent of environmental influence. Therefore, if children resemble their biological parents more than their adoptive parents, then we have grounds for concluding that genes outweigh environmental factors in their influence on the characteristic of interest. *Twin Adoption studies*, in which MZ and DZ twin pairs separated at birth are compared with twins growing up in the same family, offer a particularly powerful means to separate genetic and environmental effects. For example, if MZ twins that have been reared together are more similar than DZ twins, but no more similar than MZ twins that have been reared apart, then one would conclude that genetic factors play a strong role in the characteristic of interest. Twin adoption studies are just one example of the *combination designs* that can be achieved by mixing elements of family, adoption, and twin studies.

All of these behavioural genetic study designs have potential limitations. As noted earlier, family studies fail to disentangle genetic and environmental influences because closer relatives are more similar both genetically and environmentally. Twin studies are vulnerable to violations of the equal environments assumption and to the criticism that twins are unrepresentative of the general population. For instance, some have speculated that identical twins are treated more similarly by their parents than fraternal twins, which would exaggerate the difference in their degree of resemblance. It also might be the case that twins are so unlike other children that it is unwise to generalize from them. On the other hand, research tends to discount both of these possibilities, finding, for example, that MZ twins misclassified by their parents as fraternal are just as similar in terms of their personalities as correctly classified MZ twins, and that twins do not differ significantly from non-twins in average personality. Adoption studies are vulnerable to the same representativeness problems as twin studies, and to the possibility that adoptive and biological parents might systematically resemble one another (i.e., the problem of 'selective placement'). If in some way adoptive and biological families are matched on such criteria as social class, education, or intelligence, we can no longer have confidence that the resemblance of children to their biological parents is purely genetic or that their resemblance to their adoptive parents is purely environmental. Against this view, behavioural geneticists have shown that estimates of the effects of selective placement do not typically influence estimates of heritability.

To sum up, despite many methodological complications in behavioural genetic studies, there is general agreement that such studies are robust to these concerns. It would clearly be worrying if one method suggested that personality traits were mainly a function of genetics, while another suggested that they are mainly a function of the environment. However, the multiple methods of estimating heritability have generally led to broadly similar conclusions. This seems to suggest that the different limitations of each kind of method do not strongly undermine their usefulness for assessing the heritability of traits.

The heritability of personality

As noted above, estimates of heritability concern the extent to which individuals' genetic similarity accounts for their similarity to one another on a given trait. This can be derived from simple correlations. For example, a twin study might assess a personality trait in 100 pairs of MZ twins plus 100 pairs of DZ twins, and then examine the trait correlation for each twin group. High correlations would indicate that the twin pairs are highly similar on the personality trait, while low correlations would indicate that the twin pairs are largely dissimilar. An estimate of heritability can then be calculated as:

$H^2 = 2 \times (r_{MZ} - r_{DZ})$, where

H^2 = the proportion of variance in a trait that is due to genetic factors,

r_{MZ} = the correlation between personality scores in a population of MZ twins (i.e., a correlation of 1 would mean that all pairs of MZ twins were identical in terms of their personality scores), and

r_{DZ} = the correlation between personality scores in a population of DZ twins.

We can see how this works by considering the following scenarios. First, suppose that variation in a personality trait was due entirely to genetic influences – 100% heritable – then the trait correlation for the MZ twin group would be approximately 1.00. In contrast, as the DZ twin pairs only share half of their genes, this correlation would be half the size of that for the MZ group – approximately 0.50. In other words, the size of the trait correlation would be a direct function of the degree of genetic relatedness. Accordingly, H^2 would be calculated as $2 \times (1.00 - 0.50) = 1.00$, i.e., 100% heritability. Alternatively, if variation in the trait were entirely due to effects of upbringing and family dynamics – features of what behavioural geneticists call the *shared environment* – we would expect a correlation of approximately 1.00 for *both* the MZ and the DZ twin groups. This is because the size of the trait correlation would be a direct function of the family environment, which all of the twin pairs would share. As a result, H^2 would be calculated as $2 \times (1.00 - 1.00) = 0.00$, i.e., 0% heritability. Finally, suppose that the trait is entirely due to the unique experiences of each twin, such as might be obtained at school or in peer interactions. Behavioural geneticists call this the *unique environment*. In this case we would expect a correlation approaching zero for *both* the MZ and the DZ twin groups. This is because the main drivers of personality variation would not be shared by any of the twin pairs. In this case our calculation of H^2 would be $2 \times (0.00 - 0.00) = 0.00$, i.e., 0% heritability.

So, what is the heritability of personality traits? Behavioural geneticists have conducted a great many studies of the inheritance of personality characteristics, and these have consistently shown that virtually every personality trait examined is moderately heritable, with estimates of H^2 generally being in the range of .4 to .6 (Bouchard, 2004; Zuckerman, 2005; Riemann & Kandler, 2010). As a frame of reference, consider that the heritability of physical height is typically around .8, while the heritability of social and political attitudes is around .3. We can therefore say that personality is moderately heritable, a discovery which came as a surprise to some psychologists. Before these studies were conducted, many felt that a genetic basis for personality and other psychological characteristics was just a few steps short of preposterous. This view relates to the idea – highly influential throughout the 20th century – that we are essentially 'blank slates' at birth, and that the slate is only 'written on' through our experience (see Pinker, 1997). Our experiences are indeed important, but the extreme notion of the blank slate is simply false. Indeed, the significance of research findings in behavioural genetics has been summarized as showing 'The nature–nurture debate is over … all behavioural traits are heritable' (Turkheimer, 2000).

Often when people hear about the substantial heritability of personality traits they disagree and point out how different they are from their family members. However, high heritabilities do not entail strong correlations among close relatives. For instance, the correlation between a parent's level of Extraversion and that of their children is only .16, while the correlation between their biological children is only .20 (Loehlin, 1992). Correlations of this magnitude indicate that if you are an extravert (i.e., above the population mean on Extraversion), the probability that any particular sibling or parent of yours is also an extravert is roughly 58–60%, not much better than chance. This number is so low because you only share half of your genes with these first-degree relatives (the chance of you being extraverted if your identical twin is extraverted rises to 76%), and also as a result of environmental influences on personality – which we will come to shortly.

Another common confusion is to interpret heritability as an estimate of the genetic contribution to an *individual's* personality. It is not the case that a heritability estimate of .5 means that half of your Extraversion results from your genes – in fact, such a statement is somewhat incoherent (what exactly is 'half of your Extraversion'?). To be clear, heritability represents the proportion of *variation in a characteristic within a particular population* that is due to genetic influences. Because of this, heritability estimates can be influenced in surprising ways by various features of the specific population being studied. For instance, if the population was subject to a vast range of environmental influences, the proportion of genetic influences might be small in comparison. But this would not necessarily mean that genetics did not influence the trait. Conversely, if this hypothetical environment were somehow tightly constrained, such that its influences on individuals were highly homogeneous and socially equitable, the genetic influence on variation in traits would approach 100%. This is because if there is no variation in environmental influences then there can be no *co*-variation between environmental influences and trait characteristics. For this reason, it has been suggested that in a perfectly equitable, even-handed society we would observe perfect heritability of traits (this is known as *Herrnstein's Paradox*). In sum, one should be very clear about the precise meaning of heritability, and bear in mind that the information it provides might be particular to the time and place in which it was estimated.

Perhaps the most troublesome misinterpretation of heritability data is the widespread assumption that any characteristic that is influenced by genetics must be fixed and unchangeable. In other words, genetic *influence* is confused with genetic *determinism* – an idea we have touched on already. Genetics do completely determine *some* individual characteristics. For example, Huntington's Disease is 100% heritable, caused by a single genetic mutation – if you have that mutation then you will develop Huntington's Disease, however favourable your environmental circumstances. But very few inherited characteristics are analogous to HD, and any heritability estimates below 100% leave room for environmental influences. Even height – one of the most highly heritable characteristics ever studied – is subject to environmental influences, as demonstrated by dramatic increases in average height over the last century as a result of improved nutrition. In sum, heritability implies a statistical propensity to have a certain characteristic, not an inevitability.

The role of the environment

Behavioural genetic research on personality not only illuminates the heritable influences on personality, but has also generated some intriguing findings about the nature of environmental influences. Two findings are particularly important. First, the environmental factors that are most influential for personality are not those that people within a family have in common (i.e., the *shared environment*), but rather those that are distinctive to individual family members and make them different from one another (i.e., the *non-shared environment*). Second, many apparently 'environmental' influences are, in fact, genetically influenced.

The first finding – that the shared environment contributes very little to personality variation – was surprising to the many psychologists who had assumed that personality is primarily influenced by shared within-family experiences such as child-rearing practices, parental beliefs and values, socio-economic status, divorce, and parental bereavement. If factors such as these were important determinants of personality we might expect adoptive parents to closely resemble their children, and we would expect these biologically unrelated children to closely resemble one another. However, studies consistently show virtually no such resemblance, indicating that the shared environment of the adoptive family has very little influence on personality. The same conclusion emerges from studies of non-adoptive families. Importantly, this does not mean that within-family influences have no impact on personality development and construction. Rather it suggests that any influence of these factors on personality *are not shared* among siblings. Indeed, we know that within-family experiences, such as parenting or divorce, impact differently on different family members. These factors are thus candidates for *non-shared* environmental influences on personality (Plomin, 2011).

In contrast to the weak influence of the shared environment, non-shared environmental influences on personality are considerable. For instance, MZ twins reared together are often far from identical in personality, typically correlating at around .45 (Plomin, DeFries, McClearn, & Rutter, 1997), despite having identical genes and essentially identical shared environments. Given that most estimates of the heritability of personality traits are around .5, and the contribution of shared environment to personality variation is close to zero, the proportional contribution of non-shared environment to personality variation – i.e., the remainder – must also lie around .5. That is, around half of the variation in personality is due to environmental influences that are not shared within a family, which might include distinctive school experiences and peer interactions, but also within-family experiences that impact differently on different family members. In short, our circumstances and experiences influence our personalities about as much as our genes do, but in ways that make us different from, not similar to, our family members. An important caveat to this point, however, is that the exact meaning of 'non-shared environment' is far from clear. For this reason, the most circumspect way to think of the non-shared environmental influences on personality is that these represent all environmental influences on our personality that make is less similar to our family members.

The second major finding of behavioural genetics is that some environmental influences are themselves subject to genetic effects. For instance, susceptibility to accidents and divorce are partly heritable, which seems paradoxical because we tend to think of these as external, non-biological events. The solution to this puzzle is that heritable personality traits have some impact on whether or not these things happen to us – genes can therefore influence our environment via our personalities. We also actively expose ourselves to environments that match or fit our genetic dispositions. For example, extraverts gravitate towards excitement, and towards more stimulating work and social environments than introverts. Genetic dispositions also influence the responses that we evoke from the environment. For example, children with difficult temperaments tend to engage in risky and antisocial activities and to join delinquent peer groups, and thereby evoke more punitive and critical responses from their parents and teachers. In addition to influencing the environments that we passively endure, actively seek, and evoke from others, genes influence how we *experience* life events, so that people with different genetic dispositions may respond very differently to the same events. A stressful environment will impact more strongly on a person who, due to their genetic make-up, is highly susceptible to stress. The picture that emerges from this research is that people's genetic dispositions, revealed in their personalities, can profoundly shape the environments that they inhabit and experience.

ILLUSTRATIVE STUDY

How animal experiments can help illuminate genetic influences on personality

The fact that some children are twins and some are adopted can be thought of as natural experiments that behavioural geneticists have used to their advantage. Obviously, however, ethical and legal concerns prevent us from ever conducting an actual experiment of this kind (e.g., randomly assigning half of the babies in a study to be adopted). However, such concerns can be relaxed somewhat in animal research. Research into the heritability of animal personality can therefore offer a methodologically rigorous paradigm to complement the behavioural genetics literature.

Possibly you have just re-read that last sentence with a furrowed brow, perplexed by the absurd notion of 'animal personality'. Alternatively, you may have owned multiple pet animals in your lifetime and therefore find this notion a straightforward matter of fact. It turns out that pet owners are right to think this. Although personality in non-human animals has taken some time to gain scientific credibility, a range of species display stable patterns of individual differences, often resembling the major dimensions of human personality (Gosling & John, 1999). Interestingly, the only species in which all of the Big Five personality traits have been described is in Chimpanzees – the closest genetic relatives of human beings.

(Continued)

119

(Continued)

One of the most important chapters in the animal personality literature, in terms of demonstrating the heritability of traits, was the *Maudsley Strains*. These refer to two genetic strains of brown rat developed by psychologists at the Maudsley Hospital in London, England. The focus of this research was on individual differences in emotional reactivity, with the rodent behaviour under investigation perhaps being analogous to human neuroticism. One widely-accepted indicator of emotional stress is defecation – thus a 'defecation criterion' (number of faecal boli produced when placed in the kind of open, well lit area that rodents typically try to avoid) was used to classify 'reactive' and 'non-reactive' rats. To develop two genetically separate rodent strains, reactive rats were inter-bred separately from non-reactive rats for several generations. After 15 generations of genetic separation the reactives and non-reactives showed dramatic differences in defecation score. It seemed that this indicator of 'rat neuroticism' had a genetic basis.

You might protest that the Maudsley Strains suffer from the same problems as a family study design. That is, differences in emotional reactivity might have been passed down through successive generations as a result of the family environment. That is, offspring of the original reactive rats might have acquired their emotional reactivity as a result of the shared environment. However, this explanation was cleverly ruled out by the technique of *cross fostering*, where the litters of reactive and non-reactive rodents were switched (sometimes while still in the womb!). It turned out that reactive pups were just as reactive, whether or not they were raised by – or indeed born to – their biological mother or a non-reactive surrogate. Through such techniques, research using the Maudsley Strains was able to demonstrate that individual differences in rodent emotional reactivity are heritable, and not greatly influenced by the shared environment. This chimes closely with findings from behavioural genetic studies of human personality. If you would like read more about the Maudsley Strains, please refer to Broadhurst (1976) in the reference list.

Molecular genetics

It is surprising when one first learns that behavioural genetic methods, the powerhouse of genetic research for at least the last 50 years, involve no direct examination of genes. Although the evidence amassed in this literature is compelling and informative in what it tells us about the heritability of traits, it is also incomplete. That is, it says nothing about which genes influence personality or how they do so. These questions are addressed in the field of *molecular genetics*.

Genes are segments of a long two-stranded molecule known as DNA. The strands of the DNA molecule are held apart by pairs of four simpler molecules known as bases. The sequence of these *base pairs* contains information that our cells 'read' to synthesize the proteins that build, maintain, and regulate our bodies. One of the most important chapters in the history of molecular genetics was the *Human Genome Project*. This international collaborative effort sought to provide a 'roadmap' of human DNA and to shed light on genetic functions – primarily to advance knowledge of genetic diseases. Results made available in 2001–2004, along with data gathered in other species, yielded some surprising findings. First, it was found that human DNA contains about 25,000 genes, comprising about 3 billion base pairs. This may sound like a lot, but it is far fewer than anticipated – after all, this is less than twice the number of genes possessed by fruit flies and roughly the same number found in mice. Second, it turns out that 99.9% of these base pairs are identical for all people, and therefore cannot be the source of individual differences in personality or any other characteristics. This overlap only shifts down to about 98.5% when we compare humans to our closest non-human relatives, Chimpanzees. Overall, these findings suggest that the salience of visible individual differences – both within and between species – is not an intuitive guide to the magnitude of genetic differences. Of course, we should keep in mind that the 'tiny' 0.1% of our genetic material that does vary between individuals amounts to roughly 3 million base pairs, potentially accommodating trillions of base pair combinations. Indeed, an individual's genome – the sum-total of their genetic make-up – is analogous to their fingerprint in that there are no two alike (except in the case of MZ twins).

Genetic variations are the result of mutations, known as 'polymorphisms', and genetically-based differences in personality arise due to the functional consequences of these polymorphisms. For example, the particular allele of a gene that you inherit may result in a slight difference in some brain process that underpins personality. One major strategy in molecular genetic personality research is to identify a genetic polymorphism that has a known impact on some process that is relevant to a particular personality trait, which is known as the *candidate gene approach*. Many candidate gene studies have taken advantage of rapidly accumulating knowledge about the role of polymorphic genes in the functioning of neurotransmitter systems. **Neurotransmitters** are chemicals in the brain that transmit signals between neurons, and certain neurotransmitter systems have been linked with particular personality traits (as we will discover in more detail in the next chapter). Therefore, if a particular gene is known to influence the functioning of a neurotransmitter with which a personality trait has been linked, then one might predict that gene to influence scores on the personality trait. One landmark candidate gene study (Lesch et al., 1996) focused on the Serotonin Transporter (5-HTT) gene, which encodes for the Serotonin Transporter – a protein that regulates levels of the neurotransmitter serotonin. Because previous research had linked serotonin with mood and anxiety states, Lesch and colleagues predicted that a polymorphism in the 5-HTT gene would be associated with anxiety-related traits such as Neuroticism. In support of this prediction, they found that individuals with higher scores on these traits were more likely to carry the allele of the 5-HTT gene that had been associated with reduced serotonin levels. Over the subsequent years, many other researchers adopted the candidate gene approach, providing the first glimpses of the genes that may influence our personality and the way in which they might do so.

The candidate gene approach has a few drawbacks that are worth considering. Most obviously, in order to select a candidate gene, you first need to have some understanding of its function. While this arguably forces a more theory-based, hypothesis-driven approach, it also means that you must wait for the primary genetic research to be conducted. It also means that if this primary research turns out to be on the wrong track (e.g., the gene you thought was involved in serotonin function is not), or your theory is on the wrong track (e.g., the trait you thought was influenced by serotonin function is not), then your expensive project might be a wild goose chase. This uncertainty may be the reason that the findings from many candidate gene studies have not been replicated. Another problem is the fact that, as we have already discussed, personality traits are likely to be influenced by large numbers of genes each exerting a small influence (e.g., in the study by Lesch and colleagues, variation in the 5-HTT gene accounted for only around 3% of the variance in anxiety-related traits). The candidate gene approach, examining one promising gene at a time, might simply be too slow and clumsy a process to advance our understanding of the genetic bases of personality.

A more powerful alternative to the candidate gene approach is the *genomewide association* approach (or genomewide scan), a technique for examining hundreds of thousands of genetic polymorphisms simultaneously. The first study to employ this technique in relation to all of the Big Five personality traits was conducted by Terracciano and colleagues in 2010. In a sample of 2,250 individuals, around 300 genetic polymorphisms were found to have a significant association with all of the Big Five traits (45 with Neuroticism, 54 with Extraversion, 59 with Openness, 112 with Agreeableness and 33 with Conscientiousness). Some of these gene-trait associations made fairly good sense. For instance, Neuroticism was associated with a gene polymorphism that has a known role in the mental disorders for which neuroticism is a putative risk factor. Despite the excitement of finding so many genes with a potential role in personality variation, there were two fairly crucial caveats that probably kept the cork in the champagne bottle on this occasion. First, when one is conducting hundreds of thousands of statistical tests, many of these are likely to be statistically significant purely by chance. The authors had therefore adopted a much stricter threshold for statistical significance than is typically used in psychology research. However, when they evaluated their findings using the even stricter threshold recommended specifically for studies of this kind (known as *genomewide significance*) they observed absolutely no significant associations! Moreover, when the authors attempted to replicate the strongest and seemingly most promising relationships in three follow-up studies, they were largely unsuccessful.

As studies such as these illustrate, molecular genetic research in personality has not yet produced the triumphant findings that were anticipated in the wake of the Human Genome Project. Meta-analyses and replication studies have repeatedly cast doubt on the reliability of many promising findings. Even the most robust results consist of disappointingly small effect sizes. Given that all major personality traits are at least moderately heritable, it is surprising that the search for the genes responsible has proven so difficult. Geneticists refer to this puzzle as the *missing heritability problem*, referring to the significant shortfall in the personality variation accounted for by genetic polymorphisms, relative to the heritability estimates provided by behavioural geneticists. Note that the missing heritability problem is not specific to personality traits, but applies widely to mental disorders, physical diseases and other characteristics. Consider, for instance, that barely 5% of the variance in physical height has been accounted for by specific gene variants, despite the fact that it is one of the most highly heritable characteristics we know of (Johnston, 2010).

Several explanations for the molecular genetic shortfall have now been advanced. For instance, perhaps we have grossly under-estimated the number of genes that influence variation in a trait, and how tiny an effect each one of those genes has. Detecting tiny statistical effects requires massive sample sizes. However, in such large samples many small relationships will emerge purely by chance (as was perhaps the case in Terracciano and colleagues' genomewide scan). It has also been suggested that personality traits and other characteristics might be primarily influenced by rare genetic variants. The candidate gene approach focuses our attention on particularly common genetic polymorphisms, as it is these common variants that have been identified and understood more quickly. The genomewide scan approach has a similar problem in that it too focuses on the common form of genetic polymorphism (called a *single nucleotide polymorphism*, involving a mutation in just one base pair). A further possibility is that genetic influences on traits may involve complex interactions among multiple genes – where, for instance, the relationship between a polymorphism and a personality trait depends on which allele of any number of other genes the person has also inherited. Typical molecular genetic methods focus only on *additive effects* – examining only the effect each gene has on its own – while behavioural genetic estimates of heritability also reflect any *interactive effects* – where the effect of one gene depends on that of another gene. This discrepancy may go a long way towards explaining the missing heritability problem.

The apparent severity of the missing heritability problem might lead us to wonder if behavioural geneticists have been wrong all along. Is it possible that heritability has tended to be grossly over-estimated and molecular genetics is now revealing how trivial an influence our genes really have on our personality? There are many reasons why we might not want to leap to this conclusion. For one thing, as we have already seen, different kinds of behavioural genetics studies make different assumptions and yet lead to similar conclusions. Contrastingly, findings from molecular genetics have so far proven highly unreliable. It seems short-sighted to dismiss an advanced field whose methods have been rigorously evaluated, and whose findings have been consistently replicated, simply because its conclusions differ from a more emerging field. Moreover, the view that molecular genetic studies have provided a full and accurate account of heritability could lead to some implausible conclusions – for instance, that genes have a negligible impact on height. As geneticist Eric Turkheimer (2011, p. 232) remarked in consideration of this issue: 'Of course height is heritable, in the simple sense that it is possible to predict the heights of children from the heights of their biological parents, and, in the absence of widespread disease or malnutrition, to do so as well for adopted-away children as for children raised in their biological homes.' Both behavioural and molecular genetic methods have various limitations, and these may indeed have some role in accounting for the missing heritability problem, but it is very unlikely that all of the error will come down on the side of behavioural genetics.

Despite the vexing issue of the missing heritability problem, solutions might lie just around the corner. One recent methodological advance that encourages this optimism is *genomewide complex-trait analysis* (GCTA). This method examines the genetic information that is gathered via a genomewide scan and examines the extent to which variation in this information is associated with variation in a trait characteristic of interest. The logic of GCTA can be understood by contrasting it with the design of a twin study: while twin studies consist of comparing trait similarities for groups of individuals whose genetic similarities are 1.00 (MZ twins) and .50 (DZ twins), GCTA studies compare trait similarities for individuals within a population whose genetic similarities vary between much lower values. These studies typically find higher associations between genetic and trait variation than candidate gene studies or genomewide scans (e.g., Vinkhuyzen et al., 2012). For some individual differences (e.g., general cognitive ability), the GTCA estimate of heritability is only slightly smaller than estimates based on twin studies (e.g., Plomin et al., 2013). Such findings reaffirm the view that the genes are 'out there' to be found. They are also consistent with the view that rare genetic variants and complex genetic effects may partially account for missing heritabilities. This is because GTCA focuses on the same common variants and simple additive relationships as other molecular genetic approaches. Identification of rare polymorphisms and estimation of more complex gene–trait relationships might therefore reduce the missing heritability margin even further.

Conclusions

The idea that our personalities are influenced by genes, which are in turn sifted and sorted by the blind hand of Natural Selection, is for many an unsettling and unwelcome notion. It is therefore worth reiterating some key points – particularly in relation to the genetic inheritance of personality. First, genetic influences on personality are not overwhelming: usually at least half of the variation in personality characteristics is non-genetic. Second, genes do not 'determine' personality in the sense of fixing it within narrow limits before birth. They simply exert influences that push and pull personality development and brain functioning in particular directions, influences that for each individual gene are very small. There is *no such thing* as 'a gene' for aggression, or intelligence, or anxiety – and we should find this profoundly reassuring. Third, and as a consequence of the second point, 'genetic' does not mean immutable. Genetic influences are non-determining and may therefore be modified or compensated for by a variety of environmental factors. The construction of a personality is a flexible and multiply-determined process, guided by genes, environments, and blind luck.

Chapter summary

- One important set of explanations for individual differences in personality refers to its biological basis. This level of explanation includes theories about the way personality has been shaped by evolution, as well as genetic influences on personality traits.

- From the standpoint of evolutionary psychology, we all share a genetically encoded 'human nature', composed of psychological adaptations. However, evolutionary accounts of personality have identified multiple explanations for systematic variations around this universal design. For example, balancing selection suggests that variation in personality traits may be owing to different behavioural or psychological 'strategies' being equally adaptive as a result of different selection pressures being applied as a function of time and place.
- Behavioural genetic research uses a variety of methods to study the contribution of genetic variation to personality. Family studies examine the extent to which people of different levels of genetic relatedness within families resemble one another, twin studies compare the resemblance of identical and fraternal twins, and adoption studies investigate the extent to which adopted children resemble their biological and adoptive parents.
- This research consistently finds that the heritability of personality characteristics (i.e., the proportion of their variation that is explained by genes) is between .4 and .5. It also demonstrates that most of the non-genetic contributions to personality are due to 'non-shared environment' – influences that are distinctive to individuals rather than shared within families.
- Molecular genetic research attempts to identify the specific genes that influence variation on major personality traits. Although many such genes have now been identified, these typically account for far less variance than one might expect based on findings from behavioural genetics. This may suggest that genetic influences on personality comprise complex interactions between tens or even hundreds of genes. If so, detection of these effects will pose a formidable challenge for this field.

Further reading

Penke, L., Denissen, J. J. A., & Miller, G. F. (2007). The evolutionary genetics of personality. *European Journal of Personality*, *21*, 549–87.
One of the most important and comprehensive papers concerning evolutionary accounts of personality variation. Penke and colleagues provide a comparative review of mechanisms that potentially explain the evolution of personality traits as well as cognitive abilities.

Pinker, S. (1997). *The blank slate*. New York: Penguin.
A riveting and popular science book concerning the nature–nurture controversy. Pinker considers the enduring idea that we are 'blank slates' at birth, and the overwhelming evidence against it.

(Continued)

(Continued)

Plomin, R., DeFries, J. C., Knopik, V. S., & Neiderhiser, J. M. (2013). *Behavioural genetics* (6th ed.). New York: Worth.
Arguably the most authoritative scholarly text on behavioural genetics, with significant coverage of the heritability of personality.

Munafò, M. R., & Flint, J. (2011). Dissecting the genetic architecture of human personality. *Trends in Cognitive Sciences*, *15*(9), 395–400.
A short yet comprehensive review of molecular genetic personality research and the challenge presented by the missing heritability problem.

Biological Approaches Part 2: Brain Structure and Function

Learning objectives

- To distinguish proximal biological influences on personality (i.e., brain structure and function) from distal biological influences on personality (i.e., evolution and genetics).
- To understand and describe major biological theories of personality in terms of the neural systems they identify as underlying personality traits.
- To appreciate the role that technology has played in the development of the field known as personality neuroscience.
- To identify the key challenges that personality neuroscience faces today.

Personality traits – like all other psychological and behavioural phenomena – are produced and constrained by biological processes in the brain. As the previous chapter demonstrated, genetic influences on personality are well established, and there are several ways in which these may have been shaped through evolution by natural selection. Nevertheless, evolutionary theory and genetics offer incomplete explanations of personality differences, because the mere existence of genetic influences does not illuminate the biological processes that underlie personality variation. Genes do not directly affect behavioural dispositions; they only do so indirectly by influencing brain development, brain structure, and brain chemistry. Genes code for the production of proteins that regulate brain functioning – indeed, about one-third of all our genes are expressed only in the brain – and if we want to account for the biological processes that directly underpin personality, it is at brain structures and functioning that we should look. Processes occurring in the brain directly explain why at any moment we might feel anxious, behave aggressively, or try hard to complete a difficult task. For this reason, a major goal of *Personality Neuroscience* is to identify specific brain systems that account for regularities in affect, behaviour, and cognition, which is to say, personality.

Research into the brain structures and processes underlying personality has tended to be guided by specific, biologically-oriented theories of personality. For this reason, this chapter is organized in terms of the major theories in this area, which are presented in rough chronological order. Some of the theories we will review were proposed over 50 years ago, before many of the tools and concepts used regularly today in psychobiology were even conceived. The progenitors of these theories could not build their explanations on a complete understanding of brain functions because science at the time had not provided a complete understanding of brain functions (it still hasn't). So, what early theorists did was refer to a Conceptual Nervous System (CoNS) – a working model of the actual Central Nervous System (CNS). The idea of a CoNS can be attributed to Skinner (1938, pp. 421–7), who coined the term apparently to criticize those who claimed to be directly studying biological processes but were only doing so conceptually. However, it actually turned out to be a very useful way of theorizing, and pre-empted the style of theory-building that would characterize much of psychology throughout the 20th century (Pickering et al., 1997). Whenever we refer to a structure or process (or coherent network of structures and/or processes) in terms of the functions or characteristics we think it might have, we are implicitly referring to a CoNS. For example, we might refer to the 'pleasure system' being activated when we are feeling happy (Kringelbach & Berridge, 2010), or our 'working memory system' being taxed when someone gives us complex street directions and we are trying to hold them 'in mind' (Baddeley, 2007). Postulating a CoNS is a bit like inserting a 'black box' in a causal chain. Initially the black box may have very little in the way of concrete details, but we can fill in and revise these details as we understand more of the biological factors responsible for the functions which are captured by the conceptual system.

The biological variables we attempt to map on to our CoNS can be referred to broadly as brain structure and function. *Brain structure* refers to static architectural features or regions of the brain. This includes both grey matter (dense concentrations of cell bodies) and white matter (tracts of nerve fibre connecting different brain regions). A helpful analogy is to think of the brain as a computer laboratory, in which the various computer systems represent the grey matter while the cables connecting the systems represent the white matter. *Brain function* refers to the role served by activity in specific regions of the brain. In our computer lab analogy, one of our machines might function primarily as a server while another might be primarily used for backup data. Theory building in biological psychology might begin by postulating a CoNS in functional terms (e.g., a 'pleasure system') and then attempt to find the structures in the brain that perform these functions. Alternatively, it might begin by studying a particular brain structure, and attempting to identify the functions it performs.

Studying brain structure and function requires advanced and expensive equipment, and personality neuroscience has developed relatively slowly due to its reliance on technological advances. Long ago, the only way to understand the functions of certain brain structures was to study people who had sustained some kind of brain injury and observe how they had changed psychologically. A classic illustration is provided by Phineas Gage, the 19th-century construction worker who suffered damage to frontal areas of his brain in a blasting accident that he miraculously survived. Gage's pronounced changes in personality – which largely consisted of increased impulsivity and short-sighted behaviour – were noted in detail by his physician, while his friends remarked that he was 'no longer Gage'. Researchers who study the region of the brain that was damaged in Gage's accident, called the ventromedial prefrontal cortex, continue to see his case as informative (Damasio, 1994). In recent years, modern brain-imaging (or *neuroimaging*) methods have made it much easier to study the neural systems underlying personality. Perhaps the most popular methods at present are magnetic resonance imaging (MRI), which quantifies the size or volume of certain brain structures, and functional magnetic resonance imaging (fMRI), which quantifies brain activity in terms of blood flow to different regions of the brain. These technological advances have had a noticeable impact on the growth of personality neuroscience as well as other areas of neuroscience.

The remainder of this chapter will be organized around the most influential theories about the biology of personality. Each theory is presented roughly in chronological order, so that we start with the earliest speculations about brain structures and functions involved in personality and finish at the cutting edge of modern personality neuroscience. You will notice that the early theories rely most heavily on conceptual mechanisms (i.e., the CoNS), while later theories become increasingly detailed in terms of biological mechanisms (i.e., the CNS). This is a direct consequence of the fact that progress in neuroscientific theory and research has often depended on methodological and technological advances.

The Four Humours

We begin with the oldest known model of personality, which is also the first recorded *biological* perspective on personality. This theory has been attributed to two great thinkers of antiquity: Hippocrates (from Ancient Greece, 460–370 BC) and Galen (from Ancient Rome, AD 131–200). Both are primarily renowned as fathers of Western Medicine, and among their legacies is the 'Hippocratic Oath' – an ethical code by which medical practitioners abide even today. The Hippocrates-Galen model drew upon what is known as *Humourism*: a belief that health and wellness is dependent upon the balance of certain bodily fluids (called humours – deriving from the Greek word for fluid). The model identified four humours – black bile, yellow bile, blood, and phlegm – as underlying not only personality but also physical and psychological well-being. The Four Humours were linked to the four classical elements of nature (earth, fire, air, and water) reflecting the belief that humans are part of nature and reflect its structure. Each humour was thought to give rise to a specific personality type. Black bile resulted in a depressive temperament referred to as *Melancholic*; yellow bile produced a fiery, quick-tempered personality type called *Choleric*; blood resulted in a cheerful and enthusiastic disposition known as *Sanguine*; and phlegm produced a calm, 'slow to warm up' temperament labelled *Phlegmatic*. Thus, personality could be distinguished in terms of four basic types with a biological basis in the balance of the four humours.

The Hippocrates-Galen model demonstrates that personality has been discussed and attributed to biological causes for almost 2,500 years. Of course, the four personality types provide a crude taxonomy in comparison to something like the Big Five, and the notion that bile, blood, and phlegm drive complex patterns of affect, behaviour, and cognition looks preposterous through modern eyes. Nevertheless, Humourism sustained an intellectual influence for a remarkably long period. For instance, bloodletting was practised by physicians seeking to balance the bodily fluids of an ill person until well into the 19th century, despite the fact that it was only ever likely to be harmful to patients (American President George Washington is thought to be among the many who died from extensive bloodletting). Similarly, the typological model of Hippocrates-Galen had a long influence on thinking about the structure of personality. This point was made by Gordon Allport (1937), one of the fathers of modern personality psychology, who suggested that the durability of the four humoural types may lie in the flexibility with which they could be fitted to one's own thinking. They essentially provided a basic 2×2 classification system, which is the kind of system that many thinkers have gravitated towards when attempting to describe basic psychological phenomena. Two notable examples are the personality models developed by two of the 20th century's most well-known figures in psychology – Ivan Pavlov and Hans Eysenck – to whom we will now turn.

Pavlov's typology

The Russian physiologist Ivan Pavlov is most famous in psychology for demonstrating the phenomenon of classical conditioning (Pavlov, 1927), also known as associative learning. He noticed that experimental animals (dogs, in this case) would salivate upon the appearance of a laboratory technician who would usually feed them. Subsequently, he showed that if a neutral stimulus (e.g., a bell), which he referred to as a 'conditioned stimulus' (CS), was repeatedly presented alongside an 'unconditioned stimulus' (UCS; e.g., delicious food) that produces an innate reflex – the 'unconditioned response' (UR; e.g., salivation) – then eventually the CS would directly elicit the response. That is, the CS and the UCS would become associated, at which point the innate reflex, now under the control of the CS, becomes known as the 'conditioned response' (CR). Much of Pavlov's work was focused specifically on innate unconditioned responses to stress and pain (e.g., startle reflexes in response to an electric shock). An important observation was the finding that with extreme stress or pain a subject would stop responding and fall unconscious. He labelled this process Transmarginal Inhibition (TMI), and suggested that it may function to protect the organism from the (presumably harmful) effects of intense stimulation. The threshold of TMI can be defined as the point at which the strength of CS increases but the magnitude of the CR decreases. One cannot help but pity the poor animal subjects that endured these experiments in the name of science!

The relevance of this work to personality comes from Pavlov's observation that there were marked individual differences in the tolerance of his experimental dogs. Some dogs would reach the threshold of TMI at much lower levels of pain and stress, while others would endure this for longer and at higher intensity. Pavlov believed that this variation in tolerance was a basic, heritable individual difference and that a difference in tolerance indicated 'a fundamentally different type of nervous system' (Rokhin, Pavlov, & Popov, 1963). As his ideas developed, he proposed that there were three key features of these different kinds of nervous system. Although these referred explicitly to the actual nervous system, they were so abstract that they were best described in terms of a CoNS. The first feature was the strength of the nervous system. Pavlov distinguished between strength of excitation, which referred to the capacity to withstand intense stimulation without succumbing to TMI, and strength of inhibition, which reflected the capacity to withstand conditioned inhibitory processes such as extinction (e.g., continuing to respond to the CS long after its pairing with the UCS has ceased). The balance of these two strengths was a second nervous system property theorized by Pavlov: a balanced nervous system was one in which strengths of excitation and inhibition were in equilibrium, while in an unbalanced system strength of excitation diverged from strength of inhibition. Finally, the mobility of the nervous system concerned the ease and speed with which one could change responding in accordance with a change in the environment. A mobile nervous system can adapt rapidly and flexibly to changes in the environment, relative to a slow nervous system.

Pavlov suggested that combinations of these three properties of the nervous system (represented in conceptual terms of a CoNS, but corresponding to actual biological processes) resulted in different types of nervous system. Persons with weak nervous systems were simply known as 'weak' types – their nervous system could not be distinguished further in terms of balance and mobility. Persons with a 'strong' nervous system could either be strong and 'unbalanced' or strong and 'balanced'. Those who were strong and unbalanced could not be distinguished further, but those who were strong and balanced could be 'slow' or 'mobile' types. Thus, we have four types of nervous system in Pavlov's Typology: (1) Weak; (2) Strong and unbalanced; (3) Strong, balanced, and slow; (4) Strong, balanced, and mobile. Pavlov related these to personality types using the framework provided by Hippocrites and Galen, as follows: First, a melancholic temperament results from weak nervous systems, which characterize individuals with relatively low thresholds for TMI. Second, a choleric temperament results from a strong, but unbalanced nervous system, while a phlegmatic temperament results from a strong, balanced, but relatively immobile nervous system. Finally, a sanguine temperament is underpinned by a strong, balanced, mobile nervous system.

Although aspects of nervous system functioning were his key explanatory constructs, none of Pavlov's research involved the study of actual brain structures and processes. For this reason, Pavlov's typology is perhaps best seen as a *forerunner* of personality neuroscience. This is not to deny the influence of his theory – indeed, Pavlov's typology was the driving force of research in personality and individual differences in the Soviet Union for much of the 20th century. Moreover, his CoNSs have been noted to have had a broad influence on biologically-oriented personality psychologists in Western countries such as the UK – most notably Hans Eysenck and Jeffrey Gray (Strelau, 1997), who we will encounter next.

Eysenck's General Arousal Theory

The first modern theory in personality neuroscience – that is, one which referred to specific brain structures and processes that may underlie personality traits – was proposed by Hans Eysenck. As we saw in Chapter 2, Eysenck also laid claim to one of the most influential taxonomies of personality, consisting of two dimensions that would ultimately be retained in the integrative Big Five taxonomy: Extraversion and Neuroticism. (Recall that Eysenck added a third dimension to his model, Psychoticism, although his ideas about the biological bases of this trait were never fully developed, and therefore we shall not discuss that dimension here.) Eysenck's two-factor system was largely based on the factor analytic approach described in Chapter 2, but he also sought conceptual ties with earlier personality theorists. Like Pavlov, Eysenck found the description of personality provided by the Four Humours at least heuristically useful, and often portrayed his two-factors in relation to the four types of Hippocrates/Galen. Specifically, the choleric type could be described by a combination of high Extraversion and high Neuroticism while the melancholic type could be described by a combination of low Extraversion and high Neuroticism. Conversely, the sanguine type could be described by a combination of high Extraversion and low Neuroticism, while the phlegmatic type could be described by a combination of low Extraversion and low Neuroticism.

According to Eysenck (1967), individual differences in Extraversion and Neuroticism are based in the functions of two brain systems that regulate our levels of arousal or stimulation. For this reason, his theory came to be known as General Arousal Theory. Eysenck suggested that our standing on the dimension of extraversion–introversion is a behavioural expression of our brain's chronic level of generalized physiological arousal or stimulation, which is regulated by a brain system known as the reticulo-cortical loop. This consists of neural pathways between the Ascending Reticular Activating System (ARAS) – a bundle of neurons in the brainstem – and the cerebral cortex. He thought of the ARAS as a kind of 'volume control' that determines the impact of incoming sensory stimuli on the regions of the brain that process those stimuli. A second brain system, the reticulo-limbic loop, was thought

Table 6.1 From Hippocrates to Eysenck: Early theories of the biology of personality

Type	Hippocrates /Galen	Pavlov	Eysenck
Melancholic (Depressive)	Black bile	Weak nervous system	Low cortical arousal + high limbic arousal
Choleric (Quick tempered)	Yellow bile	Strong, unbalanced nervous system	High cortical arousal + high limbic arousal
Phlegmatic (Calm, sluggish)	Phlegm	Strong, balanced, slow nervous system	Low cortical arousal + low limbic arousal
Sanguine (Cheerful)	Blood	Strong, balanced, mobile nervous system	High cortical arousal + low limbic arousal

to underlie differences in trait Neuroticism. This consisted of neural connections between the ARAS and the limbic system, a group of structures in the midbrain whose main functions are concerned with emotion. Thus, while the reticulo-cortical loop regulates general arousal, relating to our feelings of alertness and activation, the reticulo-limbic loop regulates emotional arousal, relating to feelings such as stress and tension.

In what way might the reticulo-cortical loop and reticulo-limbic loop relate to Extraversion and Neuroticism? Eysenck hypothesized that extraverts experience chronically low levels of cortical arousal as a result of low activity in the reticulo-cortical loop. This proposal drew on the classic Yerkes-Dodson Law, which states that an intermediate level of arousal is optimum for performing a given task (Yerkes & Dodson, 1908). In effect, Eysenck's view was that extraverts are typically under-aroused, and will therefore try to raise their arousal levels towards a more optimum level. This supposedly explained why extraverts are drawn to situations and activities that are exciting, novel, and stimulating. Introverts, in contrast, were suggested to be relatively over-aroused, and would therefore try to lower their arousal to reach a more optimal level. This was supposed to account for the introvert's preference for familiar and solitary activities. Eysenck's theory therefore suggests that extraverts will be more prone to boredom, while introverts will find novel activities unpleasantly over-stimulating as a result of their chronic differences in cortical arousal. Like many people, you might find this general idea extremely intuitive and see yourself either as someone who thrives on hustle and bustle (extraverts) or rather as someone who needs to 'recharge' after too much stimulation (introverts) – although most of us will fall somewhere between these two extremes.

Eysenck's theory was proposed long before the advent of modern neuroimaging methods such as MRI and fMRI. However, a promising indirect method for studying the brain, still popular and useful today, was to record electrical activity from the scalp via electroencephalogram (EEG). This electrical activity reflects the sum-total activity of neurons throughout the cerebral cortex, and researchers in this area suggested that this might provide a good proxy for cortical arousal. Many studies employing EEG-derived measures of cortical arousal appeared to confirm that introverted individuals did indeed show higher levels of arousal than extraverts, particularly when the experimental conditions in which the EEG recording took place were moderately stimulating (Gale, 1983).

Other support for Eysenck's theory came from a number of experiments showing that increases in arousal improved the performance of extraverts (as they approach an optimum level of arousal) but impaired the performance of introverts (who become over-stimulated). For instance, Revelle, Amaral, and Turriff (1976) administered three equivalent tests of verbal ability to participants under three conditions: (1) relaxed conditions, (2) with pressure to complete the test within 10 minutes after receiving a placebo, and (3) again with time pressure, this time after receiving 200 milligrams of caffeine (roughly equivalent to that contained in a double-espresso). Revelle and his colleagues found that, *on average*, the higher levels of arousal induced by the caffeine and time pressure did not influence performance on the verbal ability tests. However, when participants were divided up into high and low scorers on a measure of Extraversion, a striking picture emerged. Consistent with Eysenck's theory, increased levels of stimulation produced better performance for extraverts, whereas introverts performed best in the least stimulating conditions. This seems consistent with the notion that extraverts are normally below the optimum level of arousal, while introverts are at or even above the optimum level of arousal. In addition to supporting Eysenck's theory, these studies indicate that having a strong cup of coffee right before a challenging task, such as an exam, may either help or hurt your performance – depending on who you are!

As for Neuroticism – the second personality trait in General Arousal Theory – Eysenck proposed that highly neurotic individuals had a more reactive reticulo-limbic loop. This meant that, for such individuals, even relatively mild emotional stimuli would be likely to activate the limbic areas of the brain and thereby trigger the 'stress responses' of the sympathetic nervous system. This supposedly accounted for the higher levels of emotional instability that characterize individuals who score highly on measures of Neuroticism. Again, given that tools for studying brain activity directly are a relatively recent addition to the psychologists' tool-kit, most of Eysenck's tests of this hypothesis were relatively indirect. One useful measure is known as Electrodermal Activity (EDA), which involves passing a small amount of electric current between two electrodes placed on the skin. This provides an index of sympathetic nervous activity, which should be higher in neurotic individuals, especially in emotionally arousing situations (e.g., under stress). Disappointingly, a number of reviews of the research concurred that this prediction has generally not been supported (Eysenck & Eysenck, 1985; Zuckerman, 1991). Somewhat better support has been obtained using subjective indicators of emotional arousal: Neuroticism has been consistently associated with higher self-reported measures of tension and negative affect, and more neurotic individuals appear to experience more tension and negative affect in response to stressful or negatively valenced stimuli (Matthews & Gilliland, 1999).

Eysenck's theory generated a large volume of research that would come to provide the bedrock of modern Personality Neuroscience. His theory was notable for being the first to specify actual brain systems underlying personality in a reasonable level of detail. In addition, his descriptive model of personality has been more or less preserved within modern personality taxonomies such as the Big Five. This means that we can read papers of Eysenck's dating back to the 1940s concerning the same personality constructs that continue to be investigated today. We can even directly build on his work by conducting new tests of his theory as new methods become available to us.

Despite its historical importance, however, the influence of General Arousal Theory began to dwindle towards the end of the 20th century. There seem to be at least three reasons for this decline. First, while Eysenck's account for the biological processes underlying Extraversion enjoyed a reasonable level of support, the evidence concerning his theory of Neuroticism was largely inconclusive. Second, the reticulo-cortical loop turned out to be much more complicated than had been assumed by Eysenck's theory. Specifically, the ARAS was found to consist of *multiple* arousal systems regulated by different neurotransmitters serving different functions. This meant that the idea of a single, general cortical arousal dimension underlying trait Extraversion was not considered to be biologically plausible (Rammsayer, 1998). Third, some of the most robust findings concerning Extraversion and Neuroticism were not well accounted for by Eysenck's theory. A case in point is the evidence that extraverts are susceptible to positive mood states while neurotics are susceptible to negative mood states (Larsen & Ketelaar, 1991). The latter finding seems consistent with the notion that Neuroticism reflects emotional arousal (assuming that negative emotions are particularly arousing), but the tendency for extraverts to experience high levels of positive affect is not predicted by Eysenck's theory. In fact, because positive affect is a somewhat aroused state, it potentially *disconfirms* the hypothesis that extraverts are chronically under-aroused. Nevertheless, General Arousal Theory remains one of the most important contributions to this literature, and provided a powerful springboard for other biologically-oriented personality theorists.

Gray's Reinforcement Sensitivity Theory

A major successor to Eysenck's General Arousal Theory was proposed by Jeffrey Gray, who completed his doctoral studies under Eysenck's supervision in London. While Eysenck's approach was first to identify major personality traits, and then to develop a theory regarding the underlying brain systems (i.e., to proceed in a 'top down' direction), Gray argued in favour of the opposite approach (i.e., to proceed in a 'bottom up' direction). This preference was motivated by certain limitations to the method of factor analysis which Eysenck had relied on, at least in part, to argue in favour of his two-dimensional system for describing personality. Specifically, factor analysis can't tell us for sure that Extraversion and Neuroticism provide the *best* two dimensions for representing variation in personality. An alternative pair of dimensions, rotated away from Extraversion and Neuroticism, would be mathematically equivalent descriptors of 'personality space', but could differ in terms of how closely they are aligned with underlying influences on personality (see Figure 6.1). If Eysenck was wrong about the fundamental dimensions of personality, then he will have looked in the wrong places for the fundamental brain systems underlying personality. To avoid this problem, Gray argued that we should *first* develop a theory about the major brain systems underlying personality and *then* identify the aspects of personality that most closely capture individual variation in the functions of those systems. Ever since he made this argument, personality psychologists have debated the relative merits of a 'top down' or 'bottom up' approach to personality theory.

Gray's theory was influenced by the work of animal learning theorists who studied behavioural responses of experimental animals (e.g., rats) to rewarding and punishing stimuli. This literature had its roots in Operant Conditioning, which concerns the processes through which rewards and punishments change behaviour. (Operant Conditioning can be contrasted with Pavlovian Classical Conditioning, which – as we saw earlier – concerns the learning of associations between stimuli.) Gray suggested that different responses to various motivationally-salient stimuli could be organized in terms of three conceptual systems. His description of these systems evolved over time as he refined his theory (see Corr, 2008, for a thorough review), and the most up-to-date version is as follows: First, the **Behavioural Approach**

System (BAS) regulates behaviour towards rewarding or appetitive stimuli. The function of the BAS can be thought of as providing the motivational 'energy' to pursue desired goals, ranging from money and recognition to sex and drugs. BAS activation is thought to elicit motivated feelings of enthusiasm, sometimes described as 'hope' or 'desire'. Second, the Fight/Flight/Freeze System (FFFS) regulates behaviour away from punishing or aversive stimuli, and underlies the emotion of fear. If you have ever experienced the 'fight/flight' response – a moment of blind panic and withdrawal (e.g., recoiling from a striking snake) – then you will already have some understanding of the functions of the FFFS. The inclusion of 'freezing' within the FFFS reflects the fact that an organism presented with an inescapable, terrifying threat will sometimes become completely motionless. Finally, the **Behavioural Inhibition System (BIS)** processes signals of goal conflict, such as a situation that is both potentially rewarding and potentially threatening. The BIS can be thought of as a risk assessment system that makes us stop what we are doing and check for danger, and is thought to underlie feelings of anxiety. You might have experienced such goal conflict when walking home to your house late at night; your main goal is to get to your front door, but the dark street seems dangerous and you feel the urge to run the other way. If you have been in such a situation, you may remember feeling very alert, and found yourself scanning the street and listening closely for potential danger – in other words, in risk assessment mode. Goal conflict may also describe the experience many of us have when chatting to a potential romantic partner. This experience can be anxiety-provoking because the potential rewards (sex, companionship) conflict with the potential threats (rejection, embarrassment).

The major contribution of Gray's Reinforcement Sensitivity Theory was the provision of a 'fully fledged neuroscience of personality' (Corr, 2004, p. 317). Most of Gray's work from the 1970s through to the late 1990s was focused on providing a detailed map of the neural architecture of the BIS, FFFS and, to a lesser degree, the BAS. This work culminated in a detailed scholarly book called *The Neuropsychology of Anxiety* (Gray & McNaughton, 2000), a title that reflected Gray's primary interest in understanding the BIS. This CoNS was mapped to a network of brain systems, at the heart of which was the *septo-hippocampal system* (i.e., two tightly interconnected structures called the septum and hippocampus). The hippocampus was thought to receive and process goal-related information and to detect instances of goal conflict (as might occur when walking down a dark street to your house). Although detection of goal conflict is the core function ascribed to the BIS, the anxiety triggered by conflict detection involves activation of not only the septo-hippocampal system but also the amygdala, among other brain regions. The amygdala is also a core anatomical module in the brain system comprising the FFFS. This is consistent with the view by many theorists that the amygdala is critically involved in the experience of fear (e.g., LeDoux, 2003). According to Gray and McNaughton (2000), fear also involves the activation of a range of other brain regions, such as the periaqueductal gray (a gray matter structure surrounding a region extending from the brainstem called the cerebral aqueduct). As for the BAS, Gray had always suggested that this CoNS consists of the 'brain reward system' famously discovered by James Olds in the 1960s. This comprises a major branch of the dopamine system connecting several structures in the midbrain including the ventral tegmental area, striatum, and nucleus accumbens (Pickering & Gray, 1999).

Gray suggested that dispositional variation in the sensitivity of these three biologically-based reinforcement systems would be likely to have major consequences for human personality. The central focus in much of Gray's work was on the BIS as the neuropsychological basis of anxiety. Gray and his colleagues had shown in animals that the common action of all clinical drugs with anxiolytic (i.e., anxiety-reducing) properties was to disrupt the behavioural functions of the BIS by acting on the septo-hippocampal system. That is, animals injected with these drugs would no longer respond to goal conflict situations with characteristic 'risk assessment' behaviour. Gray then reasoned that, if the BIS was indeed a major brain system underlying personality, then trait anxiety was likely to be a major dimension of personality. In terms of Eysenck's two-dimensional trait system, measures of trait anxiety lay roughly between the low end of Extraversion and the high end of Neuroticism. Gray therefore suggested that such an anti-clockwise rotation of Eysenck's Neuroticism axis would align it more closely with the underlying neural causes of personality.

The role that the FFFS might play in personality has long been a point of ambiguity within Reinforcement Sensitivity Theory. It supposedly forms the biological basis for a trait comprising fearfulness, consistent with its role in generating emotional states describable as fear or panic, but it is not clear where this trait might lie within the Eysenckian two-dimensional framework. In more recent times it has been suggested that trait fear and anxiety are likely to be related but distinct traits, both lying somewhere close to Neuroticism. The role of the BAS has also been ambiguous: Gray originally speculated that this brain system might give rise to trait impulsivity, which he located between the high Extraversion and high Neuroticism pole. Figure 6.1 depicts Gray's suggested personality taxonomy in relation to

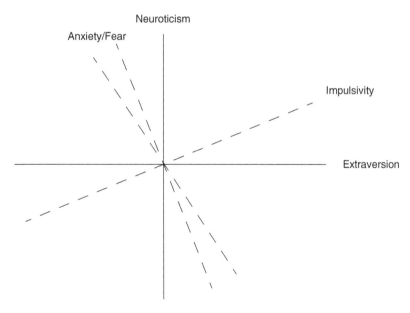

Figure 6.1 Gray's (dashed lines) suggested modification to Eysenck's (solid lines) personality dimensions

137

Eysenck's. In descriptive terms, the difference between these two models seems very slight – Gray simply suggested a 30-degree rotation of the Extraversion and Neuroticism axes. Indeed, the major difference between the two models concerns the proposed biological bases of personality, rather than the descriptive organization of personality.

An unfortunate consequence of Gray's 'bottom-up' approach has been lack of clarity regarding which personality traits one should measure when conducting tests of his model. One approach has been to use existing measures of fear, anxiety, and impulsivity – Gray's suggested trait manifestations of the FFFS, BIS, and BAS. A problem here is that there are many different ways that researchers can conceptualize these traits. For instance, impulsivity can be conceptualized as the tendency to act before thinking through the consequences of the action. This aspect of impulsivity focuses on lack of premeditation, and is captured in the old adage that one should 'look before you leap' (Whiteside & Lynam, 2001). Another way in which someone can be impulsive is to disengage readily from a task and leave things unfinished. Imagine an individual who sits down at their desk to complete their work, but then finds themselve wandering into the kitchen looking for a snack. They start to make a sandwich, but then abandon this task as well because they suddenly remember to text someone about an upcoming party. This person is demonstrating a clear lack of perseverance, another form of impulsivity (Whiteside & Lynam, 2001). From the outset, it was unclear which conceptualization of impulsivity would best reflect BAS functioning, and, after much research into the matter, many concluded that Gray might have been wrong to link the BAS with impulsivity. Today, it is generally agreed that impulsivity has more to do with the effective *regulation* of motivated behaviour, rather than motivated behaviour *per se*. In other words, it is not strong desire for a particular reward that distinguishes the impulsive individual, but rather the capacity to regulate one's response to such rewards.

Another approach to testing Reinforcement Sensitivity Theory has been to develop purpose-built FFFS, BIS, and BAS scales. In this case, rather than ask which *existing* trait reflects, for instance, 'sensitivity to reward', the strategy here is to directly measure a trait conceptualization of sensitivity to reward. One of the most famous attempts to do this was Carver and White's (1994) BIS/BAS scales. Behavioural and biological investigations have offered some support for the validity of the BIS/BAS as measures of reinforcement sensitivity. For instance, Beaver and his colleagues (2003) used fMRI to show that individuals with high scores on the BAS scale respond more strongly at a neural level (i.e., activation of key structures in the brain reward system) to pictures of appetising food (e.g., chocolate cake). It is not clear, however, to what extent such data constitute evidence in support of Reinforcement Sensitivity Theory. They may simply show that self-report measures of reinforcement sensitivity are correlated with other types of measures of reinforcement sensitivity (i.e., neural activation). In addition to this problem, there has been much disagreement about how best to conceptualize trait constructs based on Gray's biological systems. Since the BIS/BAS scales were published, several alternative measures have been developed, and there still does not seem to be a consensus regarding which questionnaire is best.

A third approach to researching Gray's model is to suggest that motivational systems may form a partial biological basis for personality, but that the organization of underlying biological systems may not have a one-to-one mapping with the structure of personality. Perhaps the most likely individuals to hold this view would be those who view the Big Five personality traits as a valid system for describing personality. For instance, it might be suggested that the BIS and FFFS contribute to different aspects of trait Neuroticism, which is not dramatically different from the view that they underlie two separate traits that are somewhat similar to Neuroticism (as depicted in Figure 6.1). In fact, even if the latter were true, it is still the case that the Big Five describe the major lines of covariation among all personality traits. Thus, whatever traits most clearly reflect individual differences in reinforcement sensitivity, they are likely to be accommodated by the Big Five. One exciting study that seems to fit well with this idea showed that the two major sub-components (or 'aspects') of Neuroticism, called volatility and withdrawal, were both related to activation of the amygdala, a central anatomical node within both the BIS and FFFS (Cunningham et al., 2010). Volatility, which captures relatively strong negative emotional responses such as anger (potentially reflecting some of the functions of the FFFS, e.g., 'fight'), predicted stronger amygdala activation in response to threatening stimuli. Conversely, withdrawal, which seems to reflect worry and anxiety (potentially reflecting some of the functions of the BIS), predicted stronger amygdala activation to both threatening and rewarding stimuli when the participant was required to virtually 'approach' the stimulus (potentially causing conflict). These and other studies encourage the view that it may be possible to reconcile the brain systems of Reinforcement Sensitivity Theory with descriptive approaches to personality such as the Big Five (see Corr, DeYoung, & McNaughton, 2013).

Gray's Reinforcement Sensitivity Theory has significantly advanced our understanding of the neuropsychological systems that underlie behavioural variation in humans and other animals. As an explanatory approach to personality it continues to have a clear impact on the field. A particularly commendable feature of Gray's model is that he and other associated researchers have been receptive to criticism, and willing to revise the theory in order that it may better account for the available data. This is why the details of the Reinforcement Sensitivity Theory have changed progressively over the last 40 years. As a result, the three brain systems that comprise this model continue to reflect current understanding in neuroscience and neurobiology. In comparison, one might regard the brain systems identified by theorists such as Eysenck and Pavlov as relics of history. Despite its many strengths, ambiguity surrounding the identification and measurement of relevant personality traits has been a perennial challenge to evaluating Reinforcement Sensitivity Theory (Smillie, Pickering, & Jackson, 2006). A potential solution to this problem is that the influences of brain systems on personality might best be organized in terms of robustly established descriptive taxonomies such as the Big Five (Corr et al., 2013).

Neurotransmitter theories

Eysenck and Gray focused primarily on the neuro*anatomical* structures and pathways that may underlie individual differences in personality. Other theorists have focused in more detail upon neuro*chemical* aspects of brain functioning. Neurobiological systems are not just grey matter structures and the white matter pathways that connect them. They are also networks through which information is communicated by chemicals in the brain that are released from one neuron and 'bind' to the next. These *neurotransmitters* are often specific to particular brain systems and pathways, and distinctive patterns of behaviour occur when recreational drugs or psychiatric medications alter their functioning. Many neurotransmitters are found in a broad range of species, and research on animals has generated a great deal of information about their likely function in humans, and their potential influence on the long-term regularities in behaviour and experience captured by personality traits.

One theory of personality that focused on how different neurotransmitters might influence personality was proposed by C. Robert Cloninger. The conceptual architecture of Cloninger's (1987) model was largely inspired by Reinforcement Sensitivity Theory. There was a Behavioural Activation System (BAS) and a Behavioural Inhibition System (BIS), which had similar functions to the systems of the same name proposed by Gray, and were thought to underlie two personality traits termed Novelty Seeking and Harm Avoidance. Individuals high on Novelty Seeking are outgoing thrill-seekers, and willing to try new things and explore their environment for potential rewards. Conversely, individuals high on Harm Avoidance are more anxious and withdrawn, and shy away from the possibility of danger. Cloninger also postulated a third Reward Dependence System (RDS), which was thought to underlie a personality trait also called Reward Dependence. Individuals with high scores on this dimension are ambitious and industrious, and not easily discouraged if they don't achieve their goals. Cloninger linked Novelty Seeking with dopamine function, Harm Avoidance with serotonin, and Reward Dependence with norepinephrine (also called noradrenaline). Tests of these propositions have yielded quite mixed findings, with no clear support for any of the links that Cloninger drew between the three neurotransmitters and his three personality factors (Paris, 2005). In addition, it has become clear that his model of the structure of personality traits has some serious limitations (Farmer & Goldberg, 2008). Indeed, some have shown that one can more easily recover the familiar Big Five personality factors from Cloninger's personality questionnaire than the traits he had originally postulated (Markon, Krueger, & Watson, 2005).

A more successful neurotransmitter theory was developed by Richard Depue. Depue has focused primarily on three personality traits known as Agentic Extraversion (which is similar to Big Five Extraversion), Affiliation (which is similar to Agreeableness) and Constraint (which is similar to Conscientiousness) (Depue & Lenzenweger, 2005). Like Cloninger, Depue focused on the functions of major neurotransmitters such as dopamine and serotonin, as well as other neurochemicals such as oxytocin and endogenous opioids. Perhaps the most thoroughly-supported aspect of Depue's theory is that concerning the role of dopamine in Agentic Extraversion (Depue & Collins, 1999). Dopamine is the central neurotransmitter in what Depue called the Behavioural Facilitation System (BFS), which seems largely synonymous with Gray's BAS and is more generally called the brain reward system. The functions of the BFS are primarily described in terms of incentive motivation, which is expressed in behaviours that direct the organism towards rewarding goals. Various studies have now supported the idea that individual differences in the functioning of this system underlie variation in trait Extraversion. A particularly elegant example was published by Depue and Fu (2013) concerning neural processes that associate contexts with reward. The idea here is that environments that are associated with reward should engage the BFS, producing the incentive motivation that drives us towards rewarding goals. Depue and Fu administered a dopamine-boosting drug in a relatively mundane laboratory context (thus linking it with reward system activity) and then examined the power of this context to facilitate the actions of this same drug on BFS outputs, including motor activity (measured by using a simple finger tapping task) and positive affect (using a self-report measure). They found that this process was very strong in highly extraverted participants, but virtually non-existent in highly introverted participants. This indicates that extraverted individuals should be much more likely to experience incentive motivation (expressed in terms of behavioural activation and feelings of excitement) in a broad range of situations. This is because they are more susceptible to the neural processes that associate those situations with reward.

Interestingly, the theory that Extraversion is based in dopaminergic function and the brain reward system has helped solve one of the puzzles encountered by Eysenck's General Arousal Theory. Recall that Eysenck was unable to explain why extraverts are susceptible to positive affect. Also, as positive affective states are states of arousal (as in the case of feeling 'excited' or 'up beat'), this association seemed to contradict his theory that extraverts were chronically *under*-aroused. From the perspective of Depue's theory the link between Extraversion and positive affect makes perfect sense in terms of the functions of the BFS. Specifically, when encountering or pursuing reward, BFS-engagement will produce strong feelings of excitement and enthusiasm, and extraverts should be more susceptible to this than introverts. This prediction also follows from reinterpretations of Gray's theory, which suggest that Extraversion is more closely related to the functioning of the BAS than is impulsivity.

Trait affiliation is an aspect of personality concerned with interpersonal warmth and the enjoyment of close personal bonds. Depue (2006) suggested that affiliation is closely related to the Big Five trait of Agreeableness, while others have suggested that it may combine aspects of Extraversion and Agreeableness (DeYoung, Weisberg, Quilty, & Peterson, 2013). In any case, Depue's theorizing about the neurobiological basis of trait affiliation has focused on endogenous opioids – a naturally occurring group of neurochemicals that mimic the pain-relieving effects of drugs such as morphine. Opioids are released in the brain during a range of close interpersonal behaviours, such as gentle touch, and seem to facilitate the maintenance of close social bonds. In support of this idea, individuals given the drug naltrexone, which blocks opioid release, are more likely to spend time alone and experience a reduction in the pleasantness of interactions with friends (Depue & Morrone-Strupinsky, 2005). Depue and Morrone-Strupinsky also used naltrexone to test the hypothesis that trait affiliation has a basis in the functioning of endogenous opioids. Participants in this study viewed a film clip that was designed to induce strong feelings of interpersonal warmth – that sappy feeling you might experience after watching a romantic movie. For individuals scoring high on trait affiliation, the film clip produced an increase in two indicators of opioid release: subjective ratings of warmth-affection and pain tolerance (recall that opioids function as a pain reliever or 'analgesic'). Neither of these increases was observed for individuals with low scores on affiliation, or for highly affiliative individuals who had received the opioid blocker. This latter result helped to confirm that the strong responses of the (non-drugged) high-affiliation participants to the film clip were indeed attributable to opioid release.

Another of Depue's influential contributions to personality neuroscience is the suggestion that serotonin underpins trait Constraint, which is similar to Conscientiousness. According to Depue (1995), low levels of serotonin are linked with (1) strong and unstable emotional responses, (2) exaggerated behavioural responses, particularly to rewarding stimuli, and (3) general irritability and sensory sensitivity. While high serotonin levels are manifested in rigid, constrained behaviour and emotions, low levels are manifested in impulsivity, aggressiveness, irritability, and emotional instability. Importantly, serotonin is known to have an inhibitory influence on dopamine and appears to constrain the functions of the BFS. Depue suggested that a way to make sense of all of this data is to view serotonin as setting a threshold for facilitating emotional responses, both positive and negative. When serotonin levels are low the threshold is also low, so that the brain systems involved in positive and negative emotionality are easily and strongly activated, resulting in impulsive reward-seeking and unstable emotional states. With higher serotonin levels the threshold is higher, so activity in these neural systems is constrained, such that impulsive and emotional behaviours are kept in check. In effect, this view of serotonin may explain why individuals who score highly on measures of constraint, such as Conscientiousness, are less likely to be ruled by their impulses and emotions.

In more recent years, the link between serotonin and Constraint has been explored further by Charles Carver and his colleagues. Carver, Johnson, and Joorman (2008) observed that serotonin has been repeatedly linked with two broad classes of psychological phenomenon. The first of these is impulsive agression: low serotonin function has been linked with a wide range of impulsive behaviours that often manifests in violent or antisocial behaviour. The second phenomenon is clinical depression: low serotonin function appears to confer a vulnerability to depression, and drugs that raise serotonin levels are effective for treating depression. These links are puzzling because depressed people are typically not described as impulsive or aggressive, and yet both classes of psychological problem appear to share a common biological basis. Carver's explanation involved the postulation of a CoNS that borrows from classic 'two-mode' models of psychological functioning (see Figure 6.2). These models suggest that behaviour is controlled by *reflexive* systems concerned with approach of rewards and avoidance of threats – that is, the kind of systems that are described in Gray's Reinforcement Sensitivity Theory. However, in two-mode models the reflexive systems can be countermanded by a higher-level, *reflective* system. The reflective system prevents us from rushing after every shiny reward that might catch our eye, or fleeing hysterically at the first sign of danger. It also helps us do things that – in reflexive mode – we might otherwise avoid (e.g., exercise, hard work). Carver and colleagues (2008) suggested that the reflective

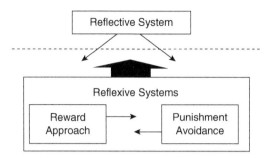

Figure 6.2   The 'two-mode' model described by Carver and colleagues (2008)

system appears to capture the key features of trait Conscientiousness. Consistent with Depue, Carver and his colleagues have argued that serotonin appears to perform the functions of the reflective system – restraining the power that basic, emotion-fuelled approach and avoidance systems have over our behaviour.

Cloninger, Depue, and Carver are just some of the theorists who have attempted to understand personality variation in terms of the functions of major neurotransmitter systems. Depue's theory is perhaps most notable for amassing at least reasonable empirical support, particularly with respect to his theory of Agentic Extraversion. Other aspects of his theory, such as Constraint, are extremely well-developed conceptually, but have not yet attracted many direct empirical evaluations to help gauge validity. A potential pitfall with some of these theories is the implausibility that single traits will be underpinned by single neurotransmitters. The reality is neurotransmitters have multiple functions and interact with one another – as we saw in the case of serotonin's inhibitory influence on dopamine. Nevertheless, it is also likely that the multiple actions of neurotransmitters may serve some overarching and coherent set of psychological functions, and a key challenge for personality neuroscience is to understand what role those functions may play in personality.

Recent trends in personality neuroscience

Personality Neuroscience today is a dynamic and rapidly unfolding field. A major driver of the current pace and variety of research has been the increasing availability of modern technologies. In earlier times, the most ambitious biologically-oriented personality psychologist was largely restricted to peripheral measures of brain and nervous system activity, such as cardiovascular measures, skin conductance, and electroencephalogram (EEG). Today it is possible to study the structure of both gray matter (using magnetic resonance imaging, MRI) and white matter (using diffusion tensor imaging, DTI); to study blood flow to different regions of the brain (using functional magnetic resonance imaging, fMRI); to selectively alter specific neurochemical systems (through psychopharmacology); and to directly influence neuronal activity (using transcranial magnetic stimulation). All of these methods have increased in their availability and ease of use, while decreasing in cost. As a result, they regularly appear in the personality neuroscience literature, and are continuing to improve our understanding of the brain structures and functions that underlie personality.

Another visible influence on the field has been the unification of personality description provided by the Big Five traits. DeYoung and Gray (2009) described the Big Five as a common language for describing personality, through which research in personality neuroscience can be organized and the results of different studies conducted by different research teams can be easily compared. This has facilitated integration across theories that have developed in relative isolation. For instance, Kennis, Rademakera, and Geuze (2013) recommend combining the three systems from Gray's theory with the constraint (or reflective control) system described by Carver and Depue. The result is a neuroscience framework that provides reasonably good coverage of variation in personality as described by the Big Five. Such integrative approaches contrast starkly with the major theories we have described in this chapter, each of which has been wedded to slightly different trait taxonomies. For example, we saw that Depue's trait dimensions were slightly different from Gray's, which were different from Eysenck's, and so on. Because each theory is focused on explaining a different set of descriptive traits, they are difficult to compare and contrast in terms of their explanatory power. A further advantage of using comprehensive trait taxonomies to organize research in personality neuroscience is that it can reveal theoretical gaps. A good example of this is trait Openness to Experience – a major personality domain that none of the theories we have examined in this chapter addresses in terms of its biological underpinnings. It is only very recently that a theory has begun to develop, comprising neural processes responsible for exploring or engaging with information and aesthetic stimuli (DeYoung, 2014). This system is grounded in a branch of the dopamine system that is somewhat separate from the reward-processing circuitry we have already discussed in relation to trait Extraversion.

ILLUSTRATIVE STUDY

The Big Five traits and associated brain structures

As we have seen in this chapter, most biologically-oriented personality theorists had a preferred taxonomy of traits that they liked to work with. Gray focused on anxiety and impulsivity, Eysenck focused on Extraversion and Neuroticism, and Carver has focused on Constraint. Meanwhile, those personality psychologists who were interested in developing a unifying taxonomy for personality description – culminating in the Big Five – were less concerned about linking that taxonomy with biological processes. This has recently started to change, and some researchers are beginning to examine how the Big Five traits can be linked with specific brain structures and functions.

A good example of this shift in focus is provided by DeYoung and colleagues (2010), who examined whether individual differences in the size of different structures in the brain are associated with individual differences in the Big Five traits. They generated their hypotheses by first identifying the key *psychological* processes that seemed central to each trait, and then identifying the specific *brain regions* that had been linked with those psychological processes. Their predictions were as follows:

1   Extraversion, as we have seen, has been linked with reactivity to reward and with the susceptibility to increases in positive affect. It was therefore predicted that Extraversion would be associated with the volume of key reward-processing structures such as the nucleus accumbens, amygdala, and orbitofrontal cortex.
2   Neuroticism, on the other hand, has been linked with reactivity to threat stimuli and with susceptibility to negative affect. This implicated brain structures involved in fear and anxiety, such as the amygdala and hippocampus.
3   Agreeableness is centrally concerned with altruistic and prosocial tendencies. It was therefore predicted that this trait would be associated with the volume of structures involved in empathy and social cognition, which includes the superior temporal sulcus, temporo-parietal junction, and posterior cingulate cortex.
4   Conscientiousness captures the tendency to be organized, diligent, persistent, and to constrain one's impulses. This strongly implies the involvement of prefrontal regions of the brain, such as the lateral prefrontal cortex.
5   Finally, Openness/Intellect has been linked with effective processing of aesthetic and perceptual information, and with cognitive functions such as working memory. This also implicates a number of regions within the prefrontal cortex.

DeYoung and colleagues used structural magnetic resonance imaging (MRI) to support all but one of their hypotheses – Openness/Intellect was not associated with the predicted regions, although there were some encouraging trends in other regions of the brain that seemed to fit broadly with the psychological processes connected with this trait. These findings were an exciting step forward in personality neuroscience. Moreover, given that the Big Five traits can be thought of as a framework for organizing all variation in personality, it should be possible – in principle – to relate these findings to any of the theories we have encountered in this chapter. For instance, the findings concerning Extraversion and Neuroticism can be related to Eysenck's, Gray's, and Depue's theories, while the findings concerning Conscientiousness – which is very similar to Constraint – can be examined in light of Depue's and Carver's theories.

The Big Five are not the only means to achieve theoretical integration within personality neuroscience. One notable theorist, whose contributions to this field are approaching a half century, is Marvin Zuckerman. Zuckerman (1991, 2005) subscribes to a variation on the Big Five traits that he calls the 'Alternate Five'. The Alternate Five preserves Big Five

Neuroticism, divides Extraversion into sociability and activity, and adds impulsive sensation-seeking (which overlaps with low Conscientiousness) and aggression-hostility (which overlaps with low Agreeableness). Using this descriptive framework, Zuckerman has drawn broadly on emerging findings in personality neuroscience, incorporating elements from Eysenck's, Gray's, and Depue's theories, in addition to his own theorizing. The result is a composite of some of the more robustly established mechanisms in the field. A noteworthy feature of this theoretical mosaic is the extent to which it recognizes that the biological bases of personality traits are likely to consist of a complex interaction between multiple neural processes. For instance, Zuckerman suggests that dopamine function underlies both Extraversion *and* impulsive sensation-seeking (consistent with both Gray's and Depue's theories); that the sex hormone testosterone and an enzyme called monoamine oxidase additionally influence both traits; and that serotonin function is inversely associated with impulsive sensation-seeking (consistent with both Depue's and Carver's theories). There is obviously a loss in parsimony when one compares this account of Extraversion with the seemingly more elegant frameworks provided by Eysenck or Depue. On the other hand, Zuckerman's model may paint a more realistic picture of the messiness and complexity of biological influences on personality.

Like any field, the recent trends in personality neuroscience have not consisted only of successes and celebrations; there have also been some formidable challenges. For instance, a broad concern that has swept through many areas of psychology (see Simmons, Nelson, & Simonsohn, 2011) relates to our confidence that published findings are reliable and will replicate. Some specific features of personality neuroscience have made studies in this area particularly vulnerable to such concerns. One example is the sheer financial expense of some neuroscience methodologies, such as fMRI. The high costs of running such a study may dissuade researchers from collecting sufficiently large samples or from running a particular study twice to confirm that findings replicate. Worryingly, many findings in personality neuroscience (and neuroscience more generally) hinge on a single study with a small sample size, which means that some such findings may be chance results (Mar, Spreng, & DeYoung, 2013). Another example is the extensive number of judgement calls that must often be made in the analysis of data collected using neuroscience methods. For example, when analyzing fMRI data one must carefully decide how to define the anatomical region of interest (e.g., the amygdala) within the brain images that have been recorded. A controversial paper by Vul and colleagues (2009) argued that some approaches to this problem are more biased than others, and may lead to substantial over-estimation of the relationship under investigation. Indeed, this paper showed that studies that had employed more biased methods than others reported implausibly strong associations between personality characteristics and aspects of brain structure and function. This suggests that some of the stronger and seemingly ground-breaking findings in the literature are exactly the kinds of findings that we should treat with suspicion. The success with which personality neuroscientists can address these problems will determine the likelihood of this emerging field developing, maturing, and genuinely expanding our knowledge of the mechanisms underlying personality.

Conclusions

The neurobiological theories briefly reviewed have made great strides towards explaining the brain mechanisms and processes that underlie personality. As we saw in the previous chapter, roughly half of the variance in personality can be attributed to genetic factors, which means that there must exist certain biological intermediaries – called *endophenotypes* – that mediate the effects that our genes (*genotype*) have on our personality (*phenotype*). Furthermore, we know that *all* sources of personality variation, both genetic and environmental, can only influence personality traits via processes in the brain. Therefore, in order to fully understand the causes of personality variation we must be able to specify these brain structures and processes. Personality neuroscientists have begun to close in on a variety of brain pathways, structures, and neurotransmitters, and specify how these might form integrated systems that underpin major personality dimensions. However, this field is essentially still in its early infancy, and it may be many years before a robust picture emerges of how complex, interacting processes in the brain make us who we are.

Chapter summary

- All human behaviour and experience arises from activity in the human brain. This is true regardless of whether we are interested in the impact of genetics or the environment on personality. Therefore, attempts to fully explain stable regularities in behaviour and experience – captured by major personality traits – must specify the brain structures and processes underlying personality.
- Early biological theories of personality relied strongly on a Conceptual Nervous System (CoNS) – a working model of the actual brain. For example, Pavlov's notions of different types of nervous system – characterized by variations in *strength*, *balance*, and *mobility* – were never clearly linked to actual biological parameters. It is only as methods for studying the actual brain have become increasingly viable that theories have been able to specify actual neural pathways and systems in some detail.
- Eysenck's General Arousal Theory of personality suggested that Extraversion was based in the functioning of a *reticulo-cortical loop* (underlying cortical arousal), while Neuroticism was based in the functioning of a *reticulo-limbic loop* (underlying emotional arousal). Despite having a profound influence on personality neuroscience, Eysenck's theory is no longer considered tenable.
- Gray suggested that personality neuroscience should proceed from the 'bottom up', by starting with the major brain systems that seem likely to influence personality. His Reinforcement Sensitivity Theory proposed that three systems, the BAS (reward sensitivity), the FFFS (threat sensitivity) and the BIS (conflict sensitivity), were likely to have an important influence on personality variation.

(Continued)

(Continued)

- Depue and Carver have developed theories regarding the role of specific neurotransmitters in personality variation. Depue's theory, which links Extraversion to dopamine function, appears consistent with Gray's theory regarding the BAS. Both Depue and Carver link serotonin function with constraint, a trait that appears similar to Conscientiousness.
- Recent trends in personality neuroscience are characterized by increasingly sophisticated methods for studying brain structure and function, and also by increasing emphasis on integration. This integration has been facilitated by adopting the Big Five as an organizing framework for this field.

Further reading

Canli, T. (2006). *Biology of personality and individual differences*. New York: Guilford Press.
An edited volume consisting of chapters contributed by some of the leading figures in personality neuroscience. Chapters provide detailed and highly readable summaries of the theories of Depue, Gray, and Zuckerman, among others, and summarize emerging developments in the field.

DeYoung, C. G. (2010). Personality neuroscience and the biology of traits. *Social and Personality Psychology Compass, 4*, 1165–80.
A succinct overview of modern personality neuroscience, organized in terms of the Big Five factors of personality.

Matthews, G., & Gilliland, K. (1999). The personality theories of H. J. Eysenck and J. A. Gray: A comparative review. *Personality and Individual Differences, 26*, 583–626.
An influential and detailed side-by-side comparison of the evidence for Eysenck's and Gray's theories, and a general critique on the success of attempts to explain personality in terms of brain structure and function.

Zuckerman, M. (2005). *Psychobiology of personality* (2nd ed.). New York: Cambridge University Press.
One of the most thorough, integrative reviews of personality neuroscience that has ever been conducted. Zuckerman's book is organized in terms of his own Alternative Five personality taxonomy.

Cognitive Approaches to Personality

Learning objectives

- To understand how cognitive approaches to personality differ from trait and other approaches.
- To develop a working understanding of the basic concepts of personal construct theory.
- To understand the concept of 'attribution' and the dimensions of attributional style.
- To understand the concept of 'coping' and the main forms of coping strategy.
- To understand the concept of 'self' and personality variables involving the evaluation and structure of the self (i.e., self-esteem and self-complexity).

This final chapter in the 'Explaining personality' section presents several ways of accounting for individual differences that share an emphasis on cognition. They all focus on the ways in which people actively make sense of their world: interpreting it, explaining events, coping with adversities, representing information about themselves, and perceiving and reasoning about emotions. We first discuss the theoretical perspectives that provide the historical context from which the cognitive approach emerged, namely behaviourist, humanistic, and social learning theories. We then turn to the work of a cognitive pioneer, George Kelly, and his psychology of 'personal constructs': ways of making sense of people and events by perceiving their similarities and differences. Following this, we investigate 'attributional style', a concept that refers to individual differences in ways of explaining the causes of events: whether something is due to factors internal to the person or to their external environment, to causes that are temporary or enduring, and so on. The implications of different styles for physical and mental well-being are discussed. Finally, we outline the varied strategies people use to deal with stress in a section on coping, and the mixed implications of viewing oneself in a positive or multifaceted fashion ('self-esteem' and 'self-complexity').

In a classic paper published in 1990, the American psychologist Nancy Cantor drew an important distinction between two ways of studying personality. One way, she wrote, is to study things that people 'have', another is to study things that they 'do'. A psychology of 'having' investigates the attributes that people possess – the characteristics that compose them and distinguish them from others. You will recognize this from Chapter 2 as trait psychology, a vigorous and successful tradition of personality research and theory that has yielded vital insights into the structure of individual differences.

You will also recall from Chapter 2 that trait psychology is not without its critics. Some criticisms have to do with the supposed abstractness and lack of explanatory power of traits. Critics contend that trait psychology represents people as collections of static properties, and fails to capture the processes that give rise to how we think, feel, and act. In a sense, traits describe the 'what' rather than the 'how' of personality. This is where Cantor's psychology of 'doing' comes to the rescue. She argues that personality psychology needs an approach that complements trait psychology by revealing the mental processes that account for how we do things. This approach, she proposes, is a cognitive one.

By 'cognition' psychologists mean mental activities such as thinking, believing, judging, interpreting, remembering, planning, and the like. A distinctly cognitive approach to psychology arose in the 1950s and 1960s, fuelled by the growing recognition that cognitive processes are indispensable for explaining behaviour. It had become clear from analyses of the nature of language and language learning that human activity is highly creative, flexible, and complex, and requires a very complex information processing system to underlie it. A basic tenet of cognitive psychology is that learning and memory are active processes. People do not relate to their environments in a passive manner, merely registering what happens to them, but meet it head on, determined to make meaning out of it. We actively filter and pay attention to incoming information according to our current concerns, actively impose patterns and meanings on it on the basis of our knowledge and expectations, and actively search our memories in order to do so. Cognitive psychologists developed many new research methods that allowed these mental processes to be studied in an impeccably controlled and scientific fashion.

Cognitive approaches to personality similarly emphasize the active, meaning-making processes that people employ in their daily lives. Proponents of these approaches study the processes people employ in interpreting their environments, explaining events, coping with life's challenges, imagining and planning for their futures, and using strategies to accomplish their goals. These emphases on cognitive process and active meaning-making distinguish cognitive approaches to personality from the biological and psychoanalytic approaches that we discussed in the previous chapters.

Unlike the biological approach, the cognitive approach refers to phenomena that are close to subjective experience. Biological theorists and researchers address the underpinnings of personality dispositions and make no attempt to study how behaviour, thought, and emotion are expressed and lived. Biological approaches also have much more to say about structures and traits ('having') than processes, focusing as they currently do on enduring genes and physiological patterns.

Psychoanalytic approaches certainly make a great deal of reference to cognitive processes – the defence mechanisms, primary and secondary process thinking, and so on – but not in a systematic fashion. Instead, psychoanalytic theorists emphasize the role of emotion and drives in the personality. Cognition in psychoanalytic theory is generally viewed as being at the mercy of desires and urges, reactive rather than pro-active, and is understood to be primarily unconscious. This view of cognition contrasts sharply with cognitive psychology's emphasis on its active, goal-pursuing, and (often) subjectively accessible nature.

To understand the cognitive approach to the study of personality, it is necessary to take a brief detour through some of the theoretical approaches to personality that led up to its development. These approaches are no longer prominent, but they provide a historical context in which the distinctness of the cognitive perspective can be appreciated.

Behaviourism

Cognitive psychology began in part as a rebellion against the previously dominant 'behaviourist' school of psychology. **Behaviourism** itself began as an attempt to develop a more rigorous, experimental approach to psychology than the approaches that preceded it. In their quest for rigour, behaviourists – most famously the American psychologist B. F. Skinner (1904–90) – argued that psychology should be the science of behaviour, rather than mind. Indeed, mental processes are so irredeemably subjective, unobservable, and difficult to pin down, they maintained, that they were not appropriate phenomena for scientific study or psychological theorizing. Psychological science should, instead, focus on what we can observe and control, specifically manifest behaviour and its relationship to observable events in the environment. Whatever happened within the organism, between the perception of an event and the 'emitting' of a behavioural response to it, was scientifically out of bounds.

Behaviourism was primarily an empirical analysis to how organisms respond to their environment, and in particular how these behavioural responses change with changes in the environment. In short, it was a psychology of learning. Behaviourists exhaustively studied how creatures modify their behaviour in response to different patterns of reward and punishment. Its understanding of learning was passive and deterministic: patterns of reward and punishment directly influence our behaviour, and our behaviour is merely a function of the rewards and punishments that we have experienced in our lifetime. The organism is not an active participant in learning, and the theory leaves no room for it to have purposes or the freedom to act as it chooses.

Behaviourism had rather serious limitations as a psychology of personality, quite apart from its portrayal of the organism as passive and determined. First, it had very little to do with what is distinctively human, and was an approach to the study of learning processes across many organisms more than a theory of human individuality. Much of its evidence base was derived from studies of rats and pigeons, and it tended to fail miserably in accounting for phenomena that are unique to our species. It is no accident that a decisive blow for cognitive psychology was struck by Noam Chomsky when he demonstrated the inability of behaviourism to make sense of human language. Second, behaviourism had no account of personality structure: the person is a collection of specific behavioural tendencies rather than having broad dimensions (as in trait psychology) or underlying components (as in psychoanalysis). Third, the behaviourist view of motivation is implausibly simple. People merely seek reward and avoid punishment, and there is no room for more elaborate needs, goals, and desires. Finally, the behaviourism approach seems to minimize the contribution of the person to behaviour. Our behaviour simply reflects our learning history, so we are essentially mere products of our environment. Individuality does not reside within the person so much as in that person's history of encounters with the external world.

It should by now be clear how cognitive psychology, and the cognitive approach to the study of personality, departed from behaviourism. Cognitivists declared mental processes to be legitimate topics for study, emphasized the active and (relatively) free nature of the person and encouraged a focus on uniquely human attributes and capacities. Despite all of its limitations, however, behaviourism did leave two important legacies to the cognitive approach to personality. First, proponents of cognitive approaches to personality retain a commitment to the scientific method as a means of studying people. Second, they retain the behaviourist belief that learning is a fundamentally important process. More than many other theories of personality, cognitive theories propose that people do not have fixed attributes but are malleable. Changing someone's personality is as easy (or as difficult) as changing their mind (i.e., their cognitions). We return to this issue of personality change in Chapter 8.

Humanistic theories

As we have seen, the cognitive approach to personality differs sharply from behaviourism in some respects but also has some affinities with it. Another approach to the psychology of personality that has some important similarities and differences with the cognitive approach is often called the 'humanistic' approach. Like behaviourism, **humanistic psychology** is no longer prominent with the field of personality psychology, but it again offers historical context for the emergence of the cognitive approach.

Two key figures in the humanistic approach to personality were Abraham Maslow (1908–70) and Carl Rogers (1902–87). Both theorists reacted against behaviourism by emphasizing the active, free, and creative aspects of human nature, by taking rationality and consciousness to be central processes in human behaviour, and by rejecting coercive attempts to control people by reward and punishment. Both theorists view people as intrinsically motivated to grow and develop in positive ways, and saw the environment not so much as a determining force in shaping people, but as a context that can enable growth and self-realization. In addition, both theorists made use of cognitive concepts.

According to Maslow's (1962) psychology, people have an internal drive to realize their potential ('self-actualization'), and will naturally tend to do this unless their social environment constrains their opportunities and choices. Providing that our basic needs for bodily sustenance, safety and security, and closeness to and esteem from others are met, we will strive for personal growth in this fashion. Social arrangements that fail to meet these needs cause neurotic suffering. As people come closer to self-actualizing, they adopt different ways of thinking, becoming less judgemental and critical.

Rogers' approach to the psychology of personality (Rogers, 1961) is similar in its optimism and belief in an intrinsic tendency to self-actualize. His personality theory unapologetically emphasized the role of subjective experience over the external environment, arguing that it is how situations and events are perceived and interpreted that determines the person's behaviour, not these external facts in themselves. The self plays a particularly central role in Rogers' psychology. It is the focus of one of our strongest needs – the need for 'positive regard' – and well-being follows when others esteem us unconditionally, enabling us to act in accordance with our 'true self'.

The humanistic approach to personality shares with the cognitive approach a rejection of the behaviourists' passive and deterministic view of people, and they also have in common the position that mental processes and subjective experience are vitally important phenomena to study. Its theorists give a central role to cognitive concepts such as self, creativity, choice, judgement, and goals. Some personality theorists who take a cognitive approach share at least part of the optimistic growth orientation of the humanistic psychologists, who in some ways can be considered precursors of that approach. The main difference between the approaches is in their relationship to the scientific method. Whereas the humanistic psychologists tended to have an ambivalent or negative relationship to scientific investigation, cognitive psychologists have tended to embrace it. In this respect, the humanistic approach to the study of personality departs further from behaviourism than the cognitive approach, although in a somewhat similar direction.

Social learning theories

Both behaviourism and humanistic psychology are precursors of the cognitive approach to the study of personality, but both are importantly different, as we have seen. More direct forerunners of the cognitive approach are the so-called '**social learning theory**' and 'social-cognitive theory'. Both of these theoretical approaches are rigorously scientific, like behaviourism, but they adopt cognitive concepts in ways that bridge behaviourist and cognitive psychology.

The main proponent of social learning theory was Julian Rotter (1916–2014). In some respects Rotter's views were clearly behaviourist: he saw behaviour as being motivated by rewards and punishments. However, he introduced an important added complexity to this simple view. Behaviour is not governed by these rewarding or punishing consequences directly, but by our 'expectancy' that our behaviour will bring them about. Expectancy is a cognitive concept: it refers to a subjective judgement about the probability of a future event. When people decide whether or not to do something, that is, they form an expectation of whether that behaviour is likely to yield a desirable outcome (e.g., 'will the movie be any good?'). The likelihood that someone will act in a particular way in a particular situation – the act's 'behavioural potential', in Rotter's terms – therefore depends both on the desirability of the behaviour's possible outcome and on how probable this outcome is judged to be.

Rotter argued that expectancies exist not only for particular behaviours, but also for behaviour in general (Rotter, 1966). One such 'generalized expectancy' is '**locus of control**', the person's beliefs about whether the outcomes of behaviour are typically under their control ('internal') or under the control of the environment ('external'). People with an internal locus believe that they are primarily responsible for what they get in life, whereas those with an external locus believe that their life outcomes are determined by other people, fate, luck, or some other factor that they cannot control. You will notice, again, that locus of control is essentially a cognitive concept, a belief about the self and the world that may not directly reflect any objective state of affairs.

The social-cognitive theory of Albert Bandura (1925–) moves us even further in a cognitive direction. More than Rotter, Bandura (1986) emphasizes the importance of the self as an active agent and as a focus of people's beliefs and expectations. Against the behaviourist view that behaviour is determined by reward and punishment, he argues that it is primarily 'self-regulated': the person, not the environment, is its primary determinant. Bandura paid special attention to beliefs about the self's capacity to bring about particular outcomes. People who are high in '**self-efficacy**' strongly believe that they are capable of behaving effectively, for instance succeeding at a demanding work task. People who are low in self-efficacy, in contrast, have low expectations that they can produce the desired behaviour, and consequently they are likely not to attempt it. Efficacy expectations such as these need not correspond closely to people's actual capabilities, so that many people may be plagued by self-doubt and fail to realize their capabilities. Bandura and colleagues have repeatedly shown that self-efficacy predicts positive outcomes in a wide variety of domains – health, job performance, academic achievement – and that by enhancing people's self-efficacy it is possible to improve their chances of benefiting from psychological treatment. Like social learning theory, then, Bandura's theory places cognitions centre stage in the study of human behaviour.

We have seen how behaviourist, humanistic, social learning, and social-cognitive theories provide a backdrop for the emergence of a distinctively cognitive approach to the study of personality. There is no single cognitive theory of personality, however. Rather, there are several distinct lines of cognitive inquiry, each focusing attention and research on specific cognitive personality characteristics. In the remainder of this chapter we will examine several ways in which the cognitive approach has contributed to and enriched the psychology of personality. These illustrative lines of theory and research will be discussed under headings that refer to a particular kind of cognitive activity.

Construing: Personal constructs

The first systematic cognitive theory of personality was developed by George Kelly (1955). Kelly's theory rests on a supremely cognitive metaphor for human nature. Biological theorists of personality represent the person as an organism and psychoanalysts as a battlefield, but Kelly saw people as scientists. Although most of us lack white coats and PhDs, we are all engaged in developing and testing theories about the world, trying to produce the best understanding of our environments and ourselves. The best personal theories are like the best scientific ones, too: they are those that are most accurate and that allow us to predict and control our environments best. As personal scientists, that is, our goal is to anticipate the future so we can best deal with it. Theories that fail to meet this goal are revised in the face of the evidence, and are ceaselessly put to the test of daily life.

The basic unit in Kelly's psychology of personality is the 'personal construct', Kelly's preferred term for the theories that everyday people develop. He once defined a construct as a way that two things are alike and different from a third thing. This may not strike you as a very enlightening definition, but it goes to the heart of Kelly's psychology. Human cognition, he argued, searches for similarities and differences, or contrasts. It is bipolar and categorical, meaning that we think and represent the world in terms of opposed categories and tend to perceive objects, events, and people as belonging to one or the other rather than falling on a continuum between them. The distinct contrasts through which we see the world are our personal construct systems.

The term 'construct' is a good one because it captures two important aspects of Kelly's theory. First, a construct is something with which – or through which – we *construe* our world; that is, how we interpret or make sense of it. By implication, personality is how we subjectively interpret the world. Second, constructs *construct* the world for us, in the sense that by interpreting our world we are actively and creatively building a coherent picture of what it is like. To a large extent, this subjective world is the one we inhabit, and our reactions to objective events and circumstances only make sense in terms of this personally constructed world. Different people may inhabit very differently constructed worlds.

Kelly laid out his theory of personal constructs as a 'fundamental postulate' and a series of 'corollaries'. The fundamental postulate expresses the basic cognitive claim that people's processes are 'channelized' – that is, formed into consistent patterns – by the way they anticipate events (i.e., their constructs). Some of the more important corollaries are easily laid out, and give a sense of Kelly's approach. First, anticipation of the future is based on construal of the past: our constructs are active and changing interpretations of evidence, and we try to improve these interpretations over time. Second, these constructs are organized in hierarchies: some are broader and basic (good vs. bad) and others more refined and specific (well-dressed vs. scruffy). Third, we tend to favour one pole of every construct: constructs are evaluative. Fourth, people construe events in different ways, and the more their construct systems diverge the more psychologically different they are. Fifth, understanding another person requires us to understand how that person construes the world, but not necessarily to share their constructs. Sixth, a person's constructs may vary in their openness to revision (i.e., their rigidity), and may conflict with one another.

All of this is fairly abstract and perhaps not very thrilling until you consider what it *doesn't* mention. There are no drives, goals, or motives of any sort, unless you count the desire to anticipate events better and grasp the world more accurately. There is no unconscious, no defence mechanisms, no emotion, no biology. All the theory refers to is our subjective ways of representing and interpreting the world. And of course that encompasses a great deal of what makes us who we are as individuals, in spite of all the theoretical concepts it leaves out. Kelly's system carves out a domain of subjectivity – our internal mental worlds – that is relatively neglected by most other theories of personality, and it does so because it is a cognitive theory.

It is worth stepping back for a moment here and thinking through how personal constructs differ from traits as units of personality. Traits are objective ways of behaving, whereas constructs are subjective ways of seeing. Traits are ways in which individuals differ along continuous dimensions, whereas constructs are ways in which each individual fits experiences into discrete categories. Traits are sources of stability and consistency that tend to change at a glacial pace, whereas constructs can in principle change as rapidly as a theory can be abandoned. Traits and personal constructs, in short, are very different theoretical concepts.

Kelly developed his theory not just to be a conceptual radical, however. His main goal was to understand individual clients in clinical settings. He recommended that therapists and counsellors assess clients' construct systems so as to understand them better, and launched a highly original method for doing so (see Chapter 9). The end result of such an assessment is a map of the client's distinctive ways of making sense of their environment, with a focus on the social environment. That is, an assessment of the client's 'construct system' primarily represents the unique ways in which they perceive differences among other people. The role of the therapist or counsellor was to determine how this construct system was not functioning well. Someone might have a system that is too simple, with a few overly dominant constructs, and someone else might have one that is full of contradictions. A client might be inhibited or prejudiced because a construct is so rigid that it narrows their thinking and prevents their construct system from developing. Someone might be disabled by anxiety because events in their lives can't be grasped by their existing constructs. Another person might be riddled with guilt because they can no longer perceive themselves as occupying the favoured pole of one of their most basic constructs. Personality psychologists in the Kellyan tradition are masters at painting revealing psychological portraits of clients' inner subjective worlds and at formulating innovative construct-based theories of conditions as diverse as stuttering and suicide.

One of the most interesting features of Kelly's cognitive approach to personality that is connected to his clinical focus may have escaped your notice. From a trait psychology perspective, a personality is characterized by locating it on a set of dimensions such as the Big Five: very high on one, low on another, average on a third, and so on. These same dimensions provide a standard descriptive framework for all people: in principle, everyone has a location within the five-dimensional space. For Kelly, however, each person has a set of constructs that is unique to him or her. Your construct system is in principle different from mine and everyone else's. It is your signature way of construing your personal world.

Some psychologists find this aspect of Kelly's theory enormously attractive and much less restrictive than the standardized formulation of personalities that trait psychology affords.

Its main disadvantage is that it makes systematic personality research quite difficult. If each personality must be characterized in it own terms, it is hard to see how generalizations about the structure or correlates of personality can be made, or even how two personalities can be compared. Generalizations and comparisons can be drawn, but Kellyan theory makes it complicated. This conflict between an approach to personality that emphasizes the uniqueness of the individual and another that seeks generalizations about personality structure is a real one in the psychology of personality. There are even two forbidding terms – '**idiographic**' (literally 'own-writing') and '**nomothetic**' (literally 'law-making') – that refer to these alternatives. The nomothetic or generalizing approach is dominant in personality psychology, a field inhabited largely by quantitative researchers, but the idiothetic or individualizing approach that Kelly represents still has its champions. We will return to the challenges of understanding the uniqueness of the individual in Chapter 11.

Kelly's approach has relatively few adherents among contemporary personality psychologists. Nevertheless, he is far from being merely a historical curiosity. His personality theory made a deep impact on the field by opening up subjectivity – the person's distinct ways of making sense of the world – as an important and legitimate field of study for personality theorists and researchers. In doing so, he contributed to the viability and popularity of the cognitive approaches to personality that followed him. We will explore some of these in the next few pages.

Explaining: Attributional style

Kelly's psychology of personal constructs gives a broad account of how we make sense of our worlds. Constructs govern how we perceive others, ourselves, and our environments, and how we fit new experiences into established beliefs and ways of thinking. Other psychologists have focused attention on a narrower form of making sense of the world, namely how we explain events. Humans, they argue, are not content to merely observe what happens around them, the passive stance towards the world that cognitive psychology debunks. Instead, we are driven to understand the *causes* of events, to actively try to grasp why they happened when or how they did. There is a reason for this, of course. If we can grasp the causes of events we are in a good position to predict and control them. We will know when similar events are likely to happen again and what sorts of responses might prevent them if they are undesirable, enable them if they are desirable, and deal with their consequences in either case.

Explanations and the causes they propose vary in many respects, but psychologists (Abramson, Seligman, & Teasdale, 1978) have argued that three dimensions are especially important. Some explanations make reference to causes that are internal to the person, such as his or her beliefs, desires, intentions, traits, and physical attributes, and some to causes that are external. External causes include other people's psychological or physical attributes as well as life events, economic or social conditions, supernatural forces, luck, and so on. Some explanations refer to causes that are stable over time and difficult to change (e.g., intelligence, genes, capitalism), whereas others refer to causes that are short-lived or unstable (e.g., moods, the weather, ill-fortune). Finally, some explanations propose causes that are broad in their implications for the person, likely to have deep and wide-ranging effects on him or her (e.g., stupidity, fate, schizophrenia), whereas others propose causes with relatively limited or specific implications for the person (e.g., spelling problems, random errors, chicken phobia).

These three dimensions are usually presented as a series of oppositions: internal vs. external, stable vs. unstable, global vs. specific. Their importance in human cognition has been established by decades of research in social psychology, especially a branch of it called '**attribution theory**', which studies how people attribute meaning, causation, and responsibility to actions and events. Any particular explanation or cause can in principle be located on each of the three dimensions. Therefore, there should be eight distinct kinds of explanation, representing combinations of the three opposed pairs (e.g., external–unstable–specific).

Many events almost demand a particular kind of explanation. Almost everyone would agree that being struck by lightning is caused by random bad luck (i.e., external–unstable–specific). However, many events are causally ambiguous and can be explained in multiple ways. For this reason, people often differ in how they account for events that they experience. Some of these differences are systematic: people may have a typical style of explaining events. Such 'explanatory styles' – more often known as '**attributional styles**' – have been the focus of a great deal of research by cognitively-oriented personality psychologists.

Although any consistent way of explaining events could be considered to be an attributional style, most psychologists have focused on a particular style that they refer to as 'pessimistic'. Pessimists tend to explain negative and positive events in quite distinctive ways. They tend to explain negative events – events that are undesirable from their perspective – in terms of causes that are internal, stable, and global. Such explanations see the negative event as caused by the self, likely to last, and likely to have widespread negative implications. In other words, pessimistic explanations lead people to blame themselves for their troubles, and to believe that these troubles are large (encouraging helplessness) and enduring (encouraging hopelessness). An example would be explaining a disappointing performance on an exam as being due to one's lack of intelligence. Pessimists tend to explain positive events very differently, with reference to external, unstable, and specific causes. Good things, that is, are seen as being out of the pessimist's control, fleeting, and having only limited implications for his or her well-being. Doing better than expected on an exam might be explained as due to a scoring error or to lucky guesses.

Optimists show the opposite pattern. Negative events are explained as externally caused, transient, and limited in their implications ('I did badly because that stupid exam was unfair') and positive events as internal, stable, and global ('I did well because I am brilliant'). Notice that both of these patterns are equally unbalanced and both are likely to be inaccurate, biased, or irrational to some extent. The extreme pessimist irrationally discounts successes and catastrophizes and takes excessive responsibility for failures, whereas the extreme optimist is self-serving, taking excessive credit for successes and making excuses for failures.

Optimism in this sense is not just a dispositional term like a trait, involving relentless cheerfulness and hope. It is, instead, a specific way of explaining events, a set of carefully described cognitive *processes*. Note how optimistic explanation by this account – e.g., ascribing negative events to causes that are external, short-lived, and narrow in their implications – has nothing directly to do with positive mood or general expectations that things will get better. Optimism here is a way of making causal sense of events, a process that can be observed whenever explanation takes place, rather than just a static trait that describes a hopeful stance towards the future.

Researchers have demonstrated that attributional style has many important implications. Pessimistic attributional style is a vulnerability factor for depression (Metalsky, Halberstadt, & Abramson, 1987). Pessimism at age 25 predicts worse physical health at age 45 (Peterson, Seligman, & Vaillant, 1988). Among university students it is associated with worse health and more doctor visits, even among students who are matched for initial health. Among students it also predicts poorer academic performance, less specific academic goals, fewer contacts with academic advisers, and dropping out prematurely (Peterson & Barrett, 1987). More pessimistic life insurance salesmen sell less insurance (Seligman & Schulman, 1986), and pessimistic competitive swimmers are more likely to perform below expectation in races, especially after another disappointing race (Seligman, Nolen-Hoeksema, Thornton, & Thornton, 1990).

Researchers have also developed ways to measure the pessimism of people who are unlikely to complete attributional style questionnaires, including historical figures, by rating spontaneous explanations extracted from speeches, diaries, letters, interviews, and even song lyrics. By this means, it has been found that most successful American presidential candidates gave a more optimistic nomination speech at their political party's pre-election convention than their rival (Zullow & Seligman, 1990). Similarly, famous American baseball players who were rated as more optimistic from explanations they gave in newspaper interviews, tended to live longer than their more pessimistic but equally successful peers (see Reivich, 1995). This method also can assess the optimism of cultures and historical periods: when top-40 song lyrics contain relatively high levels of pessimistic explanation, economic growth and consumer confidence tend to fall in the years that follow (Zullow, 1990).

All of this glowing talk about the benefits of optimism makes some students grumpy. Surely, they ask, optimism isn't always the path to everlasting health, wealth, and happiness? Aren't realism or even pessimism sometimes better approaches to take towards life? One response to these questions is to reiterate the point that optimism is often irrational and biased, reflecting a tendency to explain negative and positive events in different, self-serving ways. If it is important to you to be objective and free of illusion, then you will probably not have an unusually optimistic attributional style. However, even if optimism may be *irrational* in the sense of being distorted or inaccurate, research suggests that it may be *rational* in the sense of serving our adaptive interests most effectively. Evidence has accumulated that 'positive illusions' such as unrealistic optimism are associated with better mental health (Taylor & Brown, 1988), and that it is mildly or moderately depressed people who have the most realistic assessment of themselves and their environments (Ackermann & DeRubeis, 1991). If you strive for accurate, truthful self-knowledge you may indeed find true happiness and well-being, but research suggests you will have to push against a kind of psychological gravity to do so.

On the other hand, theorists interested in cognitive strategies have determined one way in which pessimism might not be a disadvantage in life. Cognitive strategies are defined as ways in which people apply what they know about themselves to performing specific tasks in a way that satisfies their goals. A strategy is therefore a planful way of implementing cognitive processes in real-world situations. One intriguing strategy has been called 'defensive pessimism' (Norem & Cantor, 1986). Defensive pessimists perform well on a particular kind of task, but nevertheless hold unrealistically low expectations about how well they will do each time they face new challenges. They may consistently do well on written exams, but forecast that they will do badly whenever a new one approaches. Such people imagine the worst, feel intensely worried about it, but unlike other pessimists they do not tend to withdraw effort from it and make it a self-fulfilling prophecy. Indeed, they tend to perform as well as those who pursue an optimistic strategy.

It therefore appears that defensive pessimists approach the task of performing well with the implicit goal of minimizing the disappointment they would feel if they fell short of their hopes. In a sense, they pay for a reduction in possible disappointment in the future with an increase in actual misery in the present. Presumably, they employ this strategy because it makes the most sense to them given their anticipated emotional reactions. They suffer, but they do well. This may be the best reassurance that personality psychology can offer to the pessimistic reader.

Coping: Coping strategies

Construing and explaining are two sets of cognitive processes that are quite broad and general in their implications. Kelly's personal constructs influence how we make sense of more or less everything that we encounter in life, and other people in particular. Similarly, attributional style is relevant to more or less every event that we observe: in theory at least, we are for ever seeking the causes of what happens. The next set of cognitive personality phenomena that we discuss are more specific in their focus, referring to the ways we deal with the challenges and difficulties that life throws at us. **Coping** has been defined as 'the thoughts and behaviours used to manage the internal and external demands of situations that are appraised as stressful' (Folkman & Moskowitz, 2004, p. 745). In short, people engage in efforts to cope whenever they perceive a situation as taxing their capacity to deal with life problems, and these efforts may target the situations themselves or people's internal responses to them, such as emotional distress.

Reading this definition you might see parallels with the psychoanalytic concept of defence, which was discussed in Chapter 4. The concepts of coping and defence are indeed related, but there are some important differences that reflect the theoretical differences between cognitive and psychoanalytic approaches to personality. First, coping strategies primarily deal with external stresses that the person faces – challenging events and our responses to them – whereas defence mechanisms primarily deal with internal threats such as impulses and repugnant thoughts. Second, whereas most defence mechanisms are employed unconsciously, out of the person's awareness, coping strategies are generally employed consciously. Third, 'defence' implies a reactive, damage-controlling response, whereas 'coping' implies a response that is to some extent active and future-oriented. In short, the concept of coping reflects a more active, conscious, and externally-oriented set of processes than the concept of defence mechanisms.

Coping does not refer to a single phenomenon but to any response that people make to stressful events. These responses, known usually as 'ways of coping' or 'coping strategies', are extraordinarily diverse. One review of the scientific literature found more than 400 distinct labels that have been used to describe ways of coping (Skinner, Edge, Altman, & Sherwood, 2003), and there have been numerous attempts to classify these into a more manageable set. The most widely used classification distinguishes between problem-focused and emotion-focused ways of coping (Folkman & Lazarus, 1980). Problem-focused forms of coping directly and actively address the problem that is causing the distress, and try to change it. Examples might include confronting someone about their unpleasant behaviour towards you, developing a plan of action, or actively trying to solve the problem. Emotion-focused coping, in contrast, attempts to modify the person's emotional response to the stressful situation, rather than the situation itself. For example, a person might engage in wishful thinking (i.e., imagine that an unpleasant situation would magically disappear), try to reduce their distress by drinking, distract themselves from stressful thoughts, try to relax, or try to reappraise the situation so that it doesn't seem so bad.

One reason why researchers have studied coping is to learn which ways of coping are most effective in dealing with stress. A huge volume of work has investigated the effectiveness of different ways of coping in relation to an enormous variety of stressful situations, including bereavement, cancer diagnosis, looking after an ill family member, motherhood, workplace problems, and everyday life hassles. Four main conclusions can be drawn from this work. First, most coping strategies are not intrinsically effective or ineffective, but vary according to the specific nature of the stressful situation. Particular strategies work best in particular contexts. Second, although the first point appears to be true, there is still a modest tendency for problem-focused ways of coping to be somewhat more effective than emotion-focused ways.

The third point helps to make sense of the first two. Whether a particular coping strategy is effective seems to depend on whether the person judges the stressful situation to be controllable or uncontrollable. When the situation is perceived to be potentially under the person's control (e.g., 'If I tell him off he'll stop bullying me'), then it makes sense to engage in active, problem-focused forms of coping. If, on the other hand, the person judges the situation to be unchangeable (e.g., 'Nothing I do can stop him bullying me'), these forms of coping are likely to be unproductive, and it is more appropriate for people to adapt themselves to the situation using emotion-focused strategies. Coping researchers talk about this issue in terms of the 'goodness of fit' between coping efforts and the situation: a close fit exists when people tend to engage in problem-focused coping for stressors they appraise as controllable and in emotion-focused coping for stressors they judge to be uncontrollable. Some research indicates that better fit is associated with better coping outcomes. In short, successful coping involves a capacity to engage in ways of coping that are tailored to the situation, rather than a tendency to employ a single kind of strategy in an inflexible manner.

Although the distinction between problem-focused and emotion-focused coping has been dominant in the literature, it may also be a little too coarse to encompass the diversity of coping efforts. Several additional types of coping strategy may also need to be considered, and we will briefly discuss three of them here. First, some writers have argued that although emotion-focused coping strategies often seem rather passive and inadequate, some are notably worse than others. It is possible to refer to 'avoidant' forms of coping that involve attempts to escape, either cognitively or behaviourally, from the stressful situation rather than facing it or adapting oneself to it. For example, wishful thinking, pretending the problem does not exist, avoiding people who remind you of a stressful situation, excessive sleeping, substance abuse, and simple denial, are all examples of avoidant coping. As you might expect, avoidant coping is almost always an ineffective strategy.

More effective may be a second additional kind of coping, namely the seeking of social support. Although the coping literature has tended to see coping as a relatively non-social process, in which individuals try to manage their lives single-handedly using an assortment of clever strategies, people are of course embedded in social relationships and networks. There is ample evidence that having close relationships and being a connected part of broader networks buffers people against stress and its consequences, and efforts to seek out other people appear to represent a distinct type of coping. Interestingly, support-seeking cuts across the distinction between problem- and emotion-focused coping. Other people could be sought to give active assistance in dealing with a problem we are facing, or they could be sought to console and comfort us, and to listen to our tales of woe, thereby helping us to manage our emotions.

A third, additional kind of coping involves finding meaning in adversity. Often people who are experiencing life stress, and especially stress that is lasting and severe, report that they have come to a new understanding of themselves or of life as a result of their experiences. A quote from a cancer patient, reported by Taylor (1983), is a good illustration:

> You take a long look at your life and realize that many things that you thought were important before are totally insignificant. That's probably been the major change in my life. What you do is put things in perspective. You find out that things like relationships are the most important things you have. (p. 1163)

Such efforts to find meaning and to put life and self in a new perspective are not problem-focused ways of changing the situation itself, and neither are they ways of managing emotions. Instead, they represent ways for people to reappraise or accept their fate and to reinterpret the stressful event so as to make it personally significant. Although all of this may sound woolly and philosophical, the discovery of meaning in adversity appears to have important practical implications. In a study of HIV+ men whose partners had died of AIDS, Bower, Kemeny, Taylor, and Fahey (1998) found that those men who actively engaged in cognitive processing about the meaning of their loss were more likely to find meaning in it, as indicated by a significant shift in their values and life priorities (e.g., a greater appreciation of loved ones or enhanced spirituality). Moreover, those men who found meaning showed less rapid decline in immune functioning over the next three years, and were less likely to die of AIDS-related causes (i.e., 19% of the men who found meaning compared to 50% of those who did not). Finding meaning in adversity is clearly not just a matter of philosophical navel-gazing.

The psychology of coping is an exciting area of research with important applications in a variety of applied fields. One of the most attractive features of the coping concept, and of the cognitive approach to personality more broadly, is that coping strategies are skills or ways of thinking that should be teachable. Strategies that are found to be effective by researchers could become targets for interventions aimed at people who are experiencing particular kinds of stress, so that their coping can be enhanced. The psychology of coping is therefore a solid foundation for a very practical way of improving people's lives.

Representing the self: Self-esteem and self-complexity

The three sets of concepts that we have discussed to this point in the chapter – personal constructs, explanations and attributions, and coping skills and styles – all reflect cognitive processes. All of them refer to ways in which people make active sense of their environment and respond to its challenges. However, processes are only one component of cognition, and we can also speak of cognitive products. In addition to cognitive processes, that is, people have organized knowledge of themselves and their world, and this knowledge reflects the ways in which they make sense of the world. Cognitive psychologists often refer to this structured knowledge in terms of 'representations'. People store representations of the world in their memory, and these representations, built up and modified throughout the course of our development, guide the way we process new information.

One of the most interesting and important knowledge structures or representations is the self. The self is a notoriously slippery phenomenon, and might seem to be very difficult to pin down, but when it is understood as a 'self-concept' – that is, as an organized body of knowledge about one's attributes – it becomes amenable to study by personality and social psychologists. At the most basic level, we can simply ask people to list the characteristics that they see as aspects of themselves (i.e., answers to the question 'I am ————'). Typically, people have no difficulty listing a large number of attributes. Some of these attributes refer to personal characteristics, both psychological and physical (e.g., traits, attitudes, abilities, height, hair colour), others refer to groups to which the person belongs (e.g., nationality, ethnicity, gender), and still others refer to the person's roles or relationships (e.g., father, employee, girlfriend). Sometimes these three components of the self are referred to as personal, collective, and relational selves, respectively.

Importantly, however, the self-concept is not merely a list of disconnected attributes or labels, but a structured set of beliefs. Certain attributes may be especially central to a person's self-concept but incidental to someone else's. A person's gender, or their physical appearance, or their toughness, or their ethnic group membership may be a core, defining property of their identity, for example, all other properties being secondary. In addition, the attributes within a person's self-concept are interconnected to varying degrees, and in ways that may be highly

163

distinctive for each person. In one woman's self-concept, for example, female gender may be prominently associated with traits of modesty and self-control, so that she feels most feminine when exercising self-restraint, whereas for another woman, for whom being female is an equally important aspect of self, femininity may be associated with spontaneity and seductiveness. In short, people can represent their self-knowledge in quite unique and personally revealing ways.

An enormous amount of research within personality psychology has gone into studying the self, and it is well beyond the scope of this introductory textbook to discuss most of it. However, two topics are perhaps particularly interesting and important. One refers to how we evaluate our self-concept (self-esteem) and the other to how complicated this concept is (self-complexity).

Self-esteem

Self-esteem is a concept that has successfully made the jump from the psychological literature into everyday speech, where it has thrived. People can often be heard to explain one another's behaviour in terms of the concept, and low self-esteem is commonly invoked as an explanation of everything from eating disorders to academic under-achievement. In essence, self-esteem refers to the person's overall or 'global' evaluation of their self-concept: whether they believe that their self, as they conceptualize it, is overall a good one or a not-so-good one. To have high self-esteem, then, implies that you are satisfied with and proud of the attributes that you believe yourself to possess.

When it is put this way it seems obvious that high self-esteem is a good thing. Thinking highly of oneself surely feels better than the opposite, and we would expect people who are confident in themselves to be more secure and interpersonally warm, and less prone to act in self-defeating or antisocial ways. Many people have taken the next step and argued that we should aim to promote and increase self-esteem. In the 1980s, in California, a state government task force was founded to raise self-esteem, in the hope that social pathologies as varied as teen pregnancy, crime, and poor school performance might be reduced as a result, and since then numerous organizations have advanced similar agendas. Over the past 30 years or so, for example, parents and teachers have increasingly been instructed to enhance children's self-esteem by frequent praise and by cushioning them from potentially hurtful feedback on their academic performance. Indeed, there is evidence that a cultural shift has taken place, at least in some parts of the Western world, and that self-esteem levels have been rising. Twenge and Campbell (2001) investigated the mean scores on popular self-esteem tests for American undergraduate students assessed between the 1960s and the 1990s and found that these scores have been steadily rising. At least within this population, it would seem that the prayers of the self-esteem movement are being answered and people are becoming more positive about themselves.

Recently, however, psychologists have begun to take a more critical view of self-esteem. First, they note that apparent rises in self-esteem over the past decades do not seem to have produced reductions in problem behaviours in which low self-esteem was implicated. Indeed, on many social indicators, the problems have become worse over this period. In the period covered by Twenge and Campbell's analysis, for example, rates of depression, anxiety, adolescent crime, and teen pregnancy rose, while scores on tests of educational attainment dropped. Second, evidence emerged that far from being a universal human motive, the desire for high self-esteem was difficult to establish in some cultures, such as Japan (e.g., Heine, Lehman, Markus, & Kitayama, 1999). Third, and most importantly, a body of personality and social psychology research began to challenge the causal role that self-esteem has often been assumed to play in positive behaviour. That is, self-esteem has often been understood as a psychological phenomenon that is responsible for desirable outcomes, and if it does not have such a causal role in bringing about positive outcomes then it makes little sense to raise it.

Research on this important question was reviewed by Baumeister, Campbell, Krueger, and Vohs in 2003. They concluded that although self-esteem has rather modest positive correlations with academic performance in school, there is little or no evidence that self-esteem is causally responsible for better performance and more evidence that it results from school performance. Efforts to raise self-esteem tend to produce no lasting improvement in performance. Similarly, there is little evidence that self-esteem boosts work performance. People with high self-esteem tend to see themselves as having high levels of interpersonal skill and popularity, but this view is not supported by other people's impressions of their social skills, and in some conditions, specifically when they are threatened with a loss of face, high self-esteem people are rated less likeable than low self-esteem people. According to Baumeister and colleagues (2003) there is some evidence that low self-esteem is weakly associated with delinquency, but high self-esteem people are no less likely to be aggressive than others and raising self-esteem does not lead to reductions in aggression for perpetrators of domestic violence. High self-esteem is not associated with a lower risk of alcohol and drug use, and may be linked to risky sexual behaviour. There is little evidence that it plays a significant causal role in physical health. The only desirable things with which high self-esteem is causally associated, claim Baumeister and colleagues, are positive mood and a tendency to speak up more assertively in groups.

Baumeister and colleagues' review was quite provocative in challenging established wisdom on the benefits of high self-esteem. It also seems to have been a little over-stated. For example, self-esteem does appear to have additional benefits besides those they reviewed, such as reducing vulnerability to depression (Sowislo & Orth, 2013). In addition, there is now good evidence from longitudinal research that self-esteem is a cause of some important life outcomes – in particular levels of happiness and relationship and job satisfaction, but not health or occupational status to any significant degree – rather than merely being a consequence or side-effect of these outcomes (Orth, Robins, & Widaman, 2012). However, even if it has some positive ramifications, it is clear that self-esteem is not the cure of all social and personal ills that its advocates have sometimes claimed it to be, and that it is more associated with feeling good than with behaving successfully or well.

What might account for the mixed implications of self-esteem? Several possibilities have been proposed. One possibility is that high self-esteem is beneficial when it is stable, but not when it is fragile. Kernis, Cornell, Sun, Berry, and Harlow (1993) have argued that some people with high self-esteem have a vulnerable sense of self-worth, which fluctuates in response to everyday hassles, problems, and self-doubts. For example, holding overall level of self-esteem constant, people with less stable self-esteem tend to report lower levels of well-being (Paradise & Kernis, 2002). Another explanation for the mixed implications of self-esteem is that some people who report high levels of self-esteem on questionnaires ('explicit' self-esteem) in fact have low levels of self-esteem at a less conscious or 'implicit' level. Implicit self-esteem can be assessed using an experimental procedure that examines how readily people associate themselves with desirable and undesirable stimuli (Greenwald & Farnham, 2000), and interestingly it does not correlate strongly with explicit self-esteem. People who have high explicit but low implicit self-esteem have been said to have 'defensive' self-esteem (Jordan, Spencer, Zanna, Hoshino-Browne, & Correll, 2003), because they are prone to respond more defensively than people with secure high self-esteem. Such people also appear to be high in 'narcissism', a complex trait involving arrogance, a sense of superiority and entitlement, and an exaggerated sensitivity to criticism. Narcissists tend to be particularly likely to react aggressively when their self-esteem is threatened by an insult (Bushman & Baumeister, 1998).

Self-esteem is obviously more complicated than it first appears. It does not seem to be an entirely desirable trait because it has two faces: one healthy and solid, the other unhealthily sensitive to perceived threats. It may be that high self-esteem *is* desirable, but only when it is also stable and held both explicitly and implicitly.

Self-complexity

Self-esteem refers to the person's overall *evaluation* of his or her self, but we can also ask about how, independent of its evaluation, the person's self-concept is organized or *structured*. Some personality psychologists have studied the implications of having a more or less complex self-concept. **Self-complexity** has been conceptualized and measured in several different ways, but one influential definition is 'having more self-aspects and maintaining greater distinction among self-aspects' (Linville, 1987, p. 664), where a self-aspect refers to a role or setting that defines the self (e.g., me-at-work, me-as-a-student, me-as-a-daughter). By this definition, people who report a greater number of self-aspects, and who describe these self-aspects in ways that do not overlap very much, have a more complex representation of self.

Linville, who first presented the concept, proposed that high self-complexity is beneficial because it should buffer the person against stressful events. When these events happen to someone with a complex self they may negatively affect one of the person's self-aspects, but the person has numerous other self-aspects and these should remain largely unaffected if they do not overlap. A person's self-as-student aspect may suffer in response to a bad mark on an exam, but if that person has numerous additional, unrelated self-aspects, any distress the person experiences will be confined to the one aspect. If the person's identity is almost completely wrapped up in being a student, on the other hand, and her few other self-aspects are closely related to this self-aspect (e.g., being 'smart' is an important trait for how she sees herself as a worker and family member), then the bad mark's effects should spill over to make the person generally miserable. In short, having a self that is low in complexity is like putting all one's (self-knowledge) eggs into one (cognitive) basket.

Linville's research (e.g., 1987) supported her argument that greater self-complexity buffers people against extreme emotional responses to stress, and some other studies have agreed. For example, Smith and Cohen (1993) found that people who mentally separated their romantic self-aspect from other self-aspects responded less negatively to relationship break-ups than those who did not. However, findings such as these have not been consistently obtained in other research (Rafaeli-Mor & Steinberg, 2002). Many studies have failed to find evidence that greater self-complexity reduces the negative impact of unpleasant events, and there is, instead, more evidence that it reduces the positive impact of pleasant events (i.e., the consequences of good news for one self-aspect do not spill over into self-aspects that are unrelated to it). This finding suggests that self-complexity may itself have complex and mixed implications.

This conclusion is also drawn by a number of researchers who argue that having a self composed of unrelated, non-overlapping aspects might not be a good thing. Rather than being complex, it might also be described as fragmented, disunited, conflicted, divided, con-fused, diffuse, or incoherent, characteristics that might seem pathological rather than healthy (Donaghue, Robins, Roberts, & John, 1993). For example, Campbell (1990) argued that it is healthy for people to have 'self-concept clarity', namely a self that the person can describe confidently and clearly and that is internally coherent, in the sense of not containing attributes that are contradictory. Clarity in this sense refers to an integrated rather than differentiated self, and there is some evidence that it is positively associated with psychological health and well-being. Some researchers have found that self-complexity is associated with higher levels of depression, consistent with this position (Woolfolk, Novalany, Gara, Allen, & Polino, 1995). The overall picture, then, is rather similar to the one that self-esteem presents. Having a more complex and differentiated self, like having a more positive self-evaluation, may not always be desirable, if this complexity involves a lack of integration or clarity in the self-concept.

Conclusions

In this chapter we have reviewed a variety of cognitive concepts that have been employed within personality psychology. All of them – personal constructs, attributional styles, coping strategies, and self-conceptions – refer to distinctive kinds of mental process that are involved in making sense of our world and acting competently within it. These cognitive concepts are theoretically important in that although they provide ways to describe individual differences in personality, they also offer explanations of personality in terms of the mental processes or mechanisms that generate individual differences in emotion and behaviour. These expla-nations are notably different from those we reviewed in Chapters 4, 5 and 6. They explain individuals in psychological rather than biological terms, and in terms of generally conscious cognitive mechanisms rather than generally unconscious motivations. Emphasizing the cognitive underpinnings of personality like this is theoretically and practically important because it has clear implications for intervention. If someone is engaging in ineffective coping strategies, has inflexible personal constructs or explains events in self-defeating ways, we can in principle improve their life by altering these cognitions. Altering cognitions is something that humans do rather well, and have a wide variety of methods at their disposal. Education is a prime example. In theory, it should be possible to adapt methods such as these to the correction of maladaptive ways of thinking. In short, the cognitive approach to personality implies an optimistic view of the possibility of changing people's personality, and treating their psychological disturbances.

Chapter summary

- The cognitive approach to personality differs from others in emphasizing the ways in which people actively make sense of themselves and their worlds. It explains individual differences in terms of cognitions such as beliefs, concepts, attitudes, explanations, and abilities.
- The cognitive approach arose in part out of a rebellion against the passive and deterministic view of human nature in behaviourist theory, and also resonates with some aspects of humanistic personality theories. Social learning and social-cognitive theories also introduced cognitive concepts into the study of personality.
- There is no single cognitive theory of personality, only a number of concepts that have inspired active programmes of research.
- 'Personal constructs' are cognitive structures that people use to interpret, perceive, or 'construe' the world. They are bipolar – composed of one attribute and a contrasting attribute (e.g., warm vs. cold) – and each individual has a unique, subjective repertoire of them. According to personal construct theory, our main motivation is to grasp and anticipate events in the world accurately, like scientists.
- 'Attributions' are explanations that people give for events. An event may be attributed to causes that differ in several ways. How people habitually explain events is their 'attributional [or explanatory] style'. People who typically attribute negative events to causes that are internal to themselves, lasting and broad in their implications (i.e., pessimists) are vulnerable to a variety of negative outcomes.
- 'Coping strategies' are ways of dealing with adversity, implemented when events are judged to be stressful. Different strategies are associated with better and worse coping with particular kinds of stressors.
- The self is a cognition: a mental representation of what the person is like. Self-esteem and self-complexity are ways in which these representations differ between people: how positively the self is evaluated and how many distinct aspects compose it. Both are associated with important life outcomes in interesting ways: self-esteem, for example, is not the recipe for unbridled happiness and success that it is sometimes claimed to be.

Further reading

Baumeister, R. F., Campbell, J. D., Krueger, J. I., & Vohs, K. D. (2003). Does high self-esteem cause better performance, interpersonal success, happiness, or healthier lifestyles? *Psychological Science in the Public Interest, 4*, 1–44.

Baumeister and colleagues challenge the widespread belief that self-esteem is an entirely desirable quality that social institutions should make sure to raise. They review evidence showing that self-esteem often does not contribute to positive outcomes, and that in some cases it is associated with negative ones.

Buchanan, G. M., & Seligman, M. E. P. (Eds.) (1995). *Explanatory style*. Hillsdale, NJ: Erlbaum.

This edited collection shows the wide range of topics that explanatory style can illuminate and reviews a substantial body of research on this cognitive approach to personality.

Butt, T., & Burr, V. (2005). *An invitation to personal construct psychology* (2nd ed.). New York: Wiley.

This is an accessible introduction to Kelly's personal construct psychology, with plenty of illuminating examples of this distinctive approach.

Carver, C. S., & Connor-Smith, J. T. (2010). Personality and coping. *Annual Review of Psychology, 61*, 679–704.

Carver and Connor-Smith present an excellent review of the coping literature and how Big Five traits are associated with the use of different strategies, and how these strategies and traits jointly influence physical and mental health.

Kernis, M. H. (Ed.) (2013). *Self-esteem issues and answers: A sourcebook of current perspectives*. London: Psychology Press.

This resource contains more than 50 contributions on controversies associated with the measurement, conceptualization, and consequences of self-esteem.

Section 3
Applying Personality

Personality Change and Development

Learning objectives

- To comprehend the extent to which personality traits are stable over time and the factors that contribute to this stability.
- To understand the extent of personality change and the factors that contribute to it.
- To understand the different senses of stability and change: rank-order and mean-level.
- To understand how personality develops out of childhood temperament and the stages that development follows.
- To recognize the broader implications of personality change and stability and of our beliefs about them.

The first of four chapters on applied issues in personality psychology, this chapter investigates the important question of how stable (or changeable) personality is, and how it develops from childhood. Evidence for high levels of stability in adult personality is discussed along with some of the factors that contribute to it. Equally strong evidence that the average levels of personality traits change with age is then laid out. Possible causes of these changes are discussed, including those that involve broad changes in society and culture. The chapter next reviews the ways in which child temperament develops into adult personality, and one prominent theory of the stages through which personality development proceeds. We conclude with a discussion of why the issue of change versus stability matters, pondering on some of the possible costs of believing personality to be fixed.

You are 4 years old. Your bladder control is not yet perfect. You think dinosaurs and trains are the coolest things, or play with dolls whose waists are improbably thin. You have not discovered irony or sarcasm. Your repertoire of rude words is tiny, and focused on bottoms. When you stand straight up your eyes are at the level of your parents' hips.

A researcher comes to your preschool and leads you into a room that is furnished with a table, a chair, a small bell, and a mirror. She sits you down at the table and shows you first one marshmallow and then two. She asks you which of these alternatives you prefer. You are too young to think that this is a stupid question, and say you would prefer to have two. She then says to you that she has to leave the room, but if you wait until she comes back you can have the two marshmallows. If you don't want to wait, she says, you can ring the bell and bring her back any time you want to, but if you do you only get one marshmallow. She leaves the sugary alternatives in front of you on the table and exits the room. In an act of treachery that would shock your trusting and innocent little mind, she then retreats behind the one-way mirror and times how long you withstand this torture. If you have not broken your resolve in 20 minutes she returns to the room. The average child gives up and rings the bell after eight and a half excruciating minutes.

This experiment was conducted by Shoda, Mischel, and Peake (1990), who did an innovative thing. Not content to simply observe how long or by what means children delayed gratification, they followed up their experimental participants 11 or 14 years later, assessing their personality and their academic aptitude. Length of delay at 4 years of age correlated with parental ratings of mid- to late-adolescents' planfulness, thinking ahead, using and responding to reason, tolerating stress, and being able to delay gratification. It was also correlated with standardized tests of verbal and quantitative reasoning that play a major role in college admissions in the USA, where the experiment was conducted. These correlations were substantial, averaging about .4: a child who delayed longer than average was more than twice as likely as one who didn't to be above average on these personality and academic strengths as an adolescent.

These results may surprise you, and they certainly surprised many psychologists. People often think of children as malleable creatures who undergo so many transformations over the course of development that little stability should be apparent across the 14-year gulf separating early childhood from late adolescence. Moreover, the observed correlations may *under-estimate* the real level of stability, given that the experiment represents a single observation of the children's delay tendencies. As we know from the great trait controversy (see Chapter 2), behavioural prediction improves when multiple observations, taken in different contexts and at different times, are aggregated together. Isn't it remarkable how much the adolescents' personality was foretold by one highly peculiar childhood experience?

Maybe not. Almost by definition personality is relatively stable and enduring, a source of personal continuity and predictability through time. However, this 'relatively' obscures a host of questions. Just *how* stable is personality? Is it less stable during some stages of life, such as childhood, than at others? Is there an age at which it is essentially fixed or 'set in plaster', a metaphor employed by the famous psychologist William James, who gave 30 as the answer? Even if personalities don't *tend* to change over time, does that mean that they *can't* change? To the extent that personality is stable, does this stability reflect a kind of constant momentum that traits have or a continuous process of stabilization by the person's social environment and life choices? To the extent that personality changes, what factors promote or trigger change? Does personality have the same structure in children and adults, or does the very nature of personality change? How does personality develop? This chapter will try to provide some answers to these important questions.

The stability of personality

To determine the stability of personality, researchers must conduct longitudinal studies like Shoda et al.'s (1990), in which the same people are tracked over significant periods of time. Needless to say these studies are costly and difficult to carry out, and they demand a great deal of delay of gratification on the part of researchers. University promotion committees are also generally unimpressed when scientists tell them that they expect to publish some fascinating and important findings in ten years, when the study is complete. Nevertheless, a number of longitudinal studies of personality have been conducted in recent years, often covering spans as long as 20 years. Typically they administer the same personality measure at the beginning and end of the time span and correlate participants' scores on the two occasions. These 'retest correlations' represent the degrees to which participants retain the same position relative to the other participants on the trait in question. If all participants hold the identical rank-order from the beginning to the end of the study then the correlation is perfect.

Many longitudinal studies of adult personality have used the Big Five traits reviewed in Chapter 2. Their findings have been quite consistent. Over a period of almost 20 years, the five factors all show retest correlations of about .65 (Costa & McCrae, 1994a). If you score above average on a particular trait at 30, that is, you have roughly an 83% likelihood of being above average when you turn 50. This likelihood is almost five times as great as someone who at 30 scores below average. This is surely quite impressive evidence for the stability of personality, especially as the retest correlations are probably under-estimates once again. All personality measures are subject to measurement error – random influences such as variations in mood states and attentiveness that cause a person's scores to fluctuate even over short periods – and this error reduces or 'attenuates' their ability to correlate with other measures (or with themselves years later in longitudinal studies). When measurement error is statistically removed, the 'disattenuated' correlations (i.e., estimated correlations had the trait in question been measured perfectly) rise even higher. In short, adult personality appears to be remarkably stable.

Is personality equally stable prior to adulthood, however? The evidence suggests that it isn't. Studies that track high-school-age adolescents or young adults tend to report lower retest correlations than those that follow people beginning in middle age, even when the former studies have shorter durations. These studies seem to demonstrate somewhat less stability in the personalities of people in their teens and 20s than in those in middle and old age. Costa and McCrae (1994b) conclude that 'by age 30, personality is essentially fixed' (p. 146). Although there is nothing magical about this age – you won't turn into a pumpkin on your 30th birthday – it does seem to be true that personality traits are approaching their maximum level of stability during the early-to-mid-adult years (Roberts & DelVecchio, 2000).

Sources of stability

If personality is indeed more or less fixed by early-to-mid adulthood, why is this so? One possibility, based on William James' metaphor, is that personality 'sets like plaster' at a certain time of life, remaining constant thereafter. Or to use a different metaphor, personalities moving through time, like objects moving through space, have their own momentums, carried by a steady internal force in a constant direction. These metaphors imply that in adulthood personality is intrinsically stable.

Although this way of thinking about the continuity of adult personality is pleasantly straightforward, other possibilities exist, captured by quite different metaphors. Consider water moving along a channel or a ball rolling down a groove. In both of these images, something moves in a consistent and predictable direction. However, the water and the ball do this not because it is in their intrinsic natures to be consistent and predictable, but because some external forces constrain or direct them. The channel prevents the water from flowing in different directions, despite its intrinsic capacity to do so, and the physical forces that the groove imparts on the rolling ball compel it to continue following the groove. If someone dug another channel that branched off from the main one, the water might begin to flow down this new one instead, and if the groove became shallower the ball might roll over its edge to freedom. Is it possible that the stability of personality reflects some sort of channelling process?

Maybe so. After all, people tend to inhabit environments that are quite stable over time, living under the same or similar physical and economic conditions and interacting with the same or similar people. Continuities in their personalities might therefore simply reflect continuities in the environmental influences that bear on them. In an intriguing longitudinal study of married couples, for instance, Caspi and Herbener (1990) found that people who married more similar partners showed greater stability in their personalities over the ten-year period than people who married less similar partners. By this account, then, personality stability might be at least partially shaped by the environments – or channels – in which our behaviour is expressed. Interestingly, this might help to explain the apparent increase in the stability of personality over the course of adulthood. People tend to undergo more frequent major life events and transitions in youth and early adulthood than in later adulthood – entering the workforce and long-term relationships, becoming parents, moving house, and so on – so we might expect their personalities to be more stable later in life.

Although this environmental channelling account of personality stability has some plausibility, there has been little research to establish its validity and it faces a major conceptual problem. Environments and personalities may both tend to be stable during the adult years, but can we confidently infer that the stability of the former *causes* the stability of the latter? Isn't the opposite inference equally plausible? That is, one reason why environments tend to remain stable is that people select environmental niches that suit them and express their basic dispositions. Extraverts surround themselves with friends, people high in Conscientiousness gravitate to demanding work-roles. People also elicit reactions from the environment according to their dispositions: timid people tend to be dominated by others and socially dominant people have leadership positions thrust upon them. In short, it is very risky to suppose that environmental channelling is directly responsible for the stability of personality because to some degree people's dispositions determine which channels they enter.

If environmental channelling isn't an entirely convincing account of personality continuity – although it is surely part of the explanation – other kinds of explanation are needed. Besides the intrinsic 'set like plaster' account, which might reflect genetic and maturational influences, a couple of other proposals have been put forward. One is that over the course of life people's self-perceptions tend to become crystallized (Glenn, 1980). Several implications flow from this simple claim. First, older adults should tend to open themselves to fewer new experiences that might generate personality change, because of a fixed sense of how they are and how they should live. That is, a crystallized sense of self may make people more likely to remain in their channel, or to have a more restricted view of it. By doing so, they expose themselves to familiar experiences that further reinforce the stability of their dispositions. Second, older adults' more fixed sense of self may lead them to ignore evidence of personal change that challenges their self-perceptions. This discounting of self-discrepant information may even bias people's responses to self-report personality questionnaires to minimize actual change, so that the apparent stability of personality in longitudinal studies might be exaggerated.

This explanation of the stability of personality is an important one. It suggests that personality in adulthood might be relatively stable not simply because of environmental channelling or the intrinsic fixedness of personality, but because of the basic conservatism of our ways of thinking, especially about ourselves. Our sense of who we are and what we are like tends to stabilize with age, and constrains and stabilizes the expression of our dispositions to be consistent with it. By implication, personality itself may not be intrinsically or necessarily stable in adulthood, but tends to be consistent for reasons that *are* intrinsic to human psychology, namely the self-stabilizing processes of the self-concept. The factors contributing to the continuity of personality are evidently many and complicated.

Personality change

The research that we have reviewed to this point paints a picture of continuity of the personality, particularly in middle and later adulthood, and offers several explanations for this apparent stability. The evidence for stability seems quite overwhelming. However, 'stability' turns out to be a less straightforward concept than you might imagine, and it comes in different varieties. Retest correlations reflect what is called '**rank-order stability**': they are high to the extent that people tend to maintain the same rank relative to their peers over time, so that people who rank high at the beginning of a longitudinal study still rank high at the end. However, a ranking is a *relative* ordering, referring to how people place relative to others. It is possible that people's ranks on a personality trait might be stable from one time to another, but the group's *absolute* level on the trait might change. The same people might tend to be high and low relative to their peers, but their peers might tend to undergo a shift.

As it turns out, the same studies that have found substantial rank-order stability in adult personality have also obtained evidence of significant changes in the average levels of Big Five traits. Although these changes are not huge, they complicate the picture of apparent stability that retest correlations give us, and point to typical patterns of maturational change over the course of adulthood. A particularly important study of mean-level personality change was conducted by Srivastava, John, Gosling, and Potter (2003), whose results challenged not only the 'hard plaster' view of personality – in which it is fixed at 30 – but also the 'soft plaster' view that the pace of personality change invariably slows after 30. They found that Conscientiousness rose from age 21 to 30 and continued to rise at a slower rate thereafter, but Agreeableness actually rose faster after 30 than before. Similarly, Neuroticism declined at an even rate over the adult life course (only for women), Openness declined more steeply after 30 than before. One way to summarize these developmental trajectories is to say that people tend to become more self-controlled and prudent, more interpersonally warm, less emotionally volatile, and less open to new experiences and ways of thinking. Alternatively, and more economically, one could say that with increased age people tend to have a narrower emotional range – less positive *and* negative affect – and become more socialized. More economically still, but perhaps a little uncharitably, one could say people become duller. However we look at it, though, the clear message is that some personality change – however small and gradual it may be – is normal, even during adulthood.

In addition to this work on normal, absolute changes in personality over the life-course, research on the rank-order stability of personality also reveals evidence of change. Although this research demonstrates that in adulthood broad personality traits tend to be quite stable, even in the late adult years retest correlations do not approach perfection (i.e., 1.0). Even at this time of life, a small but significant fraction of people undergo some amount of personality change. If nothing else, this shows that personality change in adulthood is entirely possible, even if it is not large or common.

This conclusion is reinforced when we look at the rank-order stability of personality prior to adulthood. In a review of 152 longitudinal studies, Roberts and DelVecchio (2000) found that retest correlations for studies of adults aged between 30 and 73 averaged about .67. The average for young adults aged 18 to 29 was about .57, and the average for children and adolescents (aged 3 to 17) was about .45. Among infants and toddlers (aged 0 to 2) the average was only .31. (All of these correlations were adjusted to refer to a retest duration of about seven years.) As you can see, personality is less and less stable the closer we get to the beginning of life, to the point that traits measured in early childhood generally do not allow confident predictions about personality in middle childhood, let alone in adulthood. Personality traits assessed at age 2 should correlate about .31 with the same traits assessed at age 9, and *this* assessment should correlate about .45 with an assessment at age 16. The stability of traits over long periods will therefore be progressively diluted. Wordsworth wrote that 'the child is father of the man', implying that adults' dispositions can be extrapolated from their childhood tendencies, but the research evidence does not bear it out strongly. This should be a comfort to parents of bratty or difficult children, and challenge the complacency of parents of little angels. Perhaps it should also challenge our willingness to extrapolate backwards from how we or others are as adults to how we were, or 'must have been', as children. The scientific study of personality suggests that such continuities may often be exaggerated or imaginary.

Personality change, both absolute and relative to one's peers (i.e., rank-order instability), seems to be quite possible. If this is the case, what might account for it? One possible influence on personality change might be genes. Although genes are often thought of only as sources of stability, they could conceivably produce distinct patterns of personality change over time, just as they may partly control the timing of pubertal changes. However, research has found little evidence for genetic influences on personality change, suggesting that change must be either random or primarily driven by environmental influences.

Several kinds of environmental influence may be responsible for changes in personality. One kind that perhaps operates most in childhood involves other people's direct attempts to change the individual's personality characteristics. A great deal of socialization and parenting can be understood in these terms, and there is considerable evidence that childhood personality can be responsive to them. For example, Kagan (1994) found that toddlers with inhibited temperament who subsequently became less inhibited had parents who exposed them to novel situations rather than being overly protective. Children whose parents allowed them to avoid the novelty that distressed them tended to remain inhibited.

Another kind of environmental influence that can account for personality change is stressful life experience. Research suggests that life stress is associated with reduced stability of the personality, and that major life transitions and changes can produce lasting reductions in self-esteem (Harter, 1993) and increases in need for intimacy (Franz, 1994). Consistent with our metaphor of the environmental channelling of personality, disruptions in the environment can produce instability and personality change.

A third kind of environmental influence can be found in the changing social roles that people occupy over the course of life. The adjustments that people make to the demands and expectations of new social positions can yield lasting changes in traits, motives, and personal preoccupations. For example, Helson, Mitchell, and Moane (1984) tracked women from their university years through their late 20s and found that those who became mothers tended to show increases in responsibility, self-control, and femininity, and decreases in self-acceptance and sociability. Women who had not become mothers did not change in this manner, suggesting that the experience of motherhood was responsible for it. The same research group found that non-mothers tend to show greater increases in independence than mothers. In another longitudinal study of male managers (Howard & Bray, 1988), those who were more successful showed a reduction in nurturance from their 20s to their 40s, whereas less successful managers showed a small increase. These various changes can be reasonably interpreted as responses to changing life challenges and opportunities.

Environmental influences on personality change can be seen in studies of adolescents and young adults. Personality change is often seen as something that occurs gradually over periods of decades, but the years of 'emerging adulthood' are witness to important shifts in personality that reflect and respond to the transitional experiences of that stage of life. On average, young people become more agreeable and conscientious and less neurotic during the transition to adulthood (Soto, John, Gosling, & Potter, 2011). Whether these positive changes occur for particular young people, however, may depend on how well they navigate the worlds of work and love. A longitudinal study by Roberts and colleagues (2003), for example, followed young adults from age 18 to 26. They found that those study participants who had more successful work experiences showed greater increases in self-confidence and sociability and greater decreases in anxiousness. A similar study by Neyer and Lehnart (2007), which followed people from their mid-20s to their early 30s, showed that the transition to their first intimate partner relationship was associated with lasting reductions in Neuroticism and shyness, and increases in Extraversion and self-esteem. Transitional experiences also trigger positive personality change at the very beginning of adulthood and in the university years. Bleidorn (2012) found that being confronted with new educational challenges during the school to adulthood transition was associated with a clear growth in Conscientiousness. And Zimmerman and Neyer (2013) found that university students who embarked on international sojourns increased in Agreeableness and Openness to Experience compared to their peers who stayed home. Thus, life experiences and new social roles can stimulate personality change and lead some people's trajectories of change to be different from others'.

The idea that personality can change in response to changing social circumstances is consistent with some fascinating work on changes in personality over the course of recent history. Just as changing social roles can bring about personality change within an individual's life, changing societal or cultural conditions appear to bring about changes in the average personality of people who grow up in different generations (different 'birth cohorts' is the preferred term). Jean Twenge and her colleagues have carried out a series of studies – using a formidable-sounding technique called 'cross-temporal meta-analysis' – that allows them to examine mean scores on personality tests for young people (usually American undergraduates) who completed these tests in many studies spanning several decades. They find striking changes in mean levels of a variety of personality traits from the 1960s to today. For example, young people at the start of the 21st century reported considerably higher average levels of self-esteem and Extraversion than they did 40 years ago (Twenge, 2001b; Twenge & Campbell, 2001). Young women became more assertive over this period (Twenge, 2001a), and showed steady increases in other stereotypically masculine traits so that gender differences in personality tended to decrease (Twenge, 1997).

Other changes were arguably less positive: samples of young people assessed in the early 1990s reported substantially higher levels of anxiety and Neuroticism than those assessed 40 years previously (Twenge, 2000), and recent samples were more likely to report that their lives were controlled by outside forces (i.e., external locus of control) rather than by internal factors such as their personal desires and abilities (Twenge, Zhang, & Im, 2004). Twenge has interpreted some of these changes in generational terms, seeing them as evidence that young people now ('Generation Me') tend to be more narcissistic and egotistical than in previous generations. This interpretation has been controversial, with some researchers (Trzesniewski & Donnellan, 2010) finding few meaningful changes in these traits, and others suggesting that cohort changes in personality have generally been positive. For example, Smits and colleagues (2011) found that on average, Dutch first-year university students became more agreeable, conscientious and extraverted, and less neurotic, from 1982 to 2007. However we interpret such changes, they indicate that mean-level personality change occurs over historical time, presumably in ways that reflect social and cultural changes. In the last half century, for example, Western societies have tended to place increasing emphasis on individual self-assertion and the feminist movement has contributed to encouraging this, especially in women. Social conditions have changed, and our personalities have changed with them.

These three forms of environmental influence laid out here – socialization, stressful life events, and changes in social roles or conditions – offer a way to think about and account for some of the rank-order instability and absolute changes in personality that we discussed earlier. It is also possible that some personality change is at least partially self-initiated rather than merely responding to environment influences. Many people report undergoing a relatively sudden change, akin to a conversion experience, in which they believed their personality to be transformed by a new insight or sense of meaning. Although these experiences often appear to be provoked by a particular event, and by a pre-existing state of emotional distress, it would be a mistake to see them merely as passive reactions to external conditions, or to doubt their validity too strenuously. They may indeed be perfectly real and lasting, however rare: psychotherapists certainly hope so! It is clearly possible for personalities to change, even in adulthood, and just as we now recognize the forces that hold them steady, we are also beginning to understand the sources of instability.

ILLUSTRATIVE STUDY

How do personality traits change over time?

American psychologists Brent Roberts and colleagues (Roberts, Walton, & Viechtbauer, 2006) set out to describe patterns of **mean-level change** in major personality traits. They employed a statistical methodology known as 'meta-analysis', which allows researchers to combine the findings of existing studies in a rigorous, quantitative fashion. They thoroughly combed the literature for studies that reported mean-level change information, and managed to locate 92 of them. They then carefully read the studies to extract information about the extent of change observed in different age ranges for six personality traits (i.e., essentially the Big Five but with Extraversion divided into 'social vitality' and 'social dominance' facets).

The findings of this meta-analysis revealed systematic patterns of change from adolescence to old age. Levels of Conscientiousness, social dominance, and emotional stability tend to increase with age, although most strongly in young adulthood. Levels of Agreeableness increase only in old age. Levels of Openness to Experience and social vitality tend to rise in adolescence, only to fall again in later life. These findings add to the growing evidence that personality traits are malleable and follow predictable trajectories over time. This evidence is especially noteworthy because – thanks to meta-analysis – it is based on a diverse assortment of studies with an enormous combined sample of 50,120 participants.

181

Temperament and personality

At this point you should have an appreciation of the ways in which personality both changes over time and remains consistent, and of the factors that influence continuity and change. However, all of these ideas about the trajectory of personality through time assume that personality itself is essentially the same sort of thing throughout the life-span. To be able to say that the average level of Extraversion decreases over the course of adulthood, or that it shows moderate rank-order stability from the teens to the 30s, requires that Extraversion be a meaningful personality trait throughout this period. If this were not the case, comparisons of 'Extraversion' over time would be invalid in a very basic way. So is it true that personality structure – the basic organization of individual differences – is constant through the life-span?

Let's think more about Extraversion, and assume for the minute that it is a valid personality factor from adolescence to senescence. Would the kinds of behaviour that express or exemplify it be the same in a 15-year-old as in a 75-year-old? On the one hand, many behavioural characteristics might well be equally expressive of Extraversion at both ends of this age spectrum, perhaps including talkativeness, number of friends, activity level, and interpersonal dominance. Remember that this does not imply the same absolute levels of these characteristics in extraverted people of each age. On the other hand, there would surely also be age differences in the behavioural manifestations of Extraversion. Teenagers are unlikely to express gregariousness by attending bingo games, or older people to express high energy levels by participating in team sports.

These differences in the behaviours that express traits at different ages can make the task of longitudinal comparison somewhat tricky. However, they do not necessarily cast doubt on a trait's continued reality or its validity as a basis for comparison. For example, if factor analyses of age-relevant behaviours in samples of teenagers reveal a factor that closely resembles one obtained in similar studies of older adults, it would be difficult to deny that the factor corresponds to essentially the same trait at both ages. This would be true even if the specific behaviours that define the factors in the two age groups differ somewhat. What matters is simply that broadly equivalent forms of behaviour define the factors at both times (e.g., the factors both encompass gregariousness, expressed in characteristically adolescent or elderly ways).

The idea that the same dimensions capture variations in personality from adolescence to old age is probably not very controversial to you. But what if we move from adolescence back to infancy and compare babies' personalities with adults'. Do babies even have 'personalities'? It is certainly hard to imagine that systems of personality description like the Big Five can make much sense of infant behaviour. Conscientiousness would not seem to be a promising way to describe differences among little savages who lack consciences, and the relevance of Openness to Experience to creatures whose lives revolve around sucking, sleeping, screaming, and excreting is questionable.

Nevertheless, as any parent will tell you, each infant comes into the world with its own distinctive behavioural style. Far from being, as the English philosopher John Locke imagined, a blank slate ('*tabula rasa*'), waiting for experience to inscribe a distinctive psychological signature on it, a baby has individuality from birth. Some rarely cry, sleep long and with regularity, and reward any face with a smile, while others fuss and scream constantly, sleep without consistency, and cry, turn purple, and grow little horns on their foreheads when they lay eyes on a friendly stranger.

Behavioural tendencies such as these – with the possible exception of horn-growth – are normally thought of as variations of temperament rather than personality. This distinction is usually based on an understanding that temperament is early-appearing, biologically grounded, and primarily related to emotional response. Our earlier question about the continuity of personality structure therefore becomes a matter of determining how temperament in infancy and early childhood is associated with adult personality. Despite appearances, the structure of temperament might map straightforwardly onto the structure of personality. Alternatively, the basic dimensions of temperament might show little correspondence with systems like the Big Five, just as the characteristics on which caterpillars differ are not the same as those that differentiate butterflies. (In a sense babies are, after all, human larvae.)

Numerous researchers have examined the structure of temperament in babies and young children. Their task is importantly different from that of the psychologists who pioneered the analysis of adult personality structure. Because infants and young children cannot rate one another's temperaments or complete self-report questionnaires, researchers must rely on ratings made by adults, usually parents or the researchers themselves. These methodological constraints present challenges, but a great deal of progress has been made in mapping temperament in spite of them. At first blush, some of these maps seem to bear little relationship to the broad adult personality factors that make up the Big Five or Big Three. Temperament researchers have identified dimensions such as distractibility, activity level, sensory sensitivity, attention span, and rhythmicity (i.e., the degree of regularity in the infant's sleeping, eating, and habits). None of these seems to have obvious parallels in adult trait dimensions.

The existence of apparently childhood-specific dimensions suggests that the structure of child temperament may differ substantially from the structure of adult personality. Research presents a more balanced picture. Martin, Wisenbaker, and Huttunen (1994) reviewed several factor-analytic studies of child temperament and found that seven dimensions emerged repeatedly. These, and the adult personality factors with which they appear to be associated, are presented in Table 8.1.

Table 8.1 indicates that, despite appearances, the structure of temperament in childhood may be not so very different from the structure of adult personality traits. Three replicated temperament factors are clearly related to single factors of the Big Five, although you should note that Activity Level is only one component of adult Extraversion. Two more temperament factors seem to be related to combinations of Big Five factors. Openness is alone among the Big Five in having no associated temperament dimension. Only biological rhythmicity and threshold seem to have no clearly corresponding adult dimensions. This may be because the variations that they capture – how well established daily cycles are and how sensitive people are to sensory stimuli – are developmentally relevant only to infants. These temperament

Table 8.1 Replicated child temperament factors, behaviours that illustrate them, and associated adult personality factors

Temperament Factor	Illustrative Behaviour	Associated Personality Factor
Activity Level	shows vigorous motor activity	Extraversion
Negative Emotionality	reacts intensely to upsets	Neuroticism
Task Persistence	is attentive and endures frustration	Conscientiousness
Adaptability	adjusts quickly and easily to change	Agreeableness + low Neuroticism
Inhibition	avoids novel situations	low Extraversion + Neuroticism
Biological Rhythmicity	has regular sleeping habits	none
Biological Threshold	is highly sensitive to new foods	none

factors also may not have sufficiently extensive behavioural implications in adulthood to emerge as broad personality dimensions.

A reasonable conclusion to draw from research on the structure of temperament is that it does not differ radically from the structure of adult personality, as represented by broad trait factors. There are differences, to be sure, and the pathways that lead from childhood temperament dimensions to adult personality factors are indistinct at times. For example, we don't know how and when Openness emerges, or whether biological threshold vanishes as a meaningful dimension at some stage of development. However, the structure of individual differences seems to be more stable over the course of development than it is unstable. Generally speaking, similar dimensions endure throughout life, even if, as we saw earlier, they are exemplified by different behaviours at different ages and individuals change where they sit on them over time.

Personality development

So far in this chapter we have focused most of our attention on change and stability in traits, with an emphasis on the broad factors identified by trait psychologists. However, these broad traits might not tell the whole story about personality change, continuity, and development. If you cast your mind back to McAdams' (1995) critique of trait psychology, you will remember that he identified levels of personality description beyond traits. For instance, he identified a level of 'personal concerns', such as motives, values, strivings, developmental issues, and life tasks. Such concerns, he argued, are more tied than traits are to specific contexts, such as particular social roles or stages of life. Consequently, McAdams suggested, the trait level of description might be the level on which the stability of personality is the most evident. Perhaps, then, a fuller picture of personality change and development might come from examining personal concerns. That is, there might be ways of thinking about personality that permit subtle – or even not-so-subtle – changes to be observed even in the face of trait stability.

Relatively little research has been conducted on the stability or change of personal concerns. However, theorists have made a variety of proposals about how such concerns might tend to undergo distinct shifts over the course of the life-span. The best-known of these theorists is Erik Erikson, who proposed that personality development consists of the person's navigation through eight distinct stages of life, each with its defining theme or issue. By this account, personality change is a basic fact of life and continues through the adult years rather than ceasing at age 30 as trait psychologists tend to maintain. Moreover, this change is not simply a gradual process of increase or decrease in certain characteristics, but reflects instead a series of qualitative transformations as the person moves from one stage to another. This is truly a different way of thinking about personality development and change.

Erikson is a romantic and charismatic figure in the history of personality psychology. Born in Germany to Danish parents, he travelled widely as a young man and subsequently moved to the USA, along the way adopting a surname that indicates his sense of self-creation (Erik son of Erik). His professional life was unusually broad, including teaching children, training as a psychoanalyst with Freud's daughter Anna in Vienna, conducting research on Native American children, and writing psychologically informed biographies of historical figures such as Mahatma Gandhi and Martin Luther. Although deeply influenced by psychoanalytic theory, he departed from it by focusing on the entirety of the life cycle and on the social and cultural aspects of psychological development rather than its sexual dimensions. Thus, his account of personality development proposes eight 'psychosocial' stages extending into old age rather than the Freudian stages of 'psychosexual' development that extend no further than childhood.

Erikson's first stage, titled 'basic trust vs. basic mistrust' covers the period of infancy that corresponds to Freud's oral stage. Ideally, in this stage the baby is consistently and sensitively cared for by parenting figures. This produces a fundamental sense of trust that the world is a beneficent place and a capacity for hope. If the baby experiences difficulties in this stage, it may come to see the world as a hostile place and be vulnerable to mental disorder. A different theme is implicated in Erikson's second stage – 'autonomy vs. shame and doubt' – where the toddler ideally develops a sense of mastery of its body and a capacity for independent actions. If its dawning autonomy is suppressed too harshly by adult authorities, however, it can be overcome with shame and self-doubt, and become rigid and over-controlled.

In 'initiative vs. guilt', Erikson's third stage, the child ideally develops a capacity to pursue goals in a purposeful, planful manner, but if its attempts to take initiatives are stifled or punished harshly, it may become inhibited and passive. As the child enters the school years, a different theme of 'industry vs. inferiority' becomes salient. In this fourth stage the child ideally learns a capacity for work and prolonged effort in the service of growing competence. Difficulties during this stage of life leave their mark on the developing personality, making the child feel inferior in comparison to peers. Erikson is best-known for his fifth stage: 'identity vs. identity confusion'. He took the key task of adolescence to be the formation of a sense of being a unique individual with a meaningful place in society. Ideally, the young person gradually develops a coherent sense of personal goals, motives, interests, tastes, and social roles. If the struggle for identity goes badly, the adolescent may develop a sense of emptiness and alienation, or prematurely choose an unexamined identity ('foreclosure'). In young adulthood the developmental theme switches from individual identity to relationships with others. The 'intimacy vs. isolation' stage ideally produces an adult who can love and be loved, but can instead result in someone who is afraid of intimacy and withdraws into loneliness, self-absorption, and shallow relationships.

Erikson described two stages in the second half of the life-span. The organizing theme of mid-life is 'generativity vs. stagnation', where the adult ideally develops a sense of contributing something meaningful to their society or culture. In the absence of this sense of meaningful contribution, the person may come to feel stuck and unfulfilled, even if they have been conventionally successful. Finally, in old age, the eighth theme of 'integrity vs. despair' comes to prominence. Ideally, there is a wise and accepting sense that one's life had meaning, for all its failures and disappointments, but otherwise there is a sense of existential despair and surrender, and a fear of death.

By Erikson's account, these 'eight ages of man' reflect a maturational blueprint or timetable, a series of stages through which people can be expected to progress as they grow older. People negotiate each stage, and the developmental task it represents, with more or less favourable outcomes. Ideally, they lay down solid foundations of basic trust, autonomy, initiative, and so on. However, if they have difficulty navigating a stage's challenges – for reasons that might be specific to an individual's life circumstances or typical of their culture and society, such as particular child-rearing practices – their personalities will be marked by the stage's characteristic weaknesses. Failure to achieve a sense of personal autonomy in early childhood creates a fault-line in the personality that might be cracked open under stress in later life, leaving the person prone to shame and intense self-doubt, as each successive stage builds on those that came before.

The Eriksonian view of personality development is interesting not only because it provides a way of thinking about personality development as a series of stages, but also because it offers a way of thinking differently about personality change. Erikson's stages represent *qualitatively* different ways in which personality can be expressed, involving different themes. As people age and mature, the nature of their concerns and preoccupations change. Most mainstream research on personality, in contrast, focuses on *quantitative* personality change: how levels of personality traits increase or decrease. People can change in both ways: the trait levels may rise and fall, and the kinds of concerns that express these traits may alter as well. Indeed, the same traits are likely to be expressed in quite different ways at different life stages. Neuroticism, for instance, may manifest itself as shame at a lack of bladder control among toddlers, as a sense of inferiority to peers among school-children, as identity confusion among adolescents, as commitment fears among young adults and as a sense of existential meaninglessness among the elderly. Erikson gives us a way to see personality change as a matter of changing subjective concerns rather than only as a matter of changing traits.

To many psychologists the openness of Erikson's approach to personality development, the way it encompasses culture, society, and the life-span, is very attractive. It is a rich and complex account, unlike the economical but static and reductive descriptive grids offered by trait psychology. However, richness and complexity have their price, and this includes the greater difficulty of pinning down and studying Eriksonian concepts. It is harder to rigorously assess people's developmentally-linked preoccupations, reflecting subtle life themes about which they may lack introspective awareness, than it is to assess standard traits with self-report questionnaires. Consequently, less research has been done on personality development from Erikson's perspective than on the stability of trait dimensions, and it has been less validated. Some supporting research has been conducted, however. For example, McAdams, de St. Aubin, and Logan (1993) found that generativity themes were more prominent in the personal strivings and autobiographical scripts of people in middle age than in those of younger and older adults. Other studies (e.g., Stewart, Franz, & Layton, 1988) have found evidence of increased intimacy and generativity concerns, and decreasing identity concerns, over the course of adulthood, again in general support of Erikson's approach. Nevertheless, this approach remains less a body of scientifically validated fact than a fruitful set of concepts for making sense of development and personality change.

How can we reconcile Erikson's portrayal of personality development as constant transformation with the trait psychology picture of considerable stability? The first thing to remember here is that there may not be much conflict to reconcile: the first five of Erikson's eight stages take place in the years over which longitudinal studies show only moderate trait stability. A second consideration is that Erikson's stage theory is more relevant to absolute than to rank-order stability: it is a theory of the normal changes that differentiate the personalities of people of different ages. The same people might tend to have relatively successful resolutions of successive stages (i.e., rank-order stability) even while different themes characterize their personalities at each stage (absolute instability). Indeed, Erikson's notion that resolution of each stage lays a foundation for resolution of the next implies just such rank-order stability: the same people who do well in one stage are likely to do well in the next.

The most important consideration, however, is that Erikson's stage theory and trait psychology operate at different levels of analysis. In McAdams' (1995) terms, the characteristic themes or preoccupations of each stage are level 2 'personal concerns' rather than level 1 traits. Eriksonian themes are more fine-grained, more difficult to identify with particular patterns of behaviour, more subtly qualitative, more contextualized by social experience and time of life. They are the sorts of personality characteristics that seem to be more changeable by nature, more responsive to new life situations, and people's changing sense of self than the broad, basic tendencies embodied by the Big Five. But this does not mean that the two languages of analysis and description – traits and Eriksonian themes – are unrelated. For instance, someone who lacks basic trust would be expected to score low on Agreeableness. Themes of industry surely have something to do with Conscientiousness, as do themes of identity with Openness. Perhaps Erikson's stages give us a way to think about how our basic underlying dispositions are manifested in, and to some extent moulded by, changing patterns of developmentally-specific and socially-shaped lived experience. That's an ugly mouthful to say, but you should say it a couple of times to digest it anyway. Ugly or not, it may come closer to the truth than simply opting for one approach – the stability of traits versus the instability of personal preoccupations – and neglecting the other.

Conclusions: Why do personality, stability and change matter?

This chapter has examined a range of questions about personality change and continuity. These issues are so interesting because they are so central to our worldviews and to the basic assumptions we hold about human nature. You may have noticed that the theories we reviewed in the second part of this book take positions on the malleability of personality. Biological approaches, especially those based on behavioural genetics, tend to emphasize stability, seeing personality development largely as the unfolding of innate behavioural tendencies mediated by brain processes that are beyond conscious control. Psychoanalytic theories tend to take an equally sceptical approach to personality change, but for different reasons. Adult personality is seen as being substantially determined by childhood experiences within the family. In addition, personality is conceptualized as a set of hard-won compromises between desires and defences, and any modification of this balance of opposed forces is resisted by fiercely conservative psychological defences.

In contrast with biological and psychoanalytic approaches, cognitive theories imply that personality is changeable. If personality is made up of ways of perceiving, thinking, and believing, then it should be modifiable by any of the processes by which cognitions change: trial-and-error learning, insight, imitation, education. The behaviourist approach from which cognitive psychology split off was even more consistent with malleability. If behaviour is governed by its consequences, as behaviourists believed, then all it should take for personality to change is for the pattern of rewards and punishments that the person receives to be altered. If these 'reinforcement contingencies' can be changed, by having people expose themselves to different environments or by engineering their environments to respond to them differently, then their dispositions should also change.

None of these theoretical approaches takes absolute positions. Even the strongest advocate of the biological basis of personality might allow that personality can change in response to pharmaceutical treatment – as in the 'cosmetic' personality change some writers have attributed to drugs like Prozac – or that our genetic inheritance dictates patterns of personality change over time. (After all, genes govern the transformations our bodies undergo as we mature, not just how we differ in enduring ways from one another.) Psychoanalysts argue that personality can change after gruelling years of psychoanalytic treatment. Likewise, cognitivists recognize that the cognitive system is conservative, often resisting change by ignoring information that challenges it or assimilating it to established ways of thinking. And behaviourism faltered partly because it had trouble accounting for the resistance of some behaviours to change in response to new patterns of reward and punishment. Nevertheless, the evidence we have considered regarding personality change and stability has definite implications for the personality theories we hold.

People have worldviews, just as theories do. If your worldview is primarily cynical, tragic, or pessimistic, you will probably believe that people don't really change, and that they have an essential nature that is determined once and for all by their early life circumstances, their biology, or their existential predicament. If your worldview is more optimistic, romantic, or otherwise sunny, you will probably have faith in the power of people to change, overcoming obstacles and flaws along the path to self-improvement or fulfilment. The evidence of this chapter is highly relevant to these deep, often unacknowledged ways of looking at the world, and offer some support for both positions. Personality is both resistant to change and capable of it: it shows inertia in some respects, such as the relative stability of fundamental, highly heritable traits, and transformation in others, such as the changing identity themes that Erikson brought to light.

Some interesting research has investigated people's beliefs about personality change and stability. Carol Dweck and her colleagues (e.g., Dweck, 1999; Levy, Plaks, Hong, Chiu, & Dweck, 2001) have studied people's 'person theories', by which they mean core assumptions about human nature. They contrast people whose theories are 'static', implying that human attributes are fixed, as distinct from 'dynamic', implying malleability. They have found that people who hold static views – '**entity theories**' – are more prone to exaggerate differences between groups to which they belong and other groups, and to endorse stereotypic beliefs about people in these groups. They are more likely to attribute group differences to innate factors, to avoid outgroup members, and to be more prejudiced. The implications of entity theories may also extend to how people think about themselves as well as others. Research suggests that entity theorists will be less likely to try to change undesirable aspects of their own behaviour. Perhaps most remarkably, promoting the abstract belief that people are malleable may even help to reduce inter-group conflicts. Halperin and colleagues (2011) showed that inducing Israelis and Palestinians to hold incremental theories of people and groups led them to become more willing to compromise for peace.

All of these findings suggest that apparently abstract, almost philosophical beliefs about human nature have very real implications for how we think and behave as social creatures. If we believe that people are not malleable, even if this belief is a tacit assumption that we barely recognize, we tend to see the social world as composed of fixed entities whose behaviour is driven by enduring internal dispositions. We correspondingly under-estimate the extent to which other people's behaviour – and perhaps our own as well – springs from social influences, the demands of the situation, or mental processes. This seems to be a recipe for an unfortunate lack of empathy and humanity towards those who are different from us.

Of course, even if it is true that holding a static view of personality may have some undesirable social consequences, this view still has some truth to it. With any luck, this chapter has given you a picture of the state of scientific knowledge about the malleability of personality, a picture that doesn't permit any extreme position on the issue. Perhaps the chapter may even lead you to consider your own beliefs about the fixedness of human nature, and their possible implications.

189

Chapter summary

- By definition, personality is at least somewhat stable over time, but how stable it is remains an important research and theoretical question.
- Longitudinal studies suggest high levels of 'rank-order stability' – stability in people's positions on trait dimensions relative to their peers – of personality traits, especially in adulthood. This stability may reflect a variety of genetic and environmental factors, and it increases with age.
- Studies of 'mean-level change' – change in the average level of traits from one age to another – demonstrate that personality is also malleable. Studies reveal predictable trajectories of mean-level change over the adult life-span, as well as changes from one historical period to another.
- Personality develops out of temperament, and there appear to be several meaningful continuities between dimensions of infant and child temperament and adult personality trait factors.
- Personality development cannot be reduced entirely to mean-level change in temperament or personality dimensions. Theorists such as Erikson propose that different stages of life involve different themes and concerns.
- The malleability or fixity of personality matters for psychological theory and practice. It may even matter in everyday thinking: people who believe personality is fixed tend to stereotype others.

Further reading

Dweck, C. S. (1999). *Self-theories: Their role in motivation, personality, and development.* Philadelphia, PA: Psychology Press.
Dweck pioneered the study of people's beliefs about the stability vs. malleability of human attributes, such as intelligence and personality, and this book reviews the many implications of these different 'self-theories'.

Erikson, E. H. (1963). *Childhood and society* (2nd ed.). New York: W. W. Norton.
Erikson's account of personality development is no longer influential or fashionable, but it remains interesting for readers who want an intimate portrait of different stages of life rather than a dry review of empirical studies.

McAdams, D. P., & Olson, B. D. (2010). Personality development: Continuity and change over the life course. *Annual Review of Psychology, 61,* 517–42.
This is a superb review of research on personality change and stability viewed through the lens of McAdams' influential work on levels of personality, from traits to personal narratives.

Roberts, B. W., & Mroczek, D. (2008). Personality trait change in adulthood. *Current Directions in Psychological Science*, *17*, 31–5.
This is a brief and accessible review of the scientific evidence of personality trait change over the adult years.

Shoda, Y., Mischel, W., & Peake, P. K. (1990). Predicting adolescent cognitive and self-regulatory competencies from preschool delay of gratification: Identifying diagnostic conditions. *Developmental Psychology*, *26*, 978–86.
Shoda and colleagues describe some of their work on the remarkable ability of childhood delay of gratification to predict important life outcomes in adolescence and early adulthood.

Soto, C. J., John, O. P., Gosling, S. D., & Potter, J. (2011). Age differences in personality traits from 10 to 65: Big Five domains and facets in a large cross-sectional sample. *Journal of Personality and Social Psychology*, *100*, 330–48.
This is a study of cross-sectional differences in personality traits that updates and elaborates the earlier study by Srivastava et al. (2003) discussed in this chapter.

The Assessment of Personality

Learning objectives

- To appreciate the complexities involved in the assessment of personality.
- To understand psychometric 'validity' and 'reliability', the basic concepts that define the quality of personality measurement.
- To recognize the strengths and weaknesses of alternative forms of personality assessment: interviews, inventories, and projective methods.
- To develop a basic understanding of alternative assessment methods.
- To recognize the difficulties involved in drawing valid inferences from personality test data.

This chapter examines the methods psychologists have developed for measuring individual differences in personality. Desirable psychometric features of assessment methods – the various forms of test validity and reliability – are outlined and a number of popular assessment methods are reviewed. The strengths and weaknesses of interviews, personality inventories, and projective tests are discussed, followed by two interesting but less commonly employed alternative assessment methods. Finally, we examine some of the problems associated with the use of personality assessment data in making judgements about people.

At this point in the book you could be forgiven for thinking that psychologists are interested in personality only for the purposes of academic research and theorizing. However, this view is quite mistaken. In the course of their professional activities, many psychologists apply personality theory and research in a wide variety of practical contexts. Industrial and organizational psychologists frequently take personality into account in personnel selection, looking for dependable employees who will not steal, be frequently absent, or cause accidents and disciplinary problems. Counselling psychologists assess their clients' personalities when advising them about career choices or solutions to life problems. Clinical psychologists often try to improve their understanding and treatment of their patients by evaluating the personality traits and dynamics in which their symptoms are embedded.

If personality information is to be used in any of these applied settings, psychologists must have systematic procedures for obtaining it. As you may have guessed from the title of this chapter, the development of assessment procedures is a major preoccupation of personality psychologists. Over the years, a huge variety of methods has emerged for assessing personality characteristics, and many psychologists have devoted themselves to studying the complex issues surrounding personality measurement. In this chapter, we will explore the alternative methods of personality assessment that are available and consider their advantages and disadvantages. Before examining the details of these methods, however, it is useful to step back for a little while and consider the broader aims of personality measurement.

Measuring personality

At first blush, the thought of measuring something as elusive as personality may seem foolish or even absurd, like trying to take the temperature of happiness or to weigh beauty. After all, personality characteristics are not quantities that can be directly perceived, and often they seem to be more like concepts dreamed up in the minds of psychological theorists than attributes of actual people. We also know that two people can often have quite different opinions about the personality of a shared acquaintance, suggesting that judgements of personality are quite subjective. In short, personality characteristics appear on the surface to be unlikely candidates for measurement because they are unobservable, because they are theoretical 'constructs', and because they are in the eye of the beholder. For these reasons the general public is often sceptical about the idea of measuring personality and other psychological variables, imagining that it amounts to measuring the unmeasurable.

But is this scepticism about psychological measurement justified? Strictly speaking, it isn't. All that is required for something to be measurable is for it to vary in detectable ways and for there to be some sensible procedure for assigning numbers to these variations. If some phenomenon varies by degrees, then it can, in principle, be measured. People usually seem quite comfortable judging one person to have more of a certain personality characteristic than another person – for instance, to be more outgoing or hostile or rigid – so there is no reason to believe that these characteristics cannot be quantified.

It is now almost universally accepted within psychology that personality characteristics can be measured. Indeed, measurement, or 'psychometrics', has always been a basic concern of psychology as a discipline, and psychologists have made fundamental contributions to its scientific understanding. Instead of asking *whether* personality can be measured, psychologists argue, we should ask *how well* it can be measured, based on serious empirical research. That is, how much *confidence* should we have in personality measurements?

This question is a deceptively complicated one, and psychologists have paid a lot of attention to it. Their analysis usually breaks the issue of measurement quality or confidence into two psychometric components: *reliability* and *validity*. A good personality measure is one that is both reliable and valid. These two concepts deserve careful examination.

Reliability refers to the *consistency* of a measure, the extent to which its scores dependably and accurately reflect the characteristic being measured. Consistency, and hence reliability, comes in three main varieties: consistency among different components (e.g., test items) of the measure ('internal consistency'), consistency in the information that different users of the measure extract from it ('inter-rater reliability'), and consistency over time in people's scores on the measure ('test–retest reliability'). To the extent that these forms of consistency are lacking in a measure, it suffers from what psychologists call 'measurement error'. A reliable measure is therefore one that enables relatively error-free assessment of a construct: its different components hang together in a coherent manner (e.g., they correlate well), it yields highly similar scores regardless of who administers it, and it provides consistent scores from one testing to another. In contrast, an unreliable measure is one whose components are not coherent, which yields discrepant scores when administered by different people, and which gives scores that differ over time. Such a measure has substantial measurement error and does not provide reliable information about the person being tested. Personality psychologists try to maximize test reliability by pre-testing items to ensure that they correlate with one another, and by ensuring that tests are given and scored in highly standardized ways to reduce variability between testers and at different times.

Validity is another somewhat complicated concept, but it boils down to two questions: first, does a measure assess what it is intended to assess, and second, does it provide practically useful information? With regard to the first question, a valid measure is one that accurately reflects the psychological construct that it is supposed to measure. That is, a test of construct A should not in fact be measuring construct B or only measuring one aspect of A. For example, a test of arrogance should not really measure self-esteem, and a test of general anxiousness should not only assess social anxiety. This kind of validity can be empirically demonstrated by showing that the measure correlates highly with other measures of the same construct ('convergent validity') and does not correlate too highly with measures of distinct constructs ('discriminant validity'). For example, a personality test measuring arrogance should correlate highly with other tests of arrogance and should not correlate highly with tests of healthy self-esteem or Extraversion. The validity of a personality test can also be supported by showing that the content of the measure truly represents the construct of interest, rather than a related construct ('content validity').

With regard to the second question, a valid measure should yield information that enables psychologists to predict criteria that the construct should be associated with ('predictive validity' or 'criterion-related validity'). For example, a Conscientiousness measure should be able to predict (i.e., correlate with) good work attendance, and a measure of trait anxiety should be able to distinguish patients suffering from anxiety-related disorders from those suffering from other disorders. Clearly, measures that cannot predict real-life criteria such as these are practically useless. It is also worth noting that a measure that does not assess its intended construct – the first kind of invalidity – is unlikely to be able to predict criteria that the construct is associated with. For example, a test of 'Conscientiousness' that actually measures willingness to lie about one's virtues will probably not correlate with being dependable in the workplace.

Reliability and validity are crucial psychometric properties of any assessment method. Without reliability and validity, assessments are incoherent, inaccurate, and practically ineffective. Fortunately, both can be established by empirical research on the correlations among measures and prediction criteria, and few measures are developed without attempting to maximize them. In addition to being individually crucial, the two properties are tightly linked such that validity cannot be high when reliability is low. That is, a measure that is inconsistent – one that is internally incoherent, yields different information to different examiners, and fluctuates over time – cannot predict validly. That is, if assessment information is riddled with measurement error, it has no practical value.

Let us briefly review our introductory discussions of personality measurement. They argued that personality characteristics are measurable in principle and that we should take an empirical approach to the question of how well they are measured in practice. Although personality variables are unobservable, are often theoretical constructs, and are to some degree subjective, they can still be assessed rigorously and well. Unobservable variables and theoretical constructs are indispensable to scientific explanation, and some degree of subjectivity is inescapable. Careful evaluation of the reliability and validity of a personality measure can tell us how much assurance we can have in the information that it provides. If we want to have confidence in personality assessments, and to make practical judgements on the strength of them, then we need to establish their psychometric credentials.

Interview methods

One way to find out about another person is, of course, to talk to him or her. When this kind of conversation is formalized and used for the purpose of assessment it can be called an interview. Interviews have been a widely-used means of gathering personality information for some time, and have been especially popular in clinical settings, where psychologists and psychiatrists use them to diagnose mental disorders. Advocates of interviews argue that they are particularly effective assessment tools because they offer multiple sources of information about the person being assessed: their overt answers to questions, their appearance, and non-verbal signs such as intonation, facial expressions, and mannerisms. In addition, they maintain, interview methods enable skilled interviewers to explore areas of special interest in greater depth and with greater flexibility than other assessment methods allow, thereby providing a unique window on the person.

Interviews vary widely in the extent to which they are standardized. In more 'free-form' interviews, interviewers are allowed to explore the domain to be assessed with as much flexibility in general approach and in the wording and order of questions as they wish. In more 'structured' interviews, interviewers are required to examine specified topics and to follow detailed instructions for question wording and order. 'Semi-structured' interviews permit an intermediate level of flexibility and organization. Psychoanalytically-oriented psychologists generally favour less-structured interviews because they give interviewers the freedom to explore the person's conflicts, defences, and resistances in all their uniqueness. Researchers and non-psychodynamic psychologists tend to favour more structured interview methods because they yield more standardized and explicit information.

Varying degrees of interview standardization have been popular over the years. Recently, psychologists have come to favour more structured interviews, largely in response to research indicating that unstructured interviews are often unreliable. Different interviewers who assess the same person using these interviews frequently show poor levels of agreement. There are several reasons for this unreliability. First, if interviewers are given flexibility to explore the person, they will ask different questions and obtain different information on which to base their assessments. Second, by giving the interviewer more power to decide how to conduct the interview, unstructured interviews increase the likelihood that each interviewer's distinctive personal experiences and theoretical biases will distort their assessments. Third, unstructured interviews make it more likely that the person being assessed will be influenced by the interviewer's attributes – such as appearance, age, and personality – and therefore respond differently to different interviewers. More structured interviews restrict the role of the interviewer and focus on the standardized content of the questions, thereby reducing this kind of influence. In sum, unstructured interviews allow increased flexibility at a high cost: increased subjectivity and unreliability in assessment, and consequently reduced validity.

Interview methods face additional problems as assessment tools. First, they are often time-consuming, frequently requiring highly trained interviewers to spend long periods with each interviewee. Second, the reliability of interviews is often adversely affected by their inescapably social quality. Compared to more impersonal assessment methods such as paper-and-pencil or computerized tests, face-to-face interviews often make people more concerned about creating a positive impression and therefore more likely to distort their responses. In addition, the intimacy of the interview setting encourages a social psychological phenomenon known as the 'self-fulfilling prophecy'. This phenomenon works as follows: the interviewer subtly communicates his or her initial impressions to the interviewee, who responds in a corresponding way that confirms the interviewer's initial impressions. For instance, an interviewer who comes to the interview with an initially unfavourable impression of the interviewee – whether or not this impression is justified – may behave in a brisk, dismissive, or condescending way that makes the interviewee anxious, awkward, or angry, thereby 'confirming' the interviewer's negative judgement even though the interviewee might not normally be like this. Moreover, initial impressions seem to be overly influential in interviewers' assessments even if the self-fulfilling prophecy does not occur. Assessment methods that are more impersonal reduce the risk of these sources of unreliability. Finally, relatively few structured interviews have been developed for the assessment of personality characteristics, more attention having been paid to assessing the symptoms of mental disorders, so their effectiveness as assessment tools is still somewhat unproven.

In general, then, most personality psychologists do not hold interviews in very high esteem as assessment methods. They are usually considered to be too unreliable, too invalid, and too time-consuming. However, it is important to mention two exceptions to this negative verdict, in which interviews are still considered to be valuable sources of personality information. First, interview methods are still widely used by clinical psychologists when they diagnose 'personality disorders' (see Chapter 10). These disorders are difficult to assess because people who suffer from them are often poor judges of how they interact with and are perceived by others, and of how deviant and self-destructive their behaviour is. In short, people with personality disorders are often incapable of giving valid self-reports. For this reason, it seems wise to employ a clinically skilled interviewer, who is given some flexibility to delve into the interviewee's ways of thinking and behaving while still following a standard series of questions to ensure reliability. Research tends to show that this sort of semi-structured interview yields a more reliable and valid assessment of personality disorders than other, less flexible methods of assessment.

A second domain in which interview methods seem to have special value is in the assessment of 'Type A' personality, which refers to a combination of traits including hostility, impatience, and competitive achievement striving. Type A personality appears to be particularly well assessed by an ingenious structured interview which illustrates the special possibilities of interviews as assessment devices. In this interview (Rosenman, 1978), the interviewee is asked a series of standard questions about Type A tendencies. However, the interviewer does not merely record the content of the interviewee's overt responses, but also notes properties of the person's speech that are indicative of Type A tendencies (e.g., its loudness, abruptness, speed, and explosiveness) and aspects of their general demeanour (e.g., boredom, irritability, and hostility). In addition, the interviewer deliberately tries to arouse hostility by sharply challenging or interrupting the interviewee's responses. Consequently, this interview combines self-report with behavioural observation, in a reasonably natural interpersonal situation where Type A behaviour might be manifested.

Personality inventories

Interviews generally allow some flexibility in how questions are worded, arranged, and answered. Personality inventories allow none. **Inventories** – also known as questionnaires or scales – present respondents with a standard list of statements, in a standard order, and with a fixed set of response options. Respondents use these options to express their agreement or disagreement with each item, usually on a computer or with a pen or pencil. Their responses are assigned ratings which are summed over groups of items to yield numerical scores. At every step, that is, personality inventories are standardized.

Personality inventories were first developed by Sir Francis Galton in the late 19th century, and since then thousands have been constructed, especially since World War II. They have become the most numerous and widely employed form of personality measure, largely because they are relatively easy to develop and use. Although their basic format of item lists and explicit response options does not vary, they differ in two main ways. First, some inventories measure a single characteristic, whereas others use multiple scales to measure personality in a more comprehensive fashion (so-called 'omnibus' tests). As a result, some single-trait inventories have as few as ten items, while other inventories may have more than 500 items distributed among more than 20 scales. Second, their response formats vary, with some inventories offering two verbal options (e.g., 'True/False') and others offering rating scales with as many as nine numbered options (e.g., from 1 'strongly disagree' to 7 'strongly agree').

The development of personality inventories is usually guided by some mixture of theoretical analysis and empirical research. Typically, a large number of items are written to reflect a preliminary understanding of the construct or constructs to be measured. These provisional items are then pre-tested on a sample of respondents so that psychometrically stronger items can be selected and weaker ones eliminated. Items may be selected according to their ability to distinguish predefined groups, their consistency with other items, and their correspondence to latent variables identified by factor analysis (see Chapter 2). For instance, potential items for a hostility inventory might be eliminated if they fail to differentiate violent from non-violent criminals, if they fail to correlate with most other items, and if they are not associated with a factor which underlies most other items. Items that survive this statistical culling are usually combined to form the new inventory. This inventory is then administered to a new sample of respondents along with other measures, so that its validity can be established. In short, inventory construction is a heavily statistical process in which efforts are made to ensure the various forms of reliability and validity.

Personality inventories have a variety of practical advantages. Compared to interviews, they are easy and quick to administer and score. They are also highly efficient, in that they can be given to many people at once, and without an examiner present. Indeed, the administration and scoring of inventories are readily computerized, and programmes now exist that can generate interpretive reports for several of them. Compared to inventories, other assessment methods are cumbersome. Finally, inventories virtually eliminate inter-rater unreliability: because they are standardized it should not matter who gives the test to the individual whose personality is being assessed.

Inventories also have certain disadvantages. Because they rely on self-report, personality inventories are particularly vulnerable to what are known as '**response biases**'. Interviewers can probe and scrutinize the interviewee's responses for evidence of dishonesty and distortion, but inventories depend on the respondent to answer truthfully and sincerely. Several response biases have been identified, including 'yea-saying' (or 'acquiescence') and 'nay-saying' (tendencies to agree and disagree with test items regardless of their content); 'faking good' and 'faking bad' (tendencies to deceptively present the self in an overly favourable and unfavourable light); and 'social desirability' (the tendency to respond in socially approved ways, but without deceptive intent). Carelessness, the tendency to respond in an unconsidered or random fashion, can also be described as a bias. All of these biases weaken test validity because they reduce the extent to which test scores accurately reflect the respondent's standing on the disposition being measured.

Developers of personality inventories have usually been alert to response biases and the threat that they pose to validity, and often take active steps to counteract them. Yea-saying and nay-saying are easily neutralized by making sure that roughly equal numbers of items within a scale require agreement and disagreement to be scored in a certain direction. For example, 'I am very outgoing' and 'I dislike meeting new people' require different responses to indicate a consistent disposition, and a test will not ascribe such a disposition to people who have tendencies to consistently agree or disagree with statements if both kinds of items are used. Other response biases can be detected using special 'validity scales'. Faking good and social desirability can be detected by 'lie scales' containing statements that only the most saintly among us could endorse or deny, such as 'I have never told a lie' and 'I never find dirty jokes amusing'. Subtler scales have also been developed to pick up more sophisticated forms of positive self-presentation, such as guardedness and defensiveness. Faking bad, which commonly occurs in some clinical and legal settings where it is called 'malingering', can be assessed by scales containing a diverse variety of self-denigrating statements and psychological symptoms. Careless responding can be detected by scales that contain items that very few people answer in a particular way, so that someone who does so repeatedly is suspected of the bias. Alternatively, highly similar items can be repeated in the inventory, and inconsistent responses taken as evidence of carelessness. In short, self-report inventories can be protected against response biases. However, as it is often difficult to determine how to adjust test scores when a bias is detected, this protection is far from absolute.

Projective methods

The preceding section argued that objective personality inventories have some attractive features, but are also subject to some potentially serious limitations. Standardized item wording and unambiguous response options improve the reliability of these measures, but they cannot ensure that people responding to them do so validly. People may display a variety of biases and respond dishonestly, defensively, and carelessly. It is understandable that people may respond in evasive or self-protective ways, especially when items ask them about unflattering or socially undesirable behaviour. Sophisticated validity scales can partially compensate for these response tendencies, but cannot eradicate them.

A second potential problem with self-report inventories is that they might not be able to assess some important personality characteristics. Inventories typically depend on respondents having some ability to introspect accurately about their dispositions and psychological processes. But what if some thoughts, feelings, desires, and motives are not readily available to the respondent's introspection? Any personality measure that directly asks people about these things might meet with the person's incomprehension, their guesses about how they ought to respond, or their distorted beliefs about what they are like. So are there some parts of our personality of which we are unaware, and about which it is pointless to question us?

As you know by now (see Chapter 4), one major strand of personality theory answers this last question with a resounding 'Yes'. Psychoanalytically-oriented psychologists argue that many parts of the human personality are inaccessible to conscious awareness, and consequently they tend to be sceptical of self-report personality inventories. It makes no sense to ask people what they are like if parts of their personalities are outside awareness or distorted by psychological defences. In place of inventories, psychoanalytically-oriented psychologists have designed personality assessment methods that do not depend on the respondent's introspective awareness and actively attempt to bypass it.

The methods that these psychologists have designed are quite diverse, but they all require people to respond in an open-ended way to a set of ambiguous stimuli. They are usually referred to as '**projective tests**' because they demand that respondents 'project' their distinctive ways of giving meaning to experience – including their conflicts, anxieties, defences, cognitive styles, and preoccupations – onto the stimuli. The most widely used projective tests require people to respond to ambiguous visual stimuli, such as ink-blots or pictures, or ambiguous verbal instructions, such as to draw an unspecified person or to complete an unfinished sentence. Because respondents do not know what characteristics these projective tests are intended to assess, and may have no introspective access to these characteristics in any case, advocates argue that projective tests can penetrate the surface of the personality and avoid the distortions and biases of inventories.

The best-known projective test is the Rorschach Ink-Blot Test, which was published by Swiss psychiatrist Hermann Rorschach in 1921 but was loosely based on a popular 19th-century European parlour game. The test uses ten standard ink-blots which are symmetrical around the vertical axis (i.e., the left and right sides are mirror images) and printed on cards. Some blots are monochromatic, some are multicoloured. Respondents are asked to tell the examiner what each blot looks like to them, giving multiple responses if they see more than one 'percept'. They are also interviewed to explain what features of the blot led them to each percept.

Many schemes for Rorschach interpretation and scoring have been developed, focusing on an enormous variety of response elements. For instance, inferences may be based on the *content* of responses, so that a negative self-image, depression, and suicidal propensities might be inferred if a respondent's percepts contain many morbid images of death, injury, and decay. (One must be careful here; one of the authors once tested someone who repeatedly saw bones in the ink-blots, but who turned out to be an undepressed X-ray technician.) Some content inferences are fairly direct and obvious, as in the case of morbid imagery, but others may refer to symbolic meanings, so that a wild animal might be inferred to represent a respondent's father. In addition to content, inferences may also be based on the *formal properties* of responses. These include the degree to which percepts clearly make use of the contours of the blot, rather than being arbitrarily imposed on it, and the extent to which percepts integrate separate components of the blot into coherent scenarios. Further response properties that

Rorschach interpreters often consider include perceptions of movement, texture, and depth, reactions to the coloured portions of the blots, and peculiarities in the wording of responses.

Another well-known projective test is the Thematic Apperception Test (TAT), which was developed by the American psychologist Henry Murray and his colleagues (1938). Like the Rorschach, the TAT uses images printed on a set of cards. Unlike ink-blots, however, these images are structured and meaningful; they are rather vague and ominous black-and-white pictures depicting people in a variety of indoor and outdoor scenes. The respondent's task is to look at each card and tell a story about what is happening, what led up to it, and what the people in the picture are thinking and feeling. These stories are usually interpreted by the psychologist in terms of the respondent's needs, preoccupations, defence mechanisms, and ways of understanding personal relationships (i.e., 'object relations'; see Chapter 4).

Although projective tests such as the Rorschach and the TAT have an attractive rationale – who could deny the appeal of laying bare the hidden organization of personality by evading the person's defences? – they have been subjected to severe criticism over the years. Some have objected to the fact that the projective test interpretation demands a theoretical orientation that is antithetical to many psychologists, requiring the use of psychoanalytic concepts, terms, and doctrines (e.g., the crucial importance of early relationships with parental figures). Others criticize the rationale for projective tests for assuming that one artificial task, such as peering at ink-blots, can adequately reveal the person's general ways of apprehending the world, if such a general style even exists. Projective tests take it for granted that people's habitual ways of making sense of themselves, their interpersonal relations, and their environments will be imposed on any ambiguous stimulus. From a practical viewpoint, projective tests have been criticized for being time-consuming to administer and score compared to the speediness of self-report inventories. In addition, they are not completely immune to defensive and distorted responding, as respondents can refuse to engage fully with the task by giving brief, guarded, or flippant responses. There is also evidence that people can 'fake bad' on projective tests, and that they are often subtly influenced by random features of the testing situation (e.g., they are more likely to draw a figure with a moustache if the examiner has one).

The most damning criticisms of projective tests, however, have focused on their lack of reliability and validity. As two psychologists have argued, 'some critics believed that Rorschach interpretation, though less messy, was no more scientific than bird hepatoscopy [i.e., examining chicken entrails, as Roman diviners once did]' (Masling & Bornstein, 2005, p. 4). When systematic research has been carried out, it has generally found disappointing levels of agreement between different projective test interpreters, and inadequate prediction by them of important criteria such as psychiatric diagnosis, suicide potential, and responsiveness to therapy. In the same way that the subjectivity and lack of standardization of unstructured interviews reduce their reliability, the flexibility of projective test interpretation makes it unlikely that two psychologists will draw similar inferences from the same projective response. And if psychologists cannot agree on what inferences should be drawn from a certain response (i.e., inter-rater unreliability), then, as we have seen, their inferences will tend to be invalid. This implies that projective tests will not become practically useful – reliable and valid – until their interpretation is standardized. A comprehensive review of projective techniques (Lilienfeld, Wood, & Garb, 2000) found that most measures based on projective tests either had inadequate validity or no scientific evidence of validity. Even standardized projective techniques tend to be no more valid than objective measures of the same constructs, and generally do not improve the prediction of important psychological phenomena (i.e., 'incremental validity') over and above these quicker and cheaper alternatives. A complex Rorschach index of depression may have some validity, but a short inventory may do so just as well, and with the expenditure of much less time, effort, and cost.

In response to these criticisms of projective tests, and the proliferation of alternative systems for interpreting them, one scoring system for the Rorschach test has been developed that is superior to its predecessors. This system, created by Exner (1986), uses explicit, standardized rules for scoring responses, thereby improving the inter-rater reliability of Rorschach information. In addition, research suggests that scores based on Exner's rules are valid predictors of several important psychological variables, such as suicide risk. These developments suggest that projective methods are capable of yielding reasonably reliable and valid personality information when they are scored in standardized and well-researched ways. On the other hand, Exner's system appears to purchase its reliability and validity at the expense of the usual rationale for projective testing: the interpretation of the person's unique psychodynamics. The personality characteristics that its improved scoring system assesses – such as stress tolerance, emotional responsiveness, coping style, social isolation, and passivity – do not require deep psychodynamic inferences, and can be readily assessed by non-projective methods, such as inventories. In short, although the Rorschach test is a fascinating assessment tool, efforts to make it reliable and valid seem to remove what is unique to it and to projective methods in general. When the test is turned into a standardized measure that yields well-normed scores for a few personality characteristics, it no longer allows the sort of interpretation that originally motivated the development of projective tests. Part of the problem here may be the intrinsic difficulty of assessing the kinds of 'deep' or 'hidden' personality characteristics that these tests try to assess. It may simply be harder to assess whether people have separation conflicts or unconscious fears of their fathers than it is to assess their levels of Extraversion or shyness. It is easier to see clearly the fish that swim near the surface than the fearsome creatures that inhabit the murky depths.

Projective tests remain popular among some personality researchers, who are often attracted to the rich narrative data that people produce in response to the TAT cards. Rigorous coding schemes have been used, for example, to assess people's use of defence mechanisms (Cramer, 1998) and their motives (McClelland, 1985). The TAT and Rorschach tests are also still widely taught to American clinical psychologists. Nevertheless, the enthusiasm for projective tests that was widespread in the 1950s and 1960s has subsided as their psychometric limitations have become clear, as psychoanalytic approaches to personality have become less popular, and as a great assortment of easy-to-use personality inventories has become available. Considerations of reliability and validity have made psychologists more sceptical about the power of projective tests to reveal the hidden depths of the personality, and more modest about what projective assessment can and should try to accomplish.

203

ILLUSTRATIVE STUDY

Measuring personality using implicit methods

Projective tests attempt to evade the distortions that can affect self-report, and to lay bare the hidden dynamics of personality. Unfortunately, they tend to suffer from some serious psychometric weaknesses. Recent approaches to the study of 'implicit' cognition – cognition that is automatic or outside conscious control – may offer a more rigorous way of assessing personality free of self-report biases. One interesting study of personality using implicit cognition methods was conducted by German psychologists Melanie Steffens and Stefanie Schulze König (2006). Steffens and Schulze König gave 89 undergraduates a popular self-report measure of the Big Five, a set of tasks intended to assess behaviour reflecting the five factors, and five versions of the Implicit Association Test (IAT; Greenwald, McGhee, & Schwartz, 1998).

The IAT is a computer-based method for assessing the 'automatic associations' that exist between concepts in people's memory. It works in an ingenious way. In one 'block' on an IAT, labels for a pair of concepts appear on the top left of the computer screen (say, 'Sweets' and 'Happiness') and another pair that are alternatives to those concepts appears on the top right (say, 'Vegetables' and 'Sadness'). A series of words then flash up in the centre of the screen, and the participant is instructed to categorize each one as belonging to the left or the right concepts as quickly as possible, by pressing response keys on the left or right of the keyboard. The words include examples of all four concepts, such as 'cake' and 'ice-cream', 'joyful' and 'jolly', 'carrot' and 'potato', and 'gloomy' and 'depressed', and are presented in a random order. In the second block of the IAT, the same words flash up but the concept labels have been switched. Now 'Sweets' is paired with 'Sadness' and 'Vegetables' is paired with 'Happiness', and the participant must again categorize the words into the left or right concepts. The computer records the person's reaction times for words in the two IAT blocks.

If the paired concepts are closely associated, then it should be easy to do the categorization task. If we associate 'Sweets' with 'Happiness', then we should be able to quickly distinguish words that exemplify either of these concepts (e.g., 'cake' and 'joyful') from those that exemplify the other concepts (e.g., 'carrot' and 'gloomy'). However, if the paired concepts are not closely associated, then the task becomes slow and difficult. Deciding whether a word exemplifies 'Sweets' or 'Sadness' vs. 'Vegetables' or 'Happiness' is not easy if, like most people, you associate sweet things with happiness. Reaction times for the 'Sweets + Happiness' IAT block should therefore be shorter (i.e., faster) than for the 'Sweets + Sadness' block.

Steffens and Schulze König adapted the IAT to assess the five personality factors. Each factor was assessed by two IAT blocks. For example, in one block the concepts

'Self' and 'Conscientious' were paired (with 'Others' and 'Unconscientious' as the alternatives), and in the second block 'Self' and 'Unconscientious' were paired (with 'Others' and 'Conscientious' as alternatives). The stimulus words that participants had to categorize reflected self (e.g., 'me', 'mine'), others (e.g., 'you', 'your'), conscientious traits (e.g., 'disciplined', 'organized') and unconscientious traits (e.g., 'untidy', 'aimless'). If a participant showed quicker reaction times for the 'Self + Conscientious' block than for the 'Self + Unconscientious' block, it could therefore be inferred that she saw herself – automatically, rather than through some deliberate process of self-report – as relatively conscientious.

The findings of this study were striking. First, the IAT-based measures of the Big Five factors correlated only weakly with the self-report questionnaire measures (mean $r = .07$). This finding suggests either that the two measures assess somewhat distinct phenomena or that one measure is flawed. If that were the case, suspicion would fall on the relatively unproven IAT measures, as the questionnaire has been extensively validated. Second, the IAT measures did appear to be valid: they predicted the behavioural tasks as well as or better than the questionnaire measures. For example, Conscientiousness was assessed by a concentration task in which participants had to cross out as many copies of a particular letter in an array that contained many similar letters. More conscientious participants should be more careful and make fewer mistakes. The IAT measure of Conscientiousness was more strongly correlated with performance on this task ($r = .36$) than the questionnaire measure ($r = .01$). In short, only the implicit measure of Conscientiousness predicted conscientious behaviour.

As yet, implicit measures of personality have not been widely used, but they are likely to become more popular in the future (see Schnabel, Asendorpf, & Greenwald, 2008, for a good discussion of their promise). These measures are certainly not 'X-rays of the soul', but they may nevertheless help us assess personality in ways that evade some of the biases that influence self-report and that supply the rationale for projective tests. Studies such as this one suggest that implicit assessment of personality is promising, in part because they show that implicit measures may sometimes predict real-life behaviour when self-report measures do not.

Alternative methods

Interviews, inventories, and projective tests do not exhaust the variety of assessment methods that have been developed by personality researchers, although they are by far the most numerous and widely used. Two alternative methods are particularly worthy of attention: the Q-sort method and the Repertory Grid.

The Q-sort method

The Q-sort method was originally developed as a means of assessing the self-concept: the person's understanding of himself or herself. It does so in an innovative way, requiring people to judge which personality attributes are more and which ones less important for defining who they are as unique individuals, instead of judging where they fall on these attributes relative to other people, the approach favoured by most personality tests. In short, Q-sorts allow people to describe themselves with reference to a purely personal, rather than normative, standard.

Q-sorts consist of a set of statements printed on cards, which people sort into several numbered piles according to how characteristic they are of themselves, ranging from 'least characteristic' to 'most characteristic'. The number of cards to be sorted into each pile is fixed in advance so that the distribution of cards is approximately normal, with few statements judged to be extremely characteristic or uncharacteristic and many judged to be intermediate between these extremes. For instance, in the popular California Q-sort (Block, 1978) there are 100 statements to be sorted into nine piles. Although at first it may seem arbitrary and restrictive, this 'forced-normal' distribution of cards has several advantages over simply presenting the same statements in an inventory with a rating scale. First, it makes people consider and judge each statement carefully and in the context of the others. Second, it does not allow them to yield to various response biases, such as indiscriminately agreeing or disagreeing with all statements (i.e., yea-saying and nay-saying). Third, it has certain statistical benefits for researchers. In return for these advantages, Q-sorts have the disadvantage of being somewhat time-consuming to complete.

Q-sorts are highly versatile methods for the intensive study of individuals. They can be used for a person's self-report and also for judgements of that person by an observer, therapist, or friend. People can also judge themselves in different ways, performing separate sorts for their 'real self' and 'ideal self', or for their personality before and after psychological treatment. Correlations between these alternative Q-sorts can reveal the extent of agreement between different observers, discrepancies between the person's self-understanding and the judgement of others, conflicts within the person, and changes in personality over time. Indeed, the Q-sort method has been used most prominently in studies of personality stability and change, allowing researchers to focus on the trajectories of individual lives rather than on normative patterns of personality change.

The Repertory Grid

The Repertory Grid test is similar in spirit to the Q-sort in that it assesses each person's individuality in its own terms rather than in relation to group norms. However, the 'Rep Test' goes even further in its attempt to capture the person's uniqueness. Whereas the Q-sort uses a standard set of descriptive statements, allowing people to select which items in the set are most important for characterizing themselves, the Rep Test allows individuals to create the descriptive attributes in terms of which they will be assessed.

The radical idea that people should be understood in terms of their unique ways of understanding the world is one that readers will remember from the discussion in Chapter 7 of George Kelly's 'constructivist' approach to personality. Kelly developed the Rep Test as a way for psychologists, particularly clinical psychologists, to determine the 'constructs' that people habitually use in making sense of one another. Although the Rep Test can be administered in many ways, typically the person who is taking the test is presented with a list of role terms – such as mother, teacher, person who dislikes you, boyfriend/girlfriend – and is asked to name someone in their life who fits each role. The examiner then selects three of these names, and asks the person to state one important way in which two of them are alike but different from the third. The attribute that the person states in response to this request is called a '**personal construct**', a way of differentiating people that is salient to him or her. The person repeats the process of eliciting constructs for many combinations of three names chosen by the examiner. The resulting set of constructs reveals the person's distinctive way of interpreting the interpersonal world in rich qualitative detail. An illustration of part of a Rep Test is presented in Figure 9.1. The first eight columns represent the role terms, the circles represent the specific roles that must be contrasted (i.e., two alike, one different), and the final two columns allow the person who is completing the test to fill in the two poles of each construct.

In settings where this kind of intimacy with the person's 'way of seeing' is crucial, as in some forms of psychotherapy, the Rep Test can have considerable value. In such settings, the

Your mother	Your father	Your spouse	Your closest friend of the same sex	A person you worked with who dislikes you	A person you'd like to know better	The most unsuccessful person you know	The happiest person you know	Column 1	Column 2
O			O			O		Warm	Cold
		O		O			O	Honest	Dishonest
	O		O		O			Cool	Dorky
		O		O		O		Demanding	Easy-going
O					O		O	Old	Young

Figure 9.1 Example segment of a Rep Grid

information that it provides can usefully complement information derived from standardized inventories. For instance, an inventory might show that two people are high on Neuroticism and depression, whereas the Rep Test might indicate that one person tends to construe others in terms of their dependability and warmth and the other in terms of their dominance and power. In one case, we might infer from the Rep Test that the person's distress is linked to their sensitivity to being abandoned and rejected (i.e., others being undependable and cold), and in the other case that the person's distress is linked to their sensitivity to feeling submissive, weak, and incompetent. These distinctive ways of construing others seem to suggest that therapy for the two people might focus on different themes.

Making use of personality assessments

The previous sections of this chapter have presented a variety of methods for the collection of personality information. All of these methods are commonly employed in applied settings, where they help psychologists to make decisions such as who to hire among several job applicants, what career a student should pursue, and whether to discharge a psychiatric patient who might be suicidal. All of these decisions are based on *predictions*: predictions that one applicant will perform better than others in the job, that the student will be most successful or fulfilled in a particular career, or that the patient will or will not attempt suicide if discharged. But how do psychologists use personality information to make predictions such as these?

This question may appear to be a simple one but it is actually quite complicated and controversial. Consider the position in which psychologists find themselves after conducting a personality assessment. Typically, they have administered more than one measure to the respondent, perhaps involving some combination of interviews, inventories, and projective tests. Each measure may yield multiple pieces of information – such as different scales on an inventory – and these pieces may differ in their format, ranging from numerical scores on inventory scales to qualitative impressions drawn from an interview. Finally, this personality information often has to be combined with additional evidence, such as biographical details of the respondent (e.g., their work history, past suicidal behaviour) and assessments of other psychological attributes (e.g., cognitive abilities or attitudes). The daunting task facing the psychologist is to integrate these multiple and diverse sources of information into a single prediction and to make this prediction as accurate (i.e., valid) as possible.

How psychologists should perform this integration is a matter of some debate, and two rival positions or philosophies can be distinguished. One position contends that psychologists should use assessment information as a basis for constructing a psychological portrait of the whole person. According to this position, a primary aim of a personality assessment is to arrive at a narrative understanding of the person, using theory, intuition, and personal experience to synthesize the assessment data. Predictions and judgements about the person can then be made from this synthesis. The other position contends that the psychologist's role should be more limited. Instead of constructing a portrait, the psychologist should use explicit rules and formulas, based on empirical research using many people, to make predictions and judgements from assessment data. They should specifically avoid the use of intuition, theory, and personal experience, as well as the urge to piece together a picture of the whole person, because doing so introduces elements of subjectivity that will weaken the validity of their predictions.

The contrast between these two positions should sound familiar by now. Remember that many of the criticisms of unstructured interviews and projective tests focused on the adverse psychometric consequences of their subjectivity and flexibility. Remember also how part of the rationale for these methods of assessment is their supposed capacity to yield a picture of the person's uniqueness and individuality. In contrast, objective assessment methods emphasize psychometric respectability and the comparison of individuals to group norms, and measure specific personality characteristics without aspiring to put them together into an integrated psychological portrait. Indeed, proponents of projective testing and unstructured interviews do tend to favour the view that assessment information should be used to construct psychological portraits, which has been dubbed the 'clinical judgement' position. Similarly, advocates of objective assessment tend to favour the 'rules and formulas' approach to the use of personality data, which is often referred to as the 'actuarial' or 'statistical judgement' position.

A great deal of research has been devoted to comparing the predictive validity of clinical and statistical methods in personality assessment. Much of this research was provoked by a ground-breaking book by Paul Meehl (1954), which reviewed a number of early studies and found overwhelming support for the superior validity of statistical methods. As Meehl's review showed, and more recent research has consistently confirmed, highly-trained psychologists who make predictions and judgements from a set of assessment data make more errors than simple statistical formulas and rules applied to the same data. Two additional points are worth making about this finding, which is now one of the best supported in all of psychology (Dawes, Faust, & Meehl, 1989). First, it holds true for all forms of assessment data, including scores from objective tests. Second, even if psychologists are given additional assessment information that is not available to the statistical formula, such as an interview, they still make less valid predictions than statistical procedures, and this additional information often makes their predictions *worse*.

The findings of this research are surprising to many people and have been vigorously challenged by psychologists who favour the use of expert clinical judgement. How might we explain this apparent inferiority of clinical judgement? There appear to be several reasons, many of which have to do with human cognitive limitations. People are simply not very good at handling multiple sources of information at once, and making single, integrated judgements from them. We tend to follow a variety of simplifying strategies for information processing, rather than making the kinds of computations that formulas and rules involve. For example, judgements are often unduly influenced by the most striking or unusual piece of information, to the neglect of less salient but equally valid evidence. Similarly, people often make premature judgements based on a subset of the information, often the first data that they see. Furthermore, they commonly use their initial judgements to bias their evaluation of the remaining information, so that they pay attention to information that confirms the initial judgement and discount information that contradicts it. People are also quite poor at reasoning with probabilities, and consequently fail to correctly judge and take into account the likelihood of particular test results and prediction criteria. These probability judgements are vitally important given the uncertainty that is always involved in psychological predictions, and it is very well handled by statistical formulas.

In addition to being weakened by cognitive limitations such as these, clinical judgement is adversely affected by a few other factors. First, judgements are often distorted by psychologists' theoretical biases, which lead them to look for assessment information that is consistent with their pre-existing beliefs rather than consider the evidence disinterestedly. Second, psychologists may hold inaccurate beliefs about how certain assessment information is associated with prediction criteria. One example is the phenomenon of 'illusory correlation', in which psychologists believe in an intuitively plausible association between a test finding and a criterion – that men who see backsides in Rorschach blots are homosexual or that individuals whose projective drawings depict people with unusually large eyes are paranoid – that is, in fact, non-existent. Third, psychologists often base their judgements on their own clinical experiences, which may be limited and unrepresentative, so that the knowledge base from which they are making their predictions is flawed. Given all of these reasons why clinical judgement is prone to error, perhaps we should not be surprised that statistical judgement tends to do better.

The lessons of this chapter are perhaps a little deflating. The idea that psychologists can, with sufficient training, perform virtuoso acts of interpretation that unmask the hidden dynamics of the personality with startling insight and accuracy has been encouraged by movies and by psychological 'experts' in the courtroom. The reality is more humble. Abundant evidence points to the modest conclusion that personality assessments can be reliable and yield valid predictions about a wide range of criteria. However, they perform best when they are conducted with standardized measures, with a focus on specific dispositions rather than holistic portraits, and with explicit prediction rules and statistical formulas. Attempts to make more ambitious and far-reaching inferences about the hidden complexities of the personality are generally ineffective: their validity crumbles under the subjectivity of the measures and the cognitive demands of clinical judgement. To modify an old saying, 'Give psychologists enough inferential rope and they will hang themselves'.

Conclusions

Personality characteristics can be assessed using a wide variety of methods, of which the most popular are interviews, objective inventories, and projective tests. Because all of these assessment methods serve practical purposes in which judgements and predictions must be made, it is important that they be psychometrically sound; that is, 'reliable' and 'valid'. Reliable measures are ones that assess a construct in a consistent and coherent fashion, yield similar scores when administered by different examiners, and yield scores that are stable over time. Valid measures are ones that assess the construct that they are intended to assess and are able to predict real-life criteria that the construct should be associated with.

Considerations of reliability and validity generally favour the use of objective over projective measures, and structured over unstructured interviews, although inventories are vulnerable to biased responding. Advocates of projective tests and unstructured interviews contend that these methods are best suited to assessing the person's underlying personality organization and psychodynamics, in all their uniqueness and individuality. However, it seems that the subjectivity and flexibility of these methods severely weaken the confidence that we can have in the 'deep inferences' that they yield.

A similar conclusion can be reached about the way in which psychologists make judgements and predictions based on personality information, regardless of the assessment methods used to generate it. Research shows that the inferences of experts are generally inferior to inferences made from statistical formulas based on empirical generalizations. The 'clinical judgement' of experts seems to be impaired by human cognitive limitations and biases, such as the difficulty of integrating multiple pieces of information and the tendency to take judgemental 'short-cuts'. For most purposes, personality assessment is best approached with standardized and empirically-validated methods, and with appropriate humility about how difficult it is to make valid inferences about another person's depths.

Chapter summary

- Personality assessment involves systematic methods for measuring individual differences. A variety of distinct methods have been developed for this purpose. All of these methods aim to yield valid and reliable assessments.
- Psychometric reliability refers to the extent to which a measure yields assessments that are consistent and does not contain measurement error. The components of the measure should be consistent with one another ('internal consistency'), different users of the measure should produce consistent assessments ('inter-rater reliability'), and the measure should yield consistent assessments when administered to the same person at different times ('retest reliability').
- Validity refers to the extent to which a measure assesses what it is intended to assess. The measure should therefore be correlated with other measures of the same construct, and predict phenomena that should be associated with the construct.
- Interview methods of personality assessment can have problems with validity and reliability if they are unstructured and not standardized: various interpersonal processes can distort inferences drawn from them. They are also labour-intensive and costly.
- Personality questionnaires or inventories are very widely used, and constructing them generally involves extensive psychometric validation. Because they are based on self-report, however, they are subject to response biases.

(Continued)

(Continued)

- Projective methods aim to avoid the distorting influence of self-report by posing ambiguous tasks whose purpose is not transparent to the person being assessed. They generally aim to access hidden personality dynamics. However, these methods have been criticized for serious problems of validity and reliability.
- A number of additional assessment methods have been developed, tailored to overcome particular assessment problems or to assess personality characteristics that are not easily assessed using standard assessment (e.g., personal constructs).
- Having a set of validly and reliably assessed pieces of information about a person does not guarantee that valid and reliable inferences will be drawn about that person. Personality assessors are vulnerable to a number of biases that limit their ability to integrate personality information optimally.

Further reading

Butcher, J. N. (2010). *Oxford handbook of personality assessment*. Oxford: Oxford University Press.
This handbook has comprehensive coverage of history, basic psychometric issues, and the practical issues involved in personality assessment.

Dawes, R. M., Faust, D., & Meehl, P. E. (1989). Clinical versus actuarial judgment. *Science, 243*, 1668–74.
Dawes and colleagues have a strong reputation for cataloguing the errors that humans (including personality psychologists) make when drawing inferences from psychological test data. This paper presents some of the evidence of how fallible assessors can be.

Lilienfeld, S. O., Wood, J. M., & Garb, H. N. (2000). The scientific status of projective techniques. *Psychological Science in the Public Interest, 1*, 27–66.
Lilienfeld and colleagues present a devastating critique of the use of projective measures such as the Rorschach Ink-Blot Test and the Thematic Apperception Test.

Wiggins, J. S. (2003). *Paradigms of personality assessment*. New York: Guilford Press.
A strength of this somewhat advanced book is the balanced attention it gives to the eclectic variety of methods available for assessing personality characteristics.

Personality and Mental Disorder

Learning objectives

- To recognize the role that personality characteristics play in making people vulnerable to mental disorders.
- To understand the diathesis–stress model of vulnerability and how it applies to particular mental disorders.
- To develop a basic understanding of the maladaptive forms of personality that are mental disorders in their own right ('personality disorders').
- To develop a basic understanding of the phenomenon of multiple personality.

This chapter examines how the study of personality can illuminate mental disorders. It begins by investigating the ways in which some personality characteristics make people vulnerable to developing particular mental disorders if they encounter stressful life events, taking depression and schizophrenia as examples. We then turn to maladaptive forms of personality that are themselves mental disorders, and examine the varied types of 'personality disorder'. We examine several approaches to understanding these disorders and some of the controversies that surround them. Finally, the chapter examines the fascinating and puzzling phenomenon of dissociative identity disorder, a controversial condition in which a person appears to have several distinct and often mutually unaware personalities.

Individual differences in personality are highly relevant to many applied areas of psychology. Psychologists who work in educational settings are interested in whether some teaching methods are more effective than others for people of differing personality, and how personality characteristics such as self-esteem, self-efficacy, and coping styles influence learning. Psychologists who provide vocational guidance try to match people's personalities with appropriate careers, and those who are involved in personnel selection select people whose personalities fit them best to particular jobs. However, personality has been an especially important focus of attention for clinical psychologists who specialize in treating, assessing, and researching mental disorders. Clinical psychologists are concerned with personality because many mental disorders can only be understood in the context of the traits and personality processes of the people who suffer from them. For example, some personality characteristics may place people at increased risk of particular disorders and make them more likely to respond in disturbed ways to stressful life events. Personality characteristics may also influence the ways in which people express certain mental disorders, and have implications for how treatment should be conducted. In addition, some personality traits, when expressed in extreme ways, may themselves be thought of as mental disorders.

In this chapter we will examine some of these varied ways in which personality is relevant to the study and treatment of mental disorders. We will begin by investigating the role of personality characteristics as risk factors or sources of psychological vulnerability, using depression and schizophrenia as illustrations. In the process, we will also discuss how personality characteristics can shape the expression of particular mental disorders. We will then spend some time examining the so-called '**personality disorders**', disorders involving personality characteristics that are so exaggerated and inflexible that they may create serious interpersonal problems and emotional disturbances for people who suffer from them. Finally, we investigate the fascinating phenomenon of multiple personality: the apparent co-existence of distinct personalities in the same person.

Vulnerability to mental disorders

Mental disorders – disturbances of emotion, behaviour, and thinking such as phobias, psychoses, addictions, and depression – are major sources of suffering and disability in modern societies. However, these disorders are not evenly distributed in the population; some groups of people are more vulnerable to them than others. Finding out which groups of people are especially vulnerable to particular mental disorders – identifying their 'risk factors' – is therefore an important research question in clinical psychology. If we can identify groups of people who are vulnerable to a particular disorder, we can intervene with them to prevent the disorder from developing. At the same time, we can learn important clues about what causes the disorder; knowing who is at risk may tell us what it is about them that places them at risk.

Many risk factors have been discovered for a wide variety of mental disorders. These include demographic variables such as gender, social class, race, and age; genetic vulnerabilities revealed by family, adoption, and twin studies (see Chapter 5); cultural characteristics such as shared beliefs about the appropriateness of particular ways of expressing distress; life events such as traumas and other stressors; and aspects of social relationships such as marital difficulties and lack of social supports. In addition to these kinds of vulnerabilities, there is now a great deal of evidence that certain personality characteristics also make people susceptible to specific forms of mental disorder. In psychology such a vulnerability is commonly referred to as a **diathesis**, meaning a predisposition to develop a specific disorder that is intrinsic to the person, a part of their 'constitution'. The search for diatheses is an important goal for many researchers in personality and clinical psychology.

Personality diatheses make up an important class of risk factors for mental disorders, often enabling us to predict who will be affected by particular disorders at least as powerfully as other kinds of risk factor. However, it is important to understand what a diathesis is and what it is not.

A diathesis is not something that invariably leads the person who has it to develop a particular disorder: it only increases the *likelihood* that this will happen. Another way of saying this is that diatheses are 'probabilistic', not 'deterministic'. Only a minority of those who have a particular diathesis may go on to develop the disorder for which it makes them susceptible. Figure 10.1 presents three possible scenarios for the relationship between a hypothetical personality trait and the mental disorder for which it is a diathesis. A person's position on the trait is represented by the proportion of people in the population who fall below that person – known as a 'percentile' – so that someone with a percentile of 60 is higher on the trait than 60% of the population. In all three scenarios, even people who are extreme on the diathesis have a less than 50% chance of developing the disorder. In scenario A, everyone is at some risk of developing the disorder, and the risk rises steadily as a person's position on the diathesis increases. Scenario B differs only in that the risk accelerates as the person's level on the trait increases, meaning that the diathesis is especially potent among people who fall high on the personality trait. Finally, in scenario C, people who fall low on the trait are at no risk

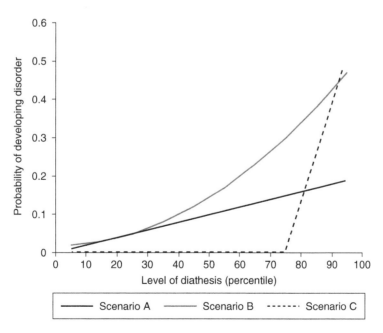

Figure 10.1 Possible relationships between diatheses and expression of mental disorders

of developing the disorder, which only affects people who have a relatively high level of the diathesis. All three of these scenarios may be true of some forms of mental disorder.

Now why is it that even people who have a high level of a diathesis for a particular mental disorder are still far from certain to develop the disorder? The answer is that most mental disorders are influenced by a complex variety of risk factors, of which personality is only one. Usually several risk factors must be combined before a person expresses a disorder, so that any one influence, such as a personality diathesis, will only lead to the disorder if other influences are also present. Someone who has a diathesis for a certain disorder but does not have other risk factors, such as poverty or harsh parenting, is therefore less likely to develop the disorder than someone who has these other risk factors. In addition, people who are predisposed to develop a disorder may also have what are known as 'protective factors', which *decrease* their likelihood of developing the disorder by making them resilient. For instance, someone whose personality makes her vulnerable to depression may also have a strong network of supportive friends and family that protects her against becoming depressed.

The existence of protective factors and the fact that most mental disorders are caused by multiple risk factors go a long way towards explaining why personality diatheses do not inevitably lead to disorder. However, a more complete explanation must also take into account the role of stressful life events in the causation of mental disorders. People who experience high levels of stress in their everyday lives – events or enduring circumstances that challenge their capacity to cope and adapt – have been shown to be at increased risk of most mental disorders. Note here that by this definition, stressful events need not be 'negative' or undesirable: events such as getting married, having a baby, and receiving a promotion also tax our capacity to adapt, and can make us more likely to develop a mental disorder. Consequently, one fundamental reason why personality diatheses are usually not sufficient to produce mental disorders is that life stress also plays an important role in determining who becomes disordered. Indeed, it is often the *combination* of diathesis and stress that best explains who becomes affected.

This simple idea is the basis for what are known as 'diathesis–stress models', which are ways of explaining the causation and development of mental disorders that are popular among psychologists. In essence, diathesis–stress models propose that for a particular disorder there is specific personality vulnerability that will only be triggered if a sufficient quantity of stress is present in the vulnerable person's life. If *either* the level of the diathesis *or* the level of life stress is low, the disorder is unlikely to develop. Only the combination of high levels of diathesis and stress is likely to result in disorder. Metaphorically, diatheses make people brittle and life stress delivers the blows that make them crack.

Diathesis–stress models of mental disorders have some interesting implications. First, they imply that the more of a diathesis a person has, the less life stress will be needed to produce a mental disorder in that person (i.e., the more brittle people are, the easier it will be to crack them). For example, if someone has an extremely high level of the predisposition to a certain disorder, a relatively minor disappointment or upset, such as an argument with a romantic partner, may be sufficient to express it. Someone with a lower level of the diathesis, on the other hand, may develop the disorder only in response to severely traumatic experiences, such as the unexpected death of a loved one or rape.

A second interesting implication of diathesis–stress models is that people will respond in quite different ways to life stress. Not only will some people be more likely than others to develop a mental disorder of any kind, but different people will also tend to develop different disorders. Because each disorder has a diathesis that is somewhat specific to it, the disorder that each one of us is likely to develop if we are sufficiently stressed will depend on which of our diatheses is the strongest. Faced with the same level of adversity and trauma in our lives, one of us may become clinically depressed, another may engage in binge eating, another may develop delusions of persecution, and another may abuse alcohol, each depending on the particular kind of diathesis that is most prominent in our personalities. In short, our personalities play a major role in determining the distinctive ways in which we become psychologically distressed.

Diathesis–stress models are appealing in their simplicity and have some interesting implications. However, these models also have some limitations. Most importantly, they give personality a rather limited role in the causation of mental disorders. In the standard diathesis–stress model, the personality diathesis is assumed to increase the risk that a given disorder will develop, without influencing the specific form that the disorder takes. In addition, the diathesis is usually considered to be triggered by any kind of sufficiently severe life stress, rather than influencing the specific kinds of stresses that may be most harmful.

Both of these assumptions of the standard diathesis–stress model restrict the role of personality in mental disorder, and both can be disputed. It is quite possible that some personality characteristics not only make people vulnerable to specific disorders, but also shape the way that affected people experience and express these disorders. More than one diathesis may exist for a given disorder, with different diatheses yielding somewhat different expressions of the disorder. It is also possible, and likely, that specific personality characteristics make people especially susceptible to specific types of stress. After all, personality influences the distinctive ways in which people make sense of their environments and respond to them. In short, diathesis–stress models may need to be refined to allow a larger and more complex role for personality.

The issues that we have discussed surrounding diathesis–stress models may all seem a bit abstract and theoretical at this point. However, they are important if we want to understand the ways in which personality influences the development of different forms of mental disorder. To illustrate how personality characteristics make people vulnerable to mental disorders, determine the experiences that trigger their vulnerabilities, and influence the way they experience their disorders, let us now investigate two disorders that produce a terrible burden of human suffering: depression and schizophrenia.

Depression

Major depression, as it is known by mental health professionals, is a serious form of emotional disturbance that affects a relatively large and apparently growing proportion of the population (about 5% of people at any particular time, and about 12% of people at some time in their lives). People who are depressed commonly suffer from a wide variety of symptoms, such as a profoundly sad mood, a loss of interest and pleasure in their everyday activities, insomnia, an inability to concentrate and make decisions, loss of appetite and weight, fatigue, guilt, and intensely self-critical and hopeless thinking. Episodes of depression commonly last for months, often recur over a person's lifetime, and have many serious complications, including an increased risk of suicide, relationship and marital problems, occupational and academic difficulties, health complaints, and abuse of alcohol and other drugs.

Given the prevalence and terrible consequences of major depression, psychologists and psychiatrists have understandably been very interested in discovering factors that predispose people to develop the disorder. The search has yielded a wide variety of factors that make some people more likely to develop major depression than others. For example, being female is a risk factor, such that two to three times as many women as men develop the disorder. Having a close relative who has been depressed also makes a person more vulnerable to depression, as does living through the death of a parent in childhood. People experiencing other serious life events, such as divorce, unemployment, and physical illness, are particularly vulnerable to developing major depression, as are people who lack social supports, such as a close, confiding relationship with a spouse.

All of these vulnerabilities are clearly important in helping us predict who is at risk of developing major depression. However, none of them refers to personality characteristics. Instead, they refer to demographic attributes (female gender), family history, past and present life stresses, and social relationships. Nevertheless, psychologists have proposed and studied several personality dispositions that also place people at increased risk of developing major depression. Four of the most extensively researched dispositions are dependency, autonomy, self-criticism, and pessimistic explanatory style. We will consider each of these in turn.

Dependency

'Dependency' can represent a fundamentally healthy tendency to enjoy and seek out connections with others: unless we are hermits, we are all dependent on others for emotional and physical well-being and for our sense of who we are. However, in the context of depression-proneness, dependency has a more pathological meaning, referring to an exaggerated need for the nurturance, guidance, and approval of others (Blatt & Zuroff, 1992). People who are dependent in this sense are deeply afraid of separation, abandonment, and disapproval, and are helpless and unable to make decisions when they are on their own. They constantly seek reassurance and advice, cling to others for support, behave submissively and passively in relationships, and tolerate being exploited because they dread losing their attachments.

Given that dependent people are heavily invested in their interpersonal relationships, it is not difficult to infer what kinds of stressful events are especially likely to tip them into depression. Not surprisingly, research has shown that highly dependent individuals are particularly vulnerable to become depressed in response to events involving interpersonal conflict, rejection, separation, and loss. These events might include romantic break-ups, arguments with family members or spouses, and the emigration or death of a loved one. Research has also suggested that when dependent people become depressed, they tend to exhibit a somewhat distinctive pattern of depressive symptoms. Although their depressions may involve all of the typical symptoms of the disorder, they are often dominated by themes of loss, emptiness, and deprivation, by crying and by active attempts to seek help.

Autonomy

Like dependency, 'autonomy' is a characteristic that can reflect a healthy independence and self-reliance that is highly esteemed in many cultures. However, some psychological writers have described a pathological form of autonomy that represents an excessive concern with personal achievement and an aversion to being controlled by or dependent on others that may lead people to sever themselves from social supports. People who are overly invested in this kind of individualistic philosophy of life, they argue, may be vulnerable to depression if they fail in their striving for personal achievement. In other words, highly autonomous people are especially susceptible to become depressed in reaction to life stresses such as losing a job, being passed over for a promotion, failing to qualify for a competitive academic course, or having the manuscript of their novel rejected by a publisher.

When events such as these happen, pathologically autonomous people may question their belief in their personal competence and their ability to control their lives, resulting in a sense of defeat and powerlessness. Some research has found support for the role of autonomy as a vulnerability factor for depression, and for the special harmfulness of stresses involving achievement-related failure. Other research further suggests that when they become depressed, autonomous people often do exhibit a symptom pattern dominated by defeat, a belief that they cannot control events in their world, and a corresponding loss of motivation and initiative that leaves them apathetic and fatigued.

Self-criticism

Self-criticism is a third personality dimension that has been proposed as a diathesis for depression. Some people, theorists argue, are especially prone to punishing self-evaluations, holding themselves to unreasonably high or perfectionistic standards. Psychoanalytic writers would describe them as suffering from a harsh super-ego. Consequently, these people are vulnerable to guilt, shame, and self-reproach in the course of their everyday lives, and if they experience significant negative events for which they feel responsible, they may become clinically depressed. When depressed, as you might expect, highly self-critical people are likely to suffer from symptoms that represent extreme expressions of their personality: severe and sometimes quite irrational guilt, believing themselves to be worthless, evil and ugly, and ruminating about the flaws that they perceive in their character. Once again, we see a personality diathesis (self-criticism) that is linked to a particular class of life stressors (negative events for which the person feels responsible) that may trigger a particular set of symptoms (self-punishing).

Pessimistic attributional style

Dependency, autonomy, and self-criticism are all personality dispositions that seem to make people vulnerable to depression. The final disposition that we shall examine differs from these in being conceptualized in explicitly cognitive terms. This disposition is based on a programme of research into the ways in which people explain life events, which we discussed in Chapter 7. Martin Seligman and his colleagues (Abramson et al., 1978) have shown that people's explanations for events differ along three 'causal dimensions', each of which has two opposed alternatives. First, events may be attributed to causes that are 'internal' (i.e., personal) or 'external' (i.e., influences outside personal control). An internal explanation might invoke personal abilities or intentions as causes of an event, whereas an external explanation might refer to other people's behaviour, to social conventions, to chance, or to fate. Second, the causes of events may be judged to be 'stable' (i.e., enduring over time) or 'unstable' (i.e., changeable). Stable causes include personality traits, societal traditions, and genes, whereas unstable causes might include moods, the weather, or unusual chance circumstances. Third, some events are attributed to 'global' causes (i.e., causes whose implications are generalized and far-reaching), others to 'specific' ones (i.e., causes having relatively narrow implications which are limited to the event in question). Intelligence, social class, and gender exemplify global causes, whereas luck, one's clothing, and skills restricted to particular tasks exemplify specific causes.

To illustrate this rather abstract review of the three explanatory dimensions, consider the following examples of explanations given by people who have just done poorly on an examination:

1. 'I did badly because I'm stupid.'
2. 'I did badly because the exam was unfair.'
3. 'I did badly because I had a toothache.'
4. 'I did badly because the educational system is biased against people like me.'

Explanation 1 invokes a cause that is internal, stable, and global. Stupidity, or low intelligence, is a characteristic that is intrinsic to the person, is unlikely to change, and is quite broad in its implications for the person's life. Explanation 2, in contrast, points to a cause that is external, unstable, and specific: the unfairness of the exam was due to someone else, future exams are not all likely to be unfair, and because the unfairness was particular to just one exam it is unlikely to have broader implications for the person's future academic performance or life. Explanation 3 proposes a cause that is unstable and specific, like explanation 2, but differs in being internal rather than external: the person claims to have been distracted by a temporary state of mind which will probably not interfere with future activities. Finally, explanation 4 contrasts sharply with explanation 3, referring to a cause that is external, stable, and global: an ongoing system of discrimination perpetrated by others.

As Chapter 7 showed, people exhibit consistent differences in their use of the three explanatory dimensions to make sense of events which are referred to as their 'attributional style'. People's ways of explaining negative events seem to be especially relevant to their vulnerability to depression, and it has been demonstrated that people who tend to attribute such events to stable and global causes are most vulnerable. In other words, people who explain negative events as outcomes of unchangeable and generalized causes – causes such as those invoked by explanations 1 and 4 – are said to have a 'pessimistic' attributional style and are depression-prone. Why this is so is not difficult to imagine. Confronted with a personally-relevant negative event, they are likely to see it as difficult to avoid, likely to continue or recur, and wide-ranging in its harmful consequences. Perceiving the event in this way is likely to leave them feeling hopeless about the future and helpless about their capacity to deal with the problem. In contrast, people who attribute negative events to unstable and specific causes – like explanations 2 and 3 – are likely to see them as transient, one-of-a-kind disruptions whose consequences are temporary and limited, and hence easily overcome. Even if, from an 'objective' standpoint, a pessimistic explanation might be more accurate – perhaps the student in explanation 2 really is not very capable and blames the 'unfair' exam as an excuse for poor performance – optimistic explanations therefore appear to protect against depression.

Pessimistic attributional style, then, is another personality diathesis for depression that can interact with a particular class of stressful events (i.e., negative ones) to produce depression. Some theorists (Abramson, Metalsky, & Alloy, 1989) have argued that people with this diathesis also tend to exhibit a characteristic pattern of symptoms when they become depressed. They propose that these people show prominent hopelessness and suicidal thinking, symptoms that are clearly consistent with a tendency to perceive negative events as unchangeable and devastating in their effects.

We have briefly reviewed four personality vulnerabilities for major depression, and found evidence that they are also associated with distinctive kinds of precipitating stresses and symptoms. It is important to recognize that these diatheses and stresses overlap: pessimistic people are likely to be self-critical, and a particular negative event, such as being insulted by one's employer, might at the same time represent an interpersonal conflict, a threat to personal competence, and a threat to self-esteem. Nevertheless, the important point to grasp here is that there are several somewhat distinct and psychologically meaningful pathways between personality and depression. All of these pathways suggest intriguing ways to understand and treat this crippling disorder.

Schizophrenia

Major depression provides a good illustration of the role that personality characteristics play in producing and shaping mental disorders. Schizophrenia provides another, which differs in interesting ways. Schizophrenia is a serious mental disorder that strikes about 1% of people at some time in their lives. The disorder is often long-lasting, with many affected people either suffering from its symptoms chronically or undergoing recurring episodes. In addition to being so enduring, the disorder is especially tragic because it severely impairs the capacity of people affected by it to engage in social relationships, to work, and to look after themselves, because these impairments often increase over time, and because the disorder usually first appears early in life, commonly in the early- to mid-20s.

The symptoms of schizophrenia are often severe and disabling. People with schizophrenia often have deeply held delusions, which are erroneous and often bizarre beliefs like having thoughts inserted in their heads by other people, being persecuted by the secret police, being eaten from within by giant insects, or being a famous historical figure. They also commonly experience hallucinations, such as hearing voices commenting on their actions, seeing visions, or smelling odours of decay. Their thinking is often disorganized and confused, and their speech is frequently incoherent, rambling, and sprinkled with invented words. Because these symptoms – delusions, hallucinations, and disorganized thinking and speech – all represent an excess or distortion of normal psychological functions, they are sometimes referred to as 'positive symptoms'. In addition to these forms of peculiarity, schizophrenic people are often very withdrawn, have a profound loss of motivation and initiative, and show a lack of emotional responsiveness to events in their lives. These symptoms are sometimes described as 'negative symptoms' because they involve a decrease or loss of normal functions.

Schizophrenia is a disorder which appears to have a substantial genetic component, indicating that some people are at higher genetic risk of developing the disorder than others. Psychologists have been eager to learn whether this genetic diathesis is expressed as a set of personality characteristics. If there is such a personality diathesis for schizophrenia, which has an at least partly genetic basis, we might be able to identify people who are at risk of developing the disorder. Indeed, psychologists have been quite successful in characterizing a personality vulnerability for schizophrenia, which is generally known as '**schizotypy**' (Meehl, 1962).

Schizotypy is a personality disposition that has several distinct aspects, which usually first reveal themselves in childhood or adolescence. As adults, schizotypal people are usually very uncomfortable in close relationships, feeling anxious and often suspecting that others have hostile intentions towards them. They tend to be solitary, and when in social situations with unfamiliar people they often come across as awkward, stiff, and unable to carry out conversation or maintain eye contact. Compounding their social difficulties, schizotypal people are commonly odd, eccentric, or peculiar in their mannerisms, and their range of emotional responses is often restricted. In addition, schizotypal people tend to show a variety of unusual cognitive and perceptual characteristics. For example, they are very superstitious, sometimes experience disorted perceptions, and often believe that they have paranormal powers, such as being able to foretell the future or magically influence other people's behaviour. In childhood and adolescence many of these schizotypal personality characteristics are manifested in social isolation and anxiety, under-achievement in school, peculiarities of behaviour and appearance that lead to teasing by peers, and active and often bizarre fantasy lives.

Schizotypal people are at an increased risk of developing schizophrenia, although not all schizophrenic adults clearly exhibit pre-existing schizotypal traits and not all people who do exhibit these traits develop schizophrenia. The precise nature of the life stresses that trigger schizophrenia in the fraction of schizotypal people who develop the disorder is not entirely clear. However, a number of physical and social stresses do seem to be involved. These stresses illustrate the wide variety of environmental influences that are involved in mental disorder in vulnerable individuals. First, there is some evidence that events during and prior to birth are influential in some cases, possibly including exposure to a virus in the womb and oxygen deprivation due to difficulties during delivery of the baby. Second, there is evidence that chaotic or inadequate child-rearing during the school years may increase the risk of schizophrenia among vulnerable, schizotypal individuals. Third, general life stress in adulthood, such as living alone for the first time, suffering the break-up of a close relationship, or receiving angry criticism or excessive demands from family members, may also play a role in precipitating schizophrenia. However, none of these stresses causes schizophrenia by itself, seeming only to do so among people who have the appropriate personality (and genetic) vulnerability.

The schizotypal diathesis is an interesting one in several respects. For one thing, it seems to be unlike many personality diatheses in being a matter of kind rather than a matter of degree (see Chapter 2). That is, people either belong to the category of schizotypes or they do not, and only the former seem to be at risk of developing schizophrenia. A second interesting aspect of schizotypy is that, like major depression, somewhat different forms of the diathesis may be precipitated by different kinds of stresses, and may result in somewhat distinctive patterns of symptoms. Some Danish research examining the children of people with schizophrenia – who are at increased risk of having the schizotypal diathesis – indicates that there are two rather distinct pathways linking the diathesis to the disorder of schizophrenia (Cannon, Mednick, & Parnas, 1990). On the one hand, some vulnerable children and adolescents tend to be socially withdrawn, emotionally unresponsive, and introverted, and often have a history of birth complications. If these individuals develop schizophrenia as adults they tend to exhibit 'negative' symptoms of the disorder (e.g., loss of motivation, profound apathy, flattened emotional expression). On the other hand, some children and adolescents with the schizotypal diathesis are impulsive, disruptive, and have peculiar mannerisms, rather than being quiet and emotionally bland. For these individuals, a chaotic family environment, including such factors as frequent moves of home, abuse, and neglect, seems to be particularly important in triggering schizophrenia. If they do develop schizophrenia, they tend to exhibit 'positive' symptoms, such as paranoid delusions, hallucinations, and disorganized speech.

Major depression and schizophrenia provide two good examples of how diathesis–stress models explain the connections between personality and mental disorder. In both cases, psychologists have discovered personality characteristics that place people at increased risk of developing the respective disorders, but are not sufficient to produce the disorders in themselves. In both cases, more than one kind of personality diathesis seems to exist, and these different diatheses seem to require somewhat different kinds of stressful events to precipitate the disorders. Moreover, the personality characteristics that make people vulnerable to the two disorders also seem to influence the ways in which they express the disorders, producing distinctive patterns of symptoms. To summarize, personality characteristics influence vulnerability, precipitating factors, and symptom patterns for mental disorders.

Our discussions of personality factors in mental disorder have focused on depression and schizophrenia, but it is worth mentioning in passing that there appear to be personality vulnerabilities for many other mental disorders. To give one example, people with social anxiety disorder, who suffer from disabling anxiety in social situations such as parties and public speaking, commonly have had what is known as 'inhibited temperament' as infants and young children (Kagan, 1994). Such children are unusually shy, are easily over-stimulated, and react fearfully and with high levels of physiological arousal to unfamiliar situations. (They are also, Kagan claims, more likely than one would expect by chance to be blue-eyed!) Having an inhibited temperament does not dictate that a child will, as an adult, become socially anxious, because many other influences, such as life stress and home and school environment, are also involved, but it does raise the odds.

To give another example, psychopaths – people who seem to lack the capacity for remorse and empathy with others, and who often engage in impulsive, violent, deceitful, and otherwise antisocial activities – seem to have the personality diathesis of unusually low fearfulness (Lykken, 1995). Once again, this diathesis does not in itself destine children to become psychopathic adults. However, by making children more impulsive and risk-seeking and less concerned and inhibited by the fear of punishment, the diathesis leaves them especially vulnerable to a variety of environmental conditions that push and pull them towards a psychopathic way of living. These conditions might include abusive, coercive, or neglectful parenting (fearless, impulsive children are apt to be frustrating and difficult to socialize), falling in with groups of older peers who introduce the child to petty criminality, being made homeless, repeatedly witnessing violent acts, and so on. In short, identifiable personality dispositions make people vulnerable for psychopathy, and these dispositions act in combination with identifiable life circumstances to produce disorder. Several additional empirically validated diatheses for mental disorders are summarized in Table 10.1, to convey a sense of the range of personality vulnerabilities that have been identified. Personality researchers are actively engaged in the important task of identifying more of these risk factors so as better to detect and intervene with people at risk.

Table 10.1 Personality vulnerabilities for selected mental disorders

Disorder	Diathesis	Definition
Anorexia nervosa	Perfectionism	A tendency to set extremely high performance standards for oneself and to be distressed when these are not met
Bipolar disorder	Hypomanic temperament	A tendency to be overly optimistic, excitable, exuberant, energetic, hyperactive, and needing less sleep than other people
Obsessive-compulsive disorder	Thought–action fusion	A tendency to see thoughts and actions as equivalent, so that having a thought about doing something wrong or inappropriate is just as bad as actually doing it.
Panic disorder	Anxiety sensitivity	A tendency to fear the physical symptoms of anxiety, such as racing heartbeat and shortness of breath

Personality disorders

Our extended discussions of depression and schizophrenia have focused on the role that personality dispositions play in making people vulnerable to mental disorders. However, in addition to influencing who develops particular disorders and how they express them, some personality dispositions can themselves be understood as disorders. These dispositions are known as 'personality disorders'. Although these disorders have been recognized forms of psychological disturbance since the 18th century, when European psychiatrists understood them in terms of moral and constitutional degeneracy, they have only been a major topic of clinical psychology research since 1980. The third edition of American psychiatry's classification of psychiatric conditions, the *Diagnostic and Statistical Manual of Mental Disorders* (DSM-III), was published in that year, and for the first time it defined personality disorders as a distinct group of conditions.

According to DSM-III and later editions – we are now up to DSM-5 (American Psychiatric Association, 2013) – the personality disorders are enduring dispositions that are inflexible and maladaptive, producing significant interpersonal difficulties and distress for people who have them. They therefore differ from most other mental disorders in several important respects. First, their primary features involve problems in the person's relations with others rather than specific abnormalities of personal behaviour, emotions, or thinking. Whereas someone with a compulsion or phobia or compulsion or psychosis suffers from specific symptoms – an urge to wash one's hands, a fear of spiders, a belief that one is being pursued by aliens – someone with a personality disorder has a broad difficulty with their interpersonal relating. Second, they are lasting rather than temporary or recurrent: unlike most mental disorders which *affect* or befall the person at distinct times, personality disorders are woven into the fabric of the person, partly defining who they *are*. Third, because personality disorders are intrinsic to the person's sense of self in a way that most disorders are not, they are seldom seen by the person as problems to be solved by psychological treatment. More often, the person sees other people as the source of their interpersonal difficulties, and only comes into treatment when their personality disorder gives rise to another disorder, such as depression. As you might expect, the existence of the personality disorder is likely to make that depression more difficult to treat, as it is linked to enduring, hard-to-change features of the person that he or she does not see as problematic.

Brief descriptions of the ten disorders recognized by the current diagnostic system (the DSM-5; American Psychiatric Association, 2013), are presented in Table 10.2. Several of the ten labels and descriptions should sound familiar. The first three – which earlier editions of DSM joined together in a so-called 'odd cluster' – bear a family resemblance to psychotic conditions such as schizophrenia, although they lack the severe symptoms of those conditions, such as hallucinations and delusions. These personality disorders do indeed have a relationship to psychoses, occurring at elevated rates among the relatives of people with schizophrenia, and 'schizotypal' personality disorder is very closely related to the concept of schizotypy, discussed earlier in this chapter as a diathesis for schizophrenia. The next four personality disorders in Table 10.2, once called the 'dramatic' cluster, are forms of maladaptive personality that are often expressed in dramatic outward displays. Antisocial personalities behave callously towards others, borderline personalities have chaotic lives marked by unstable moods, relationships, and self-image, and histrionic and narcissistic personalities demand attention is different ways. The concept of antisocial personality disorder overlaps the concept of psychopathy, and narcissistic personality disorder is an extreme form of narcissism, a characteristic discussed in Chapter 7. The final three disorders in the table, dubbed the 'anxious cluster', involve personality traits that revolve around fears and worries. Avoidant personality is associated with social anxiety disorder and obsessive-compulsive personality disorder with obsessive-compusive disorder, a condition defined by obsessive thoughts and compulsive behaviours. Readers with good memories might note that the description of obsessive-compulsive personality disorder is extremely similar to the Freudian concept of the 'anal character' (see Chapter 4).

Table 10.2 Descriptive features of the personality disorders

Personality disorder	Core personality features
Paranoid	Pervasive distrust and suspicion of others, tendency to see others as exploiting, harming or deceiving the person and to read threatening hidden meanings into benign remarks or events
Schizoid	Pervasive detachment from social relationships (i.e., preference for solitary activities and lack of desire for close relationships) and restricted or cold emotional expression
Schizotypal	Pervasive peculiarities in beliefs, perceptions, speech, and behaviour, coupled with excessive social anxiety and isolation
Antisocial	Pervasive disregard for and violation of the rights of others, shown by deceitfulness, impulsiveness, aggressiveness, irresponsibility, and remorselessness
Borderline	Pervasive instability of relationships, self-image and emotions, indicated by recurrent suicidal gestures, abandonment fears, impulsiveness, and mood-swings
Histrionic	Pervasive pattern of exaggerated emotionality and attention-seeking, shown by inappropriate exhibitionism, seductiveness, shallow displays of emotion, and self-dramatization
Narcissistic	Pervasive grandiosity, need for admiration, and lack of empathy for others, indicated by arrogance, self-importance, and feeling entitled to special treatment
Avoidant	Pervasive social inhibition, feelings of inadequacy, and over-sensitivity to negative evaluation, shown by fear of criticism and rejection
Dependent	Pervasive need to be taken care of, involving submissive and clinging behaviour and fears of separation
Obsessive-compulsive	Pervasive preoccupation with orderliness, perfectionism, and being in control, manifested by inflexibility, over-conscientiousness, excessive devotion to work, stubbornness, and miserliness

Approaches to understanding personality disorders

Personality and clinical psychologists have developed a wide variety of approaches to making sense of the personality disorders laid out in Table 10.2. One approach has been to attempt to fit the ten disorders into established frameworks for describing normal personality. For instance, it is possible that the disorders simply represent extreme positions on the Big Five trait dimensions. If this were true, scores on tests of personality disorder features should correlate strongly (positively or negatively) with scores on tests of the Big Five. Sure enough, all of the personality disorders do seem to correlate to some degree with Big Five traits. Table 10.3 summarizes these associations: 'Low' means there is a negative correlation between a disorder and a trait dimension, 'High' means there is a positive correlation, and an empty cell in the table means there is no reliable connection (the disorder is neither high nor low on the dimension).

Table 10.3 reveals a few patterns. First, high Neuroticism and low Agreeableness are shared by many of the personality disorders, implying that negative emotionality and a lack of concern for others are common features of these conditions. Second, Openness to Experience is not highly relevant to any of the disorders. Third, every personality disorder is related to two or more Big Five dimensions: each disorder has a trait 'profile' rather than being extreme on a single trait. For example, there is no disorder that simply corresponds to extreme Introversion or extreme Agreeableness. Finally, there is a lot of overlap between the trait profiles of the ten personality disorders – for example, avoidant and dependent personalities are both neurotic introverts, but dependent personalities are a little more agreeable. In sum, although the Big Five trait dimensions capture some aspects of the personality disorders and some of the features that make them distinct from one another, they do not do so perfectly.

Table 10.3 Associations between personality disorders and Big Five dimensions

	Extraversion	Agreeableness	Neuroticism	Conscientiousness	Openness
Paranoid		Low	High		
Schizoid	Low	Low			
Schizotypal	Low	Low	High		
Antisocial	High	Low	Low	Low	
Borderline		Low	High	Low	
Histrionic	High		High		
Narcissistic	High	Low			
Avoidant	Low		High		
Dependent	Low	High	High		
Obsessive-compulsive	Low	Low	High		

ILLUSTRATIVE STUDY

Do the Big Five help to illuminate personality disorders?

In collaboration with several Chinese colleagues, American psychologists Robert McCrae and Paul Costa (McCrae et al., 2001) sought to clarify how well abnormal personality can be understood in terms of the Big Five. Many writers have argued that there is no sharp, categorical distinction between normal and abnormal personality, and that models of normal personality should therefore help to make sense of personality disorders (PDs). Disorders might simply reflect extreme positions on continuous Big Five dimensions.

A considerable amount of research has shown correlations between PDs and Big Five dimensions. McCrae et al. attempted to do so in a cultural setting where this sort of research had not previously been done: the People's Republic of China. Some writers have questioned whether personality disorders that were catalogued in the West can also be found elsewhere in the world, making McCrae et al.'s effort an important scientific exercise.

McCrae et al. obtained a sample of 1,909 Chinese psychiatric patients and administered to them a carefully translated questionnaire measure of the Big Five and questionnaire- and interview-based measures of PDs. Expected or 'prototypical' Big Five profiles for each PD were generated based on Western research (for example, the profile for paranoid PD includes high Neuroticism and Conscientiousness and low Agreeableness) and the extent to which each participant fitted each profile was calculated. These Big Five-based measures of PDs were then correlated with scores for the same PDs on the PD questionnaire and interview. If these different measures correlate well, then it would appear that Big Five does a good job of making sense of the PDs in China: the same Big Five profiles that capture PDs in Western nations would capture them in that country.

Consistent with the validity of the Big Five's PD profiles in China, these profiles correlated reasonably well with the scores derived from the PD questionnaire and interview. The Big Five, a prominent model of normal personality, appears to be a useful tool for understanding abnormal personality in China as well as in the countries where the model was developed.

Personality disorders tend to involve difficulties in interpersonal relationships, so it makes sense to emphasize interpersonal traits when trying to account for them. In recognition of this point, another attempt to capture the personality disorders employs the 'interpersonal circle', another framework for describing normal personality. First developed by Timothy Leary, a personality psychologist who went on to achieve notoriety as an advocate of psychedelic drugs and a guru of the 1960s counter-culture – he famously advised us to 'tune in, turn on, drop out' – the interpersonal circle proposes that there are two main dimensions of interpersonal behaviour. One dimension, depicted as the horizontal axis in Figure 10.2, runs from cold (antagonistic and aloof) to warm (friendly and cooperative), and the other, depicted as the vertical dimension, runs from dominant (controlling and confident) to submissive (docile and dependent). Importantly, any kind of interpersonal behaviour can be understood as a blend of these two dimensions and located somewhere around a circle defined by the two dimensions. For example, resentful behaviour could be located in the circle's north-west quadrant (cold and dominant) and forgiving behaviour in the south-east (warm and submissive). Figure 10.2 labels different kinds of interpersonal behaviour at 16 compass points.

Researchers such as Wiggins and Pincus (1989) asked whether personality disorders have distinctive interpersonal signatures that could be classified on the circle. If it is true that each disorder has a particular inflexible and maladaptive interpersonal style, then people with that disorder should take an extreme position somewhere in the circle. Numerous studies have

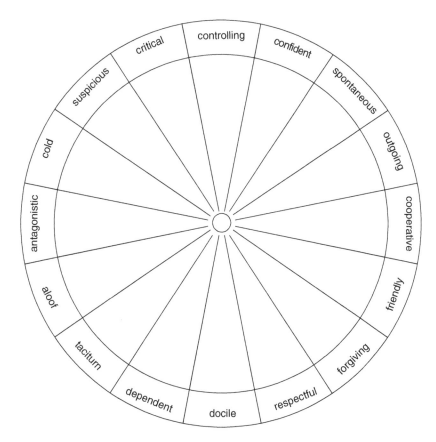

Figure 10.2 The interpersonal circle

confirmed this possibility. For example, people with dependent personality disorder tend to engage in warm and submissive behaviour to a problematic degree, with the result that they feel trampled on and used. People with avoidant and schizoid personalities have an interpersonal style that is cold and submissive, so that they are unresponsive to others and have difficulty getting close to them. People with antisocial, narcissistic, and paranoid personalities have a rigid interpersonal style in which they are overly cold and dominant, expressed in vindictive, suspicious, and disdainful behaviour towards others. Like the Big Five, then, the interpersonal circle succeeds in capturing some of the distinctive aspects of the personality disorders. Also like the Big Five, however, many different disorders look much the same according to the circle, having very similar locations. The circle also fails to capture a few of the disorders at all. For example, schizotypal and borderline personalities do not have reliable locations on the circle, indicating that it is unable to describe them.

The Big Five and the interpersonal circle help to describe the personality disorders, despite their limitations, but other approaches try to go beyond description to explain their underlying causes and mechanisms. Psychoanalytic theorists, whose work was discussed in Chapter 4, have attempted to explain the origins of personality disorders in the difficulties that children experience as they pass through the psychosexual stages. For example, according to a psychoanalytic approach, obsessive-compulsive personalities reflect fixations in the anal stage. The main features of this disorder, such as perfectionism and excessive orderliness, are reactions to deep-seated concerns about control. Psychoanalysts who study personality disorders also emphasize unconscious processes such as the defence mechanisms that people with particular disorders tend to employ.

Personality psychologists with a biological orientation (see Chapters 5 and 6) have also made contributions to our understanding of personality disorders. For example, there is now strong evidence that personality disorders have a substantial genetic component, with heritabilities similar to those of normal personality (often in the 30–50% range). One major study by Kendler and colleagues (2008) further showed that there are three main genetic factors associated with the disorders. One factor, related to negative emotionality and Neuroticism, is associated with vulnerability to most of the ten disorders. A second genetic factor is associated only with borderline and antisocial disorders, and seems to reflect impulsive aggression, and a third factor, associated only with avoidant and schizoid disorders, is linked to genetic liability for introversion. Other research has confirmed a genetic link between the 'odd cluster' disorders – paranoid, schizoid, and especially schizotypal personalities – and schizophrenia.

Other biologically-oriented researchers have shown that personality disorders have distinctive neural processes. For example, there is evidence that some brain regions associated with emotional processing, such as the amygdala, are reduced in volume among people with borderline personality disorder, who also have altered activation patterns in frontal and prefrontal brain regions that are involved in regulating emotions. These structural and functional alterations in the brain may underlie the emotional instability and impulsive behaviour that plague people with this disorder. Neurochemical abnormalities are also involved in some personality disorders. For example, schizotypal personalities often display abnormalities in the dopaminergic system of a similar sort to those that have been shown among people with schizophrenia.

Cognitive theories of personality (see Chapter 7) offer yet another way of thinking about personality disorders. Theorists such as Aaron Beck (e.g., Pretzer & Beck, 2005) argue that people with particular disorders have distinctive core beliefs or 'schemas' about themselves and others, and distinctive cognitive strategies for negotiating their interactions. For example, according to Beck and colleagues, people with avoidant personality disorder firmly believe that it is intolerable to be rejected by others but inevitable that it will happen if others come to know them as they really are. They view themselves as incompetent and vulnerable, and they view other people as highly critical, demeaning, and superior. As a result of holding their beliefs, they adopt a strategy of avoiding situations in which they might be evaluated by others. This interpersonal strategy makes perfect sense in light of their beliefs: if you are inept and fragile and others are superior, hostile, and contemptuous, it is a good idea to avoid them. Unfortunately, however, the strategy is sure to impair the person's social and work functioning, and reinforce the very sense of incompetence that drives the avoidance in the first place. Cognitive theories propose that people with personality disorders get caught in these self-perpetuating cycles, where beliefs about self and others lead to behaviour that confirms and deepens those maladaptive, self-limiting beliefs.

As we can see, personality psychology offers many ways to make sense of personality disorders, each of them clarifying some aspects of these complex phenomena. Let us take paranoid personality disorder as a case in point. Its key features are suspiciousness, distrust, a tendency to see others as malicious and devious, and an inclination to search for hidden meanings. According to the Big Five, people with this disorder are extreme on two normal personality dimensions: they are high in Neuroticism, indicating proneness to negative emotions and emotional reactivity, and low on Agreeableness, suggesting an uncooperative and antagonistic manner. According to the interpersonal circle, they have a cold and dominant style, and are therefore likely to be vindictive, bitter, domineering, and prone to aggression in their dealings with others. Psychoanalysts argue that they have an unconscious sense of weakness and inferiority, based on early problems in their relations with caregivers, and that as a result they are highly sensitive to feeling humiliated. In addition, they tend to employ the defence mechanisms of projection, disowning their self-doubts and aggressive wishes and attributing them to others. Biological researchers observe that people with paranoid personalities tend to have high loadings on a genetic factor associated with negative emotionality. Cognitive theorists propose that such people believe themselves to be innocent, vulnerable, and morally righteous, believe others to be malicious and interfering, and consequently adopt a strategy of wariness, suspicion, and pre-emptive aggression.

These alternative accounts of paranoid personality offer a variety of insights into the personality structures and processes that underpin the disorder. Each of them identifies somewhat different core disturbances and has distinct implications for how treatment of the disorder should be conducted. Any complete account of personality disorders needs to integrate these different perspectives.

Controversies in the study of personality disorders

As we have seen, personality disorders present an intriguing field of study to personality researchers and theorists. However, the field also has more than its share of controversies. Three of the main controversies relate to the co-existence and overlap of different personality disorders, whether these disorders are better understood as categories or dimensions, and whether they are highly stable over time.

It is common for more than one mental disorder to co-occur in the same individual. Someone who suffers from major depression may also have a phobia for snakes, for example. There is nothing troubling about this: the two conditions are dissimilar, have different causes, and could easily afflict the same person, just as a single, unlucky person could have both diabetes and the flu. However, the co-existence of different disorders – called 'co-morbidity' – is extremely high among personality disorders. It is relatively rare for a person to meet diagnostic criteria for a single personality disorder, and people in clinical settings often qualify for two, three or more disorders. As the junk food advertisements say, 'you can't have just one'. This creates a problem for clinical psychologists who have to treat a personality disordered client. If the person has four disorders, which one should the treatment focus on?

Many psychologists believe that the high level of co-morbidity among personality disorders means that they may not really be distinct problems. Instead, they may merely be labels that apply to different aspects of personality disturbance. That is, they may not be distinct conditions that people have, but multiple attributes of a single underlying problem. By analogy, a tennis ball does not have distinct 'yellow colour' and 'green colour' identities, but can be described both as 'yellowish' and 'greenish'. Avoidant and dependent personality disorders, for instance, may not really be distinct disorders with different causes, in the way that diabetes and flu are different diseases, but just overlapping ways of describing neurotic personality. After all, we have seen that these two disorders have high Neuroticism and low Extraversion in common (see Table 10.2), so it not surprising that they tend to be diagnosed in the same people. Rather than there truly being ten different personality disorders, as DSM-5 supposes, there may be an undifferentiated spectrum of personality disturbance.

A second controversy also relates to how personality disorders should be described. According to the DSM system, personality disorders are diagnosed categorically: a person either has a particular disorder or they do not (you can't be a little bit personality disordered, just as you can't be a little bit pregnant). This is consistent with how most mental disorders and physical illnesses are diagnosed. However, research on normal personality has shown that most personality characteristics are continuous dimensions, not categorical types (see Chapter 2). So are personality disorders best thought of as categories or dimensions?

There is now overwhelming evidence that personality disorders are dimensional. They are not only strongly associated with normal personality dimensions such as the Big Five, but there is no underlying category boundary separating people who have a disorder from those who do not. By implication, personality disorders fall on a continuum from very mild to very severe – you *can* be a little bit personality disordered – and deciding at what point along this spectrum of severity normality ends and abnormality begins is therefore somewhat arbitrary. Different disorders also appear to fall on a continuum with one another with no clear boundaries in between, a fact that helps to explain the problem of co-morbidity. If there are no boundaries between two disorders that have many overlapping features – like avoidant and dependent personality disorders – then it should come as no surprise that people will be diagnosed with both. The dimensional nature of personality disorders was finally recognized in the latest edition of the DSM system (DSM-5) in 2013, although the use of categorical labels has been retained for ease of communication. It is easier for a psychologist to tell a colleague that Mr X has borderline personality disorder than to say that he falls at the 93rd percentile on the borderline spectrum, even if the latter statement is closer to the truth.

A final controversy in the study of personality disorders concerns their stability over time. Personality disorders were defined as a separate group of conditions in DSM-III (American Psychiatric Association, 1980) largely because they were understood to be enduring characteristics of the person, unlike other disorders, which were thought of as temporary afflictions. However, longitudinal research is increasingly challenging this view and finding that personality disorders are often unstable over time. For example, among people diagnosed with a personality disorder, around 20% no longer meet diagnostic criteria for the disorder one year later (Grilo et al., 2004). The same study found that only 44% of people diagnosed with a particular personality disorder at the beginning of the study met diagnostic criteria every month during the following year. Not only are personality disorder diagnoses prone to fluctuate over time, but they may even do so more than other disorders. For instance, although DSM conceptualizes anxiety disorders as transient conditions, they appear to be more stable than personality disorders.

The apparent instability of personality has a few causes. First, levels of personality disorder traits tend to decline with age, so people who warrant a diagnosis as young adults often do not do so later on. One study of university students found that the mean number of diagnostic criteria that the sample met decreased steadily every year over a four-year period (Lenzenweger, Johnson, & Willett, 2004). Second, the measurement of personality disorders can be distorted by people's mood-states and by co-existing disorders. People with personality disorders often experience volatile moods and episodes of depression, and their personalities often appear more disturbed during these moods and episodes than when their negative moods resolve or their episodes end. It is not uncommon for a person diagnosed with a personality disorder to lose the diagnosis when their co-morbid depresson is successfully treated. What looked like enduring personality disturbance was, at least in part, merely a transient side-effect of their emotional distress.

The fact that personality is less stable over time than many psychologists originally thought should perhaps not surprise us now. As Chapter 8 showed, the last two decades of personality research have demonstrated that personality is a good deal less stable than many theorists imagined. If personality traits are prone to change, rather than set like plaster, then personality disorder traits should be expected to change as well. And if longitudinal research shows that levels of Neuroticism drop and levels of Agreeableness rise during adulthood, we would expect levels of personality disorder to decline with increasing age, Neuroticism and low Agreeableness being two shared features of many disorders (see Table 10.3). All in all, it is clear that personality disorders are less stable than was first thought. A personality disorder is not a life sentence.

Multiple personality

The personality disorders generally seem to reflect exaggerated expressions of normal personality dispositions. For this reason, many of us can recognize aspects of our own or our acquaintances' personalities when we read descriptions of these disorders. However, there is another disturbance of personality that seems so peculiar and striking that it is difficult to identify with it at all. This disturbance is often referred to as 'multiple personality disorder', although the term 'dissociative identity disorder' is more technically correct. For the sake of simplicity, we will refer to the disorder here as '**multiple personality**'.

In essence, multiple personality is the existence of two or more distinct personalities or identities, each of which takes control of the person's behaviour from time to time. Each personality has its own distinctive way of thinking and behaving, and is generally unaware of what the other personalities do when they are in charge. As a result, one personality is often unable to recall or account for long stretches of time when another personality was dominant, and may re-emerge to find itself in an unfamiliar place or activity. The person may wake up in an unfamiliar bed with someone they do not remember, or believe that someone impersonating them is withdrawing money from their bank account only to find that another personality was the culprit.

People diagnosed with multiple personality generally have a primary or 'host' personality and one or more 'alter' personalities. These alters typically have their own names, ages, mannerisms, and emotional states, and often they are of a different gender to the host personality. Different personalities often emerge predictably in different situations, and switches between them often occur during stressful interactions with others. Whereas the host personality is usually sad, dependent, and passive, the alters are often childish, hostile, seductive, or otherwise uninhibited, and are often scornful of the other personalities. The personalities seem to share general knowledge and physical skills, but may differ in many other respects. There are reports of cases whose personalities had different allergies, eye-glass prescriptions, handedness (left versus right), menstrual cycles, and patterns of blood flow in the brain.

The existence of people with multiple personalities has proven to be a controversial issue for a variety of reasons. First, it seems simply inconceivable to many people that anyone could harbour distinct identities within a single body. The idea that each of us has a single personality, whose coherence and continuity over time we prize in ourselves and rely on in making sense of other people, is deeply rooted in Western cultures. We expect others to be consistent in their behaviour and beliefs, and distrust dramatic changes in either. People who hold contradictory beliefs or behave very differently from one time to another are distrusted, and their apparent lack of a solid 'centre' is often attributed to personal weakness or immorality, or to the undue influence of others. We might accept that people act differently in different social roles or situations, but we tend to see these differences as facets of a unitary self, shallow, socially-imposed performances rather than deep divisions between alternative personalities.

A second source of scepticism about multiple personalities has to do with the recent history of the diagnosis itself, which is unusual. Until 1980 fewer than 200 cases were reported worldwide, but present estimates suggest that there may currently be tens of thousands of cases. In addition to the apparently epidemic nature of multiple personality, it is strikingly restricted to North America, with very few cases having been recorded outside the USA. Some have even claimed that the disorder is one of an exotic family of 'culture-bound' disorders, like *koro* (the intense and sometimes epidemic fear among some South and East Asian men that their penis will disappear into their body). Even within the USA, the disorder tends to congregate in a few urban areas, where a small number of psychologists and psychiatrists claim to have seen very large numbers of patients.

In addition to the intuitive strangeness and geographic limits of multiple personalities, many people are sceptical of the disorder because of the bizarre, faddish, and cult-like phenomena that sometimes adhere to it. In recent years, as more and more attention has been paid to the disorder and organized groups and conferences for sufferers have emerged, the number of alters that diagnosed cases of multiple personality present has increased, from the two or three that were typical in early reports to an average of about 12, with some cases claiming more than 100. Lately, reports of animal alters have begun to appear regularly, as have claims by patients to have been abused in gruesome rituals perpetrated by organized satanic cults or aliens. Phenomena such as these strain the credibility of many people and suggest to them that they are witnessing some mixture of fantasy, hysteria, and theatre.

Psychological theories of the origin and nature of multiple personality have been developed over the past two decades, building on important theoretical contributions made by the 19th-century-French psychiatrist Pierre Janet. Recent theories differ in their details, but most of them begin with two apparently crucial facts about multiple personality. First, almost all people diagnosed with the disorder report having been severely sexually or physically abused as children. Second, these people tend to score very high on measures of a psychological characteristic known as 'suggestibility', which refers to the capacity to become absorbed in activities and to respond to social influences. Highly suggestible people are easily hypnotized; that is to say, they are easily sent into a trance-like state of consciousness in which they are unusually responsive to other people's suggestions.

Most recent theories of multiple personality put these two observations together in an intriguing way. They argue that in response to extreme and inescapable traumatic experiences, such as being repeatedly raped by a step-father, some young children split their consciousness into one part that contains the traumatic memories and associated thoughts, and another part that has no recollection of the trauma. This splitting of consciousness is known as 'dissociation', and may represent a primitive attempt by the child to protect itself against the pain and catastrophic loss of trust and security that the traumatic abuse involves. In effect, the child tries to preserve some sense of intact selfhood by a kind of 'internal avoidance' of the trauma, in which it is isolated into a separate pocket of awareness and memory.

235

This kind of reaction has been compared to the survival tactics of animals that freeze or play dead when confronted by predators. Children who have highly suggestible personalities may be predisposed to dissociate in this way, because they are unusually capable of entering trance-like states and deflecting their attention away from unpleasant experiences. In theory, then, some children engage in an 'auto-hypnotic' reaction to protect themselves against overwhelming stress. Although this reaction may be self-protective in the short term, in the long term it creates a disintegrated personality. Moreover, children who dissociate under severe stress may learn to use dissociation as a habitual defence mechanism, which may lead them to continue to split off new identities as they progress through life.

According to this theory of multiple personality, traumatic experiences in childhood fragment an initially unitary personality in people whose suggestibility makes them predisposed to dissociate. However, this theory remains controversial to some psychologists. One in particular, Nicholas Spanos (1994), argues that multiple personality is not caused by past traumas at all. Instead, it is created by therapists who believe that multiple personality is under-diagnosed, and by a culture that recognizes it as a legitimate way of expressing psychological distress, just as in other cultures and times possession by spirits has been recognized. Spanos proposes that therapists are commonly using leading questions and hypnotic procedures to induce their patients to understand their often chaotic experiences in terms of distinct personalities. Because these patients are prone to sudden mood-swings, the idea that they have several identities is readily planted in their minds by therapists who treat their desires, emotions, and recollections *as if* they were distinct and nameable identities. The suggestibility of the patients makes them susceptible to their therapists' convictions that they have multiple personalities, even if these convictions are communicated in subtle ways, and to elaborate each newly hatched identity into a fully-fledged character. Spanos has even conducted experiments in which, using simple hypnotic instructions, several multiple personality-like phenomena can be produced in ordinary people. In short, Spanos sees multiple personality as a way for suggestible people who are struggling with identity confusions and diffuse psychological problems to make sense of their experiences. It also allows them to enact multiple social roles and personality states – such as confident sexuality, anger, authority, and innocence (i.e., the alters) – that they were unable to express prior to 'becoming a multiple'.

The two theories of multiple personality could hardly be more incompatible. One views the personalities as truly distinct products of traumatic experiences, while the other sees them as labels for poorly integrated psychological states, labels that are transformed into distinct identities by a collusion of patient and therapist. One sees multiple personality as a real disorder that is finally being recognized by enlightened mental health professionals after years of ignorance, the other as a hysterical epidemic that can be likened to previous epidemics of witchcraft and demonic possession. Wherever the truth may lie, it is clear that people diagnosed with multiple personality are not simply play-acting: they believe sincerely and passionately that their personalities are not merely roles to be enacted or personas to be juggled. The solution to the puzzle of multiple personality will be found somewhere in the grey area between two metaphors: the actor playing a series of parts and the sheet of glass shattered into pieces by a hammer.

The controversy over multiple personality is sure to continue, and it is currently the focus of vigorous debate. At this point, however, it is enough to contemplate the controversy as another fascinating intersection between the psychology of personality and mental disorder.

Conclusions

Personality characteristics are important sources of vulnerability for a variety of mental disorders, as well as for some physical illnesses. Several traits have been identified as diatheses for such crippling mental disorders as major depression and schizophrenia, as well as physical illness such as coronary heart disease and cancer. None of these diatheses is capable of producing its disorder without the contribution of other influences, such as life stresses and non-psychological risk factors. Often, the combination of personality diathesis and environmental stress is especially potent in producing mental disorder. However, personality plays a powerful role in the development of mental disorders, acting not only as a risk factor but also as an influence on the kinds of stress that are harmful to different people and on the ways in which people express and experience their disorder. Finally, some forms of personality variation can themselves be considered mental disorders. These personality disorders, as well as multiple personality, have emerged as intriguing and clinically important topics of investigation, and are open to a wide and fascinating variety of explanations.

Chapter summary

- Personality psychology intersects with clinical psychology in several intriguing ways. Personality characteristics render people vulnerable to particular kinds of mental disorder, in extreme cases they constitute disorders in themselves.
- Personality vulnerabilities ('diatheses') increase the risk for major mental disorders. Disorder usually occurs only when a diathesis is triggered by life stress. The higher the level of vulnerability, the less stress is needed to trigger it.
- Major depression and schizophrenia are two serious mental disorders that have well-established personality vulnerabilities.
- Personality disorders are extreme, inflexible, maladaptive personality variants that are associated with significant distress and interpersonal difficulties for people who are affected. Ten distinct forms are recognized by the current psychiatric classification, and these can be explained in multiple ways.
- Multiple personality ('dissociative identity disorder') is a controversial and rare condition in which the person appears to have several distinct personalities, which are often mutually unaware.

Further reading

Alloy, L. B., & Riskind, J. H. (Eds.) (2005). *Cognitive vulnerability to emotional disorders*. Mahwah, NJ: Erlbaum.
This diverse collection of chapters takes a cognitive approach to the factors that place people at risk for the development of disorders involving depression, anxiety, disturbed eating, and much more.

Claridge, G., & Davis, C. (2003). *Personality and psychological disorders*. London: Hodder Arnold.
Claridge and Davis offer a thought-provoking and clear explication of the relationship between personality variation and major mental disorders.

Clark, L. A. (2007). Assessment and diagnosis of personality disorder: Perennial issues and an emerging reconceptualization. *Annual Review of Psychology*, 58, 227–57.
Clark, a major psychological researcher in the field, presents an advanced but comprehensive review of the main controversies in the study of personality disorders.

Kihlstrom, J. F. (2005). Dissociative disorders. *Annual Review of Clinical Psychology*, 1, 227–53.
For readers interested in multiple personality ('dissociative identity disorder'), Kihlstrom provides a review of current research and theory.

Lenzenweger, M. F., & Clarkin, J. F. (2004). *Major theories of personality disorder* (2nd ed.). New York: Guilford Press.
This book contains several excellent chapters that present diverse theoretical perspectives (from the psychodynamic to the biological) on personality disorders.

Journal of Personality Disorders and *Personality Disorders: Research and Treatment*
For anyone with a deep interest in the study of personality disorders, these two academic journals are invaluable resources for the latest thinking and research findings.

Psychobiography and Life Narratives

Learning objectives

- To understand the personological approach to the study of individual personalities.
- To recognize the methodological difficulties involved in making biographical sense of lives and the weaknesses of many psychobiographies.
- To appreciate how these difficulties and weaknesses can be overcome.
- To understand the concept of 'life narrative' and how it illuminates an important dimension of the self.
- To understand some of the ways in which life narratives can be described and studied.

How personality theory and research can be used to make sense of individual lives is the focus of this chapter. We begin by examining the contentious practice of 'psychobiography', a form of biographical investigation and writing that is informed by personality psychology. Some of the theoretical and methodological problems that plague psychobiographies are discussed, followed by some of the steps that can be taken to improve their validity. We then turn to the systematic study of the stories that people tell about their own lives, and how these 'self-narratives' represent an important aspect of the self.

Adolf Hitler is the person many of us would name if we were asked to identify a historical figure who embodies evil. He was largely responsible, most historians would agree, for a war in which perhaps 50 million people lost their lives, and prosecuted a remorseless policy of extermination towards millions of Jews, homosexuals, handicapped people, 'mental defectives', Roma (gypsies) and Slavs.

Numerous attempts have been made to make sense of Hitler as a person (e.g., Redlich, 1999; see Rosenbaum, 1998, for a review). Not all of these are psychological in nature. Some writers see him as merely a symptom of the turbulent historical and political forces surging through Germany in his time. By this account, Nazism and the Holocaust were, in a sense, just waiting to happen whether or not a Hitler arose to lead and harness them, and therefore did not depend in any deep way on his personal dispositions. Others view Hitler through a theological lens, focusing on religious concepts of evil, sin, and so on. A large number of writers, however, have attempted to understand Hitler's psychology in the hope that it will illuminate the origins and dynamics of his behaviour.

Sexuality has been a dominant focus of attention for Hitler's more psychological biographers. One of the most exotic explanations makes reference to Hitler's supposed 'genital deficiency'. The tamer version of this explanation proposes that he had a congenital deformity of the penis. The more colourful alternative is that during a schoolboy prank, in which he supposedly attempted to urinate in a billy-goat's mouth, the goat objected and bit off one testicle. This story is supported by a medical examiner who examined Hitler's charred body after he had killed himself in his bunker as Berlin fell to the Allies. His scrotum – described as 'singed but preserved' – was found to lack a left testicle. Writers have argued that one or other of these genital abnormalities caused Hitler intense shame, rendered him sexually dysfunctional, and poisoned his relationships with women. It has been written that his genital condition led him to react against any femininity within himself by developing a harsh form of hyper-masculinity. This manifested itself in cruelty, mistrust of women, and the sensuousness and emotionality that they represented to him, and hatred of homosexuals and other supposedly 'feminized' groups such as Jews. Some writers have reported that Hitler had an unusual sexual perversion involving urine ('undinism'), and that the horror of participating in this may have been at least partially responsible for the suicide or attempted suicide of many of the women with whom he was intimate.

Other writers have attempted to comprehend Hitler's personality from non-sexual angles. It has been claimed that he had a physically abusive father. His anti-Semitism has been seen as rooted in his perception that a Jewish doctor mishandled the treatment of his dying mother, or as a form of displaced self-hatred because his paternal grandfather may have been Jewish. Various writers have labelled Hitler's personality psychopathic and borderline, described it as death-loving, or attributed it to a brain disorder called 'post-encephalic sociopathy'. Others have rejected efforts to attribute mental disorders to him and described him simply as an unusually cold-hearted and Machiavellian politician. A variety of symptoms and behavioural problems have been reported, ranging from hallucinations, hysterical (i.e., psychologically-caused) blindness, hypochondria, Parkinson's syndrome, facial tics and amphetamine abuse. The combined evidence of these bewilderingly diverse psychological analyses points to a clearly disturbed man, but whether they bring us closer to an understanding of a terrible genocide is perhaps debatable.

Psychobiography

Attempts such as these to make sense of Adolf Hitler's personality are examples of '**psychobiography**'. Biographies, of course, are accounts of individual lives, and what sets psychobiographies apart from run-of-the-mill biographies is their use of psychological knowledge, in the form of theory and research. A psychobiography therefore tries to situate the events of someone's life in a psychological analysis of their personality and its development.

Numerous psychobiographical studies have been published over the years. Freud conducted the first, an analysis of Leonardo da Vinci in 1910, and later collaborated on a psychobiographical study of US president Woodrow Wilson. Erik Erikson, whose eight stages of human development we encountered in Chapter 8, published widely-read psychobiographical studies of Martin Luther, founder of Protestantism, and of Mahatma Gandhi, the non-violent architect of Indian independence. Other psychobiographies have tackled famous politicians (e.g., Ronald Reagan, Margaret Thatcher, Saddam Hussein, Richard Nixon), writers and intellectuals (e.g., Virginia Woolf, Charles Darwin), and cultural icons (e.g., Elvis Presley), among many others (Schultz, 2005).

Psychobiography is one expression of a branch of personality psychology that Henry Murray, its originator, dubbed '**personology**'. Personologists try to make sense of individual lives through detailed analysis of single cases, rather than by extracting general rules or observations about groups of people, and they tend to use qualitative rather than quantitative research methods. Their focus is not just on individual personalities, in their unique complexity, but also on *lives*: they aim to understand the life-history of the person as it unfolds through time, not just to take a snapshot of the person at a particular moment.

This description of psychobiography and the personological approach should resonate with some of the themes and issues that you have come across earlier in this book. First, psychobiography clearly relates to personality development (Chapter 8), in its focus on whole lives, extended through time. Second, psychobiography is, in a sense, a form of personality assessment (Chapter 9), an effort to make informed judgements about the person on the basis of systematically collected evidence. Third, psychobiographers tend to make use of psychoanalytic theory in their work (Chapter 4). Although this is not strictly necessary, and other personality theories can be (and have been) used in psychobiographical studies, psychoanalytic theories would seem to have several advantages: they address psychological development, they are well-suited to the intensive analysis of individuals, as in clinical case studies, and they claim to penetrate beneath the surface of the personality to its underlying dynamics.

It may not surprise you to learn that psychobiography has been a controversial activity, often seen as somewhat disreputable by historians and mainstream biographers (Elms, 1994). In part this disrepute reflects the controversies surrounding two of the common threads of psychobiography mentioned above, namely psychoanalytic theory and psychological assessment. Some of the criticisms that have been thrown at psychobiography reflect the reservations that many people hold about the problematic nature of psychoanalytic theory and inference, and the limitations of certain forms of assessment. We will discuss some of these problems below, as well as a few others.

241

Weaknesses of psychobiography

Psychoanalytic theory

As we saw in Chapter 4, psychoanalysis is a controversial but influential approach to the understanding of personality. It has greater ambitions than many personality theories: to explain personality development, provide a basis for the treatment of mental disorders, interpret cultural phenomena, and, most of all, to go beneath the sometimes tranquil surface of the personality to the unpleasant truths (repressed wishes, sexual desires, unconscious fantasies, and so on) that lie beneath. It has also received a greater amount of criticism than most other theories, focusing particularly on the untestability of its theories, the weak and generally unscientific nature of its evidence base, the implausibility of some of its claims regarding human motivation and development, and the problems that plague psychoanalytic inference. The fact that with notable exceptions (e.g., Bowlby's 1991 attachment theory-based analysis of Charles Darwin) most psychobiographers make some use of psychoanalytic theory in their work leaves them open to many of the same criticisms.

Let's take an example from a psychobiography of Richard Nixon, the US president from 1969 to 1974 who left office in disgrace after it became known that he had supported the burglary of his opponents' offices to steal documents in the Watergate affair. Volkan, Itzkowitz, and Dod (1997) paint a portrait of a man who was highly moralistic but also willing to engage in criminal activities, who played the tough guy but was troubled by anxiety, and who was frequently paranoid and mistrustful of others. They also make a series of psychoanalytic inferences that might strike many readers as far-fetched and, more importantly, as going well beyond the available evidence. For example, they suggest that Nixon was especially troubled by leaks of information from the White House because they represented to him a loss of bowel control, and his personality was unconsciously dominated by such anal themes. Similarly, they argue that skills in public speaking were due in part to a sublimation of his childhood tendency to be a cry-baby, and that an inflammation of the blood vessels that he suffered reflected the operation of unconscious self-punishment. Speculations such as these are not uncommon in psychobiographies that employ psychoanalytic ideas, and to the extent that the theory can be questioned, so can the psychobiographical insights that are produced.

Inference problems

Volkan et al.'s (1997) interpretations of Nixon's personality are problematic not only because they make some questionable theoretical assumptions – for example, that unconscious guilt can cause tissue damage, that the leakage of information by one's staff is likely to be unconsciously understood as a leakage of faecal matter by one's anus – but also because the grounds for making the interpretations seem inadequate. It appears unlikely that the sort of evidence on which these inferences about Nixon's psychological dynamics were made could support them. Interpretations like these seem to go well beyond the available evidence, and rely on a form of theory-based guesswork. Such guesswork is difficult and unreliable enough when there is a living, breathing person in the psychoanalyst's consulting room, where new evidence such as dreams can at least be gathered and mental processes studied in real time. How much more difficult is it when the person is unavailable for contact and the evidence is incomplete and second-hand?

You may recall the problems with psychoanalytic inference that were discussed in Chapter 4. You will also remember the discussion of the problems with projective testing and with clinical prediction in Chapter 9 on psychological assessment. These problems can all arise in psychobiography. As with projective tests, inferences are often made about the subject's unconscious dynamics, and these inferences are often based on psychoanalytic theory, as in the case of Nixon. Similarly, the psychobiographer is required to assemble many different pieces of evidence about the person into an overall assessment, the very situation that has been shown to produce unreliable predictive judgements in clinical psychologists trying to integrate the results of multiple psychological tests. What's more, psychobiography is really not predictive at all in the sense of making judgements about the future: it usually tries to make sense of lives that have been completed, or are at least well advanced. Psychobiography is 'postdictive' not predictive, an exercise in making guesses about what has already happened. In hindsight many things look clearer than when looking into the future, and so postdictions are often more confident than they should be. For all of these reasons – the psychoanalytic licence to make judgements about the unconscious, the need to make a consistent assessment of the person out of many pieces of evidence, and the over-confidence of hindsight – psychobiographers run the risk of making serious inferential errors.

One such error – an attempt to extract deep underlying meaning from inadequate evidence – was a serious problem in the first psychobiography (Elms, 1994). Freud discussed Leonardo da Vinci's life in relation to his possible homosexuality, his illegitimacy (he was born out of wedlock to a peasant woman), his parents' separation, his remarkable creativity, and much more besides. At one point, Freud interpreted an event that Leonardo reported as an early childhood memory but that Freud took to be a fantasy. Leonardo wrote that a vulture had come down to him, opened his mouth, and repeatedly thrust its tail into it. Perhaps one does not need to be a psychoanalyst to infer a sexual meaning here, but Freud was and he did. He interpreted the fantasy as evidence of Leonardo's intense erotic relationship with his mother and of his subsequent homosexuality, based on his theory of the Oedipus complex. The interpretation was based in part on the fact that vultures are symbols of motherhood and are sexually ambiguous (the Egyptian goddess Mut was depicted as a vulture with breasts and a penis). Unfortunately, however, Leonardo had not remembered being assaulted by a vulture at all, but by a kite, a bird with no similar mythological significance. 'Vulture' was an error in the translation of Leonardo's recollection from which Freud was working. This example of an error due to the combination of inference about unconscious meanings and faulty evidence serves as a cautionary lesson for psychobiographers.

243

Nature of psychobiographical evidence

One reason why psychobiographical inference can be unreliable is that the evidence on which it is based is often of low quality or limited quantity. Making reliable judgements about people is difficult enough, as we have seen in Chapter 9, when we are assessing them with psychological tests. It is doubly difficult when, as in most psychobiographies, the author never even meets the subject and must rely on the historical record. In essence, psychobiographers are attempting to put their subjects on the couch, but these subjects are often dead or otherwise unavailable (and there is no couch). Some of the information on which inferences about personality are made, such as letters and diaries or reports on historical figures by writers of their day, may be systematically distorted. The subject's self-reports may tend to neglect or gloss over psychologically important material, or information that presents them in a poor light, and reports on them by other writers may be biased by the writers' own interests and purposes. Data from validated psychological tests are almost never available, and even if the subject is alive and consents to interviews with the psychobiographer, these interviews are prone to the same difficulties that beset that method of assessment (see Chapter 9).

Determinism

Critics of psychobiographies sometimes complain that they over-simplify the lives of their subjects by emphasizing a cause that is presented as if it inevitably determines the person's distinctive characteristics and behaviour later in life. That cause might be a childhood trauma, a troubled relationship with a parent, or some other explanation. Erikson referred to one form of this determinism as 'originology': the idea that a life's shape is determined by some traumatic event in its first few years. In addition to being deterministic, by imagining that an early cause produces later personality, such explanations can also be called reductionistic, because they reduce the causes of a personality to a single dominant factor. Needless to say, the psychoanalytic approach offers some encouragement to originology, given the importance it places on the early psychosexual development of the child and the fundamental role that family relationships are taken to play in personality formation. However, as we have seen in Chapter 8, personality is not set like plaster at age 30, let alone at age 3, and change is at least as much a fact of life in the study of personalities as is continuity from childhood. Moreover, single events rarely have the power to exert lifelong influence over a person's personality. Some psychobiographies have even taken the point of origin back to the time of birth: one writer (Whitmer, 1996) located the source of Elvis Presley's distinctive personality in the fact that he had a stillborn twin brother, Jesse, and that his intra-uterine bond with this twin exerted a lasting influence on his life.

Another form that determinism can take in psychobiographical studies is a neglect of non-psychological factors in the person's behaviour. Numerous writers, for example, have speculated about the oddities of Britain's King George III (1738–1820), who had recurring episodes of incessant talking, delusions, deep confusion, agitation, and excitement in which he sometimes foamed at the mouth. Many have argued that King George suffered from some form of madness, and have speculated about the psychological dynamics that might explain it. Medical scholarship, however, indicates that his behaviour was probably due to porphyria, a metabolic disease that causes psychiatric symptoms (Runyan, 1988). Similarly, the empirical fact that personality traits are to a considerable degree heritable (Chapter 5) implies that the sorts of environmental factors on which psychobiographers focus – the life events, family relationships, and the like – do not tell the whole story of a person's adult personality. Another way in which non-psychological factors can be neglected is a lack of consideration of the cultural or historical context. Especially when the psychobiographer is investigating a figure from a very different background, or one who lived centuries ago, it may be difficult to judge what is normal or abnormal in the person's behaviour or upbringing. Social norms have often been wildly different in other times and places, and what might at first blush seem to be clearly pathological behaviour may turn out to have been entirely typical in its context, when the appropriate historical or anthropological background is discovered.

The challenge for the psychobiographer, then, is to recognize that early events and relationships can be important determinants of a life's course, but must always be placed in the context of the many other factors, emerging throughout the life-span, that alter, dilute, or compensate for these early experiences. Similarly, psychobiographers must not spare basic research on the historical and cultural context in which their subject's life was led.

'Pathography'

Another common pitfall of psychologically informed biographies is an emphasis on abnormality or mental disorder. Psychobiographies sometimes seem to concentrate primarily on the dark side of their subjects, and to speculate that their behaviour had disturbed roots. Of course, this concentration makes for fascinating reading and strong book sales, and finding what is hidden – which tends to be more negative than what is open to public view – is one of the reasons why we want to read about famous people. However, psychobiographies can sometimes seem to show an excessive emphasis on abnormality, complete with clinical jargon. Some readers object that this sort of work can be little more than a hatchet job masquerading as science: an attempt to discredit a person while pretending to adopt the impartial stance of a psychological professional. This strikes some people as especially dubious when the subject of the psychobiographer is no longer alive to rebut a negative portrayal, and when the inferences that are made about deviant desires are made without the sort of careful clinical evaluation that would be required if the person were receiving a real psychological assessment.

Sometimes this focus on abnormality appears as a kind of reductionism: the person is assigned a psychiatric diagnosis, and this becomes the primary explanation for most of their behaviour. Does it really help to understand Hitler's complexity to classify him as a psychopath, or to classify Elvis as having a 'split personality', as some psychobiographers have done? It may well be true that subjects of psychobiography had mental disorders, and that these disorders had important implications for how their lives proceeded, but people

245

cannot, of course, be reduced to their disorders (any more than they can be reduced to their gender, ethnic background, social class, and so on). As we saw in Chapter 10, although some mental disorders have a pervasive influence on behaviour and are woven into the fabric of the personality (i.e., personality disorders), others are superimposed on it rather than being part of it, are not lasting, and may have little relationship to enduring personality dispositions. Responsible psychobiographers must therefore recognize the existence of mental disorders in their subjects – as in Virginia Woolf's bipolar disorder or Charles Darwin's anxiety – without taking these disorders as all-consuming explanations.

A final concern with pathography is that it often leaves unanswered the important question of life success. The subjects of psychobiographies have often led accomplished and creative lives, and an exclusive focus on their psychological problems and dark motives makes it difficult to understand where this accomplishment and creativity came from. Although the famous and influential are not immune to psychological disturbance, of course, it is difficult to view life successes merely as symptoms or to explain how, in spite of disturbance, greatness came about. Pathographies are therefore unsatisfying portraits of real people, in much the same way that standard biographies that dwell too much on the desirable qualities of their subjects – sometimes dubbed 'hagiographies', a term referring to accounts of lives of the saints – are unsatisfying. One-dimensionally positive or negative biographies dehumanize their subjects: without a little ambivalence a life story lacks depth, complexity, and credibility.

Improving psychobiographies

At this point you might think that psychobiography is hopelessly riddled with problems, and that perhaps we would be better off without it. However, it is important to remember that there are also many problems with orthodox biographies, which can also be full of incorrect inferences, wrong-headed theories, deterministic explanations, and so on. It also seems fair to say that an account of someone's life that failed to grapple seriously with the person's psychology would be seriously lacking. 'Just the facts' may be an appropriate motto for a police report, but it is inadequate when we want to make sense of real lives: something is missing in a life story that focuses exclusively on dates, places, and social context with no appreciation of the person's psychological individuality. Psychology, and personality psychology in particular, has amassed a body of knowledge and a set of methods of inquiry that should be able to enrich biographical studies. Rather than abandoning psychobiography, then, perhaps we should try to improve it and find ways to safeguard it against the problems we have identified.

One attempt to do so was made by Runyan (1981), who offered a set of guides for choosing between alternative psychobiographical explanations. As an example, Runyan examined 13 distinct explanations that have been offered for why Vincent van Gogh cut off his ear. These included that the act was a symbolic self-castration based on a conflict over homosexual impulses; that it was an emulation of Jack the Ripper's mutilation of his victims, which had received much media attention at the time; that it imitated the practice of bullfighters who gave the severed ear of the bull to the lady of their choice, just as Vincent gave his to a favourite prostitute; and that it was an attempt to stop the auditory hallucinations that troubled him. Runyan notes that human behaviour often has multiple causes, so that no single explanation need be correct, but that nevertheless there are principled ways to decide between the alternatives.

First, explanations should be logically sound and have no internal contradictions. Second, they should account for multiple aspects of the relevant events, the more comprehensively the better. Weaker explanations may appear to make sense of one aspect of the situation but be unable to account for many others. Third, better explanations should be able to pass attempts to falsify them. It should be possible to derive predictions from them and see whether these are supported. Fourth, explanations should be consistent with what we know about people in general. If an explanation departs markedly from ordinary human psychology, it is likely to be mistaken. Finally, a good explanation should be more credible than other explanations, when these are directly compared. These guidelines for improving psychobiographical explanation may seem somewhat obvious at some level, but they are radical in their implications for how psychobiographers should work. Rather than simply coming up with free-wheeling interpretations of a person's life, they should approach psychobiography as an attempt to build a systematic scientific theory of the individual. Like a theory, a psychobiography should be internally consistent, capable of accounting for a wide variety of facts, able to survive efforts to falsify it, and consistent with other well-supported theories, and it should be critically examined in relation to competing theories.

Psychobiography has a long way to go before it can be considered a science, and it will always involve a certain amount of non-scientific (but not necessarily unscientific) interpretation of meaning. However, writers such as Runyan (1981) show how it cannot be exempt from scientific criteria if it is to be credible. Other writers have proposed additional methodological advice to psychobiographers in an effort to improve it. Alexander (1990), for example, offers a series of criteria for deciding what information psychobiographers should pay attention to, in the vast quantities that may be available. Among these, for example, he proposes that people should heed: (a) what the person says most frequently ('frequency'; e.g., repetitive themes); (b) what they say or write first ('primacy'; e.g., early memories); (c) what they emphasize ('emphasis'); (d) what they say that seems peculiar and jarring ('isolation'); (e) what they present as unique and unprecedented in their lives ('uniqueness'); and (f) what they say that they are not ('negation'; e.g., 'I am not like my mother'). Considerations such as these, which are based on solid psychological research evidence, help to establish the 'salience' or importance of information about a person. Like Runyan's criteria for choosing between explanations, these criteria should help to improve the quality and credibility of psychobiographies.

Life narratives

As we have seen, psychobiographies are psychologically informed accounts of individual lives. They are, in effect, stories – although not entirely fictional – about particular individuals, generally those who are famous. However, not all life stories are told by professional psychobiographers about celebrated people. Some are told by ordinary people, about ordinary people: themselves. Psychologists who study '**life narratives**' argue that every one of us is engaged in an ongoing process of telling his or her own life story, and that such autobiographical life stories are crucial aspects of the self.

This narrative approach to the study of personality is different from most of the approaches that we have encountered to this point in several respects. First, unlike most personality research, studies of life narratives emphasize the uniqueness of the individual rather than attempting to fit each person into a standard descriptive framework, such as a set of trait dimensions. Accordingly, studies of life narratives tend to focus on single individuals rather than large samples of people. Second, studies of life narratives are 'person-centred' rather than 'variable-centred'. The focus of attention is on understanding the individual person rather than examining the relationships that personality characteristics have with one another or with other variables (e.g., how Extraversion is related to attachment style or to age). Third, whereas most personality psychology is relatively static, aiming to give a snapshot of people at a particular time, the narrative study of lives is intrinsically temporal. Lives unfold through time and must be understood as extended through past, present, and future. Finally, whereas most personality psychology employs quantitative research methods and seeks to clarify the causes of behaviour, the narrative approach to personality is not normally quantitative and aims to enlighten us about the meanings of behaviour (Josselson, 1995). That is, rather than trying to formulate explanatory laws about the causes and effects of personality characteristics, narrative psychologists try to interpret the complexities of individual lives in terms of human intentions, motivations, and beliefs.

If you cast your mind back to the end of Chapter 2, you will remember that after reviewing a variety of alternative units for describing personality it was proposed that they represent a distinct level of personality: Level II (personal concerns, such as motives, values, and constructs) vs. Level I (traits). McAdams (1995), who proposed this distinction, further argued that there is a third level of personality that is distinct from both traits and personal concerns, which he refers to as the level of 'integrative life stories'. Levels I and II offer a picture of the person as a static list of characteristics, but beginning in adolescence, at least, people seek a sense of personal identity that gives them unity, purpose, and coherence over time. People need to have an answer to the question 'Who am I?' that has a historical or temporal component: that presents them as a unique person with a connected past, present, and imagined future. Such Level III life stories, self-narratives or 'personal myths' are the basis of personal identity, which you will remember from Chapter 8 as a core developmental task of adolescence in Erikson's theory.

To refer to identity as a life story or **self-narrative** is to propose that we are all engaged in a process of self-construction or 'self-narration'. There is no single life story that is discovered and fixed early in adulthood. Rather, people continually and actively revise their life story to encompass, connect, and integrate new events, new hopes and fears, and new understandings of their pasts. There is no single 'true self' or identity, on this view, just a revisable history of the self. The events of one's life do not dictate a particular life story, and the same events can, in principle, be narrated in quite different ways, much as we can tell a story seriously or for laughs. Indeed, some writers argue that psychotherapy works by enabling people to develop new and more satisfying ways of understanding (or narrating) their pasts (Spence, 1980).

Making sense of self-narratives

Psychologists have developed a variety of ways of assessing and analyzing people's life stories. Given the complexities of these narratives, their irreducible uniqueness to each person, it is a challenge to describe them in a systematic way. Even so, there is a rich tradition of work in literary studies for making sense of stories, and many of the concepts that can be employed in the analysis of novels, myths, movies, and plays can be put to use in the autobiographical narratives that everyday people produce. Four core concepts that are of particular interest are narrative tone, narrative themes, characters, and narrative forms. McAdams has been at the forefront of the study of self-narratives, and our discussions lean heavily on his work.

Narrative tone

Perhaps the simplest characteristic of life narratives is their overall evaluative quality or tone. Some life stories are consistently positive, presenting past events in a favourable light and looking towards the future with optimism. Note that a life story does not need to be without sadness and adversity to have such a positive tone. The narrator may acknowledge problems, losses, or setbacks but present them as opportunities for growth rather than as crippling blows that destroyed their faith in the world, others, or themselves. Stories with a negative tone, in contrast, are full of sadness, pessimism, resignation, and distrust. However, they need not be litanies of sorrow and hardship. The narrator may report past happiness that has since been lost for ever or that turned out to be illusory. What makes narrative tone positive or negative is therefore not simply the desirability or undesirability of the events that compose the story, but the psychological attitude towards them, whether it is one of hope and trust or of pessimism and disillusion.

McAdams (1996) has argued that the roots of narrative tone can be traced to the earliest stages of personality development. According to attachment theory, people who were securely attached to caregiving figures in infancy and early childhood develop just the sort of confidence, openness, optimism, and trust in others that shine through in stories with a positive tone. Insecurely attached infants – those whose attachment style is avoidant or anxious-ambivalent (see Chapter 2) – are more likely to think of other people, and also the world beyond, as unreliable and unsafe. Similarly, Erikson's theory of psychosocial development views the first stage, Trust vs. Mistrust, as the foundation for a basic sense of security and optimism: trust not just in other people, but in the world's capacity to provide us with what we want and need. Although it is controversial to propose that early childhood experiences of caregiving and attachment are directly carried forward into adult patterns of behaviour in this way, there is an obvious resonance between the meaning of these early experiences and later narrative tone.

249

Narrative themes

A second aspect of life narratives refers not to their overall emotional colour, but to the sorts of themes that appear in their content. Themes refer to 'recurrent patterns of human intention' (McAdams, 1996, p. 67), specifically the kinds of desires and motives that animate the characters in the narrative. What kinds of desires, needs, and preoccupations are repeatedly expressed by people in the story? In a self-narrative, of course, these desires and motives are largely those of the self.

There could, in principle, be as many themes as there are motives, or perhaps more, given that different themes might exist when a certain motive is fulfilled or thwarted. However, McAdams (1996) suggests that themes can usefully be classified according to broad motivations, such as those identified by McClelland and colleagues (e.g., McClelland, 1985), who proposed that human behaviour springs from needs for power, achievement, and intimacy. You may also remember from Chapter 9 that these needs are typically assessed using projective methods, specifically the Thematic Apperception Test (TAT). The TAT is a method that explicitly requires people to generate stories about ambiguous pictures and, as its name suggests, it aims to extract the themes that appear in these stories. If strivings for influence (power), success relative to others (achievement), and love (intimacy) are core motivational themes in TAT stories, they may similarly be core themes in self-narratives.

McAdams proposes that McClelland's three basic needs can be simplified further into two distinct types of theme. 'Communal' themes are simply those in which the primary motive is intimacy. Self-narratives with communal themes emphasize the person's striving for connection, love, submergence in a larger group or in a close relationship. Successfully or unsuccessfully, the character seeks union with others. 'Agency' themes, in contrast, are those in which the character is driven by desires for independence, autonomy, and personal efficacy. The character strives to assert and enhance the self as an independent agent. Power and achievement needs are both *agentic* in this sense, placing emphasis on distinguishing the self from others through personal effort rather than linking the self to others.

Self-narratives may therefore be dominated by agentic or communal themes, although many will contain both to some extent. One person's life story may be a tale of drive for career accomplishment, triumphs over setbacks, and ultimate glory in personal achievement or a position of influence. Another's may tell of relationships forged and lost, of romantic joys and disappointments, and of successes and failures shared with important social groups. Yet another person's self-narrative may record one-dimensional striving for personal accomplishment in the early years of life that gives way – perhaps after a crisis or flash of insight – to a belated appreciation of the importance of relationships and family.

The relative importance of these themes in self-narratives is likely to alter as people age, and may also vary by gender. Agentic themes may often diminish in importance, perhaps especially for men at mid-life. Men who have striven for personal accomplishment, conforming to the high value many cultures place on male agency and independence, may often question the meaningfulness of what they have achieved at this time. Another common variant runs in the opposite direction. An early life remembered as overly submerged in relationships or groups – caring for others or being trapped in the tight embrace of a family or group – is left behind as the person seeks independence and self-realization. This sequence may be more common among women. The important thing to remember, however, is that self-narratives are always works in progress, and the themes that they contain may be reworked over the course of life.

Characters

All stories are populated by human characters, or at least by entities that have been endowed with human-like attributes (e.g., anthropomorphized animals or aliens, intelligent robots, or gods). Self-narratives are no different. The self is the main figure in its own life story, accompanied by a supporting cast of significant others. However, even though the self may be the primary figure, it may not be represented by a single character. McAdams (1996) proposes that in life stories the self is often carried by multiple characters. The need for multiple characters comes from the sheer complexity of our selves, both real and imagined. First, people tend to hold several social roles at the same time (wife, mother, daughter, employee, club president), each with its own set of expectations for appropriate behaviour. Second, people are often internally conflicted or confused about their personal identity, holding an inconsistent view of who they are or ought to be. Third, over the life-course the definition of self may change, so that it is meaningful to talk about past and future selves. Finally, given that self-narratives are not only histories but also look towards the future, we must also consider possible selves, which can be desired (successful novelist) or dreaded (homeless person).

According to McAdams, we simplify this multiplicity of self by constructing what he calls 'imagoes'. An imago is an image of the self that is simplified and personified, in the sense of being a 'stock character' that exemplifies one core component of self. These imagoes resemble figures of myth or legend, as they stand in for a particular idea or quality. Rarely does a person's self-narrative contain only a single imago, but neither do life stories contain distinct imagoes for every possible social role or facet of the personality. Instead, people refine their multiple aspects or roles into a few imagoes, each of which encompasses several such aspects and roles. A woman's roles as wife, mother, and employee might be personified in a 'caregiver' imago, whose relevance extends beyond each specific role, whereas a 'maker' imago embodies her roles as a productive and organized employee and club president. By this means, people have available a small set of story characters that can capture their internal conflicts and confusions without being unmanageably complex.

Just as self-narratives may have communal and agentic themes, the characters who embody these motives can be classified as communal or agentic imagoes. McAdams (1996) proposes a variety of possible imago figures, many drawn from Greek mythology. Communal imagoes include the lover, who strives for passionate intimacy in close relationships; the caregiver, who nurtures others with devotion and self-sacrifice; and the friend, who seeks a loyal and cooperative relationship with equals. Agentic imagoes include the warrior, who embodies vigour, courage, and self-assertion; the traveller, who is always in motion and seeks novelty, freedom from constraint, and adventure; and the sage, who seeks wisdom and deep knowledge above all. Commonly, self-narratives will include conflict between an agentic and

251

a communal imago, reflecting the conflict between autonomy and relatedness that figures in many life stories. Different imagoes may become prominent at different times in the narrative, as if jostling for the starring role, and the narrative is given dramatic tension by this conflict.

Narrative form

Narrative tone sets the overall emotional quality of the story, themes provide the recurring motivational content, and characters supply the cast, who embody this content. None of these narrative elements captures the ways in which stories unfold through time. Narrative form, the final element, refers to the temporal trajectory of stories, and to the assortment of distinct trajectories that appear repeatedly.

One interesting model of narrative form was developed by Ken and Mary Gergen (1983), who argued that many self-narratives seem to follow a few basic patterns. These narrative trajectories can vary on a dimension of positive versus negative evaluation, so that different points on a trajectory represent desirable or undesirable states of affairs. Thus, a narrative form represents a particular way in which a life story unfolds in good or bad ways. The Gergens propose seven basic forms, many of which can be observed in literary works such as novels. These forms are presented in Figure 11.1.

The simplest form, depicted in the first graph, is the 'stability' narrative. In it, the person sees his or her life as unchanging over time, maintaining a steady way of living and fixed attributes from the past into the imagined future. The evaluative tone of such narratives can be consistently positive or negative: people may see their lives as comfortably settled and have a fixed self-definition, or they may see themselves as stuck in an unending rut. Change rather than stability is the basic feature of the 'progressive' and 'regressive' narratives depicted in the second graph, which reflect life trajectories that gradually rise or decline. Progressive narratives reflect a sense of continual self-improvement that is popular in self-help books, according to which people can move from a lacklustre present towards a golden future by following a few simple steps. This sort of self-narrative appears to be very widespread. People are motivated to see themselves as steadily improving, and in the service of this goal they may remember their past self as if it were less positive than it was in fact (Ross, 1989). Regressive narratives, in contrast, portray the self as on a steady downward path from earlier glories.

Other narrative forms are more complex. Instead of reflecting a straightforward linear pathway, they have points at which the story changes direction or turns, and they may involve combinations of the simpler forms. The 'happily-ever-after' narrative, presented in the third graph, involves a combination of the progressive and stability forms: things get better and better until they reach a stable plateau of contentment (e.g., an older person looking back on life leading up to retirement, or a younger one looking forward to marriage and Prince Charming). The 'tragic' narrative, presented in the fourth graph, represents a similar variation on the regressive form, with the decline being relatively sudden and abrupt, a turning point often brought about by a loss or fall from grace. Typically, the narrative themes are agentic: a heroic individual acts contrary to social convention and as a result is isolated from others by a cruel world. Like regressive narratives, tragedy has a negative tone, but this is made more poignant by the suddenness of the decline.

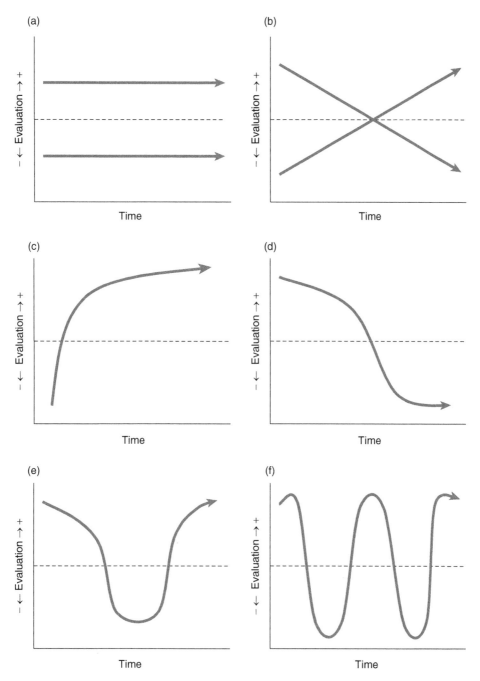

Figure 11.1 Narratives forms from Gergen and Gergen (1983): (a) stability (positive and negative); (b) progressive and regressive; (c) 'happily-ever-after'; (d) tragic; (e) comedy-melodrama; (f) romantic saga

The final two narrative forms are more complex still. Gergen and Gergen (1983) describe as 'comedy-melodrama' a self-narrative in which events become increasingly troubled, as in tragedy, but the problems are then rapidly overcome and happiness is restored. The dominant narrative themes in this form tend to be communal: the trouble is often resolved through love or togetherness. The 'romantic saga', finally, is a narrative form in which cycles of progressive and regressive elements are repeated. Someone with this sort of narrative identity sees himself or herself in heroic, questing terms, engaged in a continuing process of overcoming ill-fortune or evil. As in tragedy, the narrative themes tend to be agentic; however, the tone is more positive, as the heroic individual battles successfully against all obstacles.

One very important point about the Gergens' classification is that the choice of which narrative forms to use for telling one's own story is not dictated by the objective events of one's life. At least to some degree, the same series of life events can be narrated in many different ways. Looking back at your years as a student from some time in the future, you might see it as a period of unrelenting bliss or boredom (stability), as a steady process of enlightenment or disillusionment (progression and regression), as the gradual finding of a steady identity or love (happily-ever-after), as an abrupt loss of heart (tragedy: hopefully not triggered by a personality course), as an intellectual trial by fire that you overcame (comedy), or as a series of struggles (romantic saga). Different ways of 'storying' your past may arise at different times, or even in different states of mind. Crucially, though, the way you narrate the events of life will organize and frame your experiences in a way that gives them personal meaning at the time.

The Gergens also did not propose that their seven narrative forms were exhaustive, or that every possible life story could be assigned to just one form. More complex narratives can be described. For example, McAdams (2006) discusses an intricate 'redemption narrative' that he found to be common among highly generative mid-life Americans. According to this narrative, people see themselves early in life as having a special gift or advantage and experience empathy for the suffering of others. They come to develop a firm belief system that rules their life, experience a series of episodes where bad events are swiftly followed by good ones that redeem them, feel a conflict between desires to advance the self and to connect with others, and look forward to contributing more to society. This redemption narrative form has an upward gradient, as in the progressive form, a strong sense of personal consistency, as in the stability narrative, and also romantic elements, as in the alternation of bad then good events and the struggle between different motives. The narrative forms are building blocks from which self-narratives may be constructed.

Final notes on self-narratives

Self-narratives link up life events into a coherent plot, but theorists emphasize that there is no necessary connection between the actual events of someone's life and the narrative form that they superimpose on them. Life is often quite ambiguous, in the sense that there are often many alternative ways in which it can be made coherent. The important basic observation that writers on self-narratives make is that the way we comprehend our lives, as stories, may have profound implications for how we behave and how we view our identities. For this reason, self-narratives are fundamentally important aspects of our personalities.

Self-narratives are not the only kinds of narratives, of course. A culture contains a large repository of narratives, whether in the form of books, television shows, and movies, or as myths, oral histories, and fables. We are constantly exposed to our culture's available scripts. Many of these narratives exemplify the forms presented here. One important theoretical question in the study of self-narratives is what relation self-narratives bear to the narratives that circulate within a culture. Gergen and Gergen are quite clear on this point: 'life and art are interdependent' (1983, p. 261). How we make sense of our life stories is influenced by the narratives and narrative forms that we are exposed to, so that we will tend to construct self-narratives that borrow from and conform to cultural patterns. McAdams, for example, argues that the redemption narrative is a typically American product, embodying themes of self-reliance, spiritual destiny, and having a special place in the world that appear consistently in the nation's intellectual history, early autobiographies, and current cinema. Similarly, Hammack (2008) has shown how young Israeli and Palestinian people incorporate cultural narratives about national history – of triumph against adversity and of tragic loss, respectively – into their self-narratives. In short, self-narratives not only supply us with coherent individual selves: they connect us to the shared values and ways of thinking of our culture.

ILLUSTRATIVE STUDY

Turning point narratives of young adults

The stories that people tell about themselves can have profound implications for their well-being. This is especially true when those autobiographical stories relate to challenging personal experiences and life transitions. Being able to find meaning in change and adversity, and being able to embed that meaning in a coherent life story and sense of identity, may well be an important way of dealing with the slings and arrows of life.

A study by Canadian psychologists Kate McLean and Michael Pratt (2006) examined this possibility in a longitudinal study of self-narratives among young adults. McLean and Pratt examined a sample of 17-year-old high school students, following some of them up two years later and then surveying them again when they were 23. These young people were asked to write a 'turning point narrative' about an important transition or change with respect to their sense of themselves. The researchers coded these narratives for evidence that the writers had extracted personal meaning from the life transition, such as insights into themselves or their worlds. The students also completed measures of mature identity

(Continued)

(Continued)

based on Erikson's work (see Chapter 8), optimism, and 'generative concerns' (i.e., their feeling that they had made valuable contributions to the world).

McLean and Pratt found that meaning-making in their participants' turning-point narratives was related to a variety of positive factors. Young adults whose stories at age 23 contained more personal meanings and insights tended to have more mature identities. They tended to be more optimistic and to have a stronger sense of generativity. Their stories were more likely to contain 'redemptive sequences' in which negative beginnings give way to positive endings. Interestingly, the meaning the 23-year-olds found in their stories was not related to their optimism or maturity at age 17.

This study shows that life narratives can be studied rigorously and that meaning-making in personal stories is associated with positive identity development. Seeking and reflecting on personal meanings in life transitions is an important life task for young adults. The study suggests that those who take on that task tend to develop a strong sense of identity and purpose, and to learn life's lessons well.

Conclusions

Psychobiography and the psychology of life narratives are attempts to make sense of whole lives in their fullness and complexity. Their aim is to produce and understand coherent psychological portraits of individuals in a way that is informed by personality theory and research. Psychobiography, for example, is intrinsically difficult because of the complexity of individuals and the obstacles that stand in the way of making reliable inferences about them. Information about people is often inaccurate or incomplete, there are often many alternative explanations of their behaviour, and their motives, thoughts, and wishes are often obscure, even to themselves. In addition, the subjects of psychobiographies are engaged in a process of making narrative sense of their lives, and the sense they make may conflict sharply with how they appear to others. For all of these reasons, it is not surprising that psychobiography can be done badly.

Even if that is true, the fact remains that understanding whole persons and whole lives is an ultimate goal of personality psychology. It is no less important a goal for being hard to reach. The chapters of this book up to this point, when we are about to shift focus to the psychology of intelligence, have all presented ways of addressing some aspects of the person, and with any luck they show how personality psychology can assemble scientifically justified understandings of people that can be put together to understand whole persons and lives. Understanding persons requires a broad view, and a combination of the scientific rigour we have seen in some chapters and the humanistic imagination we have seen in others, and especially in this one. This necessary breadth and complexity, and this mixture of hard and soft ways of understanding, is part of what makes the psychology of personality so fascinating.

Chapter summary

- 'Personology' is the branch of personality psychology concerned with the intensive study of individual lives. One primary example of it is psychobiography, the use of psychological research and theory in biographical writing.
- Psychobiography has been a controversial exercise for several reasons. It often relies on questionable psychoanalytic theories of personality development, makes inferences on the basis of problematic or weak historical evidence, creates over-simplified explanations that refer the subject's personality to a single determining event and reduces the subject to a diagnosis.
- Despite these serious problems, psychobiographies can be improved by following a set of systematic guidelines for responsible interpretation. These refer to the selection of evidence and the responsible and scientifically-informed testing of alternative explanations.
- Psychobiographies are narratives of other people's lives, but people also construct stories of their own lives ('self-narratives'). These stories are important components of personal identity, one critical aspect of the self.
- These can be investigated rigorously by examining their emotional tone, themes, characters, and form (i.e., the trajectory through time of the self, whether upward, downward, or mixed).

Further reading

Elms, A. C. (1994). *Uncovering lives: The uneasy alliance of biography and psychology*. New York: Oxford University Press.
This is an important text that discusses some of the difficulties involved in psychobiographical research and some of the weaknesses to which it is prone.

McAdams, D. P. (1996). *The stories we live by: Personal myths and the making of the self*. New York: Guilford Press.
McAdams is the most prominent scholar in the field of life narratives. This book lays out his approach in a very clear and compelling way, and shows how life narratives can be studied systematically but without over-simplification.

McAdams, D. P., & McLean, K. C. (2013). Narrative identity. *Current Directions in Psychological Science*, 22, 233–8.
This short article reviews the current state of the literature on identity as a story, and shows particular kinds of life narrative are associated with positive mental health and well-being.

(Continued)

(Continued)

Runyan, W. M. (1981). Why did Van Gogh cut off his ear? The problem of alternative explanations in psychobiography. *Journal of Personality and Social Psychology, 40,* 1070–7.
This short classic article is a fascinating account of the difficulties in making definitive explanations of behaviour on the basis of historical data, in the context of a particularly puzzling event.

Runyan, W. M. (2012). Psychobiography and the psychology of science: Encounters with psychology, philosophy, and statistics. In G. J. Feist, & M. Gorman (Eds.), *Handbook of the psychology of science* (pp. 353–79). New York: Springer.
An insightful reflection on the state of psychobiographical thinking, complete with fascinating psychobiographical insights into several influential psychologists, including Sigmund Freud himself.

Schultz, W. T. (2005). *Handbook of psychobiography.* Oxford: Oxford University Press.
Schultz's handbook is an excellent resource for students of psychobiography, bringing together some new contributions as well as reprinting a number of classic papers.

Section 4
Intelligence

Intelligence and Cognitive Abilities

Learning objectives

- To recognize some major intelligence tests along with the typical scoring systems and the stability and reliability of these scores.
- To develop an understanding of the different theoretical models for intelligence that have been proposed, including the hierarchical and multiple intelligence models.
- To understand the evidence for these different models.
- To know the measured heritability of intelligence and what this concept describes.
- To recognize how intelligence changes across the life-span.
- To understand how developments in brain imaging are giving us insight into the roles of brain volume and connectivity in intelligence.

This chapter introduces the science of human intelligence. Intelligence influences how well we perform many tasks and how well we learn. While school and beginning a complex new job are contexts in which intelligence differences are clear and important, intelligence has many other effects, from managing the everyday tasks of life through to health outcomes and longevity. The chapter begins with a 'hands-on' look at the types of test used to measure intelligence. We then examine how these tests were developed, reviewing concepts such as 'IQ'. Moving to models of intelligence, we show how theories have distinguished between a general ability common to all tasks and specific abilities in restricted domains such as spatial processing or language. Next, we shift focus to the very basic cognitive correlates of intelligence, such as reaction time and inspection time. The biological bases of intelligence are introduced in the context of brain structure and connectivity before focusing on the genetic and environmental causes of intelligence. In the final section, we examine important practical properties of tests, such as their stability and potential bias. With this material understood, the educational and social correlates of ability are discussed, along with their implications for educational and social policy.

> What we measure with [intelligence] tests is not what the tests measure – not information, not spatial perception, not reasoning ability. These are only means to an end. What intelligence tests measure, what we hope they measure, is something more important: the capacity of an individual to understand the world about [him or her] and [his or her] resourcefulness to cope with its challenges. (Wechsler, 1975, p. 139)

- Try and write down a definition for the word 'esoteric'.
- If 5 machines can make 5 widgets in 5 minutes, how long will 100 machines take to make 100 widgets?
- In the figure below, which shape would complete the puzzle?

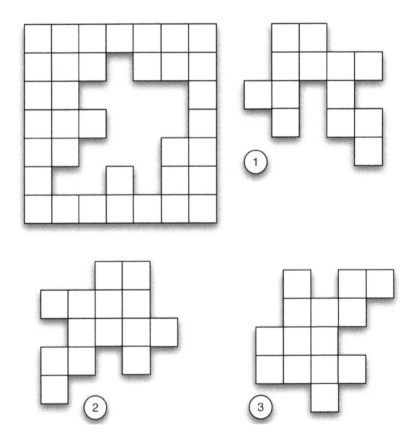

Figure 12A

How accurate were your answers?[1] These tasks assess verbal, mathematical, and spatial ability. Are there other types of ability? Are each of these abilities related to the others or independent? Why? Do tasks like these reliably measure **intelligence**? Are they valid? Could they be biased? Why do people differ on these tasks? If someone performs these tasks well, what practical guide does that give us to their ability in the workplace or in other areas of importance, such as social life or how they function after brain damage? Do genes play a role in why people differ in how well they perform on these tasks? Can changes to the environment affect performance on such tasks? The answers to these questions are the subject of intelligence research, and of this chapter.

Many of the issues we will discuss were examined first by British polymath Sir Francis Galton. Along with contributions to African exploration, analysis of finger prints, composite photography, meteorology, and developing the correlation coefficient (see Chapter 2), to name but a few of his diverse achievements, he also established the study of ability differences as a science (Wright Gillham, 2001). Galton observed that differences in ability fell along a continuum and that the distribution of these differences followed a bell-curve shape, or 'normal distribution', whereby the majority of individuals' ability scores fall close to the average score, with fewer individuals scoring at the extremely high or low end of the continuum. He saw that this ability dimension could be discerned in people's practical achievements. Individuals could be differentiated by their ability to discriminate sensory information, such that an intelligent person could discriminate very subtle changes in colour, weight, and luminance, whereas a less intelligent person could only detect greater or more obvious changes. Furthermore, Galton understood the need for theory to explain these unsuspected relations between ability and achievements in life. Finally, he examined how ability ran in families, and conceived the twin-study as a method of testing for the effects of genes and culture on intelligence.

The one thing that Galton did not do, and which has proven to be basic to advances in modern intelligence research, is develop a test of intelligence. While observers have distinguished between 'ability' and other faculties, such as personality, at least since Aristotle, the period of greatest advance in the scientific study of intelligence begins more or less with the advent of tests for ability at the beginning of the 20th century.

Binet and the origins of intelligence testing

The French psychologist Alfred Binet (1857–1911) pioneered the psychometric approach to intelligence, having been commissioned by the French government to develop a method of measuring ability to learn, so as to detect children who would face difficulties in the school system. Together with Theodore Simon, Binet published the first intelligence test in 1905 – a test that has guided most subsequent tests of intelligence. Unlike Galton, Binet did not search for a single or 'theoretically basic' measure of intelligence. Instead, he tested items from diverse areas and simply kept those items which worked, evolving the test over time based on feedback from the predictive success of the items.

Binet's test development was guided by two principles (Matarazzo, 1992):

1. Binet believed that intelligence increases through childhood: therefore, if a given item is a valid measure of ability, older children should find it easier than younger children.
2. Binet also believed that the rise in intelligence across childhood was not due to developments in sensory acuity or precision, nor was it a direct result of special education or training.

These two beliefs led to Binet's lasting contributions to intelligence test construction. First, and despite seeking to assess ability at school, he avoided any items that required experience or that resembled schoolwork. Second, he focused on tests of abstract reasoning on which, despite not being directly taught at school, performance improved with age:

> It is the intelligence alone that we seek to measure, by disregarding in so far as possible the degree of instruction which the child possesses. ... We give him nothing to read, nothing to write, and submit him to no test in which he might succeed by means of rote learning. (Binet & Simon, 1905)

Here we can see that Binet explicitly distinguishes between ability and achievement: he aims to predict subsequent achievement not from current learning or achievements, but from a measure of abstract reasoning ability. Binet's attempt to reduce dependence on special training or experience can be seen if we examine the types of item used in the 30-item 1905 Binet–Simon test of intelligence:

- Unwrap and eat a sweet.
- Define abstract words and name simple colours.
- Remember shopping lists.
- Arrange weights (3, 6, 9, 12, and 15 grams) and lines (3 cm, 4 cm) in order.
- Make rough copies of a line-drawn square, diamond, and cylinder.
- Construct sentences containing given words (e.g., 'Paris', 'fortune', and 'river').

Binet expected that all the children he tested would have been exposed to these materials many dozens of times, and that children's ability to reason and manipulate with these types of stimulus would not be dependent on differences in experience.

Within each of these item categories, various levels of item difficulty were constructed. Difficulty was defined by the average age at which the item could be answered correctly. For instance, Binet found that copying a cylinder figure was more difficult than copying a diamond figure, which in turn was more demanding than copying a square, implying that the former requires more intelligence than the latter tasks. Binet found that a typical 5-year-old could copy a square but not a diamond, and that a typical 8-year-old could copy a diamond but not a cylinder, which could in turn be copied from memory by an average 11-year-old.

Because Binet's test development has been of such lasting value, it is worth examining an item of this test in more detail. Let us take the example of figure-copying. First, Binet controlled the test situation. He showed the child a simple figure, and then removed it from view before asking them to draw the figure from memory. He also specified the criteria for marking, noting that accuracy of detail and neatness of the child's copy are unimportant. By presenting the stimulus visually rather than giving verbal instructions such as 'draw a diamond', he removed some of the role of experience and vocabulary from the situation. By removing the stimulus from view during the actual copy, he removed the possibility of a direct perceptual copy, forcing the child to rely on an internal representation of the figure. In addition to these insights in increasing the reliability of the test by controlling presentation and marking, the outcomes of the test itself help us develop a construct of intelligence. As noted above, Binet found that a square could be copied from memory by the average 5-year-old child, a diamond by age 8, and a cylinder by age 11. Why was this? What are some possible reasons why a problem is solvable at one age, but not earlier?

The problem was not perceptual or manual but rather analytic: the 8-year-old who fails at copying the diamond will have been quite able to copy the square, despite both shapes being composed of the same lines and vertices. Binet explored whether the problem was practice (which could increase with time). However, he found that the ability to copy was difficult to train, and, moreover, that training on one figure did not transfer to other equally hard figures. This suggested that, as Binet had thought, intelligence does not result from particular experiences or training, but develops largely independently of experience.

Mental age

Binet's next insight related to how to score an ability test. By having tested a large group of people, Binet could find out the age at which the average child could complete each item. His test could therefore be scored in terms of a 'mental age'. Binet developed this use of a single mental-age score for two reasons. First, he found that items within a category of related items could be arranged in terms of the mental age required to complete them. Second, he also found that children who could complete an item in one category to a given level of difficulty typically completed items from other categories to the same level of difficulty.

While Binet believed there were many distinct abilities (hence his wide choice of tests), and was initially agnostic as to the structure of intelligence, he came to speak of ability as a unitary construct. This is an important point and is worth reiterating. For example, if a 5-year-old could, in a figure-copying task, normally draw a square but not a cylinder, and could normally make a sentence containing the simpler word 'cake' but not the more difficult word 'fortune', then an average 5-year-old is expected to be able to both perform the two tasks at the same level. In our example, the 5-year-old should be able both to draw a square and make a sentence containing the word 'cake'. These apparently very different abilities somehow went together, defining a coherent 'mental age'. It was this mental age that Binet felt identified whether children would be able to cope at a given level of schooling, which was, after all, his primary task.

Binet found that children's mental age could diverge considerably from their chronological age, and that this accounted for their needing extra help at school. Some children performed as well as average children who were several years older, and some children achieved scores typical of children several years younger than themselves. If two children of different ages were found to have the same level of mental age, the younger one could be thought of as more intellectually able, given his or her age. To express these two concepts, Binet developed a distinction between mental age and chronological age.

- Chronological age – how old is this child?
- Mental age – how old would the average child be who performed at this child's level of performance?

The Binet–Simon test was therefore scored not in terms of the number of items that were correct, but in terms of the average chronological age of a child who would achieve this score, taking this as the effective mental age of the tested subject, with the child's chronological age reported for comparison.

The concept of 'IQ'

We noted above that Binet scored his test in terms of a mental age for a child, to be read along with the child's chronological age. William Stern (1912) saw that these two numbers were related and could be used to express a single value – the intelligence quotient or 'IQ':

IQ = Mental age/Chronological age × 100.

Therefore, an average child having a mental age that is commensurate with their chronological age will have an IQ of 100. This number is normally used to indicate the average IQ score. Any IQ scores higher than 100 therefore indicate higher-than-average IQ. While this definition works for children under age 17, the definition is no longer used, as scores on intelligence tests do not continue to rise with chronological age after 16–18 years of age, leading to an obvious problem: if you are an average 17-year-old (the age at which performance on the test reaches a plateau), and therefore have an IQ of 100 (17/17 × 100), what will your IQ be when you are 55, assuming your ability remains the same? After all, your ability as a 17-year-old is unlikely to continue to increase every year until you are 55 years old. You would have a mental age of 17 and a chronological age of 55, giving an IQ of just 31 (17/55 × 100), which is far below what we consider an average IQ score!

A solution to this dilemma was reached by Wechsler (1975), who recognized that the key insight to Binet's scoring system was not the use of a mental age, but the *deviation* of a child's mental age from that of the average child of his or her own age. This led to the adoption in nearly all tests of a so-called 'deviation IQ' – no longer the result of dividing mental age by chronological age, but instead based on a person's performance relative to their age cohort. In this system, the average person at any given age is given an IQ of 100, with scores above and

$$\text{Intelligence Quotient(IQ)} = \frac{\text{Mental age}}{\text{Chronological age}} \times 100$$

Figure 12B

266

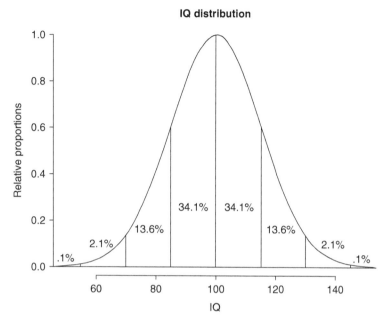

Figure 12.1 'The' normal or 'Gaussian' distribution of ability

below this scaled to give a standard deviation (SD) of 15. This is displayed in Figure 12.1, which shows the 'normal distribution' or bell-curve of IQ scores, with most people clustered in the middle around 100, and fewer people scoring either above or below this mean value. Some values to remember are that 95% of scores lie within ±2SD of the mean, i.e., between 70 and 130. Correspondingly, a score over 145 is obtained by only one person in 1,000.

The WAIS-IV: An example of a modern IQ test

In order to best understand the material of the rest of the chapter, it will be helpful to see the kinds of items in a modern ability test, what they are (and are not), and to begin to think about why they have been chosen, and how they will relate to human circumstances and outcomes.

Perhaps the most widely used and validated test of human intelligence is the Wechsler Adult Intelligence Scale, or WAIS, now in its fourth revision (the WAIS-IV: Wechsler, Coalson & Raiford, 2008). This test contains 15 sub-tests, spanning many types of item. The test can take an hour or more to complete. For reasons of copyright and of test security, the items are not shown. (It is important that the exact items of the test do not become common knowledge, lest this disrupt their valid use in selection and assessment, especially in forensic and medical contexts, such as neuropsychological assessment.) The WAIS is administered individually by a trained tester practised in the particular time limits and delivery requirements of this test. Not all of the sub-tests are presented below but here are examples:

Verbal comprehension

1. *Vocabulary*: word meanings:

   - 'What does "seasonal" mean?'
   - 'Fluctuating with the time of year' would earn more points than 'Like the weather'.

2. *Similarities*: finding what is common to two words:

   - 'Why are a boat and a car alike?'
   - 'Both are means of transport' would earn more points than 'Both are made of metal'.

Perceptual reasoning

3. *Block design*: a spatial test, in which subjects reproduce two-dimensional patterns using cubes with a range of differently coloured faces.

   - Make the pattern on the right using blocks shown on the left:

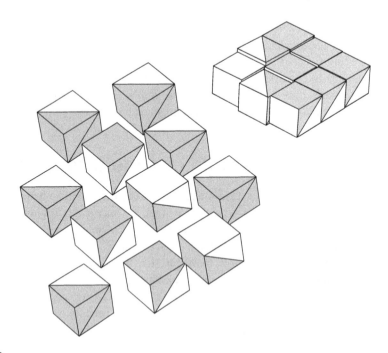

Figure 12C

4. *Matrix reasoning*: find the missing element in an array of patterned panels:

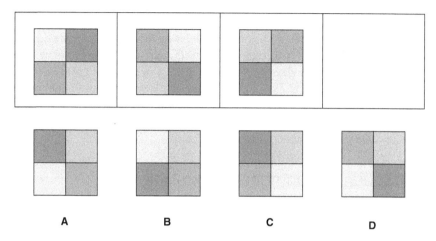

A   **B**   **C**   **D**

Figure 12D

Working memory

5. *Arithmetic*: mental arithmetic problems posed in practical situations:

   - If 1 boy takes 6 hours to make 12 widgets, how long will 3 boys take to make 6 widgets?

6. *Digit span*: the longest verbally presented number sequence that can be recalled correctly in forward, or reverse, order:

   - Read out loud at a rate of 1 per second, increasing in length until the subject reliably fails.
   - Backward span: asked to recall increasing digit strings in reverse order, again until reliably unable to do so without error.

Processing speed

7. *Coding*: re-code as many items as possible in a short time-period, using a table to map symbols such as '£, ¶, **p**' into corresponding digits.
8. *Symbol search*: mark as many lists as containing or not containing a particular target symbol as possible in a given time period.

There is a wide range of tests that is available to measure IQ and many are not as time-demanding as the WAIS-IV. Some of them can be administered in group settings and use minimal verbal instructions.

The structure of ability

We have seen how tests assess intelligence, but what exactly are they assessing? Despite a long tradition of work on the measurement of intelligence, there remains some disagreement about this most basic question. Although all scientists must deal with the same data, their explanations (theories) of these data may diverge, at least in the short term. In intelligence testing, two main approaches to explaining intelligence have been followed: one emphasizing the generality of ability, and the other focusing on differences between abilities. The first, both chronologically and in terms of its simplicity, is the general-ability theory, developed by Charles Spearman in the first quarter of the 20th century.

Charles Spearman and general intelligence

As noted earlier in relating the experience of Binet, one of the most powerful facts that confront any student of cognitive ability is the positive relationship shown across diverse ability measures. People who perform well on one ability measure also have a tendency to do well on others. This finding suggests that there may be a single organized factor underlying this correlation.

The earliest empirical studies of general cognitive ability were conducted by Charles Spearman (1863–1945), who termed this general intelligence factor 'g' (Spearman, 1904). Spearman argued that g was not a single faculty or module and therefore could never be measured directly or observed in a single behaviour. Instead, Spearman argued that intelligence was a property common to all cognitive processes, and he thought of intelligence as a 'mental energy', energizing diverse mental faculties and functions.

Binet, working on the atheoretical principle of using test items that distinguished younger from older children, found that his test was improved by using items from a broad range of domains, from defining words to drawing shapes. In similar fashion, Spearman, working from a more theory-driven perspective, argued that a good test of intelligence must concentrate not on developing a single type of *task*, but on incorporating the widest possible diversity of test items, the common element of which would emerge as general ability. This need for a wide range of items he called 'indifference of the indicator', suggesting that as g should affect all kinds of ability, the particular 'indicator' measures, or test items chosen did not matter. Instead, the more different the measures the better.

Spearman collected and studied the patterns of correlations among large numbers of distinct ability tests, observing that the clearest pattern was that all the tests, from whatever domain, correlated positively with each other. That is, if the person being tested scored very high on one test, she was likely to score very high on another test: this Spearman called 'positive manifold'. Spearman developed the statistical method of factor analysis (see Chapter 2) in part to show that these consistently positive correlations reflected an underlying general factor, implying that different ability tests are all influenced by a common underlying cause.

The general-ability factor has been confirmed in hundreds of data sets collected over the last century, where it accounts for 50% of the variance in any comprehensive and diverse

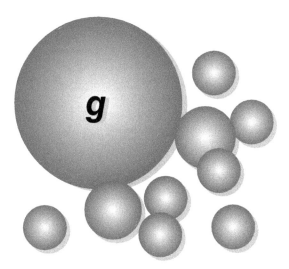

Figure 12.2 Graphical depiction of 'Spearman's' two-Factor theory

Notes: A large general factor (*g*) accounting for around half the variance in all ability, and specific factors, some of which are related to groups of tests, such as verbal ability, and some of which are very specific.

battery of tests (Carroll, 1993). Even other animals show a kind of *g* factor. While humans have evolved novel adaptations, such as generative language (Corballis, 2003), other species also appear to show general ability, suggesting that intelligence is not a simple product of language. Individual animals differ in their ability, and these differences cluster along a general factor explaining around 40% of the differences between them (Galsworthy et al., 2005). This raises the possibility of studying the biology of ability in animals, an area of research that has been neglected.

However, *g* is not the last word (or letter) on the structure of ability. In 1904, Spearman proposed that any test of ability could be decomposed into *g and* one or more specific components (see Figure 12.2). In 1937, he elaborated this theory, noting that not only did all tests correlate with each other (*g*), and single tests tended to contain variation unique to themselves (specifics), but tests also formed broad clusters such as 'verbal', 'spatial', or 'attention'. These came to be known as 'group factors'. This is suggested in Figure 12.2 by some slightly larger components of ability among the smaller, very specific elements. However, it was the work of Thurstone, who we will examine next, that most clearly emphasized these group factors.

The hierarchical model of ability: Different levels of order

While Spearman focused on the common element of all ability measures, other researchers focused on the differences between abilities, and the fact that there were individuals who were strong on one type of ability and weak on another. Principal among those emphasizing this

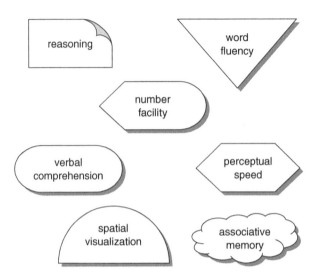

Figure 12.3 Thurstone's seven primary mental abilities

point of view was Lewis Thurstone (1887–1955), who developed a theory of 'primary mental abilities', identifying seven major different types of ability (see Figure 12.3).

Simply identifying different kinds of ability, of course, does not put Thurstone's model at odds with Binet or Spearman: all of these researchers acknowledged that different kinds of ability exist. The major distinction was that Thurstone argued that these abilities were independent or unrelated. He proposed that the apparent evidence of a general-ability factor was an artefact of testing; for instance, due to the fact that many tasks called upon more than one primary mental ability. For example, a verbally presented mathematical puzzle might be aided by spatial imagery. In a related suggestion, Thurstone and his followers argued that g was merely an 'averaging' of a person's ability on multiple independent domains. This view that there is no true underlying correlation to be found across all abilities persists today in the form of multiple intelligence theory (Gardner, 1983), which is discussed below.

Of course, if half of the variability in ability is due to a single general factor, two questions arise: What is the basis for this factor? And what is the structure of the other 50% of ability? The basis of g is addressed through the rest of this chapter, but before turning to that, it is important to understand how the overall structure of human intelligence is understood by other researchers. Carroll (1993) concluded that while half of the differences in any large test battery were due to general ability, the remaining differences had a three-tier structure similar to that intimated above by Spearman: underneath g lies what Carroll called stratum-II factors, or what Spearman called group factors. Beneath this, on what Carroll called stratum-III, lie the abilities specific to a single test or a very narrow domain of ability. This structure is well exemplified by turning again to the structure of the WAIS. Using what is called 'confirmatory factor analysis' the sub-tests of the WAIS-IV have been shown to group into four cognitive 'domains' (see Figure 12.4). Scores on the four domains inter-correlate .8 on average, supporting a single, general factor influencing each of the four abilities.

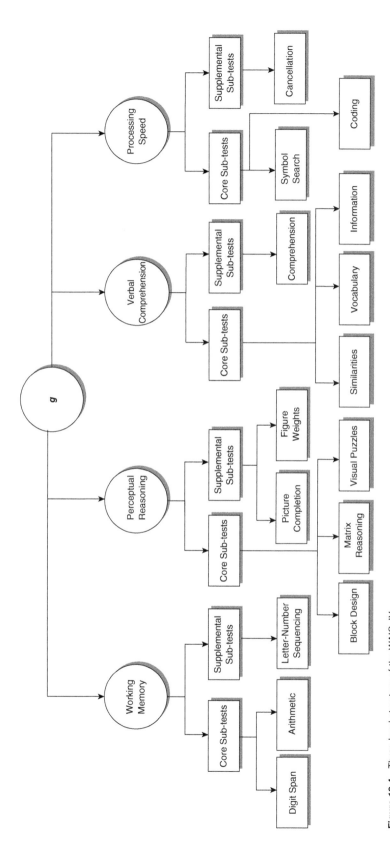

Figure 12.4 Three-level structure of the WAIS=IV

Crystallized and fluid intelligence

An alternative model of the structure of intelligence that is somewhat related to that of Spearman distinguishes between fluid ability and crystallized ability (Cattell, 1963). As we have seen above, intelligence tests can contain items that assume very little specific knowledge as well as items for which the person must have already learned the correct answer and stored it in memory. The theory of **fluid intelligence** and **crystallized intelligence** (Gf–Gc) was developed by Cattell in the 1940s and extended by Horn (1998). Cattell distinguished between fluid ability – the solving of problems where prior experience and knowledge are of little use – and crystallized knowledge – the product of education and experience, which would develop over time. Cattell and Horn argued that fluid ability should be more heritable and crystallized ability should show greater effects of family and cultural environment. The predictions have not been borne out however (Horn, 1998), and it seems likely that both fluid and crystallized ability reflect a single effect of general ability up until adulthood. During adulthood, genetic and environmental ageing factors begin to act on intelligence, with fluid ability showing greater sensitivity to these effects and declining much faster than crystallized ability (Craik & Salthouse, 2000). The Gf–Gc model has received support from a recent genomewide association study, which showed that the two proposed forms of intelligence are genetically distinct (Christoforou et al., 2014).

Gardner: Multiple intelligences

Howard Gardner (1983) proposed a theory of multiple intelligences, based on studies of 'savants' who have preserved high ability in very specific domains despite scoring very poorly on most other ability measures, neuropsychological patients who have lost relatively circumscribed ability (e.g., the ability to recognize faces), and experts showing virtuoso performance within a limited domain such as music. Gardner used these groups to contrast against the normal developmental progression observed and measured by Binet. Gardner initially proposed that the concept of intelligence should include musical, bodily-kinaesthetic, linguistic, logical-mathematical, spatial, and inter- and intra-personal abilities, but other types of intelligence have since been added to the list. This proposal in itself is not controversial: Spearman was very clear in suggesting that the best possible measure of g should include all possible abilities, and most theories of general intelligence include linguistic, logical, and spatial tasks, as well as acknowledging that behaviour results from the activity of a great range of specialized brain 'modules'. What distinguishes Gardner's theory is not its recognition of multiple abilities, but his hypothesis that these abilities do not form a general factor. In this sense, Gardner is repeating the argument of Thurstone that primary mental abilities are independent. As Gardner has not developed any scales to assess his proposed abilities, this theory remains to be tested, although the stubborn fact remains that research consistently demonstrates positive correlations among different ability tests and a powerful g factor. It does appear, for example, that intra- and inter-personal skills correlate with general ability (Mayer, Caruso, & Salovey, 1999), and that even dancing ability (presumably an aspect of kinaesthetic intelligence) is correlated with much more general cues of personal competence (Brown et al., 2005). These findings therefore appear to contradict Gardner's theory that the relevant abilities are independent of one another.

As you can see, there are a number of theories relating to how intelligence is structured, and the theories presented here are not an exhaustive list. In Chapter 14, we will encounter another different way of thinking about intelligence which relates to ability in the emotional domain.

Cognition and biology

A major goal of research into the nature of human intelligence has been to determine its biological (or neural) bases. Some of the major experimental correlates of ability include processing speed, brain volume, and brain connectivity, and these are discussed next.

Reaction time and inspection time

In a typical reaction time experiment, participants sit before a box with an array of 1–8 buttons, each with an adjacent light. When one of these lights illuminates, participants must lift their finger (often known as decision time) and move to press the correct button (often known as movement time). Hiding or inactivating some of the stimuli can produce a range of choices from 1 to 8 (see Figure 12.5).

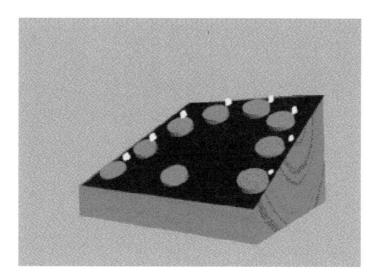

Figure 12.5   The Jensen Reaction Time Box

Each of 8 buttons has a light immediately above it. The subject rests their finger on the central 'home' key until one of the lights is illuminated, at which time they lift their finger from the home key (reaction time) and move to depress the appropriate response key (movement time).

Early on, the German psychologist Hick showed that reaction time increases linearly with the amount of information a participant must process in order to complete the reaction. Thus, perhaps surprisingly, lifting off the home key takes longer when one of four lights may illuminate on a trial, than when only one of two lights may illuminate. This effect of information processing demand on reaction time (RT) is known as 'Hick's law'. Many dozens of studies since the 1970s have shown a correlation between RT and IQ. The largest study completed to date, which examined over 900 adults, found a correlation of −.49 between IQ and four-choice RT (i.e., high intelligence correlates with relatively quick RTs), and a correlation of −.26 between IQ and the variability of RT (Deary, Der, & Ford, 2001). In addition to faster physical reactions to stimuli, researchers have examined the speed of the perceptual process itself: the so-called 'inspection time'. Inspection time (IT) refers to the shortest duration for which a stimulus can be presented – before being removed ('masked') – and the participant can still accurately report what the stimulus was. One of the reasons why researchers are interested in IT is that unlike many tasks for assessing intelligence (e.g., defining rare words, maths tasks), it is almost completely independent of culture or social learning. The typical visual stimulus used in an IT study is just a long and short line side by side, and the task is simply to report which of the two lines is longer (see Figure 12.6). Given a one-second exposure to the stimulus before it is covered by a mask, all participants can complete this task accurately on every trial. However, despite all participants knowing how to perform the task accurately, as the exposure duration is systematically reduced, some participants remain accurate while others begin to make many errors. The shortest stimulus exposure time that

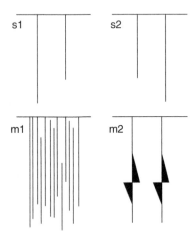

Figure 12.6 Inspection Time Stimulus

In the Inspection Time task, participants are shown one of either s1 (long line left) or s2 (long line right) and are asked to report which side the long line was on. After some practice trials, a mask is introduced: commonly a group of distracting lines (m1) or else a lightning flash (m2) that obscures the line lengths. The exposure time of the line stimulus before it is masked is varied by computer, and, by varying this duration and scoring correct and incorrect responses across a range of durations, an inspection time score can be calculated which indicates how many milliseconds exposure time before the mask a subject needs to achieve a certain percent correct, often 76%.

can be reliably discriminated by the participant at a pre-set accuracy level (e.g., 76% of stimuli exposed for a particular duration correctly identified) is that participant's IT. IT has been found to correlate strongly (negatively) with IQ scores, so that higher IQ goes with shorter IT. The effect was first reported by Australian researcher Ted Nettelbeck (1982). Since that time many dozens of studies have confirmed the effect, with a recent meta-analysis of 92 studies totalling over 4,000 participants, suggesting that IT performance correlates –.51 with general ability (Grudnik & Kranzler, 2001).

The fact that simple reaction and inspection time tasks correlate with IQ scores provides an avenue to investigating the basis of intelligence. Although these simple tasks are unlikely to replace traditional measures of intelligence, they are valuable in contributing to the current knowledge of intelligence (Deary, Austin, & Caryl, 2000).

Brain volume and connectivity

The relationship between brain volume and intelligence has been a topic of scientific debate since at least the 1830s. The idea that something as crude as brain size should be associated with intelligence may seem questionable. However, the scientific evidence now shows that brain volume is one of the strongest biological correlates of intelligence. The first rigorous report of a relation between brain volume and ability came from Nancy Andreasen (Andreasen et al., 1993), a cognitive scientist interested in creativity and exceptional performance, and numerous studies followed. A recent meta-analysis of 37 studies of the relationship between intelligence and brain volumes, derived from modern brain imaging techniques, has shown that the correlation is approximately .33 (McDaniel, 2005). It is somewhat higher for females than for males, and also higher for adults than for children. For all age and sex groups, however, brain volume is positively correlated with intelligence. In addition to that, the volume of the caudate nucleus, a subcortical brain structure that plays a role in learning, has recently been found to be related to individual differences in intelligence (Grazioplene, Ryman, Gray, Rustichini, Jung, & DeYoung, 2015).

As neuroscientific research develops, there has been an increasing focus on the search for intelligence in the brain. Studies using structural and functional neuroimaging techniques are used to examine, for example, the volume of white or grey matter in the brain in relation to intelligence, or the brain glucose metabolic rates at various brain regions in association with intelligence tests. These investigations have led to new ways of understanding brain activities in relation to intelligence, such as the Parieto-Frontal Integration Theory (P-FIT). This theory proposes that frontal and parietal brain regions in particular are related to intelligence (Jung & Haier, 2007; Haier, 2011). The connectivity between brain regions and how these regions work efficiently together is another way of examining intelligence. This focus on connectivity has led to the finding that more intelligent individuals use their brain resources more efficiently, as displayed by lower brain activation than those who are not as intelligent (neural efficiency hypothesis).

Brain volume and connectivity are genetically influenced, and some studies linking the heritability of brain structure to IQ have yielded important findings. A review of the genetics of brain structure and intelligence (Toga & Thompson, 2005) concluded that the predominant determinant of both intelligence and brain structure is genetic. Two twin-study reports

277

in the journal *Nature Neuroscience* indicate that brain size and ability are both heritable, that they correlate around .4, and that this correlation is due to shared genetic effects. This finding implies the existence of genes that control the growth of brain tissue and that also influence ability. Thompson et al. (2001) showed that although the volume of cortical grey matter is genetically influenced over all of the brain, this effect is particularly marked in the brain's frontal and language areas. The former areas are associated with performance of tasks demanding controlled attention, and a study has revealed that activation in the frontal lobe during tasks that demand controlled attention correlates highly with IQ (Gray, Chabris, & Braver, 2003). Thompson et al.'s study found that the volumes of frontal and language areas correlated particularly strongly with IQ, and were much more similar in identical twins than in dizygotic twins. This similarity therefore probably has a genetic basis. Thompson's results were confirmed in a much larger study by Dutch researcher Danielle Posthuma and colleagues (Posthuma, De Geus, Baare, Hulshoff, Kahn, & Boomsma, 2002). Her team found the heritability of brain volume to be very high (about .85), and that all of the effect of increased brain volume on increased IQ scores was due to genetic effects, rather than to environmental influences that might raise both brain size and cognitive ability. These twin study results were extended again by University of California researcher Richard Haier and his colleagues (Haier, Jung, Yeo, Head, & Alkire, 2004), who measured both the volume of particular brain regions and the activation of those regions during IQ test performance. Haier et al. replicated the brain volume–IQ correlation, and also found that the same regions that were larger in more intelligent participants were also most strongly activated during test-taking in all participants. A set of genes common to determining brain volumes and intelligence test performance is thought to account for the correlations observed between brain volumes and intelligence (van Leeuwen et al., 2009).

The brain consists not only of dense collections of nerve cells and their helpers (which appear grey in brain scans), but also of long fibres (axons) connecting these processing regions. These axons appear white because they have an insulating sheath of myelin which speeds conduction of the impulses from one grey matter nucleus to another. The organization and integrity of these fibre connections is related to cognitive ability, with correlations between .44 (Schmithorst, Wilke, Dardzinski, & Holland, 2005) and .51 (Jung et al., 2005). Thus, research has shown that IQ is related to overall brain volume, to the volume of particular brain regions, to the connectivity between different brain regions, and to the integrity of particular kinds of brain cell. At a neural level, that is, intelligence is associated with quantity, structural quality, and interconnectedness of neurons.

Genetic effects on intelligence

Heritability

As we saw in Chapter 5, behavioural genetics is the study of genetic contributions to differences between members of a population. It examines the extent and nature of these contributions.

You will recall that 'heritability' can vary from 0 to 1, and represents the proportion of variation between people that is due to genetic effects. The proportion of variability that is left unexplained by these effects is due to shared environment (i.e., effects shared within families) and non-shared environmental effects that are unique to the individual.

Many large studies estimating the heritability of IQ have been conducted, and these yield estimates between .5 and .8 (Deary, Spinath, & Bates, 2006). g has been shown to be highly heritable and increasingly heritable with age. At 9 years of age, the heritability was .41, at 12 it was .55, at 17 it was .66, and it continues to increase until late adulthood (Bouchard, 2014; Haworth et al., 2010). Conversely, environmental effects, which play a larger role than genetic factors at age 5, decrease rapidly in their influence as the individual approaches their late teens (Bouchard, 2014). These findings are illustrated in Figure 12.7. They suggest that as we develop and gain more control over our environments, the role of particular family, cultural, or social status variables ('shared environment') on intelligence are reduced. As people mature,

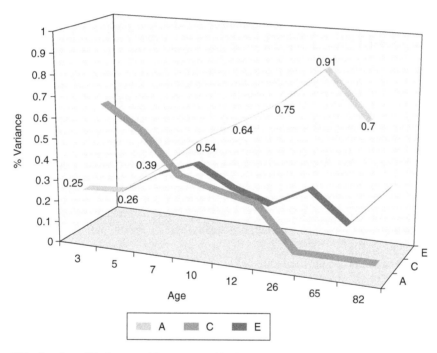

Figure 12.7   Genetic and Environmental Components of Intelligence from age 3 to age 82

Notes: A (pale) is the observed heritability, C (medium) is the effect of shared or family environment factors such as SES, and E (dark) is the remaining effects, which are unique to each individual and include measurement error. The Figure shows that at very young ages family environment has a large effect on cognitive ability, but that by young adulthood, this has been replaced with large effects of genes, which continue to rise in relative importance into old age, possibly declining again as people reach their 80s.

The data are combined results from (McClearn et al., 1997; Posthuma, De Geus, & Boomsma, 2001; Bartels, Rietveld, Van Baal, & Boomsma, 2002; Spinath & Plomin, 2003; Reynolds et al., 2005)

279

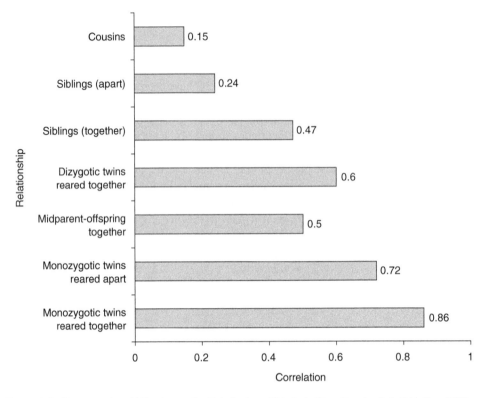

Figure 12.8 Summary of world literature on familial effects on IQ (adapted from Bouchard, Jr. & McGue, 1981)

they may begin to exercise active choice over their environment, seeking out environments and activities that are based on their internal, genetically-based personal preferences and abilities (Haworth et al., 2010).

Results of studies on the heritability of intelligence are summarized in Figure 12.8. Most of the different types of relationship presented have been examined in six or more studies, usually with at least several hundred participants. Figure 12.8 demonstrates that the resemblance between people in their intelligence increases sharply as they become more genetically similar, from relatively weak resemblance of second-degree relatives (.15 correlation between cousins) to extremely strong resemblance of monozygotic twins, especially when they are raised in the same household (.86 correlation).

Limitations of heritability research

In many samples used in heritability research, people from the lowest socio-economic status (SES) levels are under-represented, as are people from non-white backgrounds. The heritability of intelligence may differ for people from different social backgrounds. One suggestion that this is the case comes from studies of children from impoverished backgrounds who are adopted into high SES families. Although the studies reported above show limited effects of family environment on IQ by middle childhood, these adopted children show increases in IQ when compared to children who remain in the impoverished environment, their IQ often increasing to the same level as that of biological children in the adoptive family (van Ijzendoorn & Juffer, 2005). Studies such as these suggest that very poor environments have substantial negative effects on IQ, and that removing a child from such environments may have positive effects, even at age 3 or later.

The hypothesis that heritability is lower among people from very poor family environments was tested in a sample of 331 pairs of twins, aged 7 years old, who were selected from the National Collaborative Perinatal Project in the USA. The heritability of IQ was .71 in the highest SES group within the sample, but only .10 in the lowest SES groups. The effect of family environment within this subset of low SES children was a very substantial .58 (Turkheimer, Haley, Waldron, D'Onofrio, & Gottesman, 2003). This finding is consistent with the average heritability (around .4 at age 7) reported from the UK TEDS sample (Kovas et al., 2013). As the average heritability of IQ rises quite dramatically after age 7, and family effects correspondingly decrease, it is unclear whether differences in the SES groups would remain as the children grow older. However, it is interesting to note that not only was higher SES associated with higher IQ, the genetic influence on intelligence was also proportional to SES. In other words, it would appear that SES can make individual differences in intelligence even more obvious (Bates, Lewis, & Weiss, 2013).

The results of behavioural genetic studies of intelligence can be summarized in terms of two major effects: one surprising and one perhaps less surprising. The less surprising finding is that some family environments, concentrated among those of lower SES, can have large negative impacts on IQ, and these large negative effects appear to be remediable by exposure to stable and enriched environments. Perhaps more surprising is the finding that the effect of family environment on intelligence diminishes outside the most impoverished social backgrounds, suggesting, perhaps comfortingly, that most families can provide adequate environments for cognitive development.

Molecular genetics

With the advent of the human genome project in the 1990s, researchers have begun studying the individual genes that underlie human intelligence (Deary, Spinath, & Bates, 2006). The identification of possible candidate genes comes from studies of mental retardation, global cognitive function decline in older people, and memory functions, but the effects of individual genes are so small that it is more likely that the heritability of intelligence is polygenic, influenced by many different genes.

The first genomewide search for intelligence-related genes was conducted in 2005 by Danielle Posthuma and colleagues (Posthuma et al., 2005). A genomewide association study examines common variation in genes in people to see if that variation is associated with a particular trait, such as intelligence. The focus of the search is on single nucleotide polymorphisms (SNPs), which may be a variation in a nucleotide at a specific site in the genome between individuals. Posthuma et al. indicated that a gene or genes on chromosome 6 are related to intelligence. Another report (Burdick et al., 2006) has specifically implicated Dysbindin, a gene at this chromosomal site, and in 2014 a group of international researchers reported that a gene called FNBP1L was significally correlated with childhood intelligence (Benyamin et al., 2014).

Although the search for intelligence-related genes has yielded some encouraging results, it has also generated its share of frustration. One study of 7,900 children aged 7 in the UK, starting from over 350,000 SNPs, narrowed down to 28 SNPS with promising associations with intelligence, but none were ultimately validated. The authors remarked that a larger sample size and more powerful methods would be required, demonstrating the resources required for such studies. They also affirmed that intelligence is likely to be influenced by many genes of very small effect (Davis, Butcher, Docherty, Meaburn, Curtis, Simpson, Schalkwyk, & Plomin, 2010). Another study in New Zealand also failed to find genes linked to intelligence (Bagshaw, Horwood, Liu, Fergusson, Sullivan, & Kennedy, 2013). Thus it is clear that intelligence has a substantial genetic component, but the identification of the genes that compose it is a challenging task.

Environmental effects on intelligence

Much research has been devoted to attempting to understand the effects of environmental factors on intelligence. Some of this research has aimed to develop interventions to minimize or remediate the effects of early childhood deprivation on cognitive ability. While simplistic solutions such as listening to Mozart's music for a short period of time have garnered great attention (Rauscher, Shaw, & Ky, 1993), only to be rejected by careful research (Stough, Kerkin, Bates, & Mangan, 1994; Chabris, 1999), other effects bear closer scrutiny.

Schooling

Several natural experiments suggest that schooling raises IQ. One example is 'entrance staggering', which occurs when children of near identical age enter school one year apart because of birthday-related admission criteria. This creates two groups of children who would be expected to have roughly equivalent IQ (i.e., they are roughly the same age), and so any differences between them should reflect school effects. The data indicate that children who have been in school longer have higher mean IQ scores. A different kind of natural experiment occurs when schooling is interrupted for a period of time for some children but not others. Green, Hoffman, Morse, Hayes, and Morgan (1966) reported that when the schools in one Virginia county closed for several years in the 1960s to avoid racial integration, the intelligence test scores of children who did not attend school dropped by about .4 standard deviations (six points) for each missed year of school. A third natural experiment occurs when children from the same family attend different schools. Jensen (1977) reported that children learn so little at some schools that older siblings have systematically lower scores than their younger brothers and sisters attending better schools. In a recent study of primary school children from urban and rural areas of China, it was found that although age and schooling effects together play a role in intelligence, the schooling effect is stronger than the age effect. In addition, the schooling effect is larger for rural school children than for urban school children (Wang, Ren, Schweizer, & Xu, 2016). It can be concluded that attending school raises intelligence test scores, and that some schools and environments have a larger effect on intelligence than others.

When considering the effect of schooling on the different types of intelligence, such as crystallized or fluid intelligence, we would expect the effect on crystallized intelligence to increase steadily as this form of intelligence relates to school-based knowledge more than fluid intelligence. This does indeed appear to be the case. There is a steady increase in test scores relating to crystallized intelligence over time, even into the high school years, whereas the increase in fluid intelligence test scores as a result of schooling is less pronounced (Primi, Couto, Almeida, Guisande, & Miguel, 2012).

Head Start and Abecedarian studies

The first major intervention study attempting to remediate a poor or impoverished environment was 'Project Head Start', a programme giving deprived children systematic exposure to educational materials and experiences for one to two years. The results were disappointing in that while the programme did raise test scores during the course of the programme, these gains faded with time (Lee, Brooks-Gunn, Schnur, & Liaw, 1990). As this is a huge programme which has run continuously in the US since 1965, studies continue to investigate its effect. One meta-analysis of six studies, with 602 participants, showed that the gains in intelligence test performance are largely due to teachers giving children tasks that closely resemble actual intelligence tests. In addition, the gains in intelligence test scores are not matched by a rise in general intelligence, *g*. Instead, the rise in the test score is due to test-specific abilities (te Nijenhuis, Jongeneel-Grimen, & Kirkegaard, 2014). Building on the Head Start experience, other longer interventions were planned, beginning in early infancy and continuing through pre-school, of which the best example is the Carolina Abecedarian Project. This project studied 111 pre-schoolers, providing a full-day, five-day week, out-of-home pre-school intervention, from age 6 months and continuing for five years (see Figure 12.9). The study also had appropriate control groups to allow careful evaluation of the intervention. The results indicated that infants at age 2 in the programme were scoring higher on cognitive tests than control infants who had not received the intervention. Importantly, at age 12 – seven years after the programme had been completed – the experimental group maintained a five-point IQ advantage over controls, and this IQ advantage was fully reflected in school and academic achievement (Ramey & Ramey, 2004).

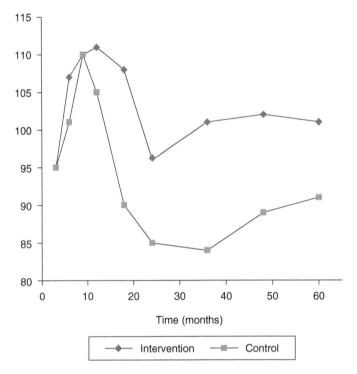

Figure 12.9   Abecedarian 5-year Intervention Data

Standardized scores on nine pre-school measurement occasions for treatment group (approximately 50 children with nutrition and health care intervention, plus full-day day care five days a week for five years) and control (nutritional and health care only) in the Abecedarian high-risk pre-school study (Ramey & Ramey, 2004).

The Flynn Effect

In the 1980s, New Zealand-based researcher James Flynn reported on an apparently very large and consistent rise in IQ scores around the world since intelligence testing began: around three IQ points per decade, and a full standard deviation since 1940. This came to be known as the 'Flynn Effect' (Dickens & Flynn, 2001). The gains were largest in 'culture fair' types of test (i.e., tests that do not rely extensively on learned material that may be less familiar to some cultural groups than to others) and smallest on knowledge-based tests such as the Scholastic Aptitude Test (SAT), where scores have actually declined (Dickens & Flynn, 2001). A study of scores of 202,486 people over 64 years on Raven's Progressive Matrices, a test thought to be culturally-fair, showed that this Flynn effect is robust. It is observed for every age group and the effect is larger in developing countries than in developed countries (Wongupparaj, Kumari, & Morris, 2015).

Several explanations for this steady rise in mean IQs have been proffered. Flynn himself argued that intelligence has not in fact increased to the level commensurate with the increase in IQ scores (Flynn, 1999). He argues that the results are so dramatic they cannot be real. For example, results from the Netherlands indicate that in 1952 only .38% of the population had IQs over 140 ('genius'), while by 1982, scored by the same norms, 12% exceeded this figure! Flynn argued that he could not see a commensurate increase in genius products and that what had changed was 'abstract problem solving ability', perhaps due to teaching that emphasizes this skill. He and Dickens have suggested that perhaps there is now a better alignment of (especially school) environments to the genetic requirements of individuals (Dickens & Flynn, 2001).

Others, citing the parallel increase in height over the same period (the average Dutch young adult male is now over six feet [1.83 metres] in height), suggested that changes in nutrition or a reduction in childhood developmental stress and infection may account for the effect. Recent studies suggest that the rise in IQ, whatever its cause, ceased in the 1990s (Teasdale & Owen, 2005) and may now have reversed in some countries. For example, performance on a spatial perception test in Austria and Germany over almost four decades seemed to increase initially but has now decreased (Pietschnig & Gittler, 2015). A similar effect has also been reported in Finland (Dutton & Lynn, 2013).

Stability of IQ

There is strong evidence that intelligence has high rank-order stability, even over long durations. IQ at age 18 is predicted very well by measures taken at age 12 ($r = .89$) or even age 6 ($r = .77$) (Jones & Bayley, 1941). If we average several test sessions at each age band to remove testing error, these correlations become even higher: for instance, the correlation of an average of measures taken at ages 11, 12, and 13 years with the average of two tests taken at 17 and 18 years is an astonishing .96, suggesting that IQ changes very little from age 11 onwards. Ability scores also remain stable across the life-span. Deary, Whalley, Lemmon, Crawford, and Starr (2000) had access to intelligence test scores for all children aged 11 in Scotland in 1932. They were able to bring 100 of this sample back to do the identical test 66 years to the day after the original test. The scores correlated .73, despite more than half a century having elapsed and the sample now being 77 years old. A recent study confirms that stability coefficients of 0.67–0.68 have been found in two longitudinal samples (Beaver, Schwartz, Connolly, Nedelec, Al-Ghamdi, & Kobeisy, 2013). It appears that IQ is relatively stable over time and the current evidence points to the contribution of both genetic and environment factors to this stability.

Group differences in intelligence

One of the most controversial and lasting aspects of intelligence testing has been the detection of group differences. One of the earliest impacts of systematic intelligence research was to disconfirm the then widely-held view that males were more intelligent on average than females, a view that was used to justify unequal access to education and democratic participation into the 20th century. Intelligence researchers demonstrated the fallacy of sex differences in intelligence, and also became active within the government of the day to push for social change based on their findings. The most reasonable conclusion to draw is that male and female general intelligence is equal on average. The picture is slightly different for performance on specific types of intelligence tests, such as those measuring verbal abilities and visuospatial abilities (Johnson & Bouchard, 2007).

Research on cognitive differences between racial groups has been more contentious. Readers are referred to Rushton and Jensen (2005) and the accompanying commentaries for a review of the literature. These contributions outline both what is known and unknown in this area of study, and help to appreciate the ethical and scientific issues involved in how the research findings should be interpreted, or whether they should be interpreted at all. What most researchers do agree on is that there is a large difference in the average test scores of self-reported black and white groups, and that this difference persists to this day even in relatively affluent societies, such as the UK and the USA. The magnitude of this difference (around 1.1 standard deviations or 16 IQ points: Neisser et al., 1996) is accepted mostly because the samples in which it has been demonstrated are among the largest and most representative ever collected in psychology (e.g., nation-wide testing for college entrance [the Scholastic Aptitude Test and Graduate Record Examinations] and in corporate and military employment screening: see Roth, Bevier, Bobko, Switzer, & Tyler, 2001).

While the difference is a matter of record, the cause of the difference has been the focus of one of the longest and most heated debates in psychology. Two elements of the race–IQ question have proven most controversial: the first is the existence of race itself as a meaningful biological construct; the second is the origin of the observed racial differences in test scores.

The existence of race has been controversial, because if racial groupings themselves have no biological basis, then neither could the observed test score differences. The validity of the concept of race has been hotly contested for many years, with many researchers arguing either that there is no biological basis for race, or that any biological correlates of race are of such little importance that research should ignore them (Rose, 2005). Biological analyses used blood-type to differentiate groups and concluded that most variation between people occurred within racial groups, rather than between them (Lewontin, 2001). The advent of human genome technologies enables a more detailed examination of possible racial differences in thousands of genetic markers. Analysis of these markers appears to validate common racial groupings, indicating that self-reported race is 96% aligned with genetic marker data (Tang et al., 2005). Yet other scholars continue to argue that there is no biological basis to race (Maglo, Mersha, & Martin, 2016). Interestingly, when human genetics scientists were interviewed, it was found that there is some variation in the definition of race being adopted in their research, rendering the use of the racial categories problematic (Hunt & Megyesi, 2008). Even if racial groupings are biologically meaningful, this does not mean that race-based differences in mean IQ have a biological basis. It is entirely possible that environmental factors that differ between racial groupings – potentially including nutrition, social norms, poverty, discrimination – contribute to these differences.

Although IQ tests generally do not suffer from significant **test bias** where race is concerned – a tendency to be relatively invalid, unsuitable or unfair for certain groups – it is possible that situational biases might exist. For example, Steele and Aronson (1995) demonstrated that when African-American students were led to believe that a difficult verbal task was diagnostic of their intelligence they performed more poorly on it than when the task was not presented in this way. They argue that being made aware of a negative stereotype about one's group creates feelings of threat and vulnerability that impair performance. When black participants are administered intelligence tests, aware that lower intelligence is part of the stereotype of their group, their performance may therefore be adversely affected. As a result, their intelligence may be under-estimated and the racial stereotype invalidly 'confirmed'. This 'stereotype threat' phenomenon may at least partly account for racial disparities in measured intelligence.

Conclusions

We can end with a definition of intelligence, provided by 52 researchers on intelligence as:

> a very general mental capability that, among other things, involves the ability to reason, plan, solve problems, think abstractly, comprehend complex ideas, learn quickly and learn from experience. It is not merely book learning, a narrow academic skill, or test-taking smarts. Rather, it reflects a broader and deeper capability for comprehending our surroundings – 'catching on,' 'making sense' of things, or 'figuring out' what to do. (Gottfredson, 1997a, p. 13)

Through studying this chapter, you will have seen that 'making sense' develops over childhood and early adolescence, that there are different elements to this trait which correlate with each other, that around half of the differences between people in 'making sense' fall under a general-ability factor, and that there are several lower-level ability factors, such as fluid and crystallized intelligence. Numerous tests have been developed to assess these abilities over the past century, with the best measures containing a broad array of abstract skills, and taking steps to ensure reliability and validity, and eliminate test bias. Improved performance on these tests during childhood is reflected in measurable cortical changes and is influenced positively by exposure to cognitively demanding environments with opportunities for structured practice, such as school. Alongside the effects of environment, genetic influences on ability are substantial and increase with age, so that roughly 70% of differences between people in their 60s is explained by genetic effects. Some portion of these genetic influences is due to effects of genes on brain structure and development, as revealed by correlations between IQ and brain volume, integrity, and connectivity. Although intelligence research has sometimes been dogged by concerns over differences in test performance between cultural groups, the IQ test is among the most stable, powerful tools developed by psychologists, with applications in medical research, neuropsychological assessment, human resources, and education, as we shall see in Chapter 13.

287

Chapter summary

- Binet assessed intelligence by assembling items that differentiated between typical children at various ages, scoring his test in terms of mental age, which formed the basis of the later 'intelligence quotient' or IQ.
- The 'deviation IQ' was first adopted by Wechsler, and differs by comparing an individual's performance against age norms, so that IQ tests have a mean of 100 and a standard deviation of 15.
- Like personality, the structure of ability is hierarchical, but unlike personality, all abilities appear to lie within a single domain.
- Authors emphasizing primary mental abilities (Thurstone) or a general ability (Spearman) are reconciled in this hierarchical model, in which g binds together more basic groups of ability, which in turn contain more specific lower-level abilities.
- Cognitive ability and the volume and connectivity of the central nervous system are related, according to imaging studies.
- Ability develops throughout childhood, and stimulation from early childhood onward, especially in the form of school-type activities, appears to be the major influence on the development of ability.
- Programmes for raising intelligence have had little lasting effect, but for children in deprived environments, full-time daycare-based care and stimulation throughout the pre-school years may have a lasting positive effect.
- Large rises in intelligence test scores in the latter half of the last century may demonstrate the effects of improved physical environment (reduced infection, improved nutrition), improvements in education, or increased practice at school of puzzle-like thinking.
- Estimates of the heritability of intelligence average around .5, with lower values in the very young and higher values in older subjects. Specific genes underlying this heritable pattern are being investigated.
- Behavioural genetic research indicates that family environment is a relatively minor contributor to cognitive ability after school begins.
- IQ scores are among the most stable measures we have of a person over time.
- Intelligence tests yield reliable race-based differences, but the causes of these differences remain obscure.

Further reading

Deary, I. J., Spinath, F. M., & Bates, T. C. (2006). Genetics of intelligence. *European Journal of Human Genetics, 14,* 690–700.
A recent review of research on the genetics of ability.

Jung, R. E. & Haier, R. J. (2007). The Parieto-Frontal Integration Theory (P-FIT) of intelligence: Converging neuroimaging evidence. *Behavioural and Brain Sciences*, *30*, 135–87.
A brain processes theory examined in many brain research studies.

Neisser, U., Boodoo, G., Bouchard, T. J., Jr, Boykin, A. W., Brody, N., Ceci, S. J., et al. (1996). Intelligence: Knowns and unknowns. *American Psychologist*, *51*, 77–101.
A comprehensive, but brief and straightforward review of intelligence, produced in the wake of the controversy over group differences in IQ.

Nisbett, R. E., Aronson, J., Blair, C., Dickens, W., Flynn, J., Halpern, D. F., & Turkheimer, E. (2012). Intelligence: New findings and theoretical developments. *American Psychologist*, *67*(2), 130–59.
A general overview of intelligence research incorporating biological approaches.

te Nijenhuis, J., Jongeneel-Grimen, B., & Kirkegaard, E. O. W. (2014). Are Headstart gains on the *g* factor? A meta-analysis. *Intelligence*, *46*, 209–15.
A summary examining the increase in IQ scores in the Head Start intervention project.

Note

1. Answers: '*esoteric*' is an adjective describing knowledge which is understood by or available to only a restricted or special group. 100 machines will take just 5 minutes to make one hundred widgets (a common incorrect answer is 100). The puzzle piece is 3.

Intelligence in Everyday Life

Learning objectives

- To develop an understanding of the contribution of intelligence to behaviour and outcomes in everyday life.
- To understand the mechanisms through which intelligence may influence life outcomes.
- To understand the challenges of researching intelligence within different domains of life.
- To know the direction of causality and conclusions that can be drawn from studies in the area.

The previous chapter showed that intelligence has played an important part in the development of psychology as a discipline. The chapter explored the structure, assessment and biological foundations of intelligence, but it did not answer the more applied question of how important intelligence is to our everyday life. That is the focus of our discussion in this chapter. More specifically, the discussion will revolve around a review of the contribution of intelligence to behaviour and outcomes in different domains of life. We hope you will have a greater appreciation for the importance of intelligence in everyday life by the end of this chapter.

This chapter will demonstrate that intelligence is fundamental to meeting many of the challenges of everyday life. We may not be conscious of its importance until new demands are made on our ability to perform a task or when we see someone else struggling with some aspects of their lives, for example coping with the effect of brain injury following a motor vehicle accident. Tasks that were originally easy to perform become a lot more difficult and demand extra effort. It is worth highlighting that when we discuss the importance of intelligence, this 'importance' refers to its role in achieving the particular goals that are valued by our society (Gottfredson, 1997b). Therefore, the value placed on a concept such as intelligence is bound by its context. Indeed, intelligence is a concept that is closely tied to cultural, social aspects of life (Sternberg, Grigorenko, & Bundy, 2001). As a result, the interpretation of what is a successful outcome in life, as a result of intelligence, ought to be considered within the context of that culture. That which is considered successful or important in one culture or society may not be so in another.

Intelligence tests: Their use and predictive validity

We cannot examine how functionally important intelligence is in everyday life without having a means of assessing it and without conducting research to find out whether intelligence assessments predict things that matter. In the previous chapter you have been introduced to the different types of tests that have been used to measure intelligence. The practical usefulness of these tests in real life will be the focus of our discussion in this section.

The use of IQ tests has been controversial and can be an issue of concern for different reasons. Concerns have been expressed about their fair use and how their results should be interpreted. Whether IQ test scores adequately represent the concept of intelligence has also been challenged. We often hear students critique a particular intelligence test by saying it does not seem to resemble the challenges presented in everyday life, thus questioning its 'ecological validity'. (We will discuss this critique later in the chapter in a discussion about intelligence and job complexity.)

Despite these concerns, intelligence tests are widely used to make important decisions, and they have been applied in many different settings. In education, they are used to inform the educational psychologist of students' relative strengths and weaknesses in order to plan an intervention programme if they are not performing academically as well as expected. In clinical or neuropsychological settings, intelligence tests are used to gauge the extent of deterioration of cognitive function following a traumatic brain injury, for example. Such an assessment of intelligence would assist in designing rehabilitation programmes or to manage the person's cognitive deficits. In organizational psychology contexts, intelligence testing may be used to assess job candidates' capacities to handle cognitively taxing work roles.

In addition to these examples of how intelligence tests can be deployed, they are used in research to examine relationships between people's level of intelligence and other facets of their life. One of the ways of doing this is to find out how well intelligence, as measured by an intelligence test, can predict life outcomes. For example, the importance of intelligence can be investigated by examining how well a group of individuals' intelligence test scores correlate with job performance. If intelligence scores predict job performance well, then there is evidence that intelligence contributes to explaining job performance, and thus showing the value and practical importance of intelligence as a concept.

The predictive capability of an intelligence test can be expressed by what is known as a criterion (or outcome) validity coefficient. This measure of predictive validity is measured by a correlation coefficient (see Chapter 2), which shows the strength of relationship between two scores – an IQ test and a supervisor's rating of job performance, for example – on a scale of −1.0 to +1.0. The closer this coefficient is to +1.0, the stronger the positive relationship between the two scores, showing the importance of intelligence in predicting the outcome (Gottfredson, 1997b). Validity coefficients can be generated from cross-sectional studies which measure intelligence and a life outcome at the same time. These are limited in the conclusions they can draw as they cannot show that one variable is causally responsible for the other (e.g., that high intelligence causes superior job performance). Validity coefficients can also be derived from longitudinal prospective studies, which measure intelligence early in life and correlate these measurements with life outcome scores later in life. This research design is less limited and provides stronger evidence on the causal relationship between the two variables. For example, it eliminates the possibility of 'reverse causality': the possibility that the positive life outcome causes high intelligence. In the absence of time travel, adult job performance cannot cause childhood intelligence. Longitudinal prospective studies can therefore provide strong evidence that intelligence is not only validly associated with life outcomes, but also that it is at least partially responsible for these life outcomes.

In the next section, we will discuss the relationship between intelligence, typically indexed by IQ scores, and life outcome measures.

Domains of life

There have now been many decades of research exploring the validity of intelligence tests as predictors of a wide assortment of life outcomes, across many domains. Intelligence has been found, through a meta-analysis of 85 data sets, to be a powerful predictor of success in education, occupation, and income (Strenze, 2007). For example, in Poland, IQ score at as young an age as 13 has been found to be a good predictor of life outcomes such as education level attained, occupational status, and financial outcomes such as family income, at age 36 (Firkowska-Mankiewicz, 2011).

The main areas that we will discuss in this section are academic achievement, work, money, and health. Before doing that, it is good to recognize that there are also other areas where intelligence research has been conducted. For example, intelligence has been found to be related to fertility indicators such as birth rate (Shatz, 2008); suicide rate (Voracek, 2004); crime indicators such as frequency of imprisonment (Levine, 2011); habitual illegal drug use (White, Mortensen, & Batty, 2012); psychosocial adaptation such as bullying behaviour (Huepe et al., 2011); juvenile offending (Moffitt, Gabrielli, Mednick, & Schulsinger, 1981); and risk and severity of mental disorders (Macklin et al., 1998). Understanding effects of intelligence on these life domains is the focus of an area of study known as cognitive epidemiology, which examines the implications of cognitive ability at a population level.

Academic achievement

There is a strong relationship between schooling and intelligence. This relationship appears to be causally complex: higher intelligence is partly responsible for positive schooling outcomes, and schooling has an effect on intelligence. Research has shown for quite some time now that not attending school for an extended duration can have a detrimental effect of up to 2 standard deviations in IQ scores (Nisbett et al., 2012). There is a strong relationship between IQ and the total years of education too, such that childhood IQ predicts the total years of education that people undertake (Neisser et al., 1996).

One of the clearest schooling-related correlates of intelligence is academic performance. Replicating Binet's original insight, it seems that aptitude for school, as measured by tests such the American SAT, simply is general intelligence, *g* (Frey & Detterman, 2004), and that *g* predicts school grades better than any other measure apart from the student's previous year's grades. Over the years, and across many studies, validity correlations between .30 and .70 have been reported for the relationship between intelligence and academic achievement (Roth et al., 2015). A recent meta-analysis of 162 studies published between 1922 and 2014, which included 105,185 participants drawn from 240 samples from 33 different countries, showed a correlation coefficient of 0.54 between IQ and academic achievement. The meta-analysis also found that the relationship between IQ and academic achievement was strongest when the IQ measure incorporated both verbal and non-verbal tests, demonstrating the importance of general intelligence, *g*. Other results from this study include the finding that intelligence seemed to become more important as school grade level increases, suggesting that as the complexity of the learning material increases, intelligence level seemed to become more important too. In terms of subject areas, intelligence is most strongly related to performance in subjects which have a clear logical structure, such as mathematics and science (Roth et al., 2015).

It is important to remember here that the correlation between intelligence and academic achievement cannot be interpreted in a simple cause-and-effect manner. The correlation between intelligence and academic achievement does not necessarily mean that intelligence is causally affecting achievement in a one-directional way, as the intelligence–academic achievement relationship is reciprocal. For example, educational interventions that promote academic achievement can affect intelligence, as shown by early childhood education intervention programmes such as the American Head Start initiative (Puma et al., 2010), which was described in Chapter 12.

Although the relationship between intelligence and academic achievement may be complex, it is undeniably strong. The Roth et al. (2015) study implies that almost 30% of the differences between people in academic achievement are related to IQ. However, this leaves over 70% of these differences unexplained by intelligence. Other factors that might account for some of the missing 70% are random influences on academic achievement, such as measurement error, and environmental factors, such as opportunities or encouragements provided to individuals, their beliefs that they can succeed, and their parental expectations (Sternberg, Grigorenko, & Bundy, 2001). Additional factors that influence academic achievement include motivation, school anxiety (Roth et al., 2015), and personality traits such as Conscientiousness (Di Fabio & Busoni, 2007), Openness to Experience and Agreeableness (Farsides & Woodfield, 2003). When intelligence, personality and **emotional intelligence** (to be discussed in Chapter 14) were investigated together in a study of high school students (Di Fabio & Palazzeschi, 2009), they all independently predicted academic achievement. Intelligence was responsible for 10% of students' differences in achievement, compared to 7% for emotional intelligence and 5% for Big Five personality traits. Therefore, although it is important to acknowledge the contribution of other factors, intelligence remains a major contributor to academic achievement.

The remainder of this section provides a snapshot of the intelligence–academic achievement relationship examined over an assortment of student groups, ranging from primary school pupils to postgraduate university students. In a longitudinal study of mid-childhood students (age 8–9), which is part of the Christchurch Health and Development Study in New Zealand, students' IQ scores were measured using the Wechsler Intelligence Scale for Children and a range of life outcomes variables, including academic success, were assessed when they were aged between 15 and 25. There was a strong and statistically positive correlation between childhood intelligence and adolescent and young adult academic success. The higher the IQ, the higher their qualifications attained, including university degree qualifications. When statistical analysis was applied to control for factors such as early childhood conduct problems and family circumstances, the relationship between IQ and academic success remained, showing that intelligence and academic outcome are associated even when these other potential contributors to academic achievement were taken into account (Fergusson, Horwood, & Ridder, 2005).

Another longitudinal study conducted in the United Kingdom (Deary, Strand, Smith, & Fernandes, 2007) examined 70,000 11-year-old children, who were administered a reasoning ability test, from which their general intelligence (g) was calculated. Their academic achievement was measured at age 16 based on performance in national examinations that determine which students could pusue further education or training. The relationship between g and academic achievement was a very strong correlation of .8. Children who achieved an average score on the intelligence test had a 58% chance of obtaining exam results that would qualify them for further education, which increased steeply to 91% chance if the student had a cognitive ability test score that is 1 standard deviation higher than the average. Together, these striking findings show the large contribution of intelligence to academic achievement in a large study that is representative of a cohort of students in a single country.

Turning from a study of 11-year-olds to a study of a sample of late teenagers, Di Fabio and Busoni (2007) investigated the relationship between fluid intelligence, personality and end-of-year academic results among 17- to 19-year-old high school students. Fluid intelligence was the strongest predictor of academic achievements, although the personality trait Conscientiousness also did so, probably in part because it contributes to diligence, organization and good study habits. At university level, a meta-analysis of 127 studies, comprising 20,352 university students, examined whether performance on the Miller Analogies Test (MAT) predicted academic performance later in the student's degree. The MAT is an analogy test – its items take the form 'A is to B as C is to ?' – that measures a combination of g and verbal ability. Scores on the MAT were found to be associated with early academic performance

295

soon after being admitted into an undergraduate course, and also to behaviours and outcomes later in the course (Kuncel, Hezlett, & Ones, 2004).

Beyond undergraduate degrees, individuals who, by the age of 13, scored in the top .01% on the SAT, a cognitive ability measure used in the USA for selection into university, showed that 51.7% of male participants and 54.3% of female participants had a doctoral-level qualification. Impressively, this is a 50 times higher rate than the 1% expected of the general population. There were also more of these individuals (21.7%) who later managed to secure permanent academic positions in the top 50 US universities as full professors compared to 6.5% of another highly capable 'control' group (Lubinski, Benbow, Webb, & Bleske-Rechek, 2006). Therefore, intelligence can predict academic success and qualifications even beyond undergraduate degree qualifications.

The world of work

The relationship between IQ and academic performance may not seem surprising. After all, IQ tests were initially designed to be relevant in the context of schooling and they are clearly related to academic skills. However, intelligence also has the capacity to predict outcomes in non-academic domains. For example, performance at work has been repeatedly shown to be best predicted by general intellectual ability (Gottfredson 1997b; Ones, Viswesvaran, & Dilchert, 2005; Ree & Earles; 1992). At work, across a range of occupations, the validity of intelligence as a predictor of eventual job level attained, job-related training performance, and actual job performance is in the high .40s–.50s range (Schmidt & Hunter, 2004). Validity coefficients as high as .74 have been reported (Ones et al., 2005). IQ also appears to be strongly predictive of performance in job training programmes as well as in jobs themselves, with researchers finding validity coefficients ranging from .30 to as high as .70 (Ones et al., 2005).

Since the 1970s, researchers have gone beyond merely documenting the strength of the relationship between intelligence and job performance and explored the relationship between different occupational *types* and intelligence. They examined how strongly ability test scores predicted job performance in various occupations. Initially, the validity coefficients were relatively low, with one even showing a negative relationship. However, when re-analyzed more appropriately, these coefficients increased in magnitude. Cognitive abilities were found to predict performance in managerial, and clerical jobs most powerfully, and to predict performance as a sales-clerk and vehicle operator least powerfully (Ones et al., 2005). High IQ scores were typically found in persons holding more 'cerebral' jobs that are thought to require more mental ability and abstract cognition (Ree & Earles, 1992), while lower IQ scores were reported in persons holding more physical and concrete jobs, such as labourer, farm worker, and lumberjack (Ree & Earles, 1992).

Research has also shown that intelligence predicts people's work trajectories. One longitudinal study (Wilk & Sackett, 1996) showed that within a five-year period, people with higher intelligence scores move upwards in the hierarchy of jobs, while those with lower intelligence scores move downwards. This job movement was related to people's intelligence and also to the complexity of the job they held originally, such that if their intelligence level was deemed to be above the complexity level of their original job, they were likely to move upwards to a job that is more complex. This tendency for individuals to gravitate towards jobs that are commensurate with their ability has been dubbed the 'gravitational hypothesis' (Wilk, Desmarais, & Sackett, 1995). Could these tendencies to move up or to remain behind be due to other confounding variables, such as opportunities that were available, or the quality of school the workers attended? Apparently not. In another study where rigorous control of variables such as family background, schools, and socio-economic status was put in place, siblings who had higher intelligence test scores had more education and held more prestigious jobs than siblings who had lower intelligence scores. This also translated into income differences – siblings who scored 120 IQ points were earning US$18,000 more than siblings who had average (i.e., 100) IQ scores. In turn, these average IQ individuals earned US$9,000 more than their siblings who had IQ scores lower than 80 (Murray, 1998).

Why should intelligence be predictive of job performance? One explanation is that both variables involve learning. Intelligence relates to the ability to learn and job performance is dependent on the learning of job-related knowledge. While job knowledge is not the same as job performance, these two aspects are closely related. As Ones, Viswesvaran, and Dilchert (2005) demonstrated, intelligence becomes a better predictor of job performance as job complexity increases, consistent with the idea that high cognitive ability is especially important for learning to master the challenges of cognitively complex work roles.

Another explanation for the role of intelligence in job performance is that intelligence relates to the successful processing of complex information, not just the amount of knowledge that workers must acquire (Gottfredson, 1997b). For example, although the tasks included in IQ tests, such as describing how two concepts are similar to each other, may seem very far removed from everyday work tasks, it is the ability to handle and manipulate complex information that is being tested. In the IQ test, the ability to abstract the key attributes of both concepts may be easier in the first few items as they only require concrete thinking. However, as the concepts become increasingly abstract as the test progresses, the complexity in the processing of thoughts becomes more salient. In the world of work, this same ability to problem-solve or process complex information is required.

The success of intelligence as a predictor of work performance is an argument in favour of the use of intelligence tests in personnel selection. Intelligence tests are especially useful in this context because the intelligence measured is not specific to particular situations or job types (Schmidt, 1988). This means that with the increasing possibility of employees moving between jobs, the selection of a suitable candidate into one role is likely to translate into the future success of the same person in another role. This may bring long-term benefit to the hiring institution. However, a problem, especially in the US context, is that certain ethnic groups, such as African Americans and Hispanics, do not fare as well as other groups in cognitive tests relating to employment selection (Schmidt, 1988). Whether this is due in part to limitations or biases in the specific ability tests used, and what should be done about it, remains very much unresolved. However, it is not self-evident or inevitable that selection using intelligence tests is intrinsically biased against particular groups. For example, using archival data of 4,462 male army recruits in 1986, researchers found that African Americans matched on intelligence level with Whites were not disadvantaged in terms of job status or income, at least in the group scoring higher than median of IQ in the total Black–White sample (Nyborg & Jensen, 2001).

Partly in response to concerns over IQ testing, Sternberg and Wagner (1993) advocated that tests of 'practical intelligence' should be used instead. These tests measure 'tacit knowledge', which involves information and skills that are not taught directly but relate to the know-how of how to succeed in a given job. Sternberg and Wagner (1993) reported that tacit knowledge predicts job performance moderately well and to a similar degree as conventional IQ tests (Sternberg & Wagner, 1993).

In an example practical intelligence test, participants rate the best options for dealing with 12 scenarios presented using a rating scale from 1 (poor solution) to 7 (excellent solution). An example of a scenario from the Sales domain is:

> You sell a line of photocopy machines. One of your machines has relatively few features and is inexpensive, at $700, although it is not the least expensive model you carry. The $700 photocopy machine is not selling well and it is overstocked. There is a shortage of the more elaborate photocopy machines in your line, so you have been asked to do what you can to improve sales of the $700 machine.
>
> Rate the following strategies for maximizing your sales of the slow-moving photocopy machine.
>
> _____ Stress with potential customers that although this model lacks some desirable features, the low price more than makes up for it.
>
> _____ Stress that there are relatively few models left at this price.
>
> _____ Arrange as many demonstrations as possible of the machine.
>
> _____ Stress simplicity of use since the machine lacks confusing controls that other machines may have.
>
> (Sternberg & Wagner, 1993, p. 4)

Thus far, we have only discussed the predictive validity of intelligence in the world of work but not whether intelligence makes a causal contribution to work performance. One piece of evidence supporting the causal role of intelligence comes from the study of military personnel in the USA. This is enabled because cognitive abilities are measured prior to military induction and training, thus minimizing the possibility of reverse causality, as mentioned earlier in this chapter. The majority of the personnel whose scores were at the higher end of the range successfully completed military training, whereas a substantially lower proportion of those who scored towards the lower end of the score distribution completed the training (Gottfredson, 1997b). In addition, training and the length of experience in the job did not substantially increase job performance. Even when provided with training, individuals with lower IQ did not seem to benefit such that their performance becomes on par with the performance of higher IQ individuals. This shows the importance of intelligence and that it cannot be readily compensated through job training. The importance of intelligence is especially salient when the nature of the jobs is not routinized but required different information-processing ability (Gottfredson, 1997b).

It would be remiss not to discuss briefly other variables that relate to work performance. Although extent of work experience and personality traits such as Conscientiousness can predict some job-related performance measures, they do not predict as well as intelligence (Schmidt & Hunter, 2004). When emotional intelligence (see Chapter 14) is investigated together with general intelligence in relation to job performance as measured by supervisors' ratings, emotional intelligence and general intelligence play a compensatory role for the other. In other words, low general intelligence employees can perform their job satisfactorily if they have high emotional intelligence and vice versa (Côté & Miners, 2006). This compensatory relationship between emotional intelligence and general intelligence has also been observed in a study which required participants to attend a simulated job interview session. The performance of individuals with lower IQ was as good as individuals with higher IQ *if* these lower IQ individuals had high emotional intelligence (Fiori, 2015). Therefore, it is important to remember that there are other factors that may compensate for a shortfall in general intelligence. However, it remains true that general intelligence is the pre-eminent psychological predictor of job performance (Gottfredson, 1997b; Ones et al., 2005).

Money matters

We have seen that intelligence predicts both academic and job performance. It also predicts measures of economic success. In a meta-analysis, 85 data sets on intelligence and income that included samples from the USA, the UK, New Zealand, Australia, Estonia, the Netherlands, Norway, and Sweden were scrutinized (Strenze, 2007). A correlation of .20 was found between intelligence and income, a figure that is lower than typical correlations between intelligence and education (.54; Roth et al., 2015), and between intelligence and occupation (.43; Strenze, 2007). This relatively low correlation between income and IQ has also been reported by other researchers. Why would income be related to IQ? Higher IQ individuals may be likely to be paid more for the more efficient production of work (Lynn, 2010), and, as we have seen, they tend to occupy better-paying occupations and be more successful in obtaining promotions within their workplaces. The famous Terman study, which examined a sample of high-achieving individuals born around 1910, offers some insight, finding that IQ, together with personality, affects the income level of these individuals. The researchers showed that IQ and personality influence income level through educational choice, such as returning to study at postgraduate level. The additional knowledge and skills acquired by individuals with high IQ through further study are viewed positively by employers, leading to higher incomes (Gensowski, 2014).

Health, morbidity, and mortality

Although links between intelligence and academic, occupational, and economic success have been well established for many years, the idea that intelligence might have a bearing on physical health has only been examined relatively recently. However, there is now strong evidence that intelligence can predict even such a fundamental phenomenon as death. Intelligence has been shown to be negatively correlated with risk of mortality, meaning that low IQ scores are related to higher likelihood of death by a particular age. To put it another way, intelligence is related positively to longevity and physical health. This has been demonstrated prospectively by studies where children with higher IQ have lower risk of mortality in adulthood. In addition to mortality risk, childhood intelligence scores are negatively correlated with morbidity risk factors, such as the development of hypertension and the uptake and continuation of smoking (Batty, Mortensen, Nybo Anderson, & Osler, 2005). Research in the growing field of cognitive epidemiology (Luciano et al., 2010) is increasingly showing that a wide range of health problems are correlated with low intelligence, including obesity, alcohol consumption, lung and stomach cancer, and proneness to physical injuries (Der, Batty, & Deary, 2009).

In terms of specific diseases, a Danish study of 6,910 school-aged boys whose intelligence was assessed at age 12 years and followed up from age 25 to 35 years old, found that childhood IQ is negatively correlated with the risk of coronary heart disease in adulthood. This relationship persisted even when birthweight and social class, which were higher in higher IQ children, were statistically controlled (Batty et al., 2005). A few explanations have been offered for this relationship. First, the *disease prevention hypothesis* posits that higher intelligence is associated with a healthier lifestyle and higher socio-economic status (SES), which hinder the development of the disease. Intelligence may be an index of low rates of exposure to early psychological or physiological childhood events that predispose people to coronary heart disease, or its link to socio-economic advantage in adulthood may be a protective factor. Alternatively, higher intelligence early in life may be related to the acquisition of healthy behaviours, such as physical activity, good diet, and avoidance of smoking (Batty et al., 2005). A second set of explanations can be described as the *disease management hypothesis*. This hypothesis proposes that individuals with higher intelligence are better equipped to manage health problems that they suffer from. For example, intelligence may assist with early detection of health problems, accessing appropriate health care, and adherence to self-administered medication regimes, and these behaviours may play an important role in maintaining health (Deary et al., 2009). A third explanation, proposed by Gottfredson and Deary (2004), is that more intelligent people may suffer less disease because they are more likely to avoid unhealthy and unsafe environments and practices.

Some light on the pathways from intelligence to health is shone by a study on risk for cardiovascular diseases (CVD). The study of 1,145 participants (Batty, Deary, Benzeval, & Der, 2010) examined the relative importance of multiple risk factors for mortality as a result of CVD within a 20-year period. The researchers found that in decreasing order of importance, the risk factors were smoking, low IQ, low income, high systolic blood pressure, and low physical activity. A second study confirmed that there is a significant correlation between low general intelligence, g, and CVD risk factors, especially heart rate, and reported that the intelligence–CVD risk factors association is mainly due to genetic rather than environmental causes. That is, intelligence and CVD risk factors are underpinned by the same genetic influences (Luciano et al., 2010). There is a clear need for research in this field to clarify the mechanisms underlying these remarkable associations between intelligence and cardiovascular disease.

It is often reported that obesity is negatively related to IQ. Although this appears to be true, the direction of causality is unclear. One of the criticisms for some of the research on this topic is that the conclusion made about obesity being linked to lower IQ are often based on cross-sectional design studies which do not allow for the direction of causality to be inferred: does high IQ protect against obesity, does obesity in some way inhibit the development of intelligence, or does some third variable account for the intelligence–obesity association? Some longitudinal studies do indicate that low IQ has some causal role in obesity. Typically, these longitudinal studies, conducted in countries including Sweden, New Zealand and the United Kingdom, have measured IQ when participants were young, and then followed them up with health indicator measurements in adulthood. By doing so, the intelligence levels of individuals have been captured prior to the development of adult disease (Kanazawa, 2014). One New Zealand study, in which 1,037 infants were tracked prospectively until they are 38 years old, found that obese adults tended to have lower adult and childhood IQ scores than non-obese adults. Obese adults showed no decline in IQ over time, indicating that lower IQ (since childhood) increases the risk of obesity, but obesity had no impact on IQ (Belsky et al., 2013).

There are other ways of investigating the relationship between intelligence and health. One way is to examine whether parents' IQ is related to their offspring's health and health behaviour. One study of 2,268 parent–offspring pairs (Whitley et al., 2013) used data from the National Child Development Study in Great Britain, health and health behaviour measures including sedentary behaviour of watching television, injuries treated at hospitals, illness not treated at hospitals, and body mass index. It found that the offspring of parents with higher IQ were less sedentary and less likely to have injuries requiring hospitalization. These findings indicate that parental IQ is related to their offspring's health and health behaviours, although because parental IQ is confounded with socio-economic status, part of the relationship may reflect the more hazardous and constrained living conditions associated with low socio-economic status.

Reverse causality can be an issue of concern in studies where somatic diseases such as hypertension may cause deterioration of intelligence rather than (low) intelligence influencing (unfavourable) health outcomes. Measuring childhood IQ and then following up people as adults can minimize this concern. A systematic review examined nine studies, conducted in Swedish, Australian, American, Scottish, Danish, and British samples, in which IQ was measured before the age of 24 and prior to the onset of disease. In all cases, IQ and mortality were inversely correlated, such that higher IQ was related to a reduced likelihood of early death (Batty, Deary, & Gottfredson, 2007). A systematic review and meta-analysis based on an initial sample size of 1.1 million participants was conducted to examine the relationship between intelligence in childhood or youth and mortality during mid- to late adulthood. The results showed that for both men and women, with one standard deviation increase in intelligence, there was a 24% reduction in mortality risk (Calvin et al., 2011). This relationship appeared to be independent of childhood socio-economic conditions as indexed by parents' occupation or income.

Links between IQ and health may also encompass mental health. In the US National Longitudinal Survey of Youth 1979 (NLSY79), 12,686 participants were given a test of intelligence at age 14–21 and tests of depression and general mental and physical health at age 40. The intelligence measure was found to be related to a range of health outcomes, both mental and physical (Der et al., 2009). Once again, the measurement of intelligence well before the health outcomes strongly suggests that the relationship between them is not due to reverse causality (i.e., poor health giving rise to reduced IQs). Instead, low intelligence appears to confer a heightened risk of ill health.

ILLUSTRATIVE STUDY

Why lower IQ predicts earlier death

Scottish psychologists Ian Deary and Geoff Der (2005) set out to study explanations for the surprising finding that people with lower IQs tend to die younger, a finding that has been replicated several times. For example, an earlier study found that if two people had IQs that differed by one standard deviation, the person with the lower IQ was only 79% as likely as the person with the higher IQ to live to age 76. Remarkably, in that study IQ was measured at age 11, indicating that childhood cognitive ability predicts adult longevity.

Deary and Der examined whether the greater mortality risk of people with lower IQs might reflect their less efficient information processing. They studied a representative sample of 898 Scottish adults in 1988, when they were aged about 54–58. These participants completed measures of verbal and numerical ability and a set of reaction time tasks, and also indicated their education, occupation, and some lifestyle data. The researchers were notified by the National Health Service of any deaths among the participants until the end of 2002. By this time 20.6% had died. Statistical analysis showed that cognitive factors (lower IQ, slower and more variable reaction times) predicted who had died even after controlling for other predictors associated with mortality risk (i.e., being male, smoking, lower socio-economic status). Moreover, reaction times were more strongly associated with death than was IQ, and appeared to explain the association between lower IQ and death. The authors speculate that reaction times may reflect an important aspect of the person's physical integrity, although the precise mechanism linking reaction times to mortality remains unclear.

Other correlates of intelligence

In this final section of this chapter, we change tack somewhat while remaining on the same course of investigating how intelligence is related to different spheres of life. Thus far our emphasis has been on the real-world correlates of intelligence that intelligence may play a role in influencing, such as academic attainment and work performance. Now we will briefly discuss the real-world factors that may play a role in influencing intelligence. Perhaps before launching into this discussion, it is worth reiterating that there is a difference between intelligence as a theoretical concept and IQ scores as a measure of the behaviour manifestation of that concept. Therefore, although we use IQ and intelligence somewhat interchangeably throughout this chapter, it is worthwhile acknowledging that there are differences between these two ideas. An ideal IQ test should be measuring intelligence purely and nothing else: that is, it should be a valid measure. It is wise to have a degree of scepticism when we hear reports about new drugs to improve intelligence, for example. The question we should ask is whether it is really intelligence that is being raised, or whether it is just IQ scores? In the following section, we will discuss the possibility of schooling, cognitive exercises, physical activities, food supplements, drugs, and environmentally hazardous metals as factors that may be associated with intelligence.

In Chapter 12, we discussed how schooling has an effect on IQ, such that absence from school for a period of time can lead to a reduction in IQ scores. Not only is the length of schooling correlated with intellectual performance (Cliffordson & Gustafsson, 2008), but schooling is also found to be strongly related to the development of intelligence (Stelzl, Merz, Ehlers, & Remer, 1995).

Formal schooling in childhood, adolescence, and young adulthood may promote intelligence, but what about the use of mental exercises or cognitive training that have become increasingly popular and heavily marketed? Do these interventions improve intelligence? One study examined this possibility using eye movement data. It showed that although a cognitive training programme led to improved scores on a test of fluid intelligence, the improvement could be accounted for by the learning of a test-taking strategy and an improved ability to use a variety of cognitive strategies flexibly for the right task. If the latter is considered a facet of fluid intelligence, then this could be evidence that intelligence can be improved. However, if that ability is seen instead as a specific, tacitly learned skill, then the increase in fluid intelligence test scores may not represent a true increase in the underlying intelligence (Hayes, Petrov, & Sederberg, 2015). Another factor that appears to be related to intelligence is physical activity. Level of aerobic physical exercise has been shown to be positively correlated with cognitive ability. In a systematic review paper, cognition, as defined as the ability to learn, reason, analyze and making judgements, was shown to be correlated with aerobic physical activity, although no inference could be made about whether exercise promotes intelligence, intelligence promotes activity, or both factors are underpinned by a hidden third variable such as physical health (Lees & Hopkins, 2013). In the absence of any evidence for the causal basis of the association between aerobic exercise and intelligence, it would be premature to engage in more exercise in the hope of turbo-charging one's intellectual powers, although there may be other good reasons for doing so.

Just as the benefits of brain training and physical exercise for mental acuity are often extolled, claims are sometimes made about the cognition-boosting effects of pharmaceutical products and nutritional supplements. Common supplements such as an Omega-3 essential fatty acid known as docosahexaenoic acid (DHA) have sometimes been thought to prevent cognitive decline. However, a study of participants aged between 44 and 77 years following 90 days of ingestion of this supplement did not show any improvement in cognitive functioning (Stough et al., 2012). Other supplements, such as Bacopa Monnieri, Gingko Biloba, and American ginseng, have also been researched in relation to specific cognitive functions such as working memory (Scholey, Pase, Pipingas, Stough, & Camfield, 2015). Although working memory is correlated with intelligence, the two capacities are not identical (Ackerman, Beier, & O'Boyle, 2005). Therefore, the effect of these supplements on intelligence is currently unclear. The same can be said for some stimulant drugs, such MDMA and d-methamphetamine. These have been found to produce deterioration in performance on some cognitive tasks and improvement in others, but these effects tend to be short-lived and affect working memory and reaction time rather than intelligence proper. At present there is no pharmaceutical short-cut to high intelligence.

In addition to the abovementioned factors that have been proposed to enhance intelligence, there are others that have been found to be related to IQ deterioration. One such factor is exposure to lead. The Port Pirie Cohort Study of 516 7-year-old children, conducted in South Australia, found that environmental exposure to lead was negatively correlated with intelligence. This effect was observed in the same cohort of children earlier, when they were age 2, and then again at age 4 (Baghurst et al., 1992). In a subsequent meta-analysis, the author asserted that, based on the strength of the relationship, the known action of lead in the brain, and cognitive function interference observed in studies of primates, it is reasonable to conclude that lead adversely affects IQ scores (Schwartz, 1994). Other researchers have reported that levels of hair arsenic and manganese in 11–13-year-old children living near a hazardous waste site in Oklahoma in the USA was negatively correlated with IQ (Wright, Amarasiriwardena, Woolf, Jim, & Bellinger, 2006). Similar findings conducted in the Great Lakes region of the USA have been reported in relation to exposure to polychlorinated biphenyls, which are found in some types of electrical equipment (Stewart et al., 2008), and also in relation to prenatal exposure to mercury (Axelrad, Bellinger, Ryan, & Woodruff, 2007). In short, a variety of environmental toxins have established damaging effects on the cognitive abilities of young people. Whether these adverse effects can be remedied and whether they naturally decline over time remains to be determined.

Conclusions

In this chapter we have explored several domains in which intelligence predicts major life outcomes (including death, the most major of all). Some of the predictive relationships were powerful. It would be simplistic to conclude that intelligence *causes* all of these outcomes. To be highly confident that intelligence causes better academic performance, job performance, or health, we would need to conduct an experiment in which people were randomly assigned to different groups and the levels of intelligence in these groups were experimentally manipulated. Needless to say, this experiment is impossible, and if it was possible, it would probably be unethical. However, we can have some confidence that intelligence is part of the complex causal stories that give rise to these outcomes. IQ measurements taken in childhood routinely predict outcomes assessed in adulthood, ruling out the possibility that the intelligence–outcome relationship operates in the reverse direction. Clarifying the role that intelligence plays in life outcomes, and determining the genetic and environmental mechanisms and pathways through which it does so, are high priorities for individual difference researchers. However, we already know a great deal. We know that intelligence, rather than merely being a statistical abstraction that is marginally relevant to a few school-related cognitive tasks, is in fact a real factor with diverse and often powerful links to outcomes in many domains of life. High intelligence is associated with academic accomplishment, with success at work, with financial status, and with better physical and perhaps even mental health. Intelligence is not the only factor that contributes to these outcomes, of course, and other individual difference variables also play significant roles. But for all the controversies surrounding its measurement and conceptualization, intelligence is a factor whose real-world implications cannot be ignored.

Chapter summary

- Intelligence is an important factor in people's capacity to function successfully in everyday life, although its importance is to some degree dependent on cultural norms and social values.
- One of the many contributions of intelligence to everyday life is through IQ tests. These tests have a range of important functions in personnel selection, clinical assessment, and education psychology settings.
- Cross-sectional research designs are limited when examining relationships between intelligence and life outcome measures, as they make it impossible to draw any causal conclusions about whether intelligence may contribute to these outcomes. The better alternative is to use longitudinal studies.
- Reverse causality is an important issue to consider when interpreting studies examining relationships between intelligence and life outcomes, as it is sometimes plausible that the 'outcomes' may influence intelligence.
- Intelligence is one of the key correlates of academic performance, and an average validity coefficient of .54 has been reported.

(Continued)

(Continued)

- The positive relationship between academic achievement and intelligence has been demonstrated from primary school through to postgraduate levels of study.
- Although other variables, such as Conscientiousness and emotional intelligence, contribute towards academic achievement, intelligence remains very important.
- Intelligence predicts job performance, the level of job status attained, and job training performance.
- The relationship between intelligence and job performance may be due to both requiring the ability to capture and deal with the complexity of information in an adaptive manner.
- Intelligence is predictive of personal income, although this effect is not as strong as the relationships between intelligence and academic or job performance.
- IQ is inversely correlated with risk of mortality.
- The disease prevention and disease management hypotheses help to explain why intelligence predicts health.
- It is likely that intelligence predicts obesity rather than obesity predicting intelligence.
- Intelligence is correlated and in some cases affected by schooling, aerobic physical exercise, food supplements, illicit drugs, and environmental toxins.

Further reading

Ceci, S. J. (1991). How much does schooling influence general intelligence and its cognitive components? A reassessment of the evidence. *Developmental Psychology*, *27*(5), 703–22.
An article focusing on the relationship between schooling and intelligence.

Gottfredson, L. S., & Deary, I. J. (2004). Intelligence predicts health and longevity, but why? *Current Directions in Psychological Science*, *13*(1), 1–4.
Provides a brief but good overview of the IQ–health relationship. It includes discussion about why intelligence predicts health in later adulthood.

Hayes, T. R., Petrov, A. A., & Sederberg, P. B. (2015). Do we really become smarter when our fluid-intelligence test scores improve? *Intelligence*, *48*, 1–14.
This article challenges the view that cognitive training will lead to enhanced cognitive ability by showing that scores on a fluid intelligence test can be improved by just changing the test-taking strategy.

Kuncel, N. R., Ones, D. S., & Sackett, P. R. (2010). Individual differences as predictors of work, educational and broad life outcomes. *Personality and Individual Differences*, *49*(4), 331–6.

A general review of life outcomes as related to intelligence (and also personality).

Ones, D. S., Viswesvaran, C., & Dilchert, S. (2005). Cognitive ability in selection decisions. In O. Wilhelm & R. W. Engle (Eds.), *Handbook of understanding and measuring intelligence* (pp. 431–68). Thousand Oaks, CA: Sage.

A review of intelligence as applied to the world of work.

Schmidt, F. L., & Hunter, J. (2004). General mental ability in the world of work: Occupational attainment and job performance. *Journal of Personality and Social Psychology*, *86*(1), 162–73.

An article about work and intelligence. It also includes a table listing jobs and the associated cognitive ability scores.

Emotional Intelligence

Learning objectives

- To develop an understanding of the main categories of theoretical models for emotional intelligence.
- To understand how emotional intelligence is measured.
- To understand the contribution of emotional intelligence to everyday life.
- To be aware of attempts to train or enhance emotional intelligence.

In the previous chapters, you have been introduced to the classical view of intelligence, which focuses on cognitive abilities. Although this view, embodied in standard intelligence tests, remains very important in psychology, alternative ways of understanding intelligence and human performance have emerged. You may recall from Chapter 12, for example, that Howard Gardner proposed the existence of multiple intelligences. Non-cognitive aspects of intelligence are also receiving increased attention, and it is widely thought that these aspects make a substantial contribution to life successes beyond the contribution of cognitive ability. One concept that has been especially visible in discussions of broader meanings of intelligence is the idea of '**emotional intelligence**' (Zeidner, Roberts, & Matthews, 2008). One reason why emotional intelligence has received so much interest from the public is the early claim that it is as important as IQ in predicting life outcomes. This claim has been refuted, but emotional intelligence is unquestionably relevant for many real-world outcomes and research on it is flourishing.

This chapter begins by introducing the development of the emotional intelligence (EI) concept. It then introduces the many theories of EI that have been proposed. Next, the application of ideas of emotional intelligence in various contexts will be explored, leading finally to a discussion of how individuals may be helped to develop their EI.

The concept of emotional intelligence

Although the popularity of EI as a concept has often been attributed to the publication of a book on the subject by Daniel Goleman in 1995, the idea of a non-cognitive aspect of intelligence had been raised much earlier. For example, 'social intelligence', the ability to understand and handle interpersonal situations, was proposed by Thorndike in the 1920s as one of three broad dimensions of intelligence (Newsome, Day, & Catano, 2000). Later, Gardner proposed interpersonal and intrapersonal intelligences as part of his multiple intelligences theory. The former relates to the understanding of other individuals and the latter to the understanding of the self.

In 1997, Mayer and Salovey proposed that EI is a broad concept that encompasses social intelligence but that is distinct from the more traditional cognitive understanding of intelligence (Newsome et al., 2000). EI specifically focuses on the ability to reason about emotions and to use emotions and knowledge about emotions in order to help with thinking through problems (Mayer, Roberts, & Barsade, 2008). EI can therefore be considered as a specific intelligence that focuses on the processing of a specific type of materials, in this case, emotions.

Approaches to studying emotional intelligence

EI has been conceptualized in many ways and the different approaches to studying it can be classified in various ways. According to Mayer, Roberts, and Barsade (2008), however, there are three main theoretical approaches. The first is the 'abilities-focused approach', where the main focus is on defining a specific skill or set of skills that is fundamental to emotional intelligence. Some of the skills include the competent use of emotional information in thinking, being accurate in labelling emotions, appraising emotions correctly, and managing one's own emotions. The second is the 'integrative model approach', which proposes that specific emotional-related abilities should be combined into a general emotional intelligence, akin to psychometric g in cognitive intelligence. The third theoretical approach to EI combines emotion-related abilities with other non-emotional abilities, and is thus called the 'mixed model approach'. It may include qualities such as stress-tolerance, adaptability, social competence, and creative thinking (Mayer et al., 2008).

A simpler way of distinguishing between different theories of EI contrasts approaches that view EI as an *ability* and those that see it as a *trait* (Petrides & Furnham, 2001). The ability view, known also as 'information-processing EI' (Petrides & Furnham, 2001), considers emotional intelligence as a cognitive ability that involves the processing of emotional information. The trait view, on the other hand, conceptualizes EI as a dispositional tendency to behave in particular ways. The two views can be referred to as Ability Emotional Intelligence (Ability EI) and Trait Emotional Intelligence (Trait EI) (Petrides, 2011). Ability EI is frequently measured using ability-type tests and may include the presentation of pictures of facial expressions from which a correct emotion should be identified. That is, just as in tests of cognitive intelligence,

Ability EI tests have objectively correct answers, and high ability is revealed by getting many correct answers. Trait EI, on the other hand, is more commonly measured using self-report questionnaires, just like personality trait measurement. Like personality tests, tests of Trait EI have no objectively correct answers, only answers that might be more socially desirable or more associated with positive outcomes. There is as yet no consensus among researchers in favour of the Ability or the Trait view of EI, although researchers have raised concerns about using the Trait EI label when the concept is closer to a type of ability and not a type of personality trait (Zeidner, Roberts, & Matthews, 2008).

One of the most influential examples of the Ability EI approach is the Mayer–Salovey four-branch model (Mayer & Salovey, 1997). The four branches involve abilities in perceiving emotion, using emotion to facilitate thought, understanding emotion, and managing emotions. In Perceiving Emotion, the ability to accurately identify the emotion in facial expressions is crucial. In Facilitating Emotion, the focus is on the ability to use emotional states to enhance effective thinking, such as employing positive mood to enable creativity. The third branch, Understanding Emotion, relates to reasoning about and understanding emotions, such as identifying the two constituent emotional states that make up a more complex emotion. Lastly, the Managing Emotion branch relates to how the person manages or regulates their own and others' emotions (Mayer, Salovey, & Caruso, 2004). This Ability EI has been reported to be related to cognitive ability, but not to major personality trait factors (O'Connor & Little, 2003).

According to researchers in the Trait EI camp, in contrast, EI is a disposition which would be expected to have only a small to moderate correlation with cognitive ability. Trait EI has instead been found to be related to personality traits, in particular Extraversion and Neuroticism, in a positive and negative direction respectively (Saklofske, Austin, & Minski, 2003). However, if Trait EI is simply another personality trait, then the concept of 'emotional intelligence' would appear to be redundant. One reassuring piece of evidence on this point comes from a study that used Trait EI measures and personality trait measures to life satisfaction and depression-proneness. Trait EI helped to predict levels of these variables over and above the personality traits, indicating that it provided additional information beyond personality traits, thus showing what is called 'incremental validity' (Saklofske et al., 2003). Incremental validity, which is discussed at greater length in the 'Exploring a concept' box below, refers to the idea that a new psychological construct or test should make a unique contribution to predicting phenomena that goes beyond existing constructs and measures. If the construct or test fails to do so, then it adds nothing unique and hence lacks this kind of validity. For Trait EI to prove its worth as a construct, it must add to our ability to predict human behaviour over and above existing individual differences variables such as cognitive intelligence and personality. Early evidence suggests that it does.

Ability EI and its measures should also demonstrate incremental validity. This was investigated by Australian researchers in 2000 using an earlier version of an ability test devised by Mayer, Salovey, and Caruso (Ciarrochi, Chan, & Caputi, 2000). Students' IQ, personality traits, and other life outcome indicators were also measured. In this study, Ability EI was not found to be related to IQ, but it was related to personality traits such as empathy and also to life satisfaction. Ability EI was found to be related to participants' ability to control their own mood, but was not related to their ability to prevent their mood from affecting their judgements. However, these two mood-related processes were found to be related to IQ. Therefore, all together, the results suggested that EI is different from IQ and also appears to provide useful additional information not otherwise available if only IQ and personality traits are measured.

You may wonder if Ability EI and Trait EI are moderately correlated. Indeed, they are. However, although they are related to one another, they correlate somewhat differently with other psychological variables (O'Connor & Little, 2003). This evidence confirms that although the two kinds of EI have some similarities, they are also importantly different, consistent with the idea of Ability EI and Trait EI differentiation, as proposed by Petrides and Furnham (2001).

Arriving at a commonly agreed understanding of EI has been difficult. In this sense, it is not entirely different from the field of cognitive intelligence, where pinning the construct down in a universally agreed manner has also proven to be a challenge. However, EI appears to be a particularly elusive concept, with a bewildering variety of definitions and measurement tools in play. It can be seen as a kind of temperament, a specific skill in emotional self-regulation, an information-processing capacity, and a set of social skills. However, regardless of the disagreement over definitions, the key pragmatic question is whether EI is useful for predicting real-world behaviour and outcomes.

Exploring a concept: Incremental validity of EI

To show incremental validity, a concept such as EI must add something extra and unique to what we already know about a phenomenon of interest. If EI as a concept had no incremental validity, relative to more established concepts, such as personality traits and intelligence, then it would serve no purpose. Similarly, a measure of EI would serve no purpose if it failed to predict anything over and above existing measures of personality and intelligence. For EI to be something more than 'old wine in new bottles', it needs to show incremental validity.

Demonstrating incremental validity for Trait EI is especially challenging because it is closely related to several personality traits, such as (high) empathy and (low) impulsivity. In fact, Trait EI has been found to correlate with all of the Big Five personality factors: positively with Agreeableness, Conscientiousness, Extraversion and Openness to Experience, and negatively with Neuroticism (Saklofske, Austin, & Minski, 2003). Any time Trait EI is found to correlate with another variable, such as job performance, it is possible that this correlation only occurs because Trait EI incorporates other Big Five traits. Those other traits may be responsible for the correlation between Trait EI and job performance. To show incremental validity, Trait EI would need to predict job performance over and above the other traits (and ideally also above intelligence), providing a unique contribution to predicting that outcome. This can be shown by measuring Trait EI, job performance, and the other Big Five traits, and examining the EI–performance correlation after statistically controlling the other traits using a statistical technique called multiple regression analysis. If Trait EI still correlates with job performance after the other traits are controlled in this way, then it has shown at least some incremental validity.

To take one example, Australian researchers administered measures of EI, personality traits, cognitive abilities, and life skills such as problem solving to a sample of university students. They found a significant correlation between EI and life skills. When they then statistically controlled for personality and cognitive abilities, an association between EI and life skills remained, but it was fairly weak, explaining only 6% of the variability in life skills in the sample (Bastian, Burns, & Nettelbeck, 2005). Thus EI had some incremental validity beyond other variables such as personality traits and cognitive abilities, but the increment was modest. Similar findings have been found in many studies: measures of EI often have incremental validity in predicting significant real-world outcomes, but their capacity to predict these outcomes is substantially reduced when measures of other traits and abilities are taken into account.

Utility of emotional intelligence

One reason for the popularity of EI in the early days of the concept was what we now know to be an exaggerated claim, namely that EI is the best psychological predictor of having a successful life and does so better than general intelligence. Subsequent investigations have shown that although EI is not the best predictor of a successful life, it does seem to be related to certain life outcomes. Trait EI, for example, is predictive of a wide range of phenomena, including prosocial and antisocial behaviours (as rated by peers and teachers), leadership, happiness, and optimism (Petrides, 2011). EI appears to be relevant in many different life domains. For example, among male students, low Ability EI is associated with illegal drug and alcohol use, deviant behaviour, such as being involved in physical fights, gambling, and poor relationship with peers. These associations remain true even after statistically controlling for other factors, such as personality and academic achievement (Brackett, Mayer, & Warner, 2004). We shall offer a few snapshots of some of the domains in which levels of EI appear to make a difference.

Academic achievement and behaviour

Evidence for a relationship between EI and academic achievement has been relatively mixed. Some studies have shown them to be positively correlated while others reported no significant relationship. Whether EI makes an incremental contribution to academic achievement beyond cognitive ability and personality also yields mixed results (Libbrecht, Lievens, Carette, & Côté, 2014). Puzzled by these inconsistent results, a study was carried out utilizing an Ability EI measure and a Mixed EI model measure (Bar-On's EQ-i; Bar-On, 1997). The researcher found that EI was not a good predictor of academic success in general: it was a weaker predictor than cognitive abilities, and just as weak as Big Five personality traits (Barchard, 2003). Another study of Trait EI found that its contribution to academic performance was small and less than that of IQ, but that the contribution was to some degree separate from IQ and personality traits (Reid, 2008), demonstrating some incremental validity for Trait EI.

However, there is more than one aspect to academic success. In some subject areas, both intellectual, knowledge-based performance and interpersonal performance contribute to success. In medical education, for example, interpersonal skills are very important when dealing with patients and developing 'bed-side manner'. Medical students' Ability EI correlates positively with their performance on doctor–patient communication courses, and in this context EI shows incremental validity beyond Conscientiousness and cognitive ability. In contrast, when predicting *intellectual* academic performance in the same group of medical students, EI does not have incremental validity beyond those same variables. Therefore, it appears that Ability EI may be important in academic domains where emotion-related content is involved (Libbrecht et al., 2014).

If we move beyond academic achievement in a narrow sense and move towards other behaviours in an academic setting, the role of EI again appears to get larger. Studies have examined whether EI is associated with school students' negative behaviour, such as being frequently absent from school, having poor relationships with fellow students, violating rules, and engaging in aggressive behaviours. In every case, low Trait EI appears to be related to these undesirable outcomes (Petrides, 2011). On the flip-side, having high Trait EI may help students with relatively low IQ manage the demands of the academic environment, perhaps by reducing their risk of engaging in self-defeating academic behaviour. Thus high EI may partially compensate for low IQ.

Success at work

In addition to its modest role in academic success and behaviour, EI appears to predict several aspects of performance in the workplace. In this domain it should surprise no one that being emotionally intelligent might enable teamwork, collaboration, and other interpersonal dimensions of successful performance in an organization. Sure enough, a meta-analytic study found that EI and job performance are positively correlated, and that EI is also related to lower levels of job stress, higher levels of job satisfaction, and stronger job commitment (Van Rooy & Viswesvaran, 2004). Other researchers have reported that EI protects workers against burnout.

Although these findings are intuitively credible, we also need to take them with a grain of salt. As we saw earlier in this chapter, measures of EI tend to correlate to some extent with some other individual difference variables, such as Conscientiousness and IQ. Thus any correlation between EI and job performance might be explained by EI's overlap with these known predictors of success at work. Again, the key question is whether measures of EI have incremental validity relative to these predictors. One meta-analysis that examined this question indicates that they do to a modest extent. The researchers found that some measures of EI were associated with workplace success largely, but not entirely, because they overlapped with other individual difference variables that predict this success. EI had some incremental validity over these other variables, but not much (Joseph, Jin, Newman, & O'Boyle, 2015).

Health

EI appears to have a strong association with mental health and some association with reporting relatively few physical health complaints. For example, one study found that people high in EI have lower rates of personality disorder and self-harming behaviour than those low in EI (Mikolajczak, Petrides, & Hurry, 2009). However, these links between EI and health seem to depend very much on how EI is conceptualized. Trait EI has clear associations with mental and physical health, but Ability EI does not (Martins, Romalho, & Morin, 2010). One possible explanation of this discrepancy is that Trait EI overlaps with (low) Neuroticism, a personality trait that has strong and well-established correlations with reports of psychological and physical symptoms.

Interpersonal relationships and behaviours

EI seems to have special relevance to close relationships, and it may go without saying that emotionally intelligent partners should have more satisfying and lasting relationships than their less emotionally intelligent peers. A meta-analysis on this topic examined six studies consisting of more than 600 individuals, and showed that Trait EI was significantly correlated with their satisfaction with their romantic relationships ($r = .32$). Having a better understanding of a romantic partner's emotional states, as well as insight into and a capacity to manage one's own emotions, is likely to increase closeness and decrease conflict. However, because the meta-analysis is only summarizing correlations we cannot be sure that EI is causally responsible for better relationships (Malouff, Schutte, & Thorsteinsson, 2014). It is also possible that having better relationships leads people to rate themselves as emotionally intelligent.

Shifting focus from love to hate, might EI contribute to lower levels of aggressive behaviour? Some research indicates that it does to some degree. For example, one study found that people's levels of emotion knowledge predicted their levels of indirect or more subtle aggressive behaviour, even after controlling for differences in their age, gender, and personality traits (Peláez-Fernández, Extremera, & Fernández-Berrocal, 2014). A recent systematic review of the relationship between EI and aggression concluded that higher EI scores – both for Trait EI and Ability EI – are associated with lower levels of aggressive behaviours. This negative association is observed across different ages and across several cultures from the USA to

Malaysia, and from Spain to China. One possible interpretation of this negative association is that aggression often results from individuals misperceiving other people's behaviour as hostile, an error that is less likely to be committed by more emotionally intelligent individuals (García-Sancho, Salguero, & Fernández-Berrocal, 2014).

Exploring a concept: Is emotional intelligence an intelligence?

The concept of EI represents a rather radical break from the traditional understanding of intelligence as cognitive ability. Some theorists have questioned whether EI is, in fact, a kind of intelligence, or whether its name is a misnomer. How would we answer this question?

Advocates of the ability approach to EI have made several arguments to support the view that EI meets the criteria for being an intelligence. First, to be an intelligence EI would need to be an ability to solve particular kinds of emotion-related problems that have objectively correct answers. Proponents of the ability approach to EI note that emotionally intelligent behaviour, such as correct answers on EI tests, can be ascertained by group consensus and expert judgement. This provides converging evidence that EI is ability-like and can be called an intelligence (Mayer, Caruso, & Salovey, 1999). Second, proponents of the ability view argue that to be an intelligence, EI should correlate with related abilities but not with other cognitive abilities, a claim that is supported by research. Finally, the proponents argue that to be an intelligence, EI should, like cognitive abilities, demonstrate developmental improvements associated with age and experience. Once again, there is ample evidence of such changes.

The status of EI as an intelligence remains somewhat controversial, however, especially among advocates of the Trait EI view (Roberts, Zeidner, & Matthews, 2001). They argue that unlike general cognitive intelligence, the scoring of 'correct' answers on Ability EI tests is sometimes problematic, and that the capacity of EI to predict real-world behaviour has not been demonstrated as thoroughly as has been done for cognitive abilities. The debate over EI's status as an intelligence is unlikely to be resolved any time soon, but the interested reader can learn more about it in articles by Locke (2005) and Brody (2004).

Measuring emotional intelligence

Earlier sections of this chapter introduced several distinct models of emotional intelligence. For these models to be practically useful they need to serve as a basis for measurement. A large number of measures of EI have been developed in recent years, and they can generally be divided into tests of Ability EI and Trait EI. Measures of these two different conceptualizations of EI are substantially different in nature. In essence, Ability EI tests aim to assess how well people perform on tasks that have objectively correct answers. People who tend to make the correct responses are judged to be more emotionally intelligent, just as people who tend to make correct responses on an IQ test are assessed as highly intelligent. Trait EI tests, in contrast, ask people to rate themselves on the extent to which they behave in emotionally intelligent ways. If you recall the discussion of the problems of self-report in Chapter 9, you should be able to anticipate some of the problems facing these Trait EI measures.

Measuring Ability EI

Ability EI tests are somewhat challenging to construct. The test developer cannot simply write a few items on which people can rate themselves. Instead she must come up with some tasks where a particular response objectively demonstrates emotionally intelligent behaviour. Such tasks tend to take longer to administer than self-report questionnaires, which simply ask people to agree or disagree with a series of short statements. It can also be difficult to establish what makes a particular response objectively correct. 'Correct' answers are often decided either on the basis of the consensus judgement of a large sample of people, so that the correct answer is the one that most people agree on, or else on the judgement of experts (Śmieja, Orzechowski, & Stolarski, 2014). Neither of these ways of establishing correctness is infallible: different groups may differ in the response they consider to be best (Zeidner, Kloda, & Matthews, 2013) and it is not always clear who relevant experts on EI should be.

One of the most prominent tests of Ability EI is the Mayer–Salovey–Caruso Emotional Intelligence Test (MSCEIT). The latest version of the MSCEIT contains 141 items divided into eight tasks that measure facets of the four branches of EI in Mayer and Salovey's Ability EI model. The tasks assess emotion perception (in faces and in landscapes), using emotions (in synaesthesia and in facilitating thought), understanding emotions (in relation to emotion blends and changes in emotions over time), and managing emotions (in oneself and in relationships). Responses to the 141 items are scored according to how they compare with consensus and expert responses. For example, in the consensus scoring method, the participant's score is the proportion of the norm group who chose the same response (Barchard, 2003). Scores can be derived for each of the four branches of EI as well an overall EI score. Despite being very popular, some concerns have been raised about the MSCEIT's claim to measure emotional intelligence and also its scoring system (Petrides, 2011).

Two additional Ability EI tests – the Situational Test of Emotional Understanding (STEU) and the Situational Test of Emotional Management (STEM) – were developed by Australian researchers. To avoid the criticisms of the consensus scoring method that were levelled at the MSCEIT, correct answers were selected not on public consensus but on a theory of emotion (MacCann & Roberts, 2008). The STEU contains 42 items, some of which are framed in workplace or personal contexts, which ask for judgements of probable emotional experiences in different situations. The STEM consists of 44 items that ask for judgements about the most effective action in particular challenging situations. The two tests were reported to predict academic achievement incrementally over measures of intelligence and personality (MacCann & Roberts, 2008). Here are two example items from the respective tests:

> An unwanted situation becomes less likely or stops altogether. The person involved is most like to feel:

> a) Regret
> b) Hope
> c) Joy
> d) Sadness
> e) Relief

A junior employee making routine adjustments to some of Teo's equipment accuses Teo of causing the equipment malfunction. What action would be the most effective for Teo?

> a) Reprimand the employee for making such accusations.
> b) Ignore the accusation, it is not important.
> c) Explain that malfunctions were not his fault.
> d) Learn more about using the equipment so that it doesn't break.

Measuring Trait EI

Tests of Trait EI rely on self-report. As we have seen in our discussion of personality inventories in Chapter 9, self-report measures are relatively quick and easy to administer. However, the validity of these measures hinges on whether people can be relied upon to respond honestly and accurately about their EI. People may be motivated to over-estimate their EI and they may lack insight into their EI levels. Some research indicates that Trait EI measures can be valid to some degree, one study showing that individuals with high self-reported EI scores performed better than individuals with low EI scores on an emotional expression identification task (Petrides & Furnham, 2003).

However, not all of the evidence has been quite so encouraging. Recently, for example, the Dunning-Kruger effect has been observed in relation to EI measurement. This effect refers to the situation where poor performers on a task over-estimate their performance because they fail to recognize how poor it has been. In essence, people sometimes lack insight into their own lack of ability. Research studies have indeed shown that individuals with low EI scores over-estimate their own EI and are also likely to dismiss feedback about their own poor EI (Sheldon, Dunning, & Ames, 2014). This phenomenon has serious implications for Trait EI measures as it implies that people may be poorly calibrated judges of their EI and may inflate their self-assessments.

Several self-report measures of Trait EI have been developed, each based on a different understanding of the components of EI. For example, the Trait Emotional Intelligence

Questionnaire (TEIQue; Petrides & Furnham, 2003) contains 144 items assessing 15 sub-scales that include Adaptability (e.g., 'I usually find it difficult to make adjustments in my lifestyle' [reverse scored]), Emotional expression (e.g., 'Others tell me that I rarely speak about how I feel' [reverse scored]), Emotion regulation (e.g., 'When someone offends me, I'm usually able to remain calm'), Empathy (e.g., 'I find it difficult to understand why certain people get upset with certain things' [reverse scored]), Self-esteem (e.g., 'I believe I'm full of personal strengths'), and Stress management (e.g., 'I'm usually able to deal with problems that others find upsetting'). Another measure, Schutte's Emotional Intelligence Scale (Schutte et al., 1998), is briefer and assesses a narrower set of four EI facets: optimism/mood regulation, emotion appraisal, social skills, and use of emotion. A popular third test, the Bar-On Emotional Quotient Inventory (EQ-i; Bar-On, 1997) contains five scales assessing Intrapersonal, Interpersonal, Adaptability, Stress Management, and General Mood.

It is clear from a brief review of these three tests that they rest on somewhat different models of Trait EI and should not be assumed to measure precisely the same underlying characteristics. Some of the measures have very broad coverage, incorporating other well-established personality traits, such as self-esteem, optimism, coping style, and so on. How well the existing Trait EI scales converge with one another, how well they have discriminant validity with tests of other personality traits (see Chapter 9), and how much they are adversely affected by the kinds of response bias that plague some self-report measures remains to be seen.

Group differences in emotional intelligence

Just as there has been some research on group differences in general cognitive intelligence, there has been some rather less contentious research on group differences in EI using some of the tests described in the preceding section. Using Schutte's Trait EI Emotional Intelligence Scale, Van Rooy and colleagues (2005) explored sex, age group, and ethnic group differences in a sample of American university students. They found that ethnic minority groups such as African Americans, and especially Hispanics, had higher EI scores than Whites. The authors speculated that Hispanic Americans inhabit a culture that is more collectivistic than White Americans, and this cultural background may offer advantages in appreciating and taking into account other people's emotional states. The authors also found age and gender differences in EI, with female students scoring higher than male students and older students scoring higher than younger ones (Van Rooy, Alonso, & Viswesvaran, 2005). The second effect is consistent with the view that EI is associated with crystallized intelligence and is strengthened by the accumulation of life experience.

Might particular kinds of life experience be especially likely to promote EI? A study by Crowne (2013) investigated whether intercultural experiences such as travel might have this sort of effect. Participants in the study were asked to indicate the overseas countries they have visited from a list of 195 countries, and also to indicate the reasons they visited these countries. The more reasons they provided, and the more countries they have visited, the more cultural exposure they were deemed to have had. Cultural exposure may have many positive

319

ramifications, but regrettably increased EI does not appear to be one of them. The measure of exposure was uncorrelated with EI but was linked to another construct that the researcher termed 'cultural intelligence' (Crowne, 2013).

Development and training in emotional intelligence

If EI predicts success in some domains of life – even if its capacity to do so may have been exaggerated (Barchard, 2003) – then the idea that it might be possible to enhance EI is very appealing. Several attempts have been made to develop training programmes for leaders, managers, and teachers in a variety of corporations, organizations, and educational settings. The efficacy of these programmes has been investigated on a few occasions. For example, in Belgium, a four-week training programme was delivered to a group of university students (Nelis, Quoidbach, Mikolajczak, & Hansenne, 2009). This group showed significantly higher EI scores than the control group at the end of the training programme. In particular, emotional identification and emotion management showed marked improvements but not emotion understanding. These improvements persisted six months after the intervention, showing that the effects of the training programme were not short-lived.

Less intensive training programmes may also have effects. Individuals in a recent study underwent a one-day, face-to-face programme focused on increasing their ability to perceive others' emotions through activities such as facial expression identification and emotion expression training using role plays and mirrors. This short EI training programme was followed up by a month-long online programme. Study participants who completed the training were compared to a control group who completed time-management skills training. At the end of the training period the EI group showed superior ability to perceive others' emotions compared to their performance prior to the training, and also compared to the control group (Herpertz, Schütz, & Nezlek, 2016). This research indicates that EI is somewhat malleable and offers support for the further development of EI training interventions.

Cautionary note

To this point we have considered EI to be something that is unambiguously positive, a source of competent interpersonal relationships, successful emotional self-management, and enhanced performance at work. However, it is fair to ask whether having high EI is always desirable. Not necessarily, it would appear. For example, some research suggests that individuals with high Trait EI scores are more prone to mood deterioration after watching an emotionally distressing video clip or recalling a past poor decision than individuals with low Trait EI (Petrides & Furnham, 2003; Sevdalis, Petrides, & Harvey, 2007). Likewise, individuals with high Trait EI scores may have to engage in more extensive coping strategies after challenges or disappointments than their lower EI scores counterparts, such as having to manage their image in the eyes of others after they have failed at a task (Petrides, 2011). Thus Trait EI's adaptive value appears to be dependent on the context, and is not invariably positive.

Conclusions

Emotional intelligence (EI) is not an entirely new concept, but it has recently gained prominence through its promotion in the popular media. The concept of EI has been taken up enthusiastically in the corporate world, where it is viewed as crucial to leadership and to employee work-stress burnout, and in educational settings, where it is viewed as important for increasing academic success and reducing delinquency. Some scholars have given EI a more solid footing by refining the concept and developing EI tests. Other scholars remained sceptical about the concept, challenging the credentials of EI as a true intelligence and questioning the incremental validity of EI tests. Nonetheless, there is a wide range of life domains within which EI may be predictively relevant. These include academic achievement and behaviour, the training of medical professionals, the promotion of physical health, mental health, psychological well-being, job performance, business leadership, and social relationships. Although the conceptualization and measurement of EI remain somewhat contentious, further research is likely to clarify this fascinating idea's relevance to everyday life.

Chapter summary

- The concept of emotional intelligence (EI) has been proposed as a form of intelligence composed of emotion-related abilities.
- Varying conceptualizations of EI have been proposed, differing on the number and organization of its component abilities, or even if it is best conceptualized as an intelligence.
- The two main theoretical approaches to EI are Ability EI and Trait EI theories. Ability EI proponents consider EI as an ability to perceive, understand, use, and manage emotions, whereas Trait EI proponents consider EI to be linked to emotion-related dispositions, and see it as a personality trait.
- EI appears to be associated with a variety of outcomes in the domains of academic and work performance. However, its incremental validity relative to intelligence and personality varies according to the domain and the type of EI measure used. For example, EI does not predict academic achievement as well as IQ.
- Ability EI has been measured using tests such as the Mayer–Salovey–Caruso Emotional Intelligence test and by several Trait EI measures that differ widely in how broadly they conceptualize EI.
- Attempts to deliver training programmes to enhance EI have shown some success in rigorous experimental studies.

Further reading

Barchard, K. A. (2003). Does emotional intelligence assist in the prediction of academic success? *Educational and Psychological Measurement*, *63*(5), 840–58.
Discusses the limited incremental validity of EI as a predictor of academic performance.

Conte, J. M. (2005). A review and critique of emotional intelligence measures. *Journal of Organizational Behavior*, *26*(4), 433–40.
Reviews some of the earlier Ability EI tests.

Davies, M., Stankov, L., & Roberts, R. D. (1998). Emotional intelligence: In search of an elusive construct. *Journal of Personality and Social Psychology*, *75*(4), 989–1015.
An examination of the EI concept, both Ability and Trait EI, in relation to the concepts of IQ and personality.

Mayer, J. D., Roberts, R. D., & Barsade, S. G. (2008). Human abilities: Emotional intelligence. *Annual Review of Psychology*, *59*, 507–36.
A general review of the state of knowledge in the study of emotional intelligence.

Petrides, K. V. (2011). Ability and Trait emotional intelligence. In T. Chamorro-Premuzic, S. Von Stumm, & A. Furnham (Eds.), *The Wiley-Blackwell handbook of individual differences* (Vol. 3) (pp. 656–78). Chichester, UK: John Wiley & Sons.
Ability EI and Trait EI are discussed, together with a good overview of Trait EI research in various life outcome measures.

Saklofske, D. H., Austin, E. J., & Minski, P. S. (2003). Factor structure and validity of a trait emotional intelligence measure. *Personality and Individual Differences*, *34*, 707–21.
An article that includes a useful discussion of Trait EI.

Zeidner, M., Roberts, R. D., & Matthews, G. (2008). The science of emotional intelligence. *European Psychologist*, *13*(1), 64–78.
An easy-to-read article that outlines some of the challenges of research in this area.

Glossary

Affect   A general term to refer to emotions and moods.

Agreeableness   One of the Big Five personality factors, involving dispositions to be cooperative, interpersonally warm, and empathic.

Anal stage   The second stage of psychosexual development in psychoanalytic theory's genetic model, in which the focus of interest is the anus and the primary developmental issue is control.

Attachment style   The tendency to approach close or romantic relationships in a particular way, as indicated by trust, dependence, and desired closeness to relationship partners. Three styles are generally recognized: secure, avoidant, and anxious-ambivalent.

Attributional style   The tendency to explain events using a particular combination of causal dimensions, the standard dimensions being internal vs. external, stable vs. unstable, and global vs. specific. A pessimistic attributional style is one in which negative events are habitually explained in terms of internal, stable, and global causes. This concept is sometimes also referred to as 'explanatory style'.

Authoritarianism   A personality trait involving rigidity, punitiveness, conventionality, distrust of introspection, and submission to authority.

Behavioural Approach System (BAS)   In Gray's theory, a neuropsychological system that underpins impulsivity, is sensitive to the possibility of rewards, and motivates people to seek them.

Behavioural Inhibition System (BIS)   For Gray, the neuropsychological system that is the basis for anxiety, is sensitive to the possibility of punishment, and motivates people to avoid it.

Behaviourism   A school of theory and research that addressed the relationships between environmental stimuli and observable behaviour, and held that mental states were not appropriate subjects of psychological investigation.

Big Five   A popular model of the five primary dimensions of personality – Agreeableness, Conscientiousness, Extraversion, Neuroticism, and Openness to Experience – derived from factor-analytic research on trait terms ('lexical' studies).

Character   The component of personality associated with integrity, self-control, and other morally-relevant dispositions. It is often analyzed in terms of character strengths and virtues.

Conscientiousness   One of the Big Five personality factors, involving dispositions to be organized, reliable, self-controlled, and deliberate.

Coping   The methods or 'strategies' that people use to manage stressful life events, generally by attempting to control the events themselves or their emotional reactions to them.

Correlation   The degree of association between two variables, measured on a scale from −1 to +1.

Crystallized intelligence   According to Cattell, the component of intelligence that depends on acquired knowledge based on education and life experience, assessed by tests of vocabulary and general knowledge, for example.

Defence mechanism   Within psychoanalytic theory, the methods (e.g., repression, denial, projection) employed by the Ego to defend itself against the anxiety caused by troublesome thoughts, wishes, and impulses.

Diathesis   A personality characteristic that confers increased vulnerability to a mental disorder, which is triggered if the person experiences a sufficient amount of life stress.

Ego   In the structural model of psychoanalytic theory, the mental agency that mediates between desire (Id), conscience (Super-Ego), and external reality. It employs a repertoire of defence mechanisms to accomplish this task.

Emotional intelligence   A set of abilities involving the perception, recognition, understanding, and regulation of emotions.

Entity theory   The belief or 'lay theory' that a psychological attribute, such as personality or intelligence, is fixed or unchangeable. The opposite belief, an 'incremental theory', posits that the attribute is malleable.

Extraversion   A Big Five personality dimension that also appears in Eysenck's system, involving sociability, high activity levels, and interpersonal dominance. The absence of these dispositions is Introversion.

Factor analysis   A statistical procedure for determining the dimensions that underlie a set of observed variables.

Five-factor model   A popular model of the five primary dimensions of personality: Agreeableness, Conscientiousness, Extraversion, Neuroticism, and Openness to Experience. Essentially equivalent to the 'Big Five', but derived from factor analyses of questionnaire items rather than lexical studies.

Fluid intelligence   According to Cattell, the component of intelligence that depends on general mental fluency and flexibility rather than acquired knowledge.

g   The general component of intelligence that underlies all cognitive abilities.

Heritability   The proportion of the differences in a characteristic between people in a population that is explained by genetic differences between people, varying from 0 to 1.

Humanistic psychology   A theoretical approach to the study of personality that emphasized motives for personal growth and self-realization, and held a very optimistic view of human nature.

Id   In the structural model of psychoanalytic theory, the mental agency that is the repository of drives and their associated wishes and impulses.

Idiographic   An approach to the study of personality that emphasizes intensive analysis of the individual's uniqueness.

Intelligence   A broad, general cognitive ability, reflected in reasoning, problem-solving, abstract thinking, mental speed, and capacity to learn.

Interactionism   A theoretical position according to which behaviour is a joint function of situational and dispositional factors.

Interest   A preference for or tendency to engage with a particular kind of activity, such as a particular kind of vocation or leisure activity.

Inventory   A form of assessment device requiring structured responses – usually self-ratings – to a standard series of test items.

Latency   In psychoanalytic theory, a period of psychosexual development in middle childhood during which sexual drives are largely dormant.

Life narrative   A biographical story of a person's life history.

Locus of control   The general expectation that events in one's life are under one's personal control (internal locus) or due to factors outside one's control, such as luck, fate, or other people (external locus).

Mean-level change   The extent to which the average level of a characteristic, such as a personality trait, differs for people of different ages.

Motive   A force that directs and energizes behaviour in particular directions. Motives may be largely outside awareness (e.g., drives, needs) or consciously accessible and future-oriented (e.g., goals, strivings).

Multiple personality   Now known as 'dissociative identity disorder', this is a rare mental disorder in which the person appears to have more than one distinct personality, with these personalities often mutually unaware.

Neuroticism   A Big Five personality dimension that also appears in Eysenck's system, involving emotional instability, proneness to experience negative emotions, vulnerability, and low self-esteem.

Neurotransmitter   A brain chemical involved in the transmission of impulses between neurons. Variation in the typical concentrations of these in the brain may be associated with differences on personality trait dimensions.

Nomothetic   An approach to the study of personality that emphasizes the development of generalizations and laws of behaviour.

Object relations   The mental representations – including unconscious ones – of self, others, and interpersonal relations that are the focus of a school of psychoanalytic theory that goes by the same name.

Openness to Experience   A Big Five trait dimension involving dispositions towards imaginativeness, aesthetic sensibility, intellectual interests, and unconventionality.

Oral stage   In the genetic model of psychoanalytic theory, the earliest stage of psychosexual development, in which the mouth is the erotic focus and dependency is the primary developmental issue.

Personal construct   In Kelly's theory, a pair of polar alternatives (e.g., 'warm vs. cold', 'old vs. young') that people use to make sense of, or 'construe', their experiences. Objects or events are construed as similar to or different from these alternatives.

Personality disorder   An extreme, inflexible, and maladaptive personality variant associated with distress, interpersonal problems, and impaired social and occupational functioning.

Personology   A school of personality psychology that focuses on the intensive study of individual lives through time, often examined using case-study and psychobiographical methods.

Phallic stage   The third psychosexual stage in psychoanalytic theory's genetic model, in which erotic interest shifts to the genitals and the difference between the sexes is a major theme. The stage terminates in the Oedipus complex.

Preconscious   In the topographic model of psychoanalytic theory, the intermediate level of the mind in which mental content that is potentially conscious resides.

Projective test   A form of personality assessment that employs ambiguous stimuli and open-ended responses in order to examine people's typical ways of imposing ('projecting') meaning on their experience, often in an attempt to delve beneath the conscious surface of the personality.

Psychobiography   The use of systematic psychological research and theory to advance the biographical understanding of individual lives, most commonly historical figures.

Psychoticism   A major trait dimension in Eysenck's system, involving aggressiveness, coldness, egocentricity, and creativity.

Rank-order stability   The extent to which levels of a characteristic, such as a personality trait, are associated from one time to another, as assessed by a 'retest correlation'.

Reliability   The extent to which a measure yields consistent assessments: the components of the measure should be consistent with one another ('internal consistency'), different users of the measure should agree in their assessments of people who they assess ('inter-rater reliability'), and the measure should yield consistent assessments when the same person is assessed on different occasions ('retest reliability'). The greater the reliability of a measure, the less its measurement error.

Response bias   The systematic tendency for people completing assessments to respond in ways that distort their responses, for example, yea-saying or nay-saying (excessive yes or no responses independent of item content), faking bad (responding as more disturbed than the person truly is), and social desirability (responding in an effort to conform to social norms).

Schizotypy   An abnormal personality variant involving social anxiety and susceptibility to unusual ideas and experiences, which appears to confer vulnerability for schizophrenia.

Self-complexity   The degree to which the self-concept is composed of multiple distinct aspects such as social roles.

Self-efficacy   The expectation that one's behaviour can effectively achieve its goals.

Self-esteem   The global evaluation, from highly negative to highly positive, that people attach to their self-concept.

Self-narrative   One component of the self-concept, involving a story-like conception of how one's life has unfolded over time which may follow a variety of narrative trajectories.

Shared environment   In behavioural genetics, those environmental influences on behaviour that are shared within families, such as social class and parental education. The remaining, non-shared environmental influences are unique to each individual.

Situationism   A theoretical position holding that behaviour is primarily a function of the situation or context in which it occurs, rather than of the person's enduring and consistent dispositions. This position directly conflicts with the trait perspective.

Social learning theory   A personality theory that modified behavioural learning theories by including cognitive constructs such as expectancies.

Super-Ego   In the structural model of psychoanalytic theory, the mental agency that represents internalized social norms in primitive form, primarily in the form of prohibitions.

Temperament   The component of personality that is believed to be biologically based, present at birth or at least early in development, and is often related to emotional expression.

Test bias   The tendency for a test to yield assessments that are less valid for one or more social groups than for another, such as having content that is unfamiliar to a group, being administered in different ways for different groups, or under- or over-predicting outcomes for particular groups.

Trait   An internal disposition to think, feel, or behave in particular ways, understood to be consistent across situations and through time, especially when referring to non-intellectual dispositions (i.e., 'personality traits').

Type   A form of personality variation in which a subset of people belong to a distinct category that share a particular characteristic, rather than varying by degrees along a personality dimension, as in standard personality trait models.

Unconscious   In psychoanalytic theory, a level of the mind whose contents (thoughts, wishes, and impulses) are prevented from entering awareness and that has its own, irrational cognitive processes.

Validity   The extent to which a measure accurately assesses the construct that it is intended to assess, and predicts phenomena that should be associated with that construct. It can be broken down into several forms. 'Content' validity refers to the extent to which the measure's elements accurately refer to the construct, 'convergent' and 'discriminant' validity refer to it being associated with other measures of the same construct and not associated with measures of other constructs, and 'predictive' validity refers to the measure's capacity to predict outcomes linked to the construct.

Value   An abstract, consciously accessible goal (e.g., 'freedom', 'respect for tradition') that applies across many situations and motivates people to behave in accordance with it.

References

Abramson, L. Y., Metalsky, G. I., & Alloy, L. (1989). Hopelessness depression: A theory-based subtype of depression. *Psychological Review, 96*, 358–72.

Abramson, L. Y., Seligman, M. E. P., & Teasdale, J. D. (1978). Learned helplessness in humans: Critique and reformulation. *Journal of Abnormal Psychology, 87*, 49–74.

Ackerman, P. L., Beier, M. E., & Boyle, M. O. (2005). Working memory and intelligence: The same or different constructs? *Psychological Bulletin, 131*(1), 30.

Ackerman, P. L., & Heggestad, E. D. (1997). Intelligence, personality, and interests: Evidence for overlapping traits. *Psychological Bulletin, 121*(2), 219–45.

Ackermann, R., & DeRubeis, R. J. (1991). Is depressive realism real? *Clinical Psychology Review, 11*, 565–84.

Adams, H. E., Wright, L. W., & Lohr, B. A. (1996). Is homophobia associated with homosexual arousal? *Journal of Abnormal Psychology, 105*, 440–5.

Adorno, T. W., Frenkel-Brunswik, E., Levinson, D. J., & Sanford, R. N. (1950). *The authoritarian personality.* New York: Harper.

Alexander, I. E. (1990). *Personology: Method and content in personality assessment and psychobiography.* Durham, NC: Duke University Press.

Allport, G. W. (1937). *Personality: A psychological interpretation.* New York: Holt.

Allport, G. W., & Odbert, H. S. (1936). Trait-names: A psycho-lexical study. *Psychological Monographs, 47*(211).

Amelang, M. & Steinmayr, R. (2006). Is there a validity increment for tests of emotional intelligence in explaining the variance of performance criteria? *Intelligence, 34*(5), 459–68.

American Psychiatric Association (1980). *The diagnostic and statistical manual of mental disorders* (3rd ed.). Washington, DC: APA.

American Psychiatric Association (2000). *Diagnostic and statistical manual of mental disorder: DSM-IV-TR.* Washington, DC: APA.

American Psychiatric Association (2013). *The diagnostic and statistical manual of mental disorders* (5th ed.). Washington, DC: APA.

Andreasen, N. C., Flaum, M., Swayze, V., O'Leary, D. S., Alliger, R., Cohen, G., et al. (1993). Intelligence and brain structure in normal individuals. *American Journal of Psychiatry, 150*, 130–4.

Axelrad, D. A., Bellinger, D. C., Ryan, L. M., & Woodruff, T. J. (2007). Dose-response relationship of prenatal mercury exposure and IQ: An integrative analysis of epidemiologic data. *Environmental Health Perspectives, 115*(4), 609–15.

Baddeley, A. (2007). *Working memory, thought, and action.* Oxford: Oxford University Press.

Baghurst, P. A., McMichael, A. J., Wigg, N. R., Vimpani, G. V., Robertson, E. F., Roberts, R. J., & Tong, S. L. (1992). Environmental exposure to lead and children's intelligence at the age of seven years: The Port Pirie Cohort Study. *New England Journal of Medicine*, *327*(18), 1279–84.

Bagshaw, A. T. M., Horwood, L. J., Liu, Y., Fergusson, D. M., Sullivan, P. F., & Kennedy, M. A. (2013). No effect of genome-wide copy number variation on measures of intelligence in a New Zealand Birth Cohort. *PLoS One*, *8*(1), e55208.

Bandura, A. (1986). *Social foundations of thought and action: A social cognitive theory*. Englewood Cliffs, NJ: Prentice-Hall.

Barchard, K. A. (2003). Does emotional intelligence assist in the prediction of academic success? *Educational and Psychological Measurement*, *63*(5), 840–58.

Bar-On, R. (1997). *Bar-On Emotional Quotient Inventory (EQ-i): Technical manual*. Toronto, Canada: Multi-Health Systems.

Barrett, L. F., & Russell, J. A. (1999) The structure of current affect: Controversies and emerging consensus. *Current Directions in Psychological Science*, *8*, 10–14.

Bartels, M., Rietveld, M. J., Van Baal, G. C., & Boomsma, D. I. (2002). Genetic and environmental influences on the development of intelligence. *Behavioral Genetics*, *32*, 237–49.

Bastian, V. A., Burns, N. R., & Nettelbeck, T. (2005). Emotional intelligence predicts life skills, but not as well as personality and cognitive abilities. *Personality and Individual Differences*, *39*(6), 1135–45.

Bates, T. C., Lewis, G. J., & Weiss, A. (2013). Childhood socioeconomic status amplifies genetic effects on adult intelligence. *Psychological Science*, *24*, 2111–16.

Batty, G. D., Deary, I. J., Benzeval, M., & Der, G. (2010). Does IQ predict cardiovascular disease mortality as strongly as established risk factors? Comparison of effect estimates using the West of Scotland Twenty-07 cohort study. *European Journal of Cardiovascular Prevention & Rehabilitation*, *17*(1), 24–7.

Batty, G. D., Deary, I. J., & Gottfredson, L. S. (2007). Premorbid (early life) IQ and later mortality risk: Systematic review. *Annals of Epidemiology*, *17*(4), 278–88.

Batty, G. D., Mortensen, E. L., Nybo Andersen, A. M., & Osler, M. (2005). Childhood intelligence in relation to adult coronary heart disease and stroke risk: Evidence from a Danish birth cohort study. *Paediatric and Perinatal Epidemiology*, *19*(6), 452–9.

Baumeister, R. F., Campbell, J. D., Krueger, J.I., & Vohs, K. D. (2003). Does high self-esteem cause better performance, interpersonal success, happiness, or healthier lifestyles? *Psychological Science in the Public Interest*, *4*, 1–44.

Beaver, J. D., Lawrence, A. D., van Ditzhuijzen, J., Davis, M. H., Woods, A., & Calder, A. J. (2003). Individual differences in reward drive predict neural responses to images of food. *Journal of Neuroscience*, *26*, 5160–6.

Beaver, K. M., Schwartz, J. A., Connolly, E. J., Nedelec, J. I., Al-Ghamdi, M. S., & Kobeisy, A. N. (2013). The genetic and environmental architecture to the stability of IQ: Results from two independent samples of kinship pairs. *Intelligence*, *41*, 428–38.

Belsky, D. W., Caspi, A., Goldman-Mellor, S., Meier, M. H., Ramrakha, S., Poulton, R., & Moffitt, T. E. (2013). Is obesity associated with a decline in intelligence quotient during the first half of the life course? *American Journal of Epidemiology*, *178*(9), 1461–8.

Benyamin, B., Pourcain, B. St., Davis, O. S., et al. (2014). Childhood intelligence is heritable, highly polygenic and associated with FBBP1L. *Molecular Psychiatry*, *19*, 253–8.

Binet, A., & Simon, T. (1905). Méthodes nouvelles pour le diagnostic du niveaux intellectuel des anormaux. *L'année psychologique*, *11*, 191–241 (E. Kite, Trans.). Reprinted in *The development of intelligence in children* (pp. 41–88). Baltimore, MD: Williams & Williams.

Blatt, S. J., & Zuroff, D. C. (1992). Interpersonal relatedness and self-definition: Two prototypes for depression. *Clinical Psychology Review*, *12*, 527–62.

Bleidorn, W. (2012). Hitting the road to adulthood: Short-term personality development during a major life transition. *Personality and Social Psychology Bulletin*, *38*, 1594–608.

Block, J. (1978). *The Q-sort method in personality assessment and psychiatric research*. Palo Alto, CA: Consulting Psychologists Press.

Borkenau, P., & Liebler, A. (1992). Trait inferences: Sources of validity at zero acquaintance. *Journal of Personality and Social Psychology*, *62*(4), 645–57.

Bouchard, T. J., Jr (2004). Genetic influence on human psychological traits: A survey. *Current Directions in Psychological Science*, 13, 148–51.

Bouchard, T. J., Jr (2014). Genes, evolution, and intelligence. *Behavior Genetics*, *44*, 549–77.

Bouchard, T. J., & McGue, M. (1981). Familial studies of intelligence: A review. *Science*, *212*, 1055–9.

Bower, J. E., Kemeny, M., Taylor, S. E., & Fahey, J. L. (1998). Cognitive processing, discovery of meaning, CD4 decline, and AIDS-related mortality among bereaved HIV-seropositive men. *Journal of Consulting and Clinical Psychology*, *66*, 979–86.

Bowlby, J. (1991). *Charles Darwin: A new life*. New York: W. W. Norton.

Brackett, M. A., Mayer, J. D., & Warner, R. M. (2004). Emotional intelligence and its relation to everyday behaviour. *Personality and Individual Differences*, *36*(6), 1387–1402.

Broadhurst, P. L. (1976). The Maudsley reactive and nonreactive strains of rats: A clarification. *Behavioural Genetetics*, *6*, 363–5.

Brody, N. (2004). What cognitive intelligence is and what emotional intelligence is not. *Psychological Inquiry*, *15*(3), 234–8.

Brown, W. M., Cronk, L., Grochow, K., Jacobson, A., Liu, C. K., Popovic, Z., et al. (2005). Dance reveals symmetry especially in young men. *Nature*, *438*, 1148–50.

Burdick, K. E., Lencz, T., Funke, B., Finn, C. T., Szeszko, P. R., Kane, J. M., et al. (2006). Genetic variation in DTNBP1 influences general cognitive ability. *Human Molecular Genetics*, *15*, 1563–8.

Bushman, B. J., & Baumeister, R. F. (1998). Threatening egotism, narcissism, self-esteem, and direct and displaced aggression: Does self-love or self-hate lead to violence? *Journal of Personality and Social Psychology*, *75*, 219–29.

Buss, D.M., Craik, K. H. (1983). The act frequency approach to personality. *Psychological Review, 90*, 105–26.

Calvin, C. M., Deary, I. J., Fenton, C., Roberts, B. A., Der, G., Leckenby, N., & Batty, G. D. (2011). Intelligence in youth and all-cause-mortality: Systematic review with meta-analysis. *International Journal of Epidemiology, 40*(3), 626–44.

Campbell, J. D. (1990). Self-esteem and clarity of the self-concept. *Journal of Personality and Social Psychology, 59*, 538–49.

Camperio Ciani, A. S., Capiluppi, C., Veronese, A., & Sartori, G. (2007). The adaptive value of personality revealed by small island population dynamics. *European Journal of Personality, 21*, 3–22.

Cannon, T. D., Mednick, S. A., & Parnas, J. (1990). Antecedents of predominantly negative and predominantly positive symptom schizophrenia in a high-risk population. *Archives of General Psychiatry, 47*, 622–32.

Cantor, N. (1990). From thought to behavior: 'Having' and 'doing' in the study of personality and cognition. *American Psychologist, 45*, 735–50.

Carroll, J. B. (1993). *Human cognitive abilities: A survey of factor-analytic studies*. New York: Cambridge University Press.

Carson, S. H., Peterson, J. B., & Higgins, D. M. (2003). Decreased latent inhibition is associated with increased creative achievement in high-functioning individuals. *Journal of Personality and Social Psychology, 85*, 499–506.

Carver, C. S., Johnson, S. L., & Joorman, J. (2008). Serotonergic function, two-mode models of self-regulation, and vulnerability to depression: What depression has in common with impulsive aggression. *Psychological Bulletin, 134*, 912–43.

Carver, C. S., & White, T. L. (1994). Behavioral inhibition, behavioral activation, and affective responses to impending reward and punishment: The BIS/BAS scales. *Journal of Personality and Social Psychology, 67*, 319–33.

Caspi, A., & Herbener, E. S. (1990). Continuity and change: Assortative mating and the consistency of personality in adulthood. *Journal of Personality and Social Psychology, 58*, 250–8.

Caspi, A., Sugden, K., Moffitt, T. E., Taylor, A., Craig, I. W., et al. (2003). Influence of life stress on depression: Moderation by a polymorphism in the 5–HTT gene. *Science, 301*, 386–9.

Caspi, A., Taylor, A., Moffitt, T. E., & Plomin, R. (2000). Neighbourhood deprivation affects children's mental health: Environmental risks identified in a genetic design. *Psychological Science, 11*, 338–42.

Cattell, R. B. (1943). The description of personality: Basic traits resolved into clusters. *Journal of Abnormal and Social Psychology, 38*, 476–506.

Cattell, R. B. (1963). The theory of fluid and crystallized intelligence: A critical experiment. *Journal of Educational Psychology, 54*, 1–22.

Ceci, S. J. (1991). How much does schooling influence general intelligence and its cognitive components? A reassessment of the evidence. *Developmental Psychology, 27*(5), 703–22.

Chabris, C. F. (1999). Prelude or requiem for the 'Mozart effect'? *Nature, 400*, 826–7.

Charness, N., Feltovich, P. J., Hoffman, R. R., & Ericsson, K. A. (Eds.) (2006). *The Cambridge handbook of expertise and expert performance*. New York: Cambridge University Press.

Chelly, J., Khelfaoui, M., Francis, F., Cherif, B., & Bienvenu, T. (2006). Genetics and pathophysiology of mental retardation. *European Journal of Human Genetics*, *14*, 701–13.

Christoforou, A., Espeseth, T., Davies, G., et al. (2014). GWAS-based pathway analysis differentiates between fluid and crystallized intelligence. *Genes, Brain and Behavior*, *13*, 663–74.

Church, A. T., & Lonner, W. J. (1998). Personality and its measurement in cross-cultural perspective. Special issue of the *Journal of Cross-Cultural Psychology*, *29*.

Ciarrochi, J. V., Chan, A. Y. C., & Caputi, P. (2000). A critical evaluation of the emotional intelligence construct. *Personality and Individual Differences*, *28*, 539–61.

Clark, L. A. (2007). Assessment and diagnosis of personality disorder: Perennial issues and an emerging reconceptualization. *Annual Review of Psychology*, *58*, 227–57.

Cliffordson, C., & Gustafsson, J.-E. (2008). Effects of age and schooling on intellectual performance: Estimates obtained from analysis of continuous variation in age and length of schooling. *Intelligence*, *36*, 143–52.

Cloninger, C. R. (1987). A systematic method for clinical description and classification of personality variants: A proposal. *Archives of General Psychiatry*, *44*, 573–88.

Cohen, J. (1992). A power primer. *Psychological Bulletin*, *112*, 155–9.

Conte, J. M. (2005). A review and critique of emotional intelligence measures. *Journal of Organizational Behavior*, *26*(4), 433–40.

Corballis, M. C. (2003). *From hand to mouth: The origins of language*. Princeton, NJ: Princeton University Press.

Corr, P. J. (2004). Reinforcement sensitivity theory and personality. *Neuroscience and Biobehavioural Reviews*, *28*, 317–32.

Corr, P. J. (Ed.) (2008). *The reinforcement sensitivity theory of personality.* Cambridge, UK: Cambridge University Press.

Corr, P. J., DeYoung, C. G., & McNaughton, N. (2013). Motivation and personality: A neuropsychological perspective. *Social and Personality Psychology Compass*, *7*, 158–75.

Costa, P. T., & McCrae, R. R. (1992). *Revised NEO Personality Inventory (NEO PI-R) and NEO Five-Factor Inventory: Professional manual*. Odessa, FL: Psychology Assessment Resources.

Costa, P. T., & McCrae, R. R. (1994a). Set like plaster? Evidence for the stability of adult personality. In T. F. Heatherton & J. L. Weinberger (Eds.), *Can personality change?* (pp. 21–40). Washington, DC: American Psychological Association.

Costa, P. T., & McCrae, R. R. (1994b). Stability and change in personality from adolescence through adulthood. In C. F. Halverson, G. A. Kohnstamm, & R. P. Martin (Eds.), *The developing structure of temperament and personality in infancy and childhood* (pp. 139–50). Hillsdale, NJ: Erlbaum.

Côté, S., & Miners, C. T. H. (2006). Emotional intelligence, cognitive intelligence, and job performance. *Administrative Science Quarterly*, *51*, 1–28.

Craik, F. I. M., & Salthouse, T. A. (Eds.) (2000). *The handbook of aging and cognition* (2nd ed.). Mahwah, NJ: Erlbaum.

335

Cramer, P. (1998). Freshman to senior year: A follow-up study of identity, narcissism, and defence mechanisms. *Journal of Research in Personality, 32,* 156–72.

Crowne, K. A. (2013). Cultural exposure, emotional intelligence, and cultural intelligence: An exploratory study. *International Journal of Cross Cultural Management, 13*(1), 5–22.

Cunningham, W. A., Arbuckle, N. L., Jahn, A., Mowrer, S. M., & Abduljalil, A. M. (2010). Aspects of neuroticism and the amygdala: Chronic tuning from motivational styles. *Neuropsychologia, 48,* 3399–3404.

Damasio, A. (1994). *Descartes' error: Emotion, reason, and the human brain.* New York: Putnam.

Darwin, C. R. (1859). *On the origin of species by means of natural selection, or the preservation of favoured races in the struggle for life.* London: Murray.

Davis, O. S. P., Butcher, L. M., Docherty, S. J., Meaburn, E. L., Curtis, C. J. C., Simpson, M. A., Schalkwyk, L. C., & Plomin, R. (2010). A three-stage genome-wide association study of general cognitive ability: Hunting the small effects. *Behavior Genetics, 40,* 759–67.

Dawes, R. M., Faust, D., & Meehl, P. E. (1989). Clinical versus actuarial judgment. *Science, 243,* 1668–74.

Dawkins, R. (1986). *The blind watchmaker.* New York: W. W. Norton.

Deary, I. J., Austin, E. J., & Caryl, P. G. (2000). Testing versus understanding human intelligence. *Psychology, Public Policy, and Law, 6*(1), 180–90.

Deary, I. J., & Der, G. (2005). Reaction time explains IQ's association with death. *Psychological Science, 16,* 64–9.

Deary, I. J., Der, G., & Ford, G. (2001). Reaction times and intelligence differences: A population-based cohort study. *Intelligence, 29,* 389–99.

Deary, I. J., Gale, C. R., Stewart, M. C., Fowkes, F. G. R., Murray, G. D., Batty, G. D., & Price, J. F. (2009). Intelligence and persisting with medication for two years: Analysis in a randomised controlled trial. *Intelligence, 37*(6), 607–12.

Deary, I. J., Spinath, F. M., & Bates, T. C. (2006). Genetics of intelligence. *European Journal of Human Genetics, 14,* 690–700.

Deary, I. J., Strand, S., Smith, P., & Fernandes, C. (2007). Intelligence and educational achievement. *Intelligence, 35*(1), 13–21.

Deary, I. J., Whalley, L. J., Lemmon, H., Crawford, J. R., & Starr, J. M. (2000). The stability of individual differences in mental ability from childhood to old age: Follow-up of the 1932 Scottish Mental Survey. *Intelligence, 28,* 49–55.

DeNeve, K. M., & Cooper, H. (1998). The happy personality: A meta-analysis of 137 personality traits and subjective well-being. *Psychological Bulletin, 124,* 197–229.

Denollet, J., Sys, S., Stroobant, N., Rombouts, H., Gillebert, T., & Brutsaert D. (1996). Personality as independent predictor of long-term mortality in patients with coronary heart disease. *Lancet, 347,* 417–21.

Depue, R. A. (1995). Neurobiological factors in personality and depression. *European Journal of Personality, 9,* 413–39.

Depue, R. A. (2006). Interpersonal behavior and the structure of personality: Neurobehavioral foundation of agentic extraversion and affiliation. In T. Canli (Ed.), *Biology of personality and individual differences*. Boston, MA: Cambridge University Press.

Depue, R. A., & Collins, P. F. (1999). Neurobiology of the structure of personality: Dopamine, facilitation of incentive motivation, and extraversion. *Behavioral and Brain Sciences*, *22*, 491–569.

Depue, R. A., & Fu, Y. (2013). On the nature of extraversion: Variation in conditioned contextual activation of dopamine-facilitated affective, cognitive, and motor processes. *Frontiers in Human Neuroscience*, *7*, 288.

Depue, R. A., & Lenzenweger, M. F. (2005). A neurobehavioural model of personality disorders. In T. Cicchetti (Ed.), *Developmental psychopathology*. New York: Wiley-Interscience.

Depue, R. A., & Morrone-Strupinsky, J. V. (2005). A neurobehavioral model of affiliative bonding: Implications for conceptualizing a human trait of affiliation. *Behavioral and Brain Sciences*, *28*, 313–50; discussion, 350–95.

Der, G., Batty, G. D., & Deary, I. J. (2009). The association between IQ in adolescence and a range of health outcomes at 40 in the 1979 US National Longitudinal Study of Youth. *Intelligence*, *37*(6), 573–80.

De Raad, B. (2005). The trait coverage of emotional intelligence. *Personality and Individual Differences*, *38*, 673–87.

Derksen, J., Kramer, I., & Katzko, M. (2002). Does a self-report measure for emotional intelligence assess something different than general intelligence? *Personality and Individual Differences*, *32*, 37–48.

DeYoung, C. G. (2006). Higher-order factors of the Big Five in a multi-informant sample. *Journal of Personality and Social Psychology*, *91*, 1138–1151.

DeYoung, C. G. (2014). Openness/intellect: A dimension of personality reflecting cognitive exploration. In R. J. Larsen & M. L. Cooper (Eds.), *The APA handbook of personality and social psychology. Volume 3: Personality processes and individual differences*. Washington, DC: American Psychological Association.

DeYoung, C. G. (2015). Cybernetic Big Five theory. *Journal of Research in Personality*, *56*, 33–58.

DeYoung, C. G., & Gray, J. R. (2009). Personality neuroscience: Explaining individual differences in affect, behaviour and cognition. In P. J. Corr & G. Matthews (Eds.), *The Cambridge handbook of personality psychology* (pp. 323–46). New York: Cambridge University Press.

DeYoung, C. G., Hirsh, J. B., Shane, M. S., Papademetris, X., Rajeevan, N., & Gray, J. R. (2010). Testing predictions from personality neuroscience: Brain structure and the big five. *Psychological Science*, *21*, 820–8. doi: 10.1177/0956797610370159

DeYoung, C. G., Quilty, L. C., & Peterson, J. B. (2007). Between facets and domains: 10 aspects of the Big Five. *Journal of Personality and Social Psychology*, *93*(5), 880–96.

DeYoung, C. G., Weisberg, Y. J., Quilty, L. C., & Peterson, J. B. (2013). Unifying the aspects of the Big Five, the Interpersonal Circumplex, and trait affiliation. *Journal of Personality*, *81*, 465–75.

Dickens, W. T., & Flynn, J. R. (2001). Heritability estimates versus large environmental effects: The IQ paradox resolved. *Psychological Review*, *108*, 346–69.

Di Fabio, A., & Busoni, L. (2007). Fluid intelligence, personality traits and scholastic success: Empirical evidence in a sample of Italian high school students. *Personality and Individual Differences*, *43*(8), 2095–104.

Di Fabio, A., & Palazzeschi, L. (2009). An in-depth look at scholastic success: Fluid intelligence, personality traits or emotional intelligence? *Personality and Individual Differences*, *46*(5), 581–5.

Digman, J. M. (1989). Five robust personality dimensions: Development, stability, and utility. *Journal of Personality*, *57*, 195–214.

Doebler, P., & Scheffler, B. (in press). The relationship of choice reaction time variability and intelligence: A meta-analysis. *Learning and Individual Differences*

Donaghue, E. M., Robins, R. W., Roberts, B. W., & John, O. P. (1993). The divided self: Concurrent and longitudinal effects of psychological adjustment and social roles on self-concept differentiation. *Journal of Personality and Social Psychology*, *64*, 834–46.

Driessen, M., Herrman, J., Stahl, K., Zwann, M., Meier, S., Hill, A., Osterheider, M., & Petersen, D. (2000). Magnetic resonance imaging volumes of the hippocampus and the amygdala in women with borderline personality disorder, and early traumatization. *Archives of General Psychiatry*, *57*, 1115–22. http://dx.doi.org/10.1016/j.lindif.2015.02.009.

Dutton, E. & Lynn, R. (2013). A negative Flynn effect in Finland, 1997–2009. *Intelligence*, *41*, 817–20.

Dweck, C. S. (1999). *Self-theories: Their role in motivation, personality, and development.* Philadelphia, PA: Psychology Press.

Elliot, A. J. (2008). *Handbook of approach and avoidance motivation.* New York: Taylor & Francis.

Elliot, A. J., & Thrash, T. M. (2002). Approach-avoidance motivation in personality: Approach and avoidance temperaments and goals. *Journal of Personality and Social Psychology*, *82*, 804–18.

Elms, A. C. (1994). *Uncovering lives: The uneasy alliance of biography and psychology.* New York: Oxford University Press.

Emmons, R. A. (1999). Motives and life goals. In R. Hogan, J. Johnson, & S. Briggs (Eds.), *Handbook of personality psychology* (pp. 485–512). New York: Academic Press.

Erikson, E. H. (1963). *Childhood and society* (2nd ed.). New York: W. W. Norton.

Exner, J. E. (1986). *The Rorschach: A comprehensive system. Volume 1: Basic foundations* (2nd ed.). New York: Wiley.

Eysenck, H. J. (1947). *Dimensions of personality.* London: Routledge & Kegan Paul.

Eysenck, H. J. (1967). *The biological basis of personality.* Springfield, IL: Charles C. Thomas.

Eysenck, H. J. (1990). Biological dimensions of personality. In L. A. Pervin (Ed.), *Handbook of personality: Theory and research* (pp. 244–76). New York: Guilford Press.

Eysenck, H. J., & Eysenck, M. W. (1985). *Personality and individual differences: A natural science approach.* New York: Plenum.

Farmer, R. F., & Goldberg, L. R. (2008). A psychometric evaluation of the revised Temperament and Character Inventory (TCI-R) and the TCI-140. *Psychological Assessment*, *20*, 281–91.

Farsides, T., & Woodfield, R. (2003). Individual differences and undergraduate academic success: The roles of personality, intelligence, and application. *Personality and Individual Differences*, *34*(7), 1225–43.

Fazio, R., Jackson, J. R., Dunton, B., & Williams, C. J. (1995). Variability in automatic activation as an unobtrusive measure of racial attitudes: A bona fide pipeline? *Journal of Personality and Social Psychology*, *69*, 1013–27.

Feldman Barrett, L., & Russell, J. A. (1999). The structure of current affect: Controversies and emerging consensus. *Current Directions in Psychological Science*, *8*, 10–14.

Fergusson, D. M., Horwood, J. L., & Ridder, E. M. (2005). Show me the child at seven II: Childhood intelligence and later outcomes in adolescence and young adulthood. *Journal of Child Psychology and Psychiatry*, *46*(8), 850–8.

Fiori, M. (2015). Emotional intelligence compensates for low IQ and boosts low emotionality individuals in a self-presentation task. *Personality and Individual Differences*, *81*, 169–73.

Fiori, M., & Antonakis, J. (2012). Selective attention to emotional stimuli: What IQ and openness do, and emotional intelligence does not. *Intelligence*, *40*(3), 245–54.

Firkowska-Mankiewicz, A. (2011). Adult careers: Does childhood IQ predict later life outcome? *Journal of Policy and Practice in Intellectual Disabilities*, *8*(1), 1–9.

Fiske, A. P., Kitayama, S., Markus, H., & Nisbett, R. (1998). The cultural matrix of social psychology. In D. T. Gilbert, S. T. Fiske, & G. Lindzey (Eds.), *The handbook of social psychology* (pp. 915–81). Boston, MA: McGraw-Hill.

Fiske, D. W. (1949). Consistency of the factorial structures of personality ratings from different sources. *Journal of Abnormal and Social Psychology*, *44*, 329–44.

Fleeson, W. (2001). Towards a structure- and process-integrated view of personality: Traits as density distributions of states. *Journal of Personality and Social Psychology*, *80*, 1011–27.

Fleeson, W., & Gallagher, P. (2009). The implications of Big Five standing for the distribution of trait manifestation in behavior: Fifteen experience-sampling studies and a meta-analysis. *Journal of Personality and Social Psychology*, *97*(6), 1097–1114.

Fleeson, W., Malanos, A. B., & Achille, N. M. (2002). An intraindividual process approach to the relationship between extraversion and positive affect: Is acting extraverted as 'good' as being extraverted? *Journal of Personality and Social Psychology*, *83*(6), 1409–22.

Folkman, S., & Lazarus, R. S. (1980). An analysis of coping in a middle-aged community sample. *Journal of Health and Social Behavior*, *21*, 219–39.

Folkman, S., & Moskowitz, J. T. (2004). Coping: Pitfalls and promise. *Annual Review of Psychology*, *55*, 745–74.

Fraley, R. C., & Shaver, P. R. (1998). Airport separations: A naturalistic study of adult attachment dynamics in separating couples. *Journal of Personality and Social Psychology*, *75*, 1198–212.

Franz, C. E. (1994). Does thought content change as individuals age? A longitudinal study of midlife adults. In T. F. Heatherton & J. L. Weinberger (Eds.), *Can personality change?* (pp. 227–49). Washington, DC: American Psychological Association.

Freud, S. (1923). *The ego and the id.* In J. Strachey (Ed. and Trans.), *The collected works of Sigmund Freud* (Vol. 14). London: Hogarth Press.

Freudenthaler, H. H., Fink, A., & Neubauer, A. C. (2006). Emotional abilities and cortical activation during emotional information processing. *Personality and Individual Differences, 41*(4), 685–95.

Frey, M. C., & Detterman, D. K. (2004). Scholastic assessment or *g*? *Psychological Science, 15,* 373–8.

Friedman, H. S., Tucker, J. S., Tomlinson-Keasey, C., Schwartz, J. E., Wingard, D. L., & Criqui, M. H. (1993). Does childhood personality predict longevity? *Journal of Personality and Social Psychology, 67,* 278–86.

Friedman, M., & Rosenman, R. H. (1974). *Type A behavior and your heart.* New York: Knopf.

Funder, D. C. (1995). On the accuracy of personality judgment: A realistic approach. *Psychological Review, 102,* 652–70.

Funder, D. C. (1997). *The personality puzzle.* New York: W. W. Norton.

Galsworthy, M. J., Paya-Cano, J. L., Liu, L., Monleon, S., Gregoryan, G., Fernandes, C., et al. (2005). Assessing reliability, heritability and general cognitive ability in a battery of cognitive tasks for laboratory mice. *Behavioral Genetics, 35,* 675–92.

Gale, A. (1983). Electroencephalographic studies of extraversion-introversion: A case study in the psychophysiology of individual differences. *Personality and Individual Differences, 4,* 371–80.

García-Sancho, E., Salguero, J. M., & Fernández-Berrocal, P. (2014). Relationship between emotional intelligence and aggression: a systematic review. *Aggression and Violent Behavior, 19*(5), 584–91.

Gardner, H. (1983). *Frames of mind: The theory of multiple intelligences.* New York: Basic Books.

Gensowski, M. (2014). *Personality, IQ, and lifetime earnings.* IZA Discussion Paper No. 8235. Bonn, Germany: Institute for the Study of Labor.

Gergen, K. J., & Gergen, M. M. (1983). Narratives of the self. In T. R. Sarbin & K. E. Scheibe (Eds.), *Studies in social identity* (pp. 254–73). New York: Praeger.

Glenn, N. D. (1980). Values, attitudes, and beliefs. In O. G. Brim & J. Kagan (Eds.), *Constancy and change in human development* (pp. 596–640). Cambridge, MA: Harvard University Press.

Goldberg, L. R. (1993). The structure of phenotypic personality traits. *American Psychologist, 48*(1), 26–34.

Goleman, D. (1995). *Emotional intelligence.* New York: Bantam.

Gosling, S. D., & John, O. P. (1999). Personality dimensions in nonhuman animals: A cross-species review. *Current Directions in Psychological Science, 8,* 69–73.

Gosling, S. D., Ko, S. J., Mannarelli, T., & Morris, M. E. (2002). A room with a cue: Personality judgments based on offices and bedrooms. *Journal of Personality and Social Psychology, 82,* 379–98.

Gottfredson, L. S. (1997a). Mainstream science on intelligence: An editorial with 52 signatories, history, and bibliography. *Intelligence, 24*(1), 13–23.

Gottfredson, L. S. (1997b). Why *g* matters: The complexity of everyday life. *Intelligence*, *24*(1), 79–132.

Gottfredson, L. S., & Deary, I. J. (2004). Intelligence predicts health and longevity, but why? *Current Directions in Psychological Science*, *13*(1), 1–4.

Gould, S. J. (1996). *The mismeasure of man* (2nd ed.). New York: W. W. Norton.

Gray, J. A. (1981). A critique of Eysenck's theory of personality. In H. J. Eysenck (Ed.), *A model for personality* (pp. 246–76). New York: Springer.

Gray, J. A., & McNaughton, N. (2000). *The neuropsychology of anxiety: An enquiry into the functions of the septo-hippocampal system* (2nd ed.). New York: Oxford University Press.

Gray, J. R., Chabris, C. F., & Braver, T. S. (2003). Neural mechanisms of general fluid intelligence. *Nature Neuroscience*, *6*, 316–22.

Grazioplene, R. G., Ryman, S. G., Gray, J. R., Rustichini, A., Jung, R. E., & DeYoung, C. G. (2015). Subcortical intelligence: Caudate volume predicts IQ in health adults. *Human Brain Mapping*, *36*, 1407–16.

Green, R. L., Hoffman, L. J., Morse, R. J., Hayes, M. E., & Morgan, R. F. (1966). *The educational status of children during the first school year following four years of little or no schooling*: Charlotteville, VA: Virginia Department of Health, Education and Welfare.

Greenwald, A. G., & Farnham, S. D. (2000). Using the Implicit Association Test to measure self-esteem and self-concept. *Journal of Personality and Social Psychology*, *79*, 1022–38.

Greenwald, A. G., McGhee, D. E., & Schwartz, J. L. K. (1998). Measuring individual differences in implicit cognition: The Implicit Association Test. *Journal of Personality and Social Psychology*, *74*, 1464–80.

Grilo, C. M., Sanislow, C. A., Gunderson, J. G., Pagano, M. E., Yen. S., et al. (2004). Two-year stability and change of schizotypal, borderline, avoidant, and obsessive-compulsive personality disorders. *Journal of Consulting and Clinical Psychology*, *72*, 767–75.

Grucza, R. A., & Goldberg, L. R. (2007). The comparative validity of 11 modern personality inventories: Predictions of behavioural acts, informant reports, and clinical indicators. *Journal of Personality Assessment*, *89*, 167–87.

Grudnik, J. L., & Kranzler, J. H. (2001). Meta-analysis of the relationship between intelligence and inspection time. *Intelligence*, *29*, 523–35.

Grünbaum, A. (1984). *The foundations of psychoanalysis: A philosophical critique*. Berkeley, CA: University of California Press.

Haier, R. J. (2011). Biological basis of intelligence. In R. J. Sternberg & S. B. Kaufman (Eds.), *The Cambridge handbook of intelligence* (pp. 351–68). Cambridge, UK: Cambridge University Press.

Haier, R. J., Jung, R. E., Yeo, R. A., Head, K., & Alkire, M. T. (2004). Structural brain variation and general intelligence. *Neuroimage*, *23*, 425–33.

Hall, C. S., & Lindzey, G. (1978). *Theories of personality* (3rd ed.). New York: Wiley.

Halperin, E., Russell, A. G., Trzesniewski, K. H., Gross, J. J., & Dweck, C. S. (2011). Promoting the Middle East peace process by changing beliefs about group malleability. *Science*, *333*, 1767–9.

341

Hamer, D. (1997). The search for personality genes: Adventures of a molecular biologist. *Current Directions in Psychological Science, 6,* 111–14.

Hammack, P. L. (2008). Narrative and the cultural psychology of identity. *Personality and Social Psychology Review, 12,* 222–47.

Hampshire, S. (1953). Dispositions. *Analysis, 14,* 5–11.

Harter, S. (1993). Causes and consequences of low self-esteem in children and adolescents. In R. Baumeister (Ed.), *Self-esteem: The puzzle of low self-regard* (pp. 87–116). New York: Plenum Press.

Haslam, N. (1997). Evidence that male sexual orientation is a matter of degree. *Journal of Personality and Social Psychology, 73,* 862–70.

Haslam, N. (2011). The return of the anal character. *Review of General Psychology, 15,* 351–60.

Haslam, N., Bain, P., & Neal, D. (2004). The implicit structure of positive characteristics. *Personality and Social Psychology Bulletin, 30,* 529–41.

Haslam, N., Bastian, B., & Bissett, M. (2004). Essentialist beliefs about personality and their implications. *Personality and Social Psychology Bulletin, 30,* 1661–73.

Haslam, N., Holland, E., & Kuppens, P. (2012). Categories versus dimensions in personality and psychopathology: A quantitative review of taxometric research. *Psychological Medicine, 42,* 903–20.

Haworth, C. M. B., Wright, M. J., et al. (2010). The heritability of general cognitive ability increases linearly from childhood to young adulthood. *Molecular Psychiatry, 15,* 1112–20.

Hayes, T. R., Petrov, A. A., & Sederberg, P. B. (2015). Do we really become smarter when our fluid-intelligence test scores improve? *Intelligence, 48,* 1–14.

Hazan, C., & Shaver, P. (1987). Romantic love conceptualized as an attachment process. *Journal of Personality and Social Psychology, 52,* 511–24.

Heaven, P. C. L., & Bucci, S. (2001). Right-wing authoritarianism, social dominance orientation and personality: An analysis using the IPIP measure. *European Journal of Personality, 15,* 49–56.

Heine, S. H., Lehman, D. R., Markus, H. R., & Kitayama, S. (1999). Is there a universal human need for positive self-regard? *Psychological Review, 106,* 766–94.

Helson, R., Mitchell, V., & Moane, G. (1984). Personality and patterns of adherence and non-adherence to the social clock. *Journal of Personality and Social Psychology, 46,* 1079–96.

Herpertz, S., Schütz, A., & Nezlek, J. (2016). Enhancing emotion perception, a fundamental component of emotional intelligence: Using multiple-group SEM to evaluate a training program. *Personality and Individual Differences, 95,* 11–19.

Hirsh, J. B., DeYoung, C. G., & Peterson, J. B. (2009). Metatraits of the Big Five differentially predict engagement and restraint of behavior. *Journal of Personality, 77,* 1085–1102.

Hirschmüller, S., Boris Egloff, B., Schmukle, S. C., Nestler, S., & Back, M. D. (2015). Accurate judgments of neuroticism at zero acquaintance: A question of relevance. *Journal of Personality, 83,* 221–8.

Hogan, J. (1989). Personality correlates of physical fitness. *Journal of Personality and Social Psychology*, *56*, 284–8.

Holland, J. L. (1997). *Making vocational choices: A theory of vocational personalities and work environments* (3rd ed.). Odessa, FL: Psychological Assessment Resources.

Horn, J. L. (1998). A basis for research on age differences in cognitive capabilities. In J. J. McArdle & R. W. Woodcock (Eds.), *Human cognitive abilities in theory and practice* (pp. 57–91). Mahwah, NJ: Erlbaum.

Howard, A., & Bray, D. (1988). *Managerial lives in transition: Advancing age and changing times*. New York: Guilford Press.

Huepe, D., Roca, M., Salas, N., Canales-Johnson, A., Rivera-Rei, Á. A., Zamorano, L., Concepción, A., Manes, F., & Ibañez, A. (2011). Fluid intelligence and psychosocial outcome: From logical problem solving to social adaptation. *PLoS One*, *6*(9), e24858, 1–9.

Hunt, L. M., & Megyesi, M. S. (2008). The ambiguous meanings of the racial/ethnic categories routinely used in human genetics research. *Social Science & Medicine*, *66*(2), 349–61.

Jackson, J. D., & Balota, D. A. (2012). Mind-wandering in younger and older adults: Converging evidence from the Sustained Attention to Response Task and reading for comprehension. *Psychological and Aging*, *27*, 106–19.

Jackson, T., Chen, H., Guo, C., & Gao, X. (2006). Stories we love by: Conceptions of love among couples from the People's Republic of China and the United States. *Journal of Cross-Cultural Psychology*, *37*, 446–64.

Jaušovec, N., & Jaušovec, K. (2005a). Sex differences in brain activity related to general and emotional intelligence. *Brain and Cognition*, *59*(3), 277–86.

Jaušovec, N., & Jaušovec, K. (2005b). Differences in induced gamma and upper alpha oscillations in the human brain related to verbal/performance and emotional intelligence. *International Journal of Psychophysiology*, *56*(3), 223–35.

Jemmott, J. B. (1987). Social motives and susceptibility to disease: Stalking individual differences in health risks. *Journal of Personality*, *55*, 267–98.

Jensen, A. R. (1977). Cumulative deficit in IQ of Blacks in the rural South. *Developmental Psychology*, *13*, 184–91.

John, O. P. (1990). The 'Big Five' factor taxonomy: Dimensions of personality in the natural language and in questionnaires. In L. Pervin (Ed.), *Handbook of personality: Theory and research* (pp. 66–100). New York: Guilford Press.

John, O. P., Caspi, A., Robins, R. W., Moffitt, T. E., & Stouthamer-Loeber, M. (1994). The 'little five': Exploring the nomological network of the five-factor model of personality in adolescent boys. *Child Development*, *65*, 160–78.

John, O. P., & Srivastava, S. (1999). The Big Five trait taxonomy: History, measurement, and theoretical perspectives. In L. A. Pervin (Ed.), *Handbook of personality: Theory and research* (Vol. 2) (pp. 102–38). New York: Guilford Press.

Johnson, W., & Bouchard, T. J., Jr. (2007). Sex differences in mental abilities: *g* masks the dimensions on which they lie. *Intelligence*, *35*, 23–39.

Johnston, W. (2010). Understanding the genetics of intelligence: Can height help? Can corn oil? *Current Directions in Psychological Science*, *19*, 177–82.

Jones, H. E., & Bayley, N. (1941). The Berkeley Growth Study. *Child Development*, *12*, 167–73.

Jordan, C. H., Spencer, S. J., Zanna, M. P., Hoshino-Browne, E., & Correll, J. (2003). Secure and defensive high self-esteem. *Journal of Personality and Social Psychology*, *85*, 969–78.

Joseph, D. L., Jin, J., Newman, D. A., & O'Boyle, E. H. (2015). Why does self-reported emotional intelligence predict job performance? A meta-analytic investigation of mixed EI. *Journal of Applied Psychology*, *100*(2), 298–342.

Josselson, R. (1995). Imagining the real: Empathy, narrative, and the dialogic self. In R. Josselson & A. Lieblich (Eds.), *Interpreting experience: The narrative study of lives* (Vol. 3) (pp. 27–44). Thousand Oaks, CA: Sage.

Jung, C. G. (1971). *Psychological types*. London: Routledge.

Jung, R. E., & Haier, R. J. (2007). The Parieto-Frontal Integration Theory (P-FIT) of intelligence: Converging neuroimaging evidence. *Behavioral and Brain Sciences*, *30*, 135–87.

Jung, R. E., Haier, R. J., Yeo, R. A., Rowland, L. M., Petropoulos, H., Levine, A. S., et al. (2005). Sex differences in N-acetyl-aspartate correlates of general intelligence: A 1H-MRS study of normal human brain. *NeuroImage*, *26*, 965–72.

Kagan, J. (1994). *Galen's prophecy: Temperament in human nature*. New York: Basic Books.

Kalichman, S. C., Heckman, T., & Kelly, J. A. (1996). Sensation seeking as an explanation for the association between substance abuse and HIV-related risky sexual behavior. *Archives of Sexual Behavior*, *25*, 141–54.

Kanazawa, S. (2014). Intelligence and obesity: Which way does the causal direction go? *Current Opinion in Endocrinology, Diabetes and Obesity*, *21*(5), 339–44.

Kaplan, H. S., & Gangestad, S. W. (2005). Life history theory and evolutionary psychology. In D. M. Buss (Ed.), *The handbook of evolutionary psychology* (pp. 68–95). Hoboken, NJ: John Wiley & Sons.

Kaufman, S. B., Quilty, L. C., Grazioplene, R. G., Hirsh, J. B., Gray, J. R., Peterson, J. B., & DeYoung, C. G. (2015). Openness to experience and Intellect differentially predict creative achievement in the arts and sciences. *Journal of Personality*, *84*, 248–58.

Kelly, G. (1955). *The psychology of personal constructs*. New York: W. W. Norton.

Kendler, K. S., Aggen, S. H., Czajkowski, N., Roysamb, E., Tambs, K., Torgersen, S., Neale, M. C., & Reichborn-Kjennerud, T. (2008). The structure of genetic and environmental risk factors for DSM-IV personality disorders: A multivariate twin study. *Archives of General Psychiatry*, *65*, 1438–46.

Kenford, S. L., Smith, S. S., Wetter, D. W., Jorenby, D. E., Fiore, M. C., & Baker, T. B. (2002). Predicting relapse back to smoking: Contrasting affective and physical models of dependence. *Journal of Consulting and Clinical Psychology*, *70*, 216–27.

Kennis, M., Rademaker, A. R., & Geuze, E. (2013). Neural correlates of personality: An integrative review. *Neuroscience and Biobehavioral Reviews*, *37*, 73–95.

Kernis, M. H., Cornell, D. P., Sun, C. R., Berry, R. J., & Harlow, T. (1993). There's more to self-esteem than whether it's high or low: The importance of stability of self-esteem. *Journal of Personality and Social Psychology, 65,* 1190–204.

Kilgour, A. H., Starr, J. M., & Whalley, L. J. (2010). Associations between childhood intelligence (IQ), adult morbidity and mortality. *Maturitas, 65*(2), 98–105.

Kovas, Y., Voronin, I., Kaydalov, A., Malykh, S. B., Dale, P. S., & Plomin, R. (2013). Literacy and numeracy are more heritable than intelligence in primary school. *Psychological Science, 24*(10), 2048–56.

Kringelbach, M. L., & Berridge, K. C. (2010). The functional neuroanatomy of pleasure and happiness. *Discovery Medicine, 9,* 579–87.

Kuncel, N. R., Hezlestt, S. A., & Ones, D. S. (2004). Academic performance, career potential, creativity, and job performance: Can one construct predict them all? *Journal of Personality and Social Psychology, 86*(1), 148–61.

Larsen, J. T., McGraw, A. P., & Cacioppo, J. T. (2001). Can people feel happy and sad at the same time? *Journal of Personality and Social Psychology, 81,* 684–96.

Larsen, R. J., & Ketelaar, T. (1991). Personality and susceptibility to positive and negative emotional states. *Journal of Personality and Social Psychology, 55,* 132–40.

Lavine, H., & Snyder, M. (1996). Cognitive processing and the functional matching effect in persuasion: The mediating role of subjective perceptions of message quality. *Journal of Experimental Social Psychology, 32,* 580–604.

LeDoux, J. E. (1996). *The emotional brain.* New York: Simon & Schuster.

LeDoux, J. E. (2003). The emotional brain, fear, and the amygdala. *Cellular and Molecular Neurobiology, 23,* 727–38.

Lee, V. E., Brooks-Gunn, J., Schnur, E., & Liaw, F. R. (1990). Are Head Start effects sustained? A longitudinal follow-up comparison of disadvantaged children attending Head Start, no preschool, and other preschool programs. *Child Development, 61,* 495–507.

Lees, C., & Hopkins, J. (2013). Effect of aerobic exercise on cognition, academic achievement, and psychosocial function in children: A systematic review of randomized control trials. *Preventing Chronic Disease, 10,* 130010.

Lenzenweger, M. F., Johnson, M. D., & Willett, J. B. (2004). Individual growth curve analysis illuminates stability and change in personality disorder features: The longitudinal study of personality disorders. *Archives of General Psychiatry, 61,* 1015–24.

Lesch, K.-P., Bengel, D., Heils, A., Sabol, S. Z., Greenberg, B. D., Petri, S., Benjamin, J., Muller, C. R., Hamer, D. H., & Murphy, D. L. (1996). Association of anxiety-related traits with a polymorphism in the serotonin transporter gene regulatory region. *Science, 274,* 1527–31.

Levine, S. Z. (2011). Elaboration on the association between IQ and parental SES with subsequent crime. *Personality and Individual Differences, 50,* 1233–7.

Levy, S. R., Plaks, J. E., Hong, Y., Chiu, C., & Dweck, C. S. (2001). Static versus dynamic theories and the perception of groups: Different routes to different destinations. *Personality and Social Psychology Review, 5,* 156–68.

Lewontin, R. (2001). *The triple helix: Gene, organism and environment.* New York: Harvard University Press.

Leyens, J.-P., Yzerbyt, V., & Schadron, G. (1994). *Stereotypes and social cognition.* London: Sage.

Libbrecht, M., Lievens, F., Carette, B., & & Côté, S. (2014). Emotional intelligence predicts success in medical school. *Emotion, 14*(1), 64–73.

Lieberman, M. D., & Rosenthal, R. (2001). Why introverts can't always tell who likes them: Multitasking and nonverbal decoding. *Journal of Personality and Social Psychology, 80,* 294–310.

Lilienfeld, S. O., Wood, J. M., & Garb, H. N. (2000). The scientific status of projective techniques. *Psychological Science in the Public Interest, 1,* 27–66.

Lillard, A. S. (1998). Ethnopsychologies: Cultural variations in theories of mind. *Psychological Bulletin, 123,* 3–32.

Linville, P. W. (1987). Self-complexity as a cognitive buffer against stress-related illness and depression. *Journal of Personality and Social Psychology, 52,* 663–76.

Little, B. R. (1989). Personal projects analysis: Trivial pursuits, magnificent obsessions, and the search for coherence. In D. M. Buss & N. Cantor (Eds.), *Personality psychology: Recent trends and emerging directions* (pp. 15–31). New York: Springer.

Little, B. R., Lecci, L., & Watkinson, B. (1991). Personality and personal projects: Linking Big Five and PAC units of analysis. *Journal of Personality, 60,* 501–25.

Locke, E. A. (2005). Why emotional intelligence is an invalid concept. *Journal of Organizational Behavior, 26,* 425–31.

Loehlin, J. C. (1992). *Genes and environment in personality development.* Newbury Park, CA: Sage.

Lopes, P. N., Salovey, P., Côté, S., & Beers, M. (2005). Emotion regulation abilities and the quality of social interaction. *Emotion, 5,* 113–18.

Lubinski, D., Benbow, C. P., Webb, R. M., & Bleske-Rechek, A. (2006). Tracking exceptional human capital over two decades. *Psychological Science, 17*(3), 194–9.

Lubinski, D., & Humphreys, L. G. (1997). Incorporating general intelligence into epidemiology and the social sciences. *Intelligence, 24*(1), 159–201.

Lucas, R. E., & Fujita, F. (2000). Factors influencing the relation between extraversion and pleasant affect. *Journal of Personality and Social Psychology, 79,* 1039–56.

Luciano, M., Batty, G. D., McGilchrist, M., Linksted, P., Fitzpatrick, B., Jackson, C., … & Porteous, D. (2010). Shared genetic aetiology between cognitive ability and cardiovascular disease risk factors: Generation Scotland's Scottish family health study. *Intelligence, 38*(3), 304–13.

Lykken, D. (1995). *The antisocial personalities.* Hillsdale, NJ: Erlbaum.

Lynn, R. (2010). In Italy, north–south differences in IQ predict differences in income, education, infant mortality, stature, and literacy. *Intelligence, 38*(1), 93–100.

MacCann, C., & Roberts, R. D. (2008). New paradigms for assessing emotional intelligence: Theory and data. *Emotion, 8*(4), 540–51.

Macklin, M. L., Metzger, L. J., Litz, B. T., McNally, R. J., Lasko, N. B., Orr, S. P., et al. (1998). Lower precombat intelligence is a risk factor for posttraumatic stress disorder. *Journal of Consulting and Clinical Psychology*, *66*, 323–6.

Macmillan, M. (1997). *Freud evaluated: The completed arc*. Cambridge, MA: MIT Press.

Maglo, K. N., Mersha, T. B., & Martin, L. J. (2016). Population genomics and the statistical values of race: An interdisciplinary perspective on the biological classification of human populations and implications for clinical genetic epidemiological research. *Frontiers in Genetics*, *7*, Article 22, 1–13.

Malouff, J. M., Schutte, N. S., & Thorsteinsson, E. B. (2014). Trait emotional intelligence and romantic relationship satisfaction: A meta-analysis. *The American Journal of Family Therapy*, *42*(1), 53–66.

Mar, R. A., Spreng, R. N., & DeYoung, C. G. (2013). How to produce personality neuroscience research with high statistical power and low additional cost. *Cognitive, Affective and Behavioural Neuroscience*, *13*, 674–85.

Markon, K. E., Krueger, R. F., & Watson, D. (2005). Delineating the structure of normal and abnormal personality: An integrative hierarchical approach. *Journal of Personality and Social Psychology*, *88*, 139–57.

Markus, H., & Nurius, P. (1986). Possible selves. *American Psychologist*, *41*, 954–69.

Marshall, G. N., Wortman, C. B., Vickers, R. R., Kusulas, J. W., & Hervig, L. K. (1994). The five-factor model of personality as a framework for personality–health research. *Journal of Personality and Social Psychology*, *67*, 278–86.

Martin, R. P., Wisenbaker, J., & Huttunen, M. (1994). Review of factor analytic studies of temperament measures based on the Thomas–Chess structural model: Implications for the Big Five. In C. F. Halverson, G. A. Kohnstamm & R. P. Martin (Eds.), *The developing structure of temperament and personality in infancy and childhood* (pp. 157–72). Hillsdale, NJ: Erlbaum.

Martins, A., Ramalho, N., & Morin, E. (2010). A comprehensive meta-analysis of the relationship between Emotional Intelligence and health. *Personality and Individual Differences*. *49*(6), 554–64.

Masling, J. M., & Bornstein, R. F. (2005). Scoring the Rorschach: Retrospect and prospect. In R. F. Bornstein & J. M. Masling (Eds.), *Scoring the Rorschach: Seven validated systems* (pp. 1–21). Mahwah, NJ: Lawrence Erlbaum Associates.

Maslow, A. H. (1962). *Towards a psychology of being*. New York: Van Nostrand.

Matarazzo, J. D. (1992). Psychological testing and assessment in the 21st century. *American Psychologist*, *47*, 1007–18.

Mathews, A., MacLeod, C. (2002). Induced processing biases have causal effects on anxiety. *Cognition and Emotion, 16*, 331–354.

Matsumoto, D. (2006). Are cultural differences in emotion regulation mediated by personality traits? *Journal of Cross-Cultural Psychology*, *37*, 421–7.

Matthews, G., & Gilliland, K. (1999). The personality theories of H. J. Eysenck and J. A. Gray: A comparative review. *Personality and Individual Differences*, 26, 583–626.

Matthews, G., Roberts, R. D., & Zeidner, M. (2004). Seven myths about emotional intelligence. *Psychological Inquiry, 15*, 179–96.

Mayer, J. D., Caruso, D. R., & Salovey, P. (1999). Emotional intelligence meets traditional standards for an intelligence. *Intelligence, 27*, 267–98.

Mayer, J. D., Lin, S. C., & Korogodsky, M. (2011). Exploring the universality of personality judgments: Evidence from the Great Transformation (1000 BCE–200 BCE). *Review of General Psychology, 15*, 65–76.

Mayer, J. D., Roberts, R. D., & Barsade, S. G. (2008). Human abilities: Emotional intelligence. *Annual Review of Psychology, 59*, 507–36.

Mayer, J. D., & Salovey, P. (1997). What is emotional intelligence? In P. Salovey & D. Sluyter (Eds.), *Emotional development and emotional intelligence: Education implications* (pp 3–31). New York: Basic Books.

Mayer, J. D., Salovey, P., & Caruso, D. R. (2004). Emotional intelligence: Theory, findings, and implications. *Psychological Inquiry, 15*, 197–215.

Mayer, J. D., Salovey, P., Caruso, D. R., & Sitarenios, G. (2001). Emotional intelligence as a standard intelligence. *Emotion, 1*(3), 232–42.

Maynard Smith, J. (1982). *Evolution and the theory of games*. Cambridge, UK: Cambridge University Press.

McAdams, D. P. (1995). What do we know when we know a person? *Journal of Personality, 63*, 365–96.

McAdams, D. P. (1996). *The stories we live by: Personal myths and the making of the self*. New York: Guilford Press.

McAdams, D. P. (2006). *The redemptive self: Stories Americans live by*. New York: Oxford University Press.

McAdams, D. P., de St. Aubin, E., & Logan, R. (1993). Generativity in young, midlife, and older adults. *Psychology and Aging, 8*, 221–30.

McClearn, G. E., Johansson, B., Berg, S., Pedersen, N. L., Ahern, F., Petrill, S. A., et al. (1997). Substantial genetic influence on cognitive abilities in twins 80 or more years old. *Science, 276*, 1560–3.

McClelland, D. C. (1985). *Human motivation*. Glenview, IL: Scott Foresman.

McCrae, R. R., & Costa, P. T. Jr. (1997). Personality trait structure as a human universal. *American Psychologist, 52*, 509–16.

McCrae, R. R., Yang, J., Costa, P. T., Dai, X., Yao, S., Cai, T., & Gao, B. (2001). Personality profiles and the prediction of categorical personality disorders. *Journal of Personality, 69*, 155–74.

McDaniel, M. A. (2005). Big-brained people are smarter: A meta-analysis of the relationship between in vivo brain volume and intelligence. *Intelligence, 33*, 337–46.

McLean, K. C., & Pratt, M. W. (2006). Life's little (and big) lessons: Identity status and meaning-making in the turning point narratives of emerging adults. *Developmental Psychology, 42*, 714–22.

Mealey, L. (1995). The sociobiology of sociopathy: An integrated evolutionary model. *Behavioral and Brain Sciences, 18*, 523–99.

Meehl, P. E. (1954). *Clinical vs. statistical prediction: A theoretical analysis and a review of the evidence*. Minneapolis, MN: University of Minnesota Press.

Meehl, P. E. (1962). Schizotaxia, schizotypy, schizophrenia. *American Psychologist, 17*, 827–38.

Meehl, P. E. (1992). Factors and taxa, traits and types, differences of degree and differences in kind. *Journal of Personality, 60*, 117–74.

Mele, A. R. (1997). Real self-deception. *Behavioral and Brain Sciences, 20*, 91–102.

Metalsky, G. I., Halberstadt, L. J., & Abramson, L. Y. (1987). Vulnerability to depressive mood reactions: Toward a more powerful test of the diathesis–stress and causal mediation components of the reformulated theory of depression. *Journal of Personality and Social Psychology, 52*, 386–93.

Meyer, G. J., & Shack, J. R. (1989). Structural convergence of mood and personality: Evidence for old and new directions. *Journal of Personality and Social Psychology, 57*, 691–706.

Mikolajczak, M., Petrides, K. V., & Hurry, J. (2009). Adolescents choosing self-harm as an emotion regulation strategy: The protective role of trait emotional intelligence. *British Journal of Clinical Psychology, 48*(2), 181–193.

Mischel, W. (1968). *Personality and assessment*. New York: Wiley.

Moffitt, T. E., Gabrielli, W. F., Mednick, S. A., & Schulsinger, F. (1981). Socioeconomic status, IQ, and delinquency. *Journal of Abnormal Psychology, 90*, 152–6.

Murray, C. (1998). *Income inequality and IQ*. La Vergne, TN: AEI Press.

Murray, H. A. (1938). *Explorations in personality*. New York: Oxford University Press.

Neisser, U., Boodoo, G., Bouchard, T. J., Jr, Boykin, A. W., Brody, N., Ceci, S. J., et al. (1996). Intelligence: Knowns and unknowns. *American Psychologist, 51*, 77–101.

Nelis, D., Quoidbach, J., Mikolajczak, M., & Hansenne, M. (2009). Increasing emotional intelligence: (How) is it possible? *Personality and Individual Differences, 47*(1), 36–41.

Nettelbeck, T. (1982). Inspection time: An index for intelligence? *Quarterly Journal of Experimental Psychology: Human Experimental Psychology, 2*, 299–312.

Nettle, D. (2005). An evolutionary approach to the extraversion continuum. *Evolution and Human Behaviour, 26*, 363–73.

Nettle, D. (2006). The evolution of personality variation in humans and other animals. *American Psychologist, 61*, 622–31.

Nettle, D., & Liddle, B. (2008). Agreeableness is related to social-cognitive, but not social–perceptual, theory of mind. *European Journal of Personality, 22*, 323–35.

Neubauer, A. C., & Fink, A. (2009). Intelligence and neural efficiency. *Neuroscience and Biobehavioral Reviews, 33*, 1004–23.

Newsome, S., Day, A. L., & Catano, V. M. (2000). Assessing the predictive validity of emotional intelligence. *Personality and Individual Differences, 29*, 1005–16.

Neyer, F. J., & Lehnart, J. (2007). Relationships matter in personality development: Evidence from an 8-year longitudinal study across young adulthood. *Journal of Personality, 75*, 535–68.

349

Nisbett, R. E., Aronson, J., Blair, C., Dickens, W., Flynn, J., Halpern, D. F., & Turkheimer, E. (2012). Intelligence: New findings and theoretical developments. *American Psychologist*, *67*(2), 130–59.

Norem, J. K., & Cantor, N. (1986). Anticipatory and post hoc cushioning strategies: Optimism and defensive pessimism in 'risky' situations. *Cognitive Therapy and Research, 10*, 347–62.

Nyborg, H., & Jensen, A. R. (2001). Occupation and income related to psychometric g. *Intelligence, 29*(1), 45–55.

O'Connor, R. M. Jr., & Little, I. S. (2003). Revisiting the predictive validity of emotional intelligence: Self-report versus ability-based measures. *Personality and Individual Differences, 35*(8), 1893–1902.

Ones, D. S., Viswesvaran, C., & Dilchert, S. (2005). Cognitive ability in selection decisions. In O. Wilhelm & R. W. Engle (Eds.), *Handbook of understanding and measuring intelligence* (pp. 431–68). Thousand Oaks, CA: Sage.

Open Science Collaboration. (2015). Estimating the reproducibility of psychological science. *Science, 349*(6251), aac4716.

Orth, J. F., Robins, R. W., & Widaman, K. F. (2012). Life-span development of self-esteem and its effects on important life outcomes. *Journal of Personality and Social Psychology, 102*, 1271–88.

Ozer, D. J., & Benet-Martínez, V. (2006). Personality and the prediction of consequential outcomes. *Annual Review of Psychology, 57*, 201–21.

Palys, T. S., & Little, B. R. (1983). Perceived life satisfaction and the organization of personal project systems. *Journal of Personality and Social Psychology, 44*, 1221–30.

Paradise, A. W., & Kernis, M. H. (2002). Self-esteem and psychological well-being: Implications of fragile self-esteem. *Journal of Social and Clinical Psychology, 21*, 345–61.

Paris, J. (2005). Neurobiological dimensional models of personality: A review of the models of Cloninger, Depue, and Siever. *Journal of Personality Disorders, 19*, 156–70.

Paunonen, S. V., & Ashton, M. C. (2001). Big Five predictors of academic achievement. *Journal of Research in Personality, 35*, 78–90.

Pavlov, I. P. (1927). *Conditioned reflexes: An investigation of the physiological activity of the cerebral cortex*. London: Oxford University Press.

Peláez-Fernández, M. A., Extremera, N., & Fernández-Berrocal, P. (2014). Incremental prediction and moderating role of the perceived emotional intelligence over aggressive behavior. *The Spanish Journal of Psychology, 17*, E15.

Penke, L., Denissen, J. A., & Miller, G. F. (2007). The evolutionary genetics of personality. *European Journal of Personality, 21*, 549–87.

Peterson, C., & Barrett, L. (1987). Explanatory style and academic performance among university freshmen. *Journal of Personality and Social Psychology, 53*, 603–7.

Peterson, C., & Seligman, M. E. P. (2002). *Character strengths and virtues: A handbook and classification*. New York: Oxford University Press & American Psychological Association.

Peterson, C., Seligman, M. E. P., & Vaillant, G. E. (1988). Pessimistic explanatory style is a risk factor for physical illness: A thirty-five year longitudinal study. *Journal of Personality and Social Psychology*, *55*, 23–7.

Peterson, J. B., & Carson, S. (2000). Latent inhibition and openness to experience in a high-achieving student population. *Personality and Individual Differences*, *28*, 323–32.

Petrides, K. V. (2011). Ability and Trait Emotional Intelligence. In T. Chamorro-Premuzic, S. Von Stumm, & A. Furnham (Eds.), *The Wiley-Blackwell handbook of individual differences* (Vol. 3) (pp. 656–78). Chichester, UK: John Wiley & Sons.

Petrides, K. V., & Furnham, A. (2000). On the dimensional structure of emotional intelligence. *Personality and Individual Difference*, *29*, 313–20.

Petrides, K. V., & Furnham, A. (2001). Trait emotional intelligence: Psychometric investigation with reference to established trait taxonomies. *European Journal of Personality*, *15*, 425–48.

Petrides, K. V., & Furnham, A. (2003). Trait emotional intelligence: Behavioural validation in two studies of emotion recognition and reactivity to mood induction. *European Journal of Personality*, *17*, 39–57.

Petrides, K. V., Pita, R., & Kokkinaki, F. (2007). The location of trait emotional intelligence in personality factor space. *British Journal of Psychology*, *98*(2), 273–89.

Petrides, K. V., Vernon, P. A., Schermer, J. A., & Veselka, L. (2011). Trait emotional intelligence and the dark triad traits of personality. *Twin Research and Human Genetics*, *14*(01), 35–41.

Pickering, A. D., Corr, P. J., Powell, J. H., Kumari, V., Thornton, J. C., & Gray, J. A. (1997). Individual differences in reactions to reinforcing stimuli are neither black nor white: To what extent are they Gray? In H. Nyborg (Ed.), *The scientific study of human nature: Tribute to Hans J. Eysenck at eighty*. Amsterdam: Elsevier.

Pickering, A. D., & Gray, J. A. (1999). The neuroscience of personality. In L. A. Pervin & O. P. John (Eds.), *Handbook of personality: Theory and research* (2nd ed.) (pp. 277–99). New York: Guilford Press.

Pietschnig, J., & Gittler, G. (2015). A reversal of the Flynn effect for spatial perception in German-speaking countries: Evidence from a cross-temoral IRT-based meta-analysis (1977–2014). *Intelligence, 53*, 145–53.

Pinker, S. (1997). *The blank slate: The modern denial of human nature*. London: Penguin.

Pinker, S. (2009). My genome, my self. *New York Times Magazine*, January 7.

Plomin, R., DeFries, J. C., McClearn, G. E., & Rutter, M. (1997). *Behavioral genetics* (3rd ed.). New York: Freeman.

Plomin, R., Haworth, C. M. A., Meaburn, E. L., Price, T. S., Wellcome Trust Case Control Consortium, & Davis, O. S. P. (2013). Common DNA markers can account for more than half of the genetic influence on cognitive abilities. *Psychological Science*, *24*, 562–8.

Plomin, R., & Kovas, Y. (2005). Generalist genes and learning disabilities. *Psychological Bulletin*, *131*, 592–617.

Posthuma, D., De Geus, E. J., Baare, W. F., Hulshoff Pol, H. E., Kahn, R. S., & Boomsma, D. I. (2002). The association between brain volume and intelligence is of genetic origin. *Nature Neuroscience, 5,* 83–4.

Posthuma, D., De Geus, E. J., & Boomsma, D. I. (2001). Perceptual speed and IQ are associated through common genetic factors. *Behavioral Genetics, 31,* 593–602.

Posthuma, D., Luciano, M., De Geus, E. J., Wright, M. J., Slagboom, P. E., Montgomery, G. W., et al. (2005). A genomewide scan for intelligence identifies quantitative trait Loci on 2q and 6p. *American Journal of Human Genetics, 77,* 318–26.

Prentice, D. A. (1990). Familiarity and differences in self- and other-representations. *Journal of Personality and Social Psychology, 59,* 369–83.

Pretzer, J. L., & Beck, A. T. (2005). A cognitive theory of personality disorders. In M. F. Lenzenweger & J. F. Clarkin (Eds.), *Major theories of personality disorder* (2nd ed.) (pp. 43–113). New York: Guilford Press.

Primi, R., Couto, G., Almeida, L. S., Guisande, M. A., & Miguel, F. K. (2012). Intelligence, age and schooling: Data from the Battery of Reasoning Tests (BRT-5). *Psicologia: Reflexão e Crítica, 25*(1), 79–88.

Protzko, J. (2015). The environment in raising early intelligence: A meta-analysis of the fade-out effect. *Intelligence, 53,* 202–10.

Puma, M., Bell, S., Cook, R., Heid, C., Shapiro, G., Broene, P., & Spier, E. (2010). *Head Start: Impact study. Final report.* Washington, DC: US Department of Health and Human Services, Administration for Children and Families.

Pytlik Zillig, L. M., Hemenover, S. H., & Dienstbier, R. A. (2002). What do we assess when we assess a Big 5? A content analysis of the affective, behavioral, and cognitive processes represented in Big 5 Personality Inventory. *Personality and Social Psychology Bulletin, 28*(6), 847–58.

Rafaeli-Mor, E., & Steinberg, J. (2002). Self-complexity and well-being: A review and research synthesis. *Personality and Social Psychology Review, 6,* 31–58.

Ramey, C. T., & Ramey, S. L. (2004). Early learning and school readiness: Can early intervention make a difference? *Merrill-Palmer Quarterly, 50,* 471–91.

Rammsayer, T. H. (1998). Extraversion and dopamine: Individual differences in responsiveness to changes in dopaminergic activity as a possible biological basis of extraversion. *European Psychologist, 3,* 37–50.

Rauscher, F. H., Shaw, G. L., & Ky, K. N. (1993). Music and spatial task performance. *Nature, 365,* 611.

Raven, J., Raven, J. C., & Court, J. H. (1998). *Manual for Raven's advanced progressive matrices.* Oxford: Oxford Psychologists Press.

Redlich, F. (1999). *Hitler: Diagnosis of a destructive prophet.* New York: Oxford University Press.

Ree, M. J., & Earles, J. A. (1992). Intelligence is the best predictor of job performance. *Current Directions in Psychological Science, 1,* 86–9.

Reid, J. (2008). Does emotional intelligence predict real-world performance? In S. Boag (Ed.), *Personality Down Under: Perspectives from Australia* (pp. 123–129). New York: Nova Science Publishers.

Reivich, K. (1995). The measurement of explanatory style. In G. M. Buchanan & M. E. P. Seligman (Eds.), *Explanatory style* (pp. 21–48). Hillsdale, NJ: Erlbaum.

Revelle, W., Amaral, P., & Turriff, S. (1976). Introversion/extraversion, time stress, and caffeine: Effect on verbal performance. *Science, 192*, 149–50.

Reynolds, C. A., Finkel, D., McArdle, J. J., Gatz, M., Berg, S., & Pedersen, N. L. (2005). Quantitative genetic analysis of latent growth curve models of cognitive abilities in adulthood. *Developmental Psychology, 41*, 3–16.

Richardson, K., & Norgate, S. H. (2015). Does IQ really predict job performance? *Applied Developmental Science, 19*(3), 153–69.

Riemann, R., Angleitner, A., & Strelau, J. (1997). Genetic and environmental influences on personality: A study of twins reared together using the self- and peer report NEO-FFI scales. *Journal of Personality, 65*, 449–76.

Riemann, R., & Kandler, C. (2010). Construct validation using multitrait-multimethod twin data: The case of a general factor of personality. *European Journal of Personality, 24*, 258–77,

Roberts, B. W., Caspi, A., & Moffitt, T. E. (2003). Work experiences and personality development in young adulthood. *Journal of Personality and Social Psychology, 84*, 582–93.

Roberts, B. W., & DelVecchio, W. F. (2000). The rank-order consistency of personality traits from childhood to old age: A quantitative review of longitudinal studies. *Psychological Bulletin, 126*, 3–25.

Roberts, B. W., Walton, K. E., & Viechtbauer, W. (2006). Patterns of mean-level change in personality traits across the life course: A meta-analysis of longitudinal studies. *Psychological Bulletin, 132*, 1–25.

Roberts, R. D., Zeidner, M., & Matthews, G. (2001). Does emotional intelligence meet traditional standards for an intelligence? Some new data and conclusions. *Emotion, 1*(3), 196–232.

Roccas, S., Sagiv, L., Schwartz, S. H., & Knafo, A. (2002). The Big Five personality factors and personal values. *Personality and Social Psychology Bulletin, 28*, 789–801.

Rogers, C. (1961). *On becoming a person.* Boston, MA: Houghton-Mifflin.

Rokhin, L., Pavlov, I., & Popov, Y. (1963). *Psychopathology and psychiatry.* Moscow: Foreign Languages Publication House.

Rose, S. (2005). *Lifelines: Life beyond the gene.* London: Vintage.

Rosenbaum, R. (1998). *Explaining Hitler: The search for the origins of his evil.* New York: Random House.

Rosenman, R. H. (1978). The interview method of assessment of the coronary-prone behavior pattern. In T. M. Dembroski, S. M. Weiss, J. L. Shields, S. G. Haynes, & M. Feinleib (Eds.), *Coronary-prone behavior* (pp. 55–69). New York: Springer.

Rosenthal, R. (1990). How are we doing in soft psychology? *American Psychologist, 45*, 775–7.

Rosenthal, R., & Rubin, D. B. (1982). A simple, general purpose display of magnitude of experimental effect. *Journal of Educational Psychology, 74*, 166–9.

Rosenwald, G. C., Mendelson, G. A., Fontana, A., & Portz, A. T. (1966). An action test of hypotheses concerning the anal personality. *Journal of Abnormal Psychology, 71*, 304–9.

Ross, M. (1989). Relation of implicit theories to the construction of personal histories. *Psychological Review, 96*, 341–57.

Roth, B., Becker, N., Romeyke, S., Schäfer, S., Domnick, F., & Spinath, F. M. (2015). Intelligence and school grades: A meta-analysis. *Intelligence, 53*, 118–37.

Roth, P. L., Bevier, C. A., Bobko, P., Switzer, F. S. I., & Tyler, P. (2001). Ethnic group differences in cognitive ability in employment and educational settings: A meta-analysis. *Personnel Psychology, 54*, 297–330.

Rotter, J. B. (1966). Generalized expectancies for internal versus external control of reinforcement. *Psychological Monographs, 80*, 1–28.

Rowatt, W. C., Cunningham, M. R., & Druen, P. B. (1998). Deception to get a date. *Personality and Social Psychology Bulletin, 24*, 1228–42.

Rozin, P., & Royzman, E. B. (2001). Negativity bias, negativity dominance, and contagion. *Personality and Social Psychology Review, 5*, 296–320.

Runyan, W. M. (1981). Why did Van Gogh cut off his ear? The problem of alternative explanations in psychobiography. *Journal of Personality and Social Psychology, 40*, 1070–7.

Runyan, W. M. (1988). Progress in psychobiography. In D. P. McAdams & R. L. Ochberg (Eds.), *Psychobiography and life narratives* (pp. 295–326). Durham, NC: Duke University Press.

Rushton, J. P., & Jensen, A. R. (2005). Thirty years of research on race differences in cognitive ability. *Psychology, Public Policy, and Law, 11*, 235–94.

Saklofske, D. H., Austin, E. J., & Minski, P. S. (2003). Factor structure and validity of a trait emotional intelligence measure. *Personality and Individual Differences, 34*, 707–21.

Salahodjaev, R. (2015). Intelligence and shadow economy: A cross-country empirical assessment. *Intelligence, 49*, 129–33.

Sandstrom, M. J., & Cramer, P. (2003). Girls' use of defence mechanisms following peer rejection. *Journal of Personality, 71*, 605–27.

Schmidt, F. L. (1988). The problem of group differences in ability test scores in employment selection. *Journal of Vocational Behavior, 33*, 272–92.

Schmidt, F. L., & Hunter, J. (1998). The validity and utility of selection methods in personnel psychology. *Psychological Bulletin, 124*, 262–74.

Schmidt, F. L., & Hunter, J. (2004). General mental ability in the world of work: Occupational attainment and job performance. *Journal of Personality and Social Psychology, 86*(1), 162–73.

Schmithorst, V. J., Wilke, M., Dardzinski, B. J., & Holland, S. K. (2005). Cognitive functions correlate with white matter architecture in a normal pediatric population: A diffusion tensor MRI study. *Human Brain Mapping, 26*, 139–47.

Schnabel, K., Asendorpf, J. B., & Greenwald, A. G. (2008). Implicit Association Tests: A landmark for the assessment of implicit personality self-concept. In G. J. Boyle, G. Matthews, & D. H. Saklofske (Eds.), *Handbook of personality theory and testing* (pp. 508–528). London: Sage.

Scholey, A., Pase, M., Pipingas, A., Stough, C., & Camfield, D. A. (2015). Herbal extracts and nutraceuticals for cognitive performance. In T. Best & L. Dye (Eds.), *Nutrition for brain health and cognitive performance* (pp. 221–50). Boca Raton, FL: CRC Press.

Schultz, W. T. (2005). *Handbook of psychobiography*. Oxford: Oxford University Press.

Schutte, N. S., Malouff, J. M., Hall, L. E., Haggerty, D. J., Cooper, J. T., Golden, C. J., & Dornheim, L. (1998). Development and validation of a measure of emotional intelligence. *Personality and Individual Differences*, *25*(2), 167–77.

Schwartz, J. (1994). Low-level lead exposure and children's IQ: A metaanalysis and search for a threshold. *Environmental Research*, *65*(1), 42–55.

Schwartz, S. H. (1992). Universals in the content and structure of values: Theoretical advances and empirical tests in 20 countries. In M. Zanna (Ed.), *Advances in experimental social psychology* (Vol. 25) (pp. 1–65). New York: Academic Press.

Schwartz, S. H. (1994). Are there universal aspects in the structure and contents of human values? *Journal of Social Issues*, *50*, 19–45.

Schwartz, S. H., et al. (2012). Refining the theory of basic individual values. *Journal of Personality and Social Psychology*, *103*, 663–88.

Seligman, M. E. P., Nolen-Hoeksema, S., Thornton, N., & Thornton, K. M. (1990). Explanatory style as a mechanism of disappointing athletic performance. *Psychological Science*, *1*, 143–6.

Seligman, M. E. P., & Schulman, P. (1986). Explanatory style as a predictor of productivity and quitting among life insurance salesmen. *Journal of Personality and Social Psychology*, *50*, 832–8.

Sevdalis, N., Petrides, K. V., & Harvey, N. (2007). Trait emotional intelligence and decision-related emotions. *Personality and Individual Differences*, *42*, 921–33.

Shatz, S. M. (2008). IQ and fertility: A cross-national study. *Intelligence*, *36*, 109–11.

Sheldon, O. J., Dunning, D., & Ames, D. R. (2014). Emotionally unskilled, unaware, and uninterested in learning more: Reactions to feedback about deficits in emotional intelligence. *Journal of Applied Psychology*, *99*(1), 125–37.

Shoda, Y., Mischel, W., & Peake, P. K. (1990). Predicting adolescent cognitive and self-regulatory competencies from preschool delay of gratification: Identifying diagnostic conditions. *Developmental Psychology*, *26*, 978–86.

Sibley, C., Robertson, A., & Wilson, M. S. (2006). Social dominance orientation and right-wing authoritarianism: Additive and interactive effects. *Political Psychology*, *27*, 755–68.

Silverman, L., & Weinberger, J. (1985). Mommy and I are one: Implications for psychotherapy. *American Psychologist*, *40*, 1296–308.

Silvia, P. J., Nusbaum, E. C., Berg, C., Martin, C., & O'Connor, A. (2009). Openness to experience, plasticity, and creativity: Exploring lower-order, higher-order, and interactive effects. *Journal of Research in Personality*, *43*, 1087–90.

Simpson, J. A., Rholes, W. D., & Phillips, D. (1996). Conflict in close relationships: An attachment perspective. *Journal of Personality and Social Psychology, 71*, 899–914.

Skinner, B. F. (1938). *The behavior of organisms: An experimental analysis.* Cambridge, MA: B. F. Skinner Foundation.

Skinner, E. A., Edge, K., Altman, J., & Sherwood, H. (2003). Searching for the structure of coping: A review and critique of category systems for classifying ways of coping. *Psychological Bulletin, 129*, 216–69.

Śmieja, M., Orzechowski, J., & Stolarski, M. S. (2014). TIE: An ability test of emotional intelligence. *PLoS One, 9*(7), e103484, 1–10.

Smillie, L. D., Pickering, A. D., & Jackson, C. J. (2006). The new reinforcement sensitivity theory: Implications for personality measurement. *Personality and Social Psychology Review, 10*, 320–35.

Smith, H. S., & Cohen, L. H. (1993). Self-complexity and reaction to a relationship breakup. *Journal of Social and Clinical Psychology, 12*, 367–84.

Smith, T. W., & Spiro, A. (2002). Personality, health, and aging: Prolegomenon for the next generation. *Journal of Research in Personality, 36*, 363–94.

Smits, I. A. M., Doan, C. V., Vorst, H. C. M., Wicherts, J. M., & Timmerman, M. E. (2011). Cohort differences in Big Five personality factors over a period of 25 years. *Journal of Personality and Social Psychology, 100*, 1124–38.

Snyder, M. (1974). The self-monitoring of expressive behavior. *Journal of Personality and Social Psychology, 30*, 526–37.

Soto, C. J., John, O. P., Gosling, S. D., & Potter, J. (2011). Age differences in personality traits from 10 to 65: Big Five domains and facets in a large cross-sectional sample. *Journal of Personality and Social Psychology, 100*, 330–48.

Sowislo, J. F., & Orth, U. (2013). Does low self-esteem predict depression and anxiety? A meta-analysis of longitudinal studies. *Psychological Bulletin, 139*, 213–40.

Spanos, N. P. (1994). Multiple identity enactments and multiple personality disorder: A socio-cognitive perspective. *Psychological Bulletin, 116*, 143–65.

Spearman, C. (1904). 'General intelligence,' objectively determined and measured. *American Journal of Psychology, 15*, 201–93.

Spence, D. P. (1980). *Narrative truth and historical truth: Meaning and interpretation in psychoanalysis.* New York: W. W. Norton.

Spinath, F. M., & Plomin, R. (2003). Amplification of genetic influence on g from early childhood to the early school years. Paper presented at the IVth Meeting of the International Society for the Study of Intelligence, Irvine, USA, 4–6 December.

Srivastava, S., John, O. P., Gosling, S. D., & Potter, J. (2003). Development of personality in early and middle adulthood: Set like plaster or persistent change? *Journal of Personality and Social Psychology, 84*, 1041–53.

Steele, C. M., & Aronson, J. (1995). Stereotype threat and the intellectual performance of African Americans. *Journal of Personality and Social Psychology, 69*, 797–811.

Steffens, M. C., & Schulze König, S. (2006). Predicting spontaneous Big Five behavior with Implicit Association Tests. *European Journal of Psychological Assessment, 22*, 13–20.

Stelzl, I., Merz, F., Ehlers, T., & Remer, H. (1995). The effect of schooling on the development of fluid and cristallized intelligence: A quasi-experimental study. *Intelligence*, *21*(3), 279–96.

Stern, W. (1912). *The psychological methods of intelligence testing* (G. Whipple, Trans.). Baltimore, MD: Warwick & York.

Sternberg, R. J. (1996). Love stories. *Personal Relationships*, *3*, 59–79.

Sternberg, R. J., Grigorenko, E. L., & Bundy, D. A. (2001). The predictive value of IQ. *Merrill-Palmer Quarterly*, *47*(1), 1–41.

Sternberg, R. J., & Wagner, R. K. (1993). The g-ocentric view of intelligence and job performance is wrong. *Current Directions in Psychological Science*, *2*(1), 1–5.

Stewart, A. J., Franz, C. E., & Layton, L. (1988). The changing self: Using personal documents to study lives. *Journal of Personality*, *56*, 41–74.

Stewart, P. W., Lonky, E., Reihman, J., Pagano, J., Gump, B. B., & Darvill, T. (2008). The relationship between prenatal PCB exposure and intelligence (IQ) in 9-year-old children. *Environmental Health Perspectives*, *116*(10), 1416.

Stough, C., Downey, L., Silber, B., Lloyd, J., Kure, C., Wesnes, K., & Camfield, D. (2012). The effects of 90-day supplementation with the omega-3 essential fatty acid docosahexaenoic acid (DHA) on cognitive function and visual acuity in a healthy aging population. *Neurobiology of Aging*, *33*(4), 824-e1.

Stough, C., Kerkin, B., Bates, T. C., & Mangan, G. (1994). Music and spatial IQ. *Personality and Individual Differences*, *17*, 695.

Stough, C., King, R., Papafotiou, K., Swann, P., Ogden, E., Wesnes, K., & Downey, L. A. (2012). The acute effects of 3, 4-methylenedioxymethamphetamine and d-methamphetamine on human cognitive functioning. *Psychopharmacology*, *220*(4), 799–807.

Strelau, J. (1997). The contribution of Pavlov's typology of CNS properties to personality research. *European Psychologist*, *2*, 125–38.

Strenze, T. (2007). Intelligence and socioeconomic success: A meta-analytic review of longitudinal research. *Intelligence*, *35*(5), 401–26.

Tan, Y., Zhang, Q., Li, W., Wei, D., Qiao, L., Qiu, J., & Liu, Y. (2014). The correlation between Emotional Intelligence and gray matter volume in university students. *Brain and Cognition*, *91*, 100–7.

Tang, H., Quertermous, T., Rodriguez, B., Kardia, S. L., Zhu, X., Brown, A., et al. (2005). Genetic structure, self-identified race/ethnicity, and confounding in case-control association studies. *American Journal of Human Genetics*, *76*, 268–75.

Taylor, S. E. (1983). Adjustment to threatening events: A theory of cognitive adaptation. *American Psychologist*, *38*, 1161–73.

Taylor, S. E., & Brown, J. D. (1988). Illusion and well-being: A social psychological perspective on mental health. *Psychological Bulletin*, *103*, 193–210.

Teasdale, T. W., & Owen, D. R. (2005). A long-term rise and recent decline in intelligence test performance: The Flynn Effect in reverse. *Personality and Individual Differences*, *39*, 837–43.

Tellegen, A. (1985). Structures of mood and personality and their relevance to assessing anxiety, with an emphasis on self-report. In A. H. Tuma & J. D. Maser (Eds.), *Anxiety and anxiety disorders* (pp. 681–706). Hillsdale, NJ: Erlbaum.

Tellegen, A., Watson, D., & Clark, L. A. (1999). On the dimensional and hierarchical structure of affect. *Psychological Science, 10*(4), 297–303.

te Nijenhuis, J., Jongeneel-Grimen, B., & Kirkegaard, E. O. W. (2014). Are Headstart gains on the g factor? A meta-analysis. *Intelligence, 46*, 209–15.

Terracciano, A., et al. (2005). National character does not reflect mean trait levels in 49 cultures. *Science, 310*, 96–100.

Terracciano, A. et al. (2010). Genome-wide association scan for five major dimensions of personality. *Molecular Psychiatry, 15*, 647–56.

Thompson, P. M., Cannon, T. D., Narr, K. L., van Erp, T., Poutanen, V. P., Huttunen, M., et al. (2001). Genetic influences on brain structure. *Nature Neuroscience, 4*, 1253–8.

Timoshanko, A., Desmond, P., Camfield, D. A., Downey, L. A., & Stough, C. (2014). A magnetic resonance spectroscopy (1 H MRS) investigation into brain metabolite correlates of ability emotional intelligence. *Personality and Individual Differences, 65*, 69–74.

Toga, A. W., & Thompson, P. M. (2005). Genetics of brain structure and intelligence. *Annual Review of Neuroscience, 28*, 1–23.

Tooby, J., & Cosmides, L. (1990). On the universality of human nature and the uniqueness of the individual: The role of genetics and adaptation. *Journal of Personality, 58*, 17–67.

Trahan, L. H., Stuebing, K. K., Fletcher, J. M., & Hiscock, M. (2014). The Flynn Effect: A meta-analysis. *Psychological Bulletin, 140*(5), 1332–60.

Trzesniewski, K. H., & Donnellan, M. B. (2010). Rethinking 'Generation Me': A study of cohort effects from 1976–2006. *Perspectives on Psychological Science, 5*, 58–75.

Turkheimer, E. (2000). Three laws of behavior genetics and what they mean. *Current Directions in Psychological Science, 9*, 160–4.

Turkheimer, E. (2011). Still missing. *Research in Human Development, 8*, 227–41.

Turkheimer, E., Haley, A., Waldron, M., D'Onofrio, B., & Gottesman, I. (2003). Socioeconomic status modifies heritability of IQ in young children. *Psychological Science, 14*, 623–8.

Twenge, J. M. (1997). Changes in masculine and feminine traits over time: A meta-analysis. *Sex Roles, 36*, 305–25.

Twenge, J. M. (2000). The age of anxiety? Birth cohort change in anxiety and neuroticism, 1952–1993. *Journal of Personality and Social Psychology, 79*, 1007–21.

Twenge, J. M. (2001a). Changes in women's assertiveness in response to status and roles: A cross-temporal meta-analysis, 1931–1993. *Journal of Personality and Social Psychology, 81*, 133–45.

Twenge, J. M. (2001b). Birth cohort changes in extraversion: A cross-temporal meta-analysis, 1966–1993. *Personality and Individual Differences, 30*, 735–48.

Twenge, J. M., & Campbell, W. K. (2001). Age and birth cohort differences in self-esteem: A cross-temporal meta-analysis. *Personality and Social Psychology Review, 5*, 321–44.

Twenge, J. M., Zhang, L., & Im, C. (2004). It's beyond my control: A cross-temporal meta-analysis of increasing externality in locus of control, 1960–2002. *Personality and Social Psychology Review*, *8*, 308–19.

van Ijzendoorn, M. H., & Juffer, F. (2005). Adoption is a successful natural intervention enhancing adopted children's IQ and school performance. *Current Directions in Psychological Science*, *14*, 326–30.

Van Leeuwen, M., Peper, J. S., van den Berg, S. M., Brouwer, R. M., Hulshoff Pol, H. E., Kahn, R. S., & Boomsma, D. I. (2009). A genetic analysis of brain volumes and IQ in children. *Intelligence*, *37*, 181–91.

Van Rooy, D. L., & Viswesvaran, C. (2004). Emotional intelligence: A meta-analytic investigation of predictive validity and nomological net. *Journal of Vocational Behavior*, *65*(1), 71–95.

Van Rooy, D. L., Alonso, A., & Viswesvaran, C. (2005). Group differences in emotional intelligence scores: Theoretical and practical implications. *Personality and Individual Differences*, *38*(3), 689–700.

Vazire, S., & Gosling, S. D. (2004). E-perceptions: Personality impressions based on personal websites. *Journal of Personality and Social Psychology*, *87*, 123–32.

Veenhoven, R., & Choi, Y. (2012). Does intelligence boost happiness? Smartness of all pays more than being smarter than others. *International Journal of Happiness and Development*, *1*(1), 5–27.

Vinkhuyzen, A. A. E., et al. (2012). Common SNPs explain some of the variation in the personality dimensions of neuroticism and extraversion. *Translational Psychiatry*, *2*, e102.

Volkan, V. D., Itzkowitz, N., & Dod, A. W. (1997). *Nixon: A psychobiography*. New York: Columbia University Press.

Voracek, M. (2004). National intelligence and suicide rate: An ecological study of 85 countries. *Personality and Individual Differences*, *37*, 543–53.

Vorst, H. C. M., & Bermond, B. (2001). Validity and reliability of the Bermond-Vorst alexithymia questionnaire. *Personality and Individual Differences*, *30*, 413–34.

Vul, E., Harris, C., Winkielman, P., & Pashler, H. (2009). Puzzlingly high correlations in fMRI studies of emotion, personality, and social cognition. *Perspectives on Psychological Science*, *4*, 274–90.

Waller, N. G. (1999). Evaluating the structure of personality. In C. R. Cloninger (Ed.), *Personality and psychopathology* (pp. 155–200). Washington, DC: American Psychiatric Press.

Wang, T., Ren, X., Schweizer, K., & Xu, F. (2016). Schooling effects on intelligence development: Evidence based on national samples from urban and rural China. *Educational Psychology*, *36*, 831–44.

Watson, D., & Clark, L. A. (1984). Negative affectivity: The disposition to experience aversive emotional states. *Psychological Bulletin*, *96*, 465–90.

Watson, D., & Clark, L. A. (1992a). On traits and temperament: General and specific factors of emotional experience and their relation to the five-factor model. *Journal of Personality*, *60*, 441–76.

Watson, D., & Clark, L. A. (1992b). Affects separable and inseparable: On the hierarchical arrangement of the negative affects. *Journal of Personality and Social Psychology, 62,* 489–505.

Watson, D., & Clark, L. A. (1993). Behavioral disinhibition versus constraint: A dispositional perspective. In D. M. Wegner & J. W. Pennebaker (Eds.), *Handbook of mental control* (pp. 506–27). Upper Saddle River, NJ: Prentice-Hall.

Watson, D., & Clark, L. A. (1997). Measurement and mismeasurement of mood: Recurrent and emergent issues. *Journal of Personality Assessment, 68,* 267–96.

Watson, D., & Tellegen, A. (1985). Toward a consensual structure of mood. *Psychological Bulletin, 98,* 219–35.

Wechsler, D. (1975). Intelligence defined and undefined: A relativistic appraisal. *American Psychologist, 30,* 135–9.

Wechsler, D. (2008). *Wechsler Adult Intelligence Scale IV.* San Antonio, TX: Psychological Corporation.

Wechsler, D., Coalson, D. L., & Raiford, S. E. (2008). *WAIS-IV: Wechsler adult intelligence scale.* San Antonio, TX: Pearson.

Westen, D. (1998). The scientific legacy of Sigmund Freud: Toward a psychodynamically informed psychological science. *Psychological Bulletin, 124,* 333–71.

Whalley, L. J., & Deary, I. J. (2001). Longitudinal cohort study of childhood IQ and survival up to age 76. *British Medical Journal, 322,* 819–22.

White, J., Mortensen, L. H., & Batty, G. D. (2012). Cognitive ability in early adulthood as a predictor of habitual drug use during later military service and civilian life: The Vietnam Experience Study. *Drug and Alcohol Dependence, 125*(1), 164–8.

Whiteside, S. P., & Lynam, D. R. (2001). The five factor model and impulsivity: Using a structural model of personality to understand impulsivity. *Personality and Individual Differences, 30,* 669–89.

Whitley, B. E. (1999). Right-wing authoritarianism, social dominance orientation, and prejudice. *Journal of Personality and Social Psychology, 77,* 126–34.

Whitley, E., Gale, C. R., Deary, I. J., Kivimaki, M., Singh-Manoux, A., & Batty, G. D. (2013). Influence of maternal and paternal IQ on offspring health and health behaviors: Evidence for some trans-generational associations using the 1958 British birth cohort study. *European Psychiatry, 28*(4), 219–24.

Whitmer, P. O. (1996). *The inner Elvis: A psychological biography of Elvis Aaron Presley.* New York: Hyperion.

Wiggins, J. S. (1997). In defence of traits. In R. Hogan, J. Johnson, & S. Briggs (Eds.), *Handbook of personality psychology* (pp. 95–115). New York: Academic Press.

Wiggins, J. S., & Pincus, A. L. (1989). Conceptions of personality disorders and dimensions of personality. *Psychological Assessment, 12,* 305–16.

Wilk, S. L., Desmarais, L. B., & Sackett, P. R. (1995). Gravitation to jobs commensurate with ability: Longitudinal and cross-sectional tests. *Journal of Applied Psychology, 80*(1), 79–85.

Wilk, S. L., & Sackett, P. R. (1996). Longitudinal analysis of ability–job complexity fit and job change. *Personnel Psychology, 49*(4), 937–67.

Williams, R. (1976). *Keywords: A vocabulary of culture and society.* London: Fontana.

Wilson, D. S. (1994). Adaptive genetic variation and human evolutionary psychology. *Ethology and Sociobiology, 15*, 219–35.

Wolf, M., van Doorn, G. S., Leimar, O., & Weissing, F. J. (2007). Life-history trade-offs favour the evolution of animal personalities. *Nature, 447*, 581–4.

Wongupparaj, P., Kumari, P., & Morris, R. G. (2015). A cross-temporal meta-analysis of Raven's Progressive Matrices: Age groups and developing versus developed countries. *Intelligence, 29*, 1–9.

Woolfolk, R. L., Novalany, J., Gara, M. A., Allen, L. A., & Polino, M. (1995). Self-complexity, self-evaluation, and depression: An examination of form and content within the self-schema. *Journal of Personality and Social Psychology, 68*, 1108–20.

Wright, R. O., Amarasiriwardena, C., Woolf, A. D., Jim, R., & Bellinger, D. C. (2006). Neuropsychological correlates of hair arsenic, manganese, and cadmium levels in school-age children residing near a hazardous waste site. *NeuroToxicology, 27*(2), 210–16.

Wright Gillham, N. (2001). *A life of Sir Francis Galton: From African exploration to the birth of eugenics.* London: Oxford University Press.

Yerkes, R. M., & Dodson, J. D. (1908). The relation of strength of stimulus to rapidity of habit-formation. *Journal of Comparative Neurology and Psychology, 18*, 459–82.

Zeidner, M., Kloda, I., & Matthews, G. (2013). Does dyadic coping mediate the relationship between emotional intelligence (EI) and marital quality? *Journal of Family Psychology, 27*(5), 795–805.

Zeidner, M., Roberts, R. D., & Matthews, G. (2008). The science of emotional intelligence. *European Psychologist, 13*(1), 64–78.

Zimmerman, J., & Neyer, F. J. (2013). Do we become a different person when hitting the road? Personality development of sojourners. *Journal of Personality and Social Psychology, 105*, 515–30.

Zuckerman, M. (1991). *Psychobiology of personality.* New York: Cambridge University Press.

Zuckerman, M. (2005). *Psychobiology of personality* (2nd ed.). New York: Cambridge University Press.

Zullow, H. M. (1990). Pessimistic rumination in popular songs and news magazines predicts economic recession via decreased consumer optimism and spending. *Journal of Economic Psychology, 12*, 501–26.

Zullow, H., & Seligman, M. E. P. (1990). Pessimistic rumination predicts defeat of presidential candidates, 1900–1984. *Psychological Inquiry, 1*, 52–61.

361

Index

Index

Index

Index